AN INTRODUCTION TO THE GREEN ECONOMY

Science, systems and sustainability

Adrian C. Newton and Elena Cantarello

Routledge
Taylor & Francis Group

LONDON AND NEW YORK

earthscan
from Routledge

First published 2014
by Routledge
2 Park Square, Milton Park, Abingdon, Oxon OX14 4RN

And by Routledge
711 Third Avenue, New York, NY 10017

Routledge is an imprint of the Taylor & Francis Group, an informa business

British Library Cataloguing-in-Publication Data
A catalogue record for this book is available from the British Library

Library of Congress Cataloging-in-Publication Data
Newton, Adrian C.
   An introduction to the green economy : science, systems and
   sustainability / Adrian C. Newton and Elena Cantarello.
      pages cm
   Includes bibliographical references and index.
   1. Sustainable development. 2. Environmental economics
   3. Environmental policy—Economic aspects. 4. Ecology—Economic
   aspects. I. Cantarello, Elena. II. Title.
   HC79.E5N45713 2014
   338.9'27—dc23
                                                          2014003827

ISBN: 978-0-415-71160-9 (hbk)
ISBN: 978-0-415-71161-6 (pbk)
ISBN: 978-1-315-88448-6 (ebk)

Typeset in Bembo
by Keystroke, Station Road, Codsall, Wolverhampton

MIX
Paper from
responsible sources
FSC
www.fsc.org   FSC® C013604

Printed and bound by CPI Group (UK) Ltd, Croydon, CR0 4YY

CONTENTS

FIGURES

TABLES

ACRONYMS AND ABBREVIATIONS

2DS	2°C scenario
3R	reduce, reuse and recycle
10YFP	10-Year Framework of Programmes
AAU	Assigned Amount Unit
AD	Activity Data
ARD	afforestation, reforestation and deforestation
BEV	battery electric vehicles
BRIC	Brazil, Russia, India and China
C&I	criteria and indicators
CAS	Complex adaptive systems
CBD	Convention on Biological Diversity
CBET	community-based ecotourism
CCA	California Carbon Allowance
CCB	Climate, Community and Biodiversity Standard
CCD	colony collapse disorder
CCS	carbon capture and storage
CDIAC	Carbon Dioxide Information Analysis Center
CDM	Clean Development Mechanism
CDR	carbon dioxide removal
CER	Certified Emissions Reductions
CHP	combined heat and power
CHPDH	combined heat and power for district heating
CITES	Convention on International Trade in Endangered Species
CITL	Community Independent Transaction Log
CMP	carbon management plan
CMS	Convention on Migratory Species
CoPs	Conferences of the Parties
CPV	concentrated photovoltaic
CREO	Committee on Recently Extinct Organisms

CSP	concentrated solar power
CSR	corporate social responsibility
DAI	dangerous anthropogenic interference
DDT	dichloro, diphenyl trichloroethane
DIC	dissolved inorganic carbon
DNA	Designated National Authority
EC	European Commission
ECHR	European Convention on Human Rights
EDC	endocrine-disrupting compound
EF	emission factor
EGS	enhanced geothermal system
EGS	environmental goods and services
EIA	environmental impact assessment
EIT	economies in transition
EJO	environmental justice organisation
EMS	environmental management system
EoLV	end of life vehicle
ERU	emission reduction unit
ETP	Energy Technology Perspective
EU	European Union
EUA	European Union Allowance
EU ETS	EU Emissions Trading Scheme
FAME	fatty acid methyl ester
FAO	Food and Agricultural Organisation
FCPF	Forest Carbon Partnership Facility
FCV	fuel cell vehicle
FDI	foreign direct investment
FMU	forest management unit
FoE	Friends of the Earth
FPAR	fraction of photosynthetically active radiation
FPIC	free, prior and informed consent
FRA	Forest Resource Assessment
FSC	Forest Stewardship Council
GATT	General Agreement on Tariffs and Trade
GDP	gross domestic product
GGEI	Global Green Economy Index
GGGI	Global Green Growth Institute
GHG	greenhouse gas
GMO	genetically modified organism
GPI	Genuine Progress Indicator
GPP	gross primary production
GSTC	Global Sustainable Tourism Criteria
Gt	gigatonne
GWEC	Global Wind Energy Council
GWP	global warming potential
GWP-100	100-year global warming potential

HANPP	human appropriation of net primary production
HDR	hot dry rock
HFC	hydrofluorocarbon
HPI	Happy Planet Index
IAIA	International Association for Impact Assessment
ICDP	integrated conservation and development project
ICE	internal combustion engine
ICM	integrated coastal management
ICZM	integrated coastal zone management
IEA	International Energy Agency
IEMA	Institute of Environmental Management and Assessment
IEO	international economic organisation
IIASA	International Institute for Applied Systems Analysis
IIASAGPI	International Institute for Applied Systems Analysis Genuine Progress Indicator
IMF	International Monetary Fund
IPBES	Intergovernmental Platform on Biodiversity and Ecosystem Services
IPCC	Intergovernmental Panel on Climate Change
IPM	integrated pest management
ISEW	Index of Sustainable Economic Welfare
ISO	International Organization for Standardization
ISWA	International Solid Waste Association
ISWM	integrated sustainable waste management
ITL	international transaction log
IUCN	International Union for Conservation of Nature
IWRM	integrated water resources management
JI	Joint Implementation
LAI	leaf area index
LCA	life cycle assessment/life cycle analysis
LCC	life cycle costing
LCOE	levelised cost of energy
LCSA	life cycle sustainability assessment
LDV	light duty vehicle
LED	light-emitting diode
LPG	liquified petroleum gas
LRTAP	long-range transboundary air pollution
LULUCF	land use, land-use change and forestry
MBT	mechanical biological treatment
MDG	Millennium Development Goal
MEA	Millennium Ecosystem Assessment
MPA	marine protected area
MSY	maximum sustainable yield
MW	megawatts
NAPA	National Adaptation Programme of Action
NF_3	Nitrogen trifluoride
NGO	non-governmental organisation

NIMBY	Not In My Back Yard
NMT	non-motorised transport
NOAA/GMD	National Oceanic and Atmospheric Administration's Global Monitoring Division
NPP	net primary productivity
NZU	New Zealand Unit
ODA	official development assistance
OECD	Organisation for Economic Co-operation and Development
PAH	polycyclic aromatic hydrocarbon
PBDE	polybrominated diphenyl ether
PCB	polychlorinated biphenyl
pCER	primary Certified Emission Reduction
PDD	project design document
PES	payments for ecosystem services
PETM	Paleocene-Eocene thermal maximum
PFC	perfluorocarbon
PFM	participatory forest management
Pg	petagram
PHEV	plug-in hybrid electric vehicle
ppmv	parts per million by volume
REDD	Reduce carbon Emissions from Deforestation and forest Degradation
RF	radiative forcing
RGGI	Regional Greenhouse Gas Initiative
RMU	removal unit
SCP	sustainable consumption and production
SER	Society of Ecological Restoration
SF_6	Sulphur hexafluoride
SFM	sustainable forest management
SLCA	social life-cycle assessment
SLF	Sustainable Livelihood Framework
SRES	Special Report on Emissions Scenarios
SRM	solar radiation management
SSF	small-scale fisheries
STEP	Sustainable Tourism Eco-certification Program
STL	supplementary transaction log
TEEB	The Economics of Ecosystems and Biodiversity
TEV	total economic value
Tg	Teragram
THC	thermohaline circulation
UN	United Nations
UNCCD	United Nations Convention to Combat Desertification
UNCED	United Nations Conference on Environment and Development
UNCSD	United Nations Commission on Sustainable Development
UNCTAD	United Nations Conference on Trade and Development
UNDESA	United Nations Department of Economic and Social Affairs
UNDP	United Nations Development Programme

UNDRIP	United Nations Declaration of the Rights of Indigenous Peoples
UNECE	United Nations Economic Commission for Europe
UNEP	United Nations Environment Programme
UNESCAP	United Nations Economic and Social Commission for Asia and the Pacific
UNESCO	United Nations Educational, Scientific and Cultural Organization
UNFCCC	United Nations Framework Convention on Climate Change
UNU-IHDP	University of the United Nations – International Human Dimensions Programme
VER	verified emissions reduction
VKM	vehicle kilometre
WBCSD	World Business Council for Sustainable Development
WEC	World Energy Council
WEEE	waste electrical and electronic equipment
WRI	World Resources Institute
WTO	World Trade Organization
WTP	willingness to pay
WWF	World Wildlife Foundation

PREFACE

Recent years have witnessed a rapid growth of interest in the green economy, resulting in its incorporation into policy at both national and international scales. This interest is driven by an attractive idea: that the green economy could help solve both the financial and environmental crises that affect the world today. Consequently, considerable investments are now being made in the development of green technology, green goods and services, renewable energy, recycling of materials and green infrastructure. However, are such approaches genuinely 'green'? How can the green economy be defined and assessed? How can it be achieved in practice? And does the green economy genuinely offer a 'win-win' solution to both environmental and economic problems?

The green economy is one of the most exciting ideas of our times. Yet there is considerable uncertainty about what it actually entails, how it should be developed, and what its impacts might be. Many aspects of the green economy are currently the focus of controversy and debate. At the same time, the green economy is developing rapidly, with new products and services continually emerging. As an illustration, renewable energy already accounts for one-fifth of global power generation, and will soon exceed all other power sources other than coal (IEA, 2013). The green economy therefore provides many new opportunities for innovation, economic development and employment.

To take advantage of these opportunities, and to help the green economy achieve its potential, there is an urgent need for people with appropriate knowledge, skills and understanding. This book has been developed to help meet this need. The text is based on a new Green Economy MSc course that we recently developed at Bournemouth University, which is the first of its kind. Our motivation for developing this course, which is entirely delivered by distance learning, was to support those people interested in developing a career in the green economy. This might be achieved either through new job opportunities or entrepreneurship, or through existing employment, for example, by driving institutional change. The information that such people might need is distributed very widely across many different academic journals, books and other sources. The aim of this book is therefore to provide an introduction to this literature, while providing a foundation for deeper learning of individual topics of particular interest.

The green economy is an enormous subject. We have therefore had to be highly selective when choosing material for this book. Inevitably, this choice has been influenced by our own interests and experience, and for these biases, we apologise. We believe that what differentiates the green economy from traditional economic approaches is its relationship to the environment, and for this reason, emphasis is placed here on the underlying ecological processes and principles. However, we also recognise that the green economy is highly interdisciplinary, and this text therefore also draws on a wide range of different sources, including social science, geography, psychology, law, sustainability science, environmental science, political science and economics. Emphasis is also placed on systems thinking, to help readers integrate information from these different disciplines.

This book examines the green economy as a type of social-ecological system, rather than focusing explicitly on economics. Readers interested in learning more about the principles and practice of green economics are encouraged to consult *Green Economics* by Cato (2009), available from the same publisher. This could usefully be viewed as a sister publication to the current book, which is designed to be complementary in terms of content and scope. While limited reference is made here to green economic theory, which Cato (2009) considers in depth, its application is explored at a number of points in this text. Perspectives such as ecological economics, sociology and environmental politics are similarly not treated here in great depth, despite their relevance to the overall theme. However, suggestions for further reading on these and other topics are provided throughout the text.

The material presented in this book is grounded firmly in the primary research literature, particularly drawing on publications in leading academic journals. In this way, we have attempted to provide an entry point into the best available evidence on each topic considered. However, the green economy is a living discipline, which is developing rapidly. As noted above, many of the issues associated with it are controversial. Many text books present a topic as if knowledge is complete or a consensus exists. This is very far from the case with the green economy, which is partly what makes it so interesting and challenging. Our intention here is not to promote a particular point of view or to identify consensus, but to encourage the reader to reflect on the evidence presented and to draw their own conclusions. We strongly believe that there is a need for critical evaluation of the concepts, approaches and evidence that have been provided by different authors. This book is designed to support such critical thinking. We have encouraged the reader to think about the issues raised in the text, and the evidence presented, through the inclusion of 'Reflection points'. These are invitations to consider the issues raised, and the questions presented, to encourage a reflective approach to learning. We have also suggested some further learning activities at various points in the text. Hopefully, readers will subsequently feel able to engage in the active, on-going debate about the future development of the green economy, and even to improve on the ideas presented.

We find the idea of a green economy deeply exciting. It offers nothing less than a better world for everyone. However, achievement of this vision will require unprecedented changes in our society and how we go about our everyday lives. While many substantial challenges remain, it is heartening to see the widespread changes that are already taking place, some of which are profiled in this book. We very much hope that you will be inspired by this text, and that it encourages you to help the green economy become a reality. Whether this book succeeds or fails in these goals, please let us know how it could be improved in future.

Acknowledgements

In preparing this book, we thank Professor Molly Cato, Roehampton University, and Tim Hardwick, our editor at Earthscan, for their help and support. We also gratefully acknowledge the contributions made by our colleagues: Jennifer Birch, John Brackstone, Tilak Ginige, Kathy Hodder, Kate Forrester and Chris Shiel.

Bibliography

Cato, M. S. 2009. *Green Economics. An Introduction to Theory, Policy and Practice*, Earthscan, London.
IEA 2013. *Medium-Term Renewable Energy Market Report 2013. Market Trends and Projections to 2018*, OECD/IEA, Paris.

Adrian C. Newton and Elena Cantarello
School of Applied Sciences
Bournemouth University
anewton@bournemouth.ac.uk
ecantarello@bournemouth.ac.uk
November 2013

1

INTRODUCTION

The term 'green economy' appears to have first been used by Pearce *et al.* (1989) in the title of their book, *Blueprint for a Green Economy*. However, the term 'green economy' is not explicitly defined or referred to in the book itself, which focuses on the concept of sustainable development. The term 'green economy' only became widely used following the global financial crisis of 2007–2008, which helped push it swiftly to the top of the political agenda. The financial crisis drove many countries into recession and into higher levels of debt, while also causing high numbers of job losses and widespread business failure. At the same time, it exacerbated a food crisis in many developing countries, as a result of rising food and fuel prices. These events coincided with increasing concern about the potential impacts of climate change caused by anthropogenic activities, particularly the increasing use of fossil fuels (UNEP, 2009). All these crises occurred against a backdrop of widespread and intensifying ecological degradation, and growing concern about its impact on human livelihoods (Millennium Ecosystem Assessment, 2005).

Development of the green economy was widely seen as offering a potential solution to these multiple global crises. For example, the United Nations Environmental Programme (UNEP) promoted the idea of 'green stimulus packages' as part of the economic recovery efforts, involving large-scale public investment in green technologies. In 2008, UNEP launched a 'Green Economy Initiative' to provide analysis and policy support for development of the green economy, and published *A Global Green New Deal* (Barbier, 2009, 2010). This identified the potential opportunity provided by these multiple crises, by supporting economic recovery while addressing other global challenges, such as reducing carbon dependency, protecting ecosystems and water resources, and alleviating poverty. This was identified as the only way of revitalising the global economy on a more sustained basis (Barbier, 2009). In 2011, UNEP's Green Economy Initiative provided a detailed report on the green economy, with the aim of providing practical guidance to policy-makers (UNEP, 2011).

A number of other commentators similarly suggested that these events might offer an opportunity for a fundamental shift in the global economy (Homer-Dixon, 2007; Jones, 2009). At the same time, many authors have identified the numerous business opportunities that can be provided by the development of the green economy (Esty and Winston, 2006; Croston, 2008; Makower, 2009; Kane, 2010; Weybrecht, 2010). Today, the green economy is growing rapidly through the development of environmentally enhancing goods and services, including cleaner and more efficient technology, renewable energy, ecosystem- and biodiversity-based products and services, chemical and waste management, and the construction or retrofitting of ecologically friendly buildings (UNEP, 2011).

This chapter provides a brief introduction to the concept of a green economy, by considering how it might be defined and how it has become incorporated into policy. Some of the economic principles on which the green economy might be based are then briefly described, to provide a context for the rest of the book.

1.1 Definition of the green economy

At the outset of its use, the term 'green economy' was treated as synonymous with the concept of sustainable development, as noted above (Pearce *et al.*, 1989; Jacobs, 1991). More recently, a variety of other definitions have been proposed, some of which are:

- UNEP (2011) defines a green economy as one that results in 'improved human well-being and social equity, while significantly reducing environmental risks and ecological scarcities'. Put another way, a green economy is 'low-carbon, resource efficient and socially inclusive'. Furthermore, 'growth in income and employment are driven by public and private investments that reduce carbon emissions and pollution, enhance energy and resource efficiency, and prevent the loss of biodiversity and ecosystem services'.
- The Green Economy Coalition (2012), which is a large multi-stakeholder alliance, defines the green economy as 'one that generates a better quality of life for all within the ecological limits of the planet'. These authors highlight the need for green economies to improve human well-being, while also improving natural capital and systems.
- The United Nations Conference on Trade and Development (UNCTAD, 2010) defines a green economy as 'an economy that results in improved human well-being and reduced inequalities, while not exposing future generations to significant environmental risks and ecological scarcities. It seeks to bring long-term societal benefits to short-term activities aimed at mitigating environmental risks'.
- The International Chamber of Commerce (2011) defines the green economy from a business perspective, as 'an economy in which economic growth and environmental responsibility work together in a mutually reinforcing fashion while supporting progress on social development'.

The Danish 92 Group (2012) defines the green economy as:

> not a state but a process of transformation and a constant dynamic progression. The green economy does away with the systemic distortions and dysfunctionalities of the current mainstream economy and results in human well-being and equitable access to opportunity for all people, while safeguarding environmental and economic integrity in order to remain within the planet's finite carrying capacity. The economy cannot be green without being equitable.

UNU-IHDP (2012) define a green economy as:

> one that focuses on enabling people around the world to pursue and achieve lives that are meaningful to them, while minimizing humanity's negative impacts on the environment. It is an economy that is measured against the yardsticks of human well-being and its productive base. It is an economy that is anchored by a passion for equity and a celebration of ingenuity.

Chapple (2008) defines the green economy as:

> the clean energy economy, consisting primarily of four sectors: renewable energy (e.g. solar, wind, geothermal); green building and energy efficiency technology; energy-efficient infrastructure and transportation; and recycling and waste-to-energy. The green economy is not just about the ability to produce clean energy, but also technologies that allow cleaner production processes, as well as the growing market for products which consume less energy. Thus, it might include products, processes, and services that reduce environmental impact or improve natural resource use.

These different definitions highlight the lack of consensus about precisely what the green economy entails. Rather, this is an area of active debate. For many commentators, particularly those in the business community, the green economy is synonymous with the 'clean energy' economy, as described by Chapple (2008). Many of the definitions listed above, however, also refer to the goals of improving human well-being and social equity. Many also explicitly mention the environment, by referring to the concept of environmental limits or carrying capacity.

Reflection point

Which of these definitions do you think best describes the green economy? How might these definitions be improved? You are encouraged to continue to consider these questions, as you consult other chapters of this book.

As noted by Peters and Britez (2010), the existence of various definitions indicates that the term 'green economy' is ambiguous and can contain multiple meanings. It is therefore important to consider what is being meant by people when they use the term, particularly when they do not provide an explicit definition. It is also important to remember that there is also a political dimension to the concept. For example, Peters and Britez caution that it could be used as an empty rhetoric device, to justify the political primacy of certain countries within the global economic system. A key issue, which is hidden within these definitions, is whether an effective green economy can be constructed within the current capitalist economic system, or whether the system requires a profound restructuring. This relates to the widely held view that green technology, such as forms of clean energy, are sufficient solutions for the current global environmental problems, widespread poverty and social inequality. The explicit incorporation of social equity and environmental quality in many definitions of the green economy is evidence of a counter-view.

Reflection point

When politicians refer to the green economy, which definition do you think they have in mind?

Other related concepts have also been widely used, including 'green growth' and the 'low carbon economy'. For example, in 2010, the Global Green Growth Institute (GGGI; http:// gggi.org/) was established as a new international organisation, which is dedicated to pioneering and diffusing a new model of economic growth in developing and emerging countries, known as 'green growth'. This simultaneously targets poverty reduction, job creation and social inclusion, together with environmental sustainability, including mitigation of climate change and biodiversity loss, and security of access to clean energy and water. Similarly at the G20 Seoul Summit in 2010, government leaders recognised green growth as an inherent part of sustainable development, focusing on creating enabling environments for the development of energy efficiency and clean energy technologies. These countries devoted some US$522 billion to such objectives as part of the fiscal stimulus measures undertaken in 2008–2009 (Allen and Clouth, 2012). A number of other international organisations have also focused on green growth, including the World Bank (2012) and the OECD (2011).

A range of different definitions for green growth have been proposed, including (Allen and Clouth, 2012):

- UNESCAP: growth that emphasises environmentally sustainable economic progress to foster low-carbon, socially inclusive development.
- OECD: fostering economic growth and development, while ensuring that natural assets continue to provide the resources and environmental services on which our well-being relies.
- World Bank: growth that is efficient in its use of natural resources, clean in that it minimises pollution and environmental impacts, and resilient in that it accounts for natural hazards and the role of environmental management and natural capital in preventing physical disasters.
- GGGI: growth that sustains economic growth while at the same time ensuring climatic and environmental sustainability.

Reflection point

Is green growth the same concept as the green economy? Note that these definitions emphasise economic growth, which is a widespread political goal. Whether or not a green economy is compatible with economic growth is a major point of debate, which will be considered later in this book.

The concept of low carbon development originates in the United Nations Framework Convention on Climate Change (UNFCCC) adopted in 1992. This is based on the approach of amending economic development planning to ensure reduced emission of greenhouse gases (GHGs), which are associated with anthropogenic climate change. Many individual countries have produced low-carbon growth plans, supported by international organisations such as UNDP, UNEP, and the World Bank. The issue of climate change and carbon management is considered further in Chapter 3.

Allen and Clouth (2012) highlight the significant overlap that exists between the concepts of the green economy and green growth, including a shared focus on environmental protection, resource efficiency, ecological sustainability, human well-being and equity. Low carbon development can best be considered as a sub-set of both green growth and the green economy. However, definitions of green growth do not refer to ecological limits (see Chapter 2), as incorporated within some definitions of the green economy. The various definitions of low carbon development, green growth and green economy can be seen to cover a spectrum of different 'shades of green', from narrow concerns about climate change at one end of the spectrum to more extensive critiques of the environmental sustainability of modern capitalism at the other.

1.2 Policy context

The green economy has recently become the focus of policy development at both the national and international scales. Most significantly, it was one of the two main themes addressed at the UN Conference on Sustainable Development (Rio+20) in 2012. This international dialogue was supported by the development of a number of reports, notably that produced by UNEP (2011) entitled *Towards a Green Economy: Pathways to Sustainable Development and Poverty Eradication*. While establishing that the green economy was now part of mainstream political dialogue, the report sought to provide guidance to governments on policy development, while highlighting its potential value in achieving both economic development and poverty alleviation.

The principal outcome document of Rio+20 was a report entitled *The Future We Want*. This recognised the green economy as an important tool for achieving sustainable development, which 'should contribute to eradicating poverty as well as sustained economic growth, enhancing social inclusion, improving human welfare and creating opportunities for employment and decent work for all, while maintaining the healthy functioning of the earth's ecosystems' (UNCSD, 2012). The document also encouraged countries to develop green economy policies, and provided some guidance for the development of such policies.

Some commentators have criticised the outcome of Rio+20 for lacking firm commitments from countries, and lacking detail on how to implement the green economy in practice (Barbier, 2012; Morrow, 2012; Borel-Saladin and Turok, 2013). However, many countries have subsequently begun to develop national strategies and plans for green economic development. These efforts are being supported by a range of international organisations, such as the OECD and the World Bank, as well as other UN agencies. At the European scale, the EU 2020 strategy aims to develop a 'smart, green and inclusive economy' (EC, 2010). At the national scale, green economic plans are under development in countries such as Indonesia, Brazil, Mexico, Ethiopia, Cambodia, Guyana, Kazakhstan, Mongolia, Papua New Guinea and the Philippines (Benson and Greenfield, 2012). Some countries have already made significant progress towards the development of such strategies. For example, South Korea has incorporated green growth into its national development strategy, and has dedicated 80 per cent of its fiscal stimulus plan to green growth projects. It is aiming to establish the first nationwide 'smart grid' system by 2030, increasing renewable energy to 11 per cent of energy supplies by 2030, and to construct 1 million green homes by 2020. In China, some US$140 billion is targeted at green investments, and its 12th Five-Year Plan (2011–2015) dedicates an entire section to green development (Benson and Greenfield, 2012). Other countries that have developed national strategies or plans for the green economy include Barbados, Canada, Grenada, Jordan, South Africa, France and the UK (Allen and Clouth, 2012).

> ### Reflection point
>
> Morrow (2012) criticises the outcome of Rio+20 for being 'pro-growth and unashamedly anthropocentric'. Do you think it might be appropriate for the green economy to be 'pro-growth' and 'anthropocentric', or not?

1.3 The green economy versus sustainable development

The focus on the green economy at Rio+20 can be viewed in terms of an attempt to apply new thinking or new impetus to the concept of sustainable development, specifically by linking it to the concept of green growth (Morrow, 2012). This therefore raises the question – what is the relationship between the green economy and sustainable development?

Sustainable development is often defined as development that 'meets the needs of the present without compromising the ability of future generations to meet their needs'. This definition comes from the report *Our Common Future* (often referred to as the Brundtland Report), which was published in 1987 (WCED, 1987). While this is often taken to be the standard definition of the concept, there are many others in the literature. The main components of sustainable development are generally agreed to be economic, environmental and social, which are often represented by three pillars or three interlocking circles (Figure 1.1a) (Kates *et al.*, 2005; Dresner, 2008).

Sustainable development has been the subject of a number of milestones in international policy. Key among these is the United Nations Conference on Environment and Development (UNCED) held in Rio de Janeiro in 1992 (the so-called 'Earth Summit'), which issued a declaration of principles, and developed Agenda 21, which provided a global action plan for future sustainable development. As a result of the Earth Summit, many national governments developed national policies or strategies for sustainable development. The commitment to

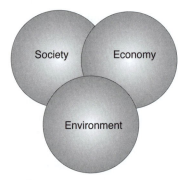

FIGURE 1.1A The conventional view of the interaction between economy, society and environment, as incorporated within the concept of sustainable development

sustainable development was reaffirmed in 2002, at the World Summit on Sustainable Development in Johannesburg, South Africa.

Another key policy initiative was the development of the Millennium Development Goals (MDGs). These were established as a direct result of the Millennium Summit in 2000, where the United Nations Millennium Declaration was adopted by many world leaders. The aim of the MDGs was to support development by improving social and economic conditions in the poorest countries, based on the recognition that there is a strong connection between poverty alleviation and sustainable development. The principal focus of the MDGs was on raising basic standards of living, which was addressed by concentrating on three areas of development: (1) strengthening human capital; (2) improving infrastructure; and (3) enhancing social, economic and political rights. The eight principal MDGs, which ranged from halving extreme poverty to providing universal primary education, defined targets to be met by 2015. A further MDG Summit took place in 2010. This concluded with the adoption of a global action plan, and the pledging of additional resources to support its implementation. While some progress has been made towards achieving the MDGs, overall this is very uneven and substantial challenges remain (Chibba, 2011).

In the wake of these policy processes, sustainable development has spread rapidly as a concept, and can now be considered a global movement that is central to the mission of many international organisations, national institutions, corporate enterprises and locales. This is despite the fact that the standard definition is highly ambiguous, resulting in a substantial and ongoing debate about what sustainable development really means in practice (Kates *et al.*, 2005; Dresner, 2008). Many authors have also questioned how the concept is interpreted. For example, Dawe and Ryan (2003) highlight a weakness of considering its three components, economic, environmental and social, as equivalent. This implies that if a compromise can be reached between our economic needs, human well-being and the environment, we can simply continue along our current economic path. However, as these authors point out, humanity can have neither an economy nor social well-being without the environment. The environment should therefore be viewed as the foundation of any economy and of human well-being.

Reflection point

Do you agree with Dawe and Ryan (2003) that the environment is the source of both the economy and human well-being, and should therefore be viewed as more significant than the others? If so, what implications does this have for the kind of economy that is required in the future?

The concept of sustainable development derived from the Brundtland Report attempted to reconcile social, economic and environmental concerns through achieving a balance between them. In practice, trade-offs between them are arguably inevitable (Morrow, 2012). Nevertheless, this concept of sustainability has been very successful in achieving buy-in by states and other participants, and its inherent flexibility or vagueness has helped to ensure its widespread support. Concerns remain, however, about the limited progress being made towards sustainable development, as highlighted by the environmental degradation that is occurring in many parts of the world (Millennium Ecosystem Assessment, 2005).

As sustainable development continues to be the overarching policy goal of the international community, the green economy is widely seen as a means of supporting its achievement (Allen and Clouth, 2012), or as an enabling component of it (UNCTAD, 2010). However, as noted by IUCN (2010), the concept of the green economy often carries a more distinctive meaning, which focuses specifically on the fundamental changes that are required to ensure that economic systems are made more sustainable. Similarly, for the Green Economy Coalition (2012), the green economy is about a different way of doing things.

> ### Reflection point
>
> Given that sustainable development is a well-established concept, is there a need for the green economy? Or might the concept of the green economy galvanise new action, for example among the business community, which could help deliver sustainable development?

1.4 Neoclassical economics

Economics can be defined as a social science that seeks to explain the economic basis of human societies, or how societies decide what, how and for whom to produce (Begg *et al.*, 2011). It therefore studies the choices that individuals, businesses, governments and societies make as they cope with the scarcity of resources, and the incentives that influence these choices (Parkin *et al.*, 2012). The subject can be divided into two main themes. *Micro-economics* is the study of the choices that individuals and businesses make, the way these interact in markets and the influence of governments. In contrast, *macro-economics* is the study of the performance of national economies and the global economy.

There are two main types of economic system, the market economy and the command economy. In a market economy, resources are allocated through the mechanism of price, and resources are primarily owned and controlled by private companies and individuals. A market can be defined as an arrangement where buyers and sellers trade commodities and resources, usually in exchange for money. In a command economy, resources are allocated by a central planning authority, and major industries and resources are both owned and controlled by the state (Hardwick *et al.*, 1999).

Mainstream (or orthodox) economics is referred to as neoclassical economics, which is based on three main assumptions (Weintraub, 2013):

1. People have rational preferences among outcomes.
2. Individuals maximise utility (which is what they obtain from consuming goods), and firms maximise profits.
3. People act independently on the basis of full and relevant information.

Based on these assumptions, neoclassical economists have developed a number of theories for understanding how scarce resources are allocated. These include profit maximisation by firms, and the use of supply and demand curves to understand production and consumption, respectively (Hardwick *et al.*, 1999). The interactions between supply and demand determine the market price. While recognising that economic systems are dynamic, neoclassical economics focuses strongly on the concept of equilibria. A market equilibrium is considered to exist when the price and quantity of a commodity match the expectations of both producers and consumers; the quantities demanded and supplied are equal.

According to neoclassical theory, economic decisions are made on the basis of maximising utility, to ensure that the preferences of as many 'agents' as possible are fulfilled to the maximum extent possible, given the limitation of available resources (Cato, 2011). In this context, agents are those actors or decision-makers involved in economic activity, such as individual consumers or firms. According to this theory, the economy is expected to grow indefinitely (ibid.), for example, as a result of developments in technology. Economic growth is the major objective of many governments, as it can lead to an increased standard of living, and can potentially eliminate poverty (Hardwick *et al.*, 1999). However, economic growth can also lead to negative impacts, both on people and the environment.

One of the defining features of neoclassical economics is the belief that the market economy is superior to other forms of economic organisation, because of its superior efficiency. Economic efficiency is achieved when the available resources are used to produce goods and services at the lowest possible cost, and in the quantities that will provide the greatest possible value or benefit (Parkin *et al.*, 2012). The relationships between costs and benefits can be assessed through a *cost-benefit analysis*, which is often used to evaluate the relative merits of different decisions or policy options (Cato, 2011).

Further details of neoclassical economics are provided by introductory texts such as Begg *et al.* (2011), Parkin *et al.* (2012) and Hardwick *et al.* (1999).

A number of authors have criticised neoclassical economic approaches, particularly in the wake of the recent financial crisis. For example Colander *et al.* (2009) highlighted the failure of the economics profession to predict the crisis, or to fully appreciate its extent. This was attributed to a failure in economic theory and associated models, which failed to capture the inherent dynamics of economic systems and the instability that accompanies its complex dynamics. The theoretical focus on the allocation of scarce resources was considered to be 'short-sighted and misleading', and was associated with a failure to fully appreciate the role of the increasing connectivity of the financial system and the interactions between actors. The authors conclude that the dominant economic paradigm has 'no solid methodological basis', and generally performs only modestly.

Similarly, Aldred (2009) provides a detailed critique of economics, highlighting the limitations of a dogmatic focus on economic growth, which widely pervades government policy. Rather, he suggests, outcomes such as improved quality of life, human well-being and happiness should be the principal objectives of such policy. These outcomes do not necessarily result from increased consumption, despite its assumed importance in economic theory. Aldred also questions the increasing monetisation of many aspects of human life, which erodes the intrinsic values that people hold, such as those arising from moral convictions. For example, rather than viewing climate change mitigation as a purely economic decision amenable to cost-benefit analysis, he argues that such mitigation should be viewed as a political and ethical decision that has major implications for future generations. Aldred highlights the fact that the assumptions underpinning neoclassical economics are often flawed, and argues strongly that it draws on hidden ethical assumptions, which should instead be made explicit.

1.5 Ecological economics

In recent decades, ecological economics has developed as an academic discipline that examines the interactions between economic systems and ecological systems (Common and Stagl, 2005). This field developed as a response to the fact that neoclassical economics has largely ignored the natural environment. Two sub-disciplines of neoclassical economics have developed since the 1970s, namely *environmental economics* and *natural resource economics*. These respectively consider the relationship between the economy and the environment, including environmental pollution, and the extraction of natural resources. However, ecological economics differs from these two sub-disciplines by explicitly viewing economic activity as occurring within an environmental context, rather than viewing the environment as a sub-set of the human economy. Ecological economics therefore considers the economy to be a sub-system of nature, whereas neoclassical approaches take an opposing view (Common and Stagl, 2005; Faber, 2008).

Some of the defining features of ecological economics include:

- An emphasis on preserving natural capital, or the stock of natural ecosystems that provides goods and services to people. This is because natural capital cannot readily be substituted by human-made capital, as assumed by neoclassical economics.
- A belief that economic growth cannot continue indefinitely. Ultimately, growth will be limited by the carrying capacity of the Earth's ecosystems and the fact that natural resources are finite. Many ecological economists envisage a steady state economy, with zero growth.
- Consideration of the scale of the economy relative to the ecosystems on which it depends.
- A focus on the economics of sustainable development, including the equitable distribution of goods and services, the incorporation of social values in decision-making, and improvement of human well-being.

In addition, ecological economics is concerned about incorporating moral values into economic decisions, and considering their ethical implications, such as the rights of future generations and treatment of the poor (Spash, 1999). Many of these issues are highly relevant to the green economy, and are considered later in this book. However, as noted by Daly and Farley (2011), ecological economics has largely been an academic endeavour to date, and has had relatively little impact on mainstream economic thinking. Detailed accounts of ecological economics are provided by Common and Stagl (2005), Daly and Farley (2011) and Shmelev (2012); see also Barbier and Markandya (2012).

1.6 Green economics

In contrast to ecological economics, green economics has not developed primarily as an academic discipline, but has emerged from the grassroots. As a consequence, it is arguably more diverse and more loosely defined than the other approaches to economics described above. Cato (2009) provides a valuable synthesis of different concepts and ideas, and traces the historical development of green economics through the contributions of key individuals. These include E. F. Schumacher, whose seminal book, *Small Is Beautiful* (Schumacher, 1973), continues to exert a powerful influence over much green thinking. For many, its emphasis on the local scale, on embedding economic activity in neighbourhoods, communities and local culture, and on keeping supply chains short, remains central to the green ethos.

Cato (2011) indicates that green economics differs from neoclassical economics in the following ways (Figure 1.1b):

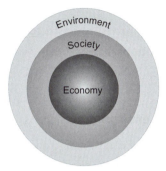

FIGURE 1.1B   The green economy paradigm; the economy operates within social relationships and the whole of society is embedded within the environment

Source: Cato (2011), with permission from Taylor & Francis.

- It seeks to include the perspectives of those who are marginalised within the present economic structure, including women and the world's poor, as well as the needs of planet Earth.
- It is inherently concerned with social justice; issues such as equality and justice take precedence over considerations such as economic efficiency.
- It has emerged from the work of environmental campaigners and green politicians, and is grounded in the process of building a sustainable economy in practice rather than in abstract theory.
- It aims to move away from the focus on economic growth towards a steady-state economy.
- It supports a shift away from the market economy to a focus on human interactions, involving an increased role for mutual and community-based economic activity, occurring within a framework of strict international regulation of environmental and social standards.
- It encourages a shift towards localisation, involving the development of locally based economies, each embedded in its environmental and cultural context, and each aiming for self-sufficiency in basic resources.

Some of these ideas are shared with ecological economics. For example, the concept of the economy being embedded within the natural environment is common to both approaches (Figure 1.2). However, Cato (2009) draws a distinction between green and ecological economics, highlighting the more academic and scientific nature of the latter, and its greater focus on measurement and valuation, often using techniques from neoclassical economics. A further key distinction is the explicit link between green economics, environmentalism and green politics. According to Cato, for many green economists, there is a need for massive, significant changes to the way our economic lives are organised, including new ways of thinking about economics itself. The outcome might be an economy that is not capitalist;

that is not dominated by transnational corporations; that does not focus solely on monetary exchange, work and production; and will not be globalised. Such radical proposals have been a feature of green politics for some time, though as Cato (2009) points out, Green Parties that have been elected into government positions have often become less radical as a result.

> **Reflection point**
>
> Which approaches to economics are relevant to the green economy? Must a green economy be based on green economics, or could it be achieved through the application of neoclassical or ecological economics?

1.7 The economy and the environment

As noted above, the economy and the environment can be viewed as two interdependent systems (Figure 1.2). What happens in the economy affects the environment, and changes in

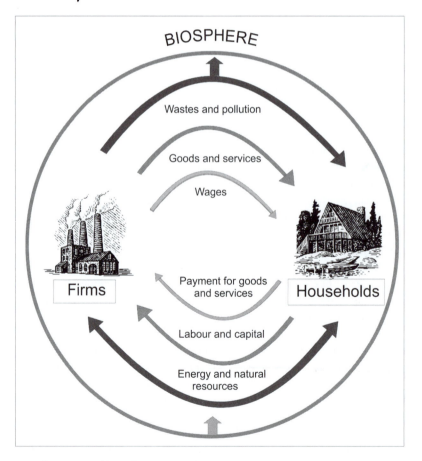

FIGURE 1.2   Illustration of how the economy links with the environment

Source: Cato (2011), with permission from Taylor & Francis.

the environment affect the economy. Specifically, there are four classes of service that the environment provides to the economy (Common and Stagl, 2005):

- *Resource supply*: Resources (often referred to as natural resources) are extracted from the environment and used in economic production. Renewable resources are those that can be replaced after they are harvested, such as those derived from biotic populations, which can reproduce. Non-renewable resources, such as minerals and fossil fuels, cannot be replaced over timescales relevant to human interest.
- *Waste sink*: Wastes arise from both production and consumption in the economy, but ultimately derive from resources. Following the law of the conservation of matter, the mass of wastes inserted into the environment must equal the mass of resources extracted from it.
- *Amenity*: The environment provides humans with sources of pleasure and stimulation, such as swimming in the ocean, hiking in nature reserves and other forms of recreation.
- *Life support*: The maintenance of the conditions necessary for human life is a precondition for human economic activity.

Many of the processes in both the economic and ecological systems can be considered in terms of *stocks* and *flows*. A stock is a quantity measured at a specific point in time, and a flow is measured over an interval of time, in other words, it is analogous to a rate. For example, a country may have capital stocks referring to the total value of equipment, buildings and other assets. The gross domestic product (GDP) refers to the amount of money spent over a time period (such as a year), and is therefore a flow variable.

The basic activities that comprise an economy are *consumption*, *production* and *investment*, defined as follows (Common and Stagl, 2005):

- *Consumption* is the use by humans of goods and services (or commodities) to satisfy their needs and wants. This includes both consumption of physical materials and energy, but also non-material services such as the aesthetic value of a painting displayed in an art gallery.
- *Production* refers to the creation of the goods and services that people consume, undertaken by firms. Production may require several kinds of inputs, including labour, energy, and the raw materials or natural resources extracted from the environment.
- *Investment* refers to that part of production added to the capital stock rather than consumed. In economics this refers to the accumulation of physical entities, such as factories, machinery and houses. In finance, investment involves putting money into an asset with the expectation of capital appreciation and/or interest earnings.

The capital stock of an economy includes: (1) the *durable* or *physical capital* used in production, and includes tools, machinery, vehicles and roads, etc.; (2) *human capital*, referring to the stock of knowledge and skills held by individuals, used to produce economic value through labour; (3) *intellectual capital*, which is the knowledge and skills used by the economy but not embodied in particular individuals, but held in books and other cultural artefacts; and (4) *social capital*, which is the set of institutions and customs that organise economic activity. In addition, (5) *natural capital* refers to those stocks in the environment that deliver services to the economy.

This brief overview of the main elements of an economy immediately highlights some of the potential environmental impacts that can arise through economic activity. These include the use of non-renewable natural resources as inputs to production, and the harmful effects of waste emissions on the environment, referred to as pollution. Such impacts will be considered further in subsequent chapters.

1.8 Is the green economy a flawed idea?

Many of the concepts used in policy and decision-making have been subjected to critical scrutiny, and the green economy is no exception to this. Morrow (2012) highlighted the debate surrounding the concept of the green economy, as developed by UNEP and other UN agencies, associated with Rio+20. Some developing countries expressed scepticism about the green economy as a creative 'fix' for flaws in the global economic system, noting that the financial crisis was largely Western in origin. Concerns about the potential negative impacts of 'green' technologies were also raised, together with the risks of 'greenwashing', or misleading claims being made about green credentials. A number of developing countries, including Bolivia, Paraguay and Ecuador, pressed for major changes in the relationship between humanity and nature, which were more radical than the concept of the green economy promoted by the UN (ibid.). A further area of concern related to international trade, including the possibility of trade protectionism, potential attempts by some countries to gain enhanced market access for their products, and the potential role of transnational corporations. This relates to the issue of power, the grabbing of land and natural resources, and ultimately who controls the green economy (ETC Group, 2011).

Allen and Clouth (2012) highlight the widely held view that the green economy should not compete with or displace sustainable development, nor focus on environmental and economic dimensions to the detriment of the social element. Conversely, Borel-Saladin and Turok (2013) and Lander (2011) highlight concerns that current conceptions of the green economy may not represent a significant enough departure from the current economic system to be effective. Other main areas of concern relate to the monetisation of nature, or the financial valuation of ecosystem goods and services, which is widely perceived as an element of the green economy (Spash, 2008; Lander, 2011). In addition, much of the recent dialogue surrounding the green economy has failed to address the issue of the potential ecological limits to economic growth (Borel-Saladin and Turok, 2013). These issues are addressed further in Chapters 2 and 4.

Many of these concerns relate to how the green economy is defined, and specifically how it was conceived by the UN agencies who encouraged debate on the topic at Rio+20. Similar issues have characterised other intergovernmental debates, such as those surrounding sustainable development and climate change (Morrow, 2012). However, it is important to remember that the green economy does not solely depend on support from intergovernmental policy processes organised by the UN. It can also be considered as a grassroots initiative involving many civil society organisations, and increasingly as a commercial imperative within the business sector.

Reflection point

If the concept of a green economy is flawed, either in terms of how it is defined or implemented, how might such problems be addressed?

At the very least, development of the green economy concept has stimulated debate of how the global economy might be improved in future, to help achieve sustainable development. Allen and Clouth (2012) suggest that this debate has stimulated global efforts to transform the current economic system, including development of operational principles and measures that can be adopted by national governments to shift to a more sustainable economic framework. However, while it is widely agreed that changes to the global economic system need to be made, there is less agreement about precisely what changes are required. In whichever way the green economy is defined, the concept is based on the need to reduce the environmental impacts of economic activity. The following chapters examine how this might be achieved, while meeting human needs.

Reflection point

Do you consider the green economy as something separate from the main economy, or a part of it, as some commentators imply? Or do you believe that the entire economic system needs to be greener?

Suggested activity

Rio+20 was an important international event, which prompted a great deal of debate concerning the green economy. You are encouraged to explore the internet resources generated by this debate:

Rio+20: http://www.uncsd2012.org/
UN Sustainable Development resources: http://sustainabledevelopment.un.org/
UNCSD: www.uncsd2012.org/publicationsgreeneconomy.html
UNEP: www.unep.org/greeneconomy/
UNESCAP: www.greengrowth.org/

Bibliography

Aldred, J. 2009. *The Skeptical Economist: Revealing the Ethics Inside Economics*, Earthscan, London.

Allen, C. and Clouth, S. 2012. *A Guidebook to the Green Economy. Issue 1: Green Economy, Green Growth and Low Carbon Development: History, Definitions and a Guide to Recent Publications*, UN Division for Sustainable Development, Department of Economic and Social Affairs (UNDESA), New York.

Barbier, E. B. 2009. *Rethinking the Economic Recovery: A Global Green New Deal*, UNEP, Geneva.

Barbier, E. B. 2010. *A Global Green New Deal: Rethinking the Economic Recovery*, Cambridge University Press, Cambridge.

Barbier, E. B. 2012. The green economy post Rio+20. *Science*, 338: 887–888.

Barbier, E. B. and Markandya, A. 2012. *A New Blueprint for a Green Economy*, Routledge, London.

Begg, D., Vernasca, G., Fischer, S. and Dornbusch, R. 2011. *Economics*, 10th edn, McGraw-Hill, Maidenhead.

Benson, E. and Greenfield, O. 2012. *Surveying the 'Green Economy' and 'Green Growth' Landscape*, Green Economy Coalition, IIED, London.

Borel-Saladin, J. M. and Turok, I. N. 2013. The green economy: incremental change or transformation? *Environmental Policy and Governance*, 23: 209–220.

Cato, M. S. 2009. *Green Economics: An Introduction to Theory, Policy and Practice*, Earthscan, London.

Cato, M. S. 2011. *Environment and Economy*, Routledge, London.

Chapple, K. 2008. *Defining the Green Economy: A Primer on Green Economic Development*, Center for Community Innovation, University of California, Berkeley, CA.

Chibba, M. 2011. The Millennium Development Goals: key current issues and challenges. *Development Policy Review*, 29: 75–90.

Colander, D., Föllmer, H., Haas, A., *et al.* 2009. *The Financial Crisis and the Systemic Failure of Academic Economics.* Discussion Papers 09-03, Department of Economics, University of Copenhagen.

Common, M. and Stagl, S. 2005. *Ecological Economics: An Introduction*, Cambridge University Press, Cambridge.

Croston, G. 2008. *75 Green Businesses: You Can Start to Make Money and Make a Difference*, Entrepreneur Press, Irvine, CA.

Daly, H. E. and Farley, J. 2011. *Ecological Economics: Principles and Applications*, Island Press, Washington, DC.

Danish 92 Group 2012. *Building an Equitable Green Economy*, The Danish 92 Group Forum for Sustainable Development, Copenhagen.

Dawe, N. K. and Ryan, K. L. 2003. The faulty three-legged-stool model of sustainable development. *Conservation Biology*, 17: 1458–1460.

Dresner, S. 2008. *The Principles of Sustainability*, Earthscan, London.

EC 2010. *Europe 2020: A Strategy for Smart, Sustainable and Inclusive Growth. COM(2010) 2020 Final*, European Commission, Brussels.

Esty, D. C. and Winston, A. S. 2006. *Green to Gold: How Smart Companies Use Environmental Strategy to Innovate, Create Value, and Build Competitive Advantage*, John Wiley & Sons, Hoboken, NJ.

ETC Group 2011. Who will control the green economy? *ETC Communiqué*, no. 107 [Online]. Available at: www.etcgroup.org (accessed 21 Sept. 2013).

Faber, M. 2008. How to be an ecological economist. *Ecological Economics*, 66: 1–7.

Green Economy Coalition 2012. *The Green Economy Pocket Book*, The Green Economy Coalition, IIED, London.

Hardwick, P., Langmead, J. and Khan, B. 1999. *An Introduction to Modern Economics*, Pearson Education, Harlow.

Homer-Dixon, T. 2007. *The Upside of Down: Catastrophe, Creativity and the Renewal of Civilization*, Souvenir Press, London.

International Chamber of Commerce 2011. *The ICC Task Force on Green Economy*, International Chamber of Commerce, Paris.

IUCN 2010. *A Guidebook for IUCN's Thematic Programme Area on Greening the World Economy (TPA5)*, IUCN, Gland, Switzerland.

Jacobs, M. 1991. *The Green Economy: Environment, Sustainable Development and the Politics of the Future*, Pluto Press, London.

Jones, V. 2009. *The Green Collar Economy: How One Solution Can Fix Our Two Biggest Problems*, HarperCollins, New York.

Kane, G. 2010. *The Three Secrets of Green Business: Unlocking Competitive Advantage in a Low Carbon Economy*, Earthscan, London.

Kates, R. W., Parris, T. M. and Leiserowitz, A. A. 2005. What is sustainable development? Goals, indicators, values, and practice. *Environment*, 47: 8–21.

Lander, E. 2011. *The Green Economy: The Wolf in Sheep's Clothing.* November 2011, Transnational Institute, Amsterdam. Available at: www.tni.org (accessed 21 Sept. 2013).

Makower, J. 2009. *Strategies for the Green Economy: Opportunities and Challenges in the New World of Business*, McGraw-Hill, New York.

Millennium Ecosystem Assessment 2005. *Ecosystems and Human Well-being: Current State and Trends*, Vol. 1, Island Press, Washington, DC.

Morrow, K. 2012. Rio+20, the green economy and re-orienting sustainable development. *Environmental Law Review*, 14: 279–297.

OECD 2011. *Towards Green Growth. A Summary for Policy Makers*, OECD, Paris.

Parkin, M., Powell, M. and Matthews, K. 2012. *Economics*, 8th edn, Pearson Education, Harlow.

Pearce, D. W., Markandya, A. and Barbier, E. 1989. *Blueprint for a Green Economy*, Earthscan, London.

Peters, M. A. and Britez, R. 2010. Ecopolitics of 'green economy', environmentalism and education. *Journal of Academic Research in Economics*, 2: 21–36.

Schumacher, E. F. 1973. *Small Is Beautiful*, Abacus, London.

Shmelev, S. E. 2012. *Ecological Economics: Sustainability in Practice*, Springer, Dordrecht.

Spash, C. L. 1999. The development of environmental thinking in economics. *Environmental Values*, 8: 413–435.

Spash, C. L. 2008. How much is that ecosystem in the window? The one with the bio-diverse tail. *Environmental Values*, 17: 259–284.

UNCSD 2012. *Report of the United Nations Conference on Sustainable Development. A/CONF.216/16*, United Nations, New York.

UNCTAD 2010. *The Green Economy: Trade and Sustainable Development Implications. Background Note Prepared by the UNCTAD Secretariat*, United Nations, New York.

UNEP 2009. *A Global Green New Deal: Policy Brief*, United Nations Environment Programme, Economics and Trade Branch, Geneva.

UNEP 2011. *Towards a Green Economy: Pathways to Sustainable Development and Poverty Eradication*, UNEP, Geneva.

UNU-IHDP 2012. *Green Economy and Sustainability: A Societal Transformation Process. Summary for Decision-Makers*, Secretariat of the International Human Dimensions Programme on Global Environmental Change (UNU-IHDP), Bonn.

WCED 1987. *Our Common Future*, Oxford University Press, Oxford.

Weintraub, E. R. 2013. Neoclassical economics, in *The Concise Encyclopedia of Economics*. Available at: www.econlib.org/library/Enc1/NeoclassicalEconomics.html (accessed 04 Sept. 2013).

Weybrecht, G. 2010. *The Sustainable MBA: The Manager's Guide to Green Business*, John Wiley & Sons, Chichester.

World Bank 2012. *Inclusive Green Growth: The Pathway to Sustainable Development*, World Bank, Washington, DC.

2

SUSTAINABILITY SCIENCE

2.1 Introduction

'Sustainability science' is a relatively new scientific discipline, focusing on the science underpinning sustainable development. It can also be considered as the science underpinning the development of the green economy. Kates *et al.* (2001), McMichael *et al.* (2003), Kates (2010) and de Vries (2012) provide useful overviews of the subject.

2.1.1 Characteristics of sustainability science

It is worth pausing a moment to consider what science is. It can be described simply as a system of acquiring knowledge, through a process of observation and experimentation. The value of an experiment is that it provides the most reliable form of evidence that there is. In the context of sustainability, you might immediately spot a problem: some aspects may be very difficult to observe, and may not be amenable to experimentation (how do we experiment on climate change, for example?). This illustrates the challenge facing the science of sustainability, and where arguably science may reach its limits. On the other hand, this is a very exciting and important challenge. We need the best scientific evidence on which to base the decisions that we are making, as they could affect our future very profoundly.

Some characteristics of sustainability science listed by Kates (2010) include:

- It is use-inspired; in other words, it is defined by the problems that it addresses rather than by the approaches employed. In this, it contrasts with curiosity-driven or 'blue skies' research. It is applied in nature, designed to meet human needs.
- It focuses on coupled human–environment systems. Integration is therefore a core theme. It is also strongly interdisciplinary, including both social and environmental sciences, as well as other fields.
- Sustainability science is rooted in values. Many proposed solutions relating to the development of the green economy depend on the values of different people. The subject therefore includes the science of identifying and analysing values and attitudes, as well as actions.

This third point is particularly profound. Much of the current debate regarding land use, economic development and environmental change arises from the contrasting values held by different people. For example, should the Arctic National Wildlife Refuge in Alaska be drilled for oil, or not? The answer to this arguably depends on your values. It might seem self-evident that we should, at all times, place human interests first. But there are other philosophical standpoints, which place the needs and rights of 'nature' as equal to those of people, such as the 'deep ecology' movement. This is an influential body of thought (e.g. see Grey 1993).

2.1.2 Context: environmental impacts of human activities

The whole concept of the green economy rests on the fact that human activities are having a major effect on the environment, at a global scale. Sustainability science examines these impacts, and attempts to identify how human needs can be met without compromising the global ecosystems on which we all depend.

It is difficult to appreciate just how profound the environmental impacts of human activities actually are. In Figure 2.1, you can see at a glance how the extent of human impact, on a range of different environmental variables, has intensified over the past few decades, particularly since 1950.

Questions you should be asking yourself about graphs like these are:

- What is this really telling us?
- How accurate are the data presented?
- How were these variables actually measured?
- What is the uncertainty, or error, around the data presented?
- Has this uncertainty changed over time? In other words, are the environmental data available at different times in the past as reliable as modern data?

As a generalisation, we always need to be cautious when interpreting data presented at the global scale. Nevertheless, they provide a striking impression of the rate and magnitude of the environmental change that is taking place.

2.1.3 Population growth

What is driving this increase in human impact? One factor is human population growth. This can be considered a major driver of environmental change. The latest population estimates produced by the United Nations Population Division suggest that the current world population of 7.2 billion is projected to reach 9.6 billion by 2050 (United Nations, 2012) (Figure 2.2).

The annual growth rate of the world population is about 1.1 per cent, which adds about 77 million people per year (ibid.). It is projected that the world's population could ultimately stabilise at about 9–10 billion people, some time later this century, but of course this projection is highly uncertain. Almost all of the projected growth will take place in the developing countries. How are we going to meet the human needs of 2 billion more people? At the same time, if global fertility continues to decline, this will lead to an increasingly aged population. How will they be cared for?

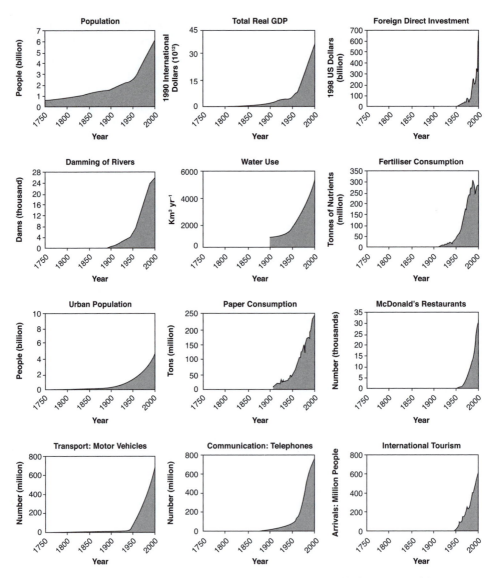

FIGURE 2.1 The increasing rates of change in human activity since the beginning of the Industrial Revolution

Source: Figure 3.67, Steffen *et al.* (2004, p. 133). With kind permission from Springer Science+Business Media.

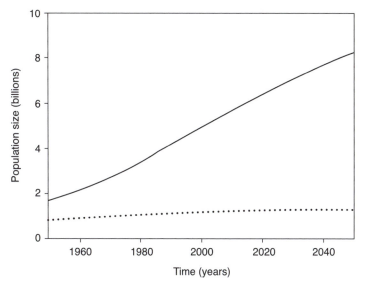

FIGURE 2.2 Trends in human population size

Source: Data provided by United Nations (2012).
Note: Dotted line, more developed regions; continuous line, less developed regions.

Reflection point

You might usefully compare the figure of population growth (Figure 2.2) with the impacts pictured in Figure 2.1. Perhaps you can see evidence of a correlation. But is this proof of a causal relationship? If there is general agreement that population growth is a major problem that needs to be solved, what can actually be done about it? As you reflect on this point, you might begin to understand why many environmental organisations, and even the United Nations, tend to avoid raising this issue.

While many commentators emphasise the problems caused by human population growth, others suggest that it is not so much population size that is important, but patterns of consumption. This is an area of very contentious debate. You might consider it self-evident that a rapidly increasing human population is a major determinant of human impacts on the global environment. However, some people – notably those in richer countries – consume a lot more than others. This question is therefore not just of academic interest, but is one of great political and ethical importance.

2.2 Earth system science

2.2.1 Introduction

In order to identify how a green economy might be developed, it is essential to understand how human activities affect the functioning of the Earth system. Scientific research has tended to focus on increasingly small scales (think of electron microscopy, biotechnology and particle physics), using so-called 'reductionist' approaches. However, it is increasingly being recognised that the Earth's ecological and biogeochemical processes cannot be understood in isolation, because they are all interlinked. This has given rise to the discipline of 'Earth system science', which has been particularly stimulated by concerns about climate change (Steffen *et al.*, 2004).

How does 'Earth system science' relate to 'sustainability science'? The distinguishing feature of Earth system science is its focus on studying processes at the global scale. As human activities are increasingly having an impact at that scale, understanding such global processes and their connection to human society is clearly an essential component of sustainability science. In addition, recent developments in Earth system science provide profound insights into how the world functions as an integrated system, of which humans are a part. For example, it is now clear that the global climate system is much less stable than was originally thought, and can change rapidly over very short timescales.

2.2.2 The Anthropocene

The term 'the Anthropocene' was first suggested by Crutzen (2002), who noted that many human activities now have greater impacts than natural processes; for example, more nitrogen today is fixed synthetically than is fixed by all the world's plants and associated microorganisms. Crutzen suggests that the current human-dominated era is somehow equivalent to the geological epochs that have been defined in the past, on the basis of stratigraphy and changes in fossil communities.

Zalasiewicz *et al.* (2010) examine the concept in more depth, and highlight the following points:

- The Anthropocene is driven by the unprecedented rise in human numbers since the early nineteenth century, which is intimately linked to a massive expansion in the use of fossil fuels. This powered the Industrial Revolution, and allowed the mechanisation of agriculture that enabled those additional billions to be fed.
- The most plainly visible physical effects of this are the growth of the world's megacities. In such 'terraforming', humans have brought about an order-of-magnitude increase in the long-term rate of erosion and sedimentation.
- The rise in atmospheric CO_2 concentrations to over a third above pre-industrial values has been demonstrated beyond reasonable doubt: by systematic measurement since the 1950s; and by the record of atmospheric composition, now nearly a million years long, preserved in the Antarctic ice.
- Other human stressors (such as land cover change) have caused a sharp increase in the rate of species extinctions, which 'looks set to become Earth's sixth great extinction event' (see Chapter 4).

- Enhanced dissolution of increased atmospheric CO_2 in the oceans is increasing their acidity. This factor alone may substantially change marine ecosystems over the next century.

2.2.3 Principles of Earth system science

In the phrase 'Earth system science', the key term is 'system'. A system is a collection of interdependent parts enclosed within a defined boundary. The Earth system is comprised of sub-systems, e.g. the physical climate system and biogeochemical cycles (Steffen *et al.*, 2004). It can also be useful to consider the atmosphere, biosphere, hydrosphere, lithosphere, and the human component (anthroposphere) as sub-systems. Some definitions:

- the *lithosphere* contains all of the cold, hard, solid rock of the planet's crust (surface), the hot semi-solid rock that lies underneath the crust, the hot liquid rock near the centre of the planet, and the solid iron core of the planet;
- the *hydrosphere* contains all of the planet's solid, liquid, and gaseous water;
- the *biosphere* contains all of the planet's living organisms;
- the *atmosphere* contains all of the planet's air.

Earth system science focuses on:

- interactions between oceans, atmosphere, living things, geological processes, land surface dynamics, and human systems;
- processes that connect biological, physical and human systems operating near the Earth's surface;
- how interrelationships between physical and biological systems impact each other and lead to changes.

Because output from one system is the input into another, none of these categories can be evaluated in isolation, leading to a holistic and systems-based approach to science (Steffen *et al.*, 2004).

2.2.4 Systems thinking

Let us consider the word 'system' in more detail. Whenever we use the words 'Earth system' or 'ecosystem', we are implying that ecological processes and communities can be considered as 'systems', but what does this word really mean?
    Systems thinkers (e.g. Meadows, 1999) consider that:

- a 'system' can be considered as a dynamic and complex whole, which interacts as a structured functional unit;
- materials, energy, and information can flow among the different parts of the system;
- systems may be regulated and tend towards equilibrium, but they can also be unstable, by exhibiting oscillating, chaotic, or exponential behaviour.

Systems approaches depend strongly on the field of *cybernetics,* which is the study of regulatory systems. Systems are typically considered to feature *feedback loops* (both positive and negative). This is a key point to understand. A common example is the regulation of a central heating system, or the temperature of an oven. When your room or your oven gets too hot, the heating switches off; this allows it to cool down. Eventually it will get too cold, when the heating will switch back on, so raising the temperature once again.

This is an example of *negative feedback* to maintain a constant value (which is called the *set point*). Negative feedback means that whenever a change occurs in a system, this automatically causes a corrective mechanism to start, which reverses the original change and brings the system back towards the set point (i.e. the 'normal' condition). It also means that the bigger the change, the bigger the corrective mechanism. This provides an example of *homeostasis*, which literally means 'same state' and refers to the process of keeping the environment in a steady state, when the external environment is changed. One key point is that in a system controlled by negative feedback, the set level is never perfectly maintained, but rather the system constantly oscillates about the set point. An efficient homeostatic system minimises the size of the oscillations. An example of homeostasis is the regulation of body temperature in mammals.

Positive feedback is very different, and occurs when A produces more of B which in turn produces more of A. An example is population growth in animals, including people. As we have more children, they will eventually grow into adults and produce more children themselves. Positive feedback often leads to *exponential growth* (Figure 2.3). All organisms have the capacity for exponential population growth, unless some other factor (such as availability of resources) reduces the ability to reproduce, or increases mortality.

Other features of systems include *emergent properties*, which can appear when a number of entities operate in an environment, and produce more complex behaviours as a collective. Swarming is a well-known example in many animal species, such as locusts, schooling fish or flocking birds (Miller, 2010). The key point about emergent properties is that they cannot be predicted by studying only the components of a system; they emerge when the components interact. For this reason, systems are often said to comprise 'more than the sum of their parts'.

Reflection point

Do you think it might make sense to consider humans as an animal species that displays complex social behaviour? In other words, does human society have any emergent properties that you could not predict just from studying the behaviour of individual people?

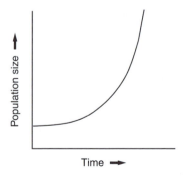

FIGURE 2.3 Exponential growth

2.2.5 The Earth as a system

Does it make sense to think of the Earth as a complete, integrated system? Many scientists now believe that it does (Reid *et al.*, 2010). Perhaps the best-known contribution in this area is the *Gaia theory*, developed by James Lovelock (e.g. Lovelock, 2006). The Gaia hypothesis (named after the Greek Earth goddess) postulates that the living organisms of Earth do not just adapt to the planet, but act upon the planet to make it fit for life, keeping its temperature and atmosphere appropriate for its inhabitants. Together, the physical and chemical environment of the Earth and its living organisms form a system that embraces the whole Earth. The idea has been highly influential, particularly with respect to environmentalism, but the theory has been widely debated by the scientific community. It is viewed as controversial, and some aspects of it are not supported by current evidence (Tyrell, 2013).

The key question is this: is the Earth really a system or not? Does it help to consider the Earth in this way? One of the problems with the Gaia theory is that it implies that the Earth's environment is highly regulated; if it changes in some way, negative feedback processes will operate to bring it back to its set point. However, we now know that the history of the Earth's environment has been highly dynamic, and sometimes it has changed rapidly to different states, which themselves have been highly stable over long periods of time.

For example, during the most recent geological period, the Pleistocene (2.5 million–11,700 years BP), the Earth has experienced at least 11 major glaciation events, plus many additional minor ones. Recent evidence suggests that the transition from full glacial to interglacial conditions can be very rapid, in some cases; perhaps just a few decades (Adams *et al.*, 1999). In contrast, during the Eocene (55.8–33.9 million years ago), the Earth heated up in one of the most rapid (in geologic terms) and extreme global warming events recorded in geologic history, called the Paleocene-Eocene thermal maximum (PETM) (Zachos *et al.*, 2005). This was an episode of rapid and intense warming (up to 7°C at high latitudes), which lasted less than 100,000 years.

Further back in time, evidence indicates that the Earth has been dynamic throughout its history. This is illustrated by the recent discovery that the entire Earth has frozen over, perhaps several times in its history (Hoffman *et al.*, 1998). This is referred to as the 'snowball Earth' theory. Aspects such as ocean currents and sea level have also changed throughout Earth's history, along with the position of the continents.

Understanding the dynamics of the Earth system therefore requires an understanding of how the Earth has changed *in the past*. Such information can be obtained from disciplines such as geology, palaeontology, palaeoecology and palaeoclimatology (Steffen *et al.*, 2004). The results of such research highlight the *different rates and scales* of various processes affecting the Earth's system (see Figures 2.4 and 2.5).

Examples of different rates:

* *Atmosphere* – formation of clouds may take minutes, but hurricanes take days, and ice ages thousands of years.
* *Hydrosphere* – flash floods can occur in minutes to hours, floods in a major river system over days to months, whereas circulation of deep ocean currents can take years.
* *Biosphere* – lifetime of a grass, months; lifetime of a tree, hundreds or thousands of years; a forest might take many thousands of years to grow.
* *Lithosphere* – landslide, minutes; volcanic eruption, hours or days; elevation of a mountain range, tens of millions of years.

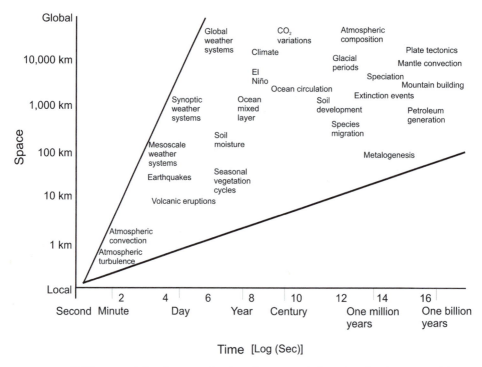

FIGURE 2.4 Different spatial and temporal scales of processes influencing the dynamics of the Earth system

Source: US National Aeronautics and Space Administration (NASA).

The implication of this is that some of the feedback mechanisms that regulate the Earth's environment operate very slowly. Consequently, the Earth's environment can change very rapidly, behave chaotically, and suddenly flip from one state to another. It is also important to remember that current rates of environmental change are very high, in historical terms, as a result of human activity.

2.3 Understanding complex systems

2.3.1 Introduction

If the Earth can be viewed as a complex system, how do such systems behave? How can an understanding of system dynamics contribute to developing the green economy?

2.3.2 Overview of complex systems

A complex system is a system composed of interconnected parts that as a whole exhibits one or more 'emergent' properties, which are not obvious from the properties of the individual parts. As illustration, think of termites building a mound. Mound building

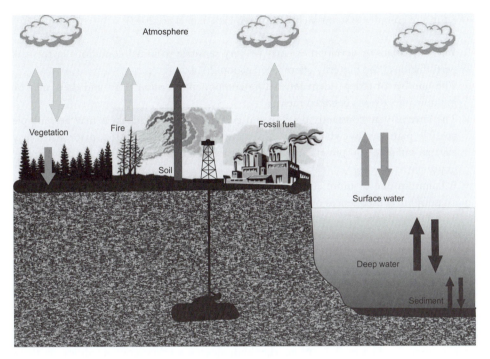

FIGURE 2.5   Rates of different processes influencing the carbon cycle

Source: Data presented in Falkowski *et al.* (2000) and IPCC (2001).

Key to arrows: very pale grey indicates the exchange process is very fast (less than one year); pale grey indicates fast (1–10 years), dark grey indicates slow (10–100 years), and very dark grey indicates very slow (more than 100 years).

is a property that emerges from the social behaviour of a group of termites; you could not predict it from an understanding of the physiology or biochemistry of individual termites.

Research investigating complex systems focuses on how parts of a system (often referred to as 'agents') give rise to the collective behaviours of the system, and how the system interacts with its environment. One of the key features of this research is that it spans many disciplines; as a consequence, there is great interest in finding out whether lessons learned from one type of complex system might be applicable to another. Examples of complex systems include social systems formed out of people, the brain formed out of neurons, molecules formed out of atoms, and the weather formed out of air flows. The field of complex systems therefore cuts across all traditional disciplines of science, as well as engineering, business management, and medicine.

In a complex system, the causes and effects are often not obviously related, which can make problems hard to understand and difficult to solve. Affecting a complex system in one place often has effects in another, because the parts are interdependent or are connected in some way. This is particularly apparent in our efforts to solve societal problems or to avoid ecological disasters resulting from human activities, which often may have unexpected outcomes (Meadows, 1999).

Features of complex systems include (e.g. see Ladyman *et al.*, 2013):

- Their dynamics or development may be very sensitive to initial conditions or to small perturbations ('the butterfly effect'; see Section 2.3.4).
- The number of independent interacting components is often large, and there may be multiple interactions between them.
- The systems may constantly develop and evolve over time, and there may be multiple possible pathways by which they can change in future. In addition, prior states may have an influence on present states. The history of a complex system may therefore be important.
- A failure in one or more components can lead to cascading failures, which may have catastrophic consequences on the functioning of the whole system.
- The components of a complex system may themselves be complex systems. For example, an economy is made up of organisations, which are made up of people, which are made up of cells – all of which are complex systems. Such systems are said to be *nested*.
- Both negative (damping) and positive (amplifying) feedback loops are typically found in complex systems.

To illustrate this complexity, consider the Earth system (see Figure 2.6) and human impacts upon it (Figure 2.7). Note the high degree of interconnectedness in these diagrams.

> **Reflection point**
>
> Imagine what would happen if you changed one of the variables (or boxes) on these diagrams; what would the impacts be on other system components? Also, can you spot any feedback loops in any of these diagrams? (You can find these by following the arrows around from box to box, to see whether any of them create loops.)

Given this complexity, how can we begin to understand such systems? The field of complex systems science provides a number of tools to understand these relationships, including concepts and approaches for describing, modelling or simulating these systems. Systems models are becoming increasingly sophisticated, involving the simulation of many individuals (in what are termed 'agent-based models'; Railsback and Grimm, 2012). Examples of complex systems for which models have been developed include ant colonies, human economies and social structures, climate, nervous systems, cells, living organisms (including human beings), as well as modern energy and telecommunication infrastructures. There is currently great interest in how best to manage and model the global financial system, which itself is highly complex (e.g. Farmer *et al.*, 2012). However, one of the characteristics common to all complex systems is that they are hard to understand, and models are difficult to verify. We should therefore always be cautious when using such models.

Physical climate system
Atmospheric physics / dynamics
Climate change
External forcing
Sun
Volcanoes
Stratospheric chemistry / dynamics
Ocean dynamics
Terrestrial energy / moisture
Global moisture
Soil
CO_2
Human activities
Marine biogeochemistry
Terrestrial ecosystems
Land use
Tropospheric chemistry
CO_2
Pollutants
Biogeochemical cycles

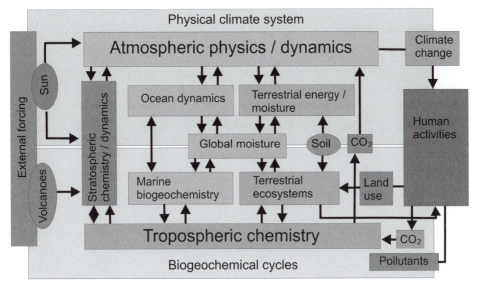

FIGURE 2.6 Illustration of the Earth system

Source: NASA (1988).

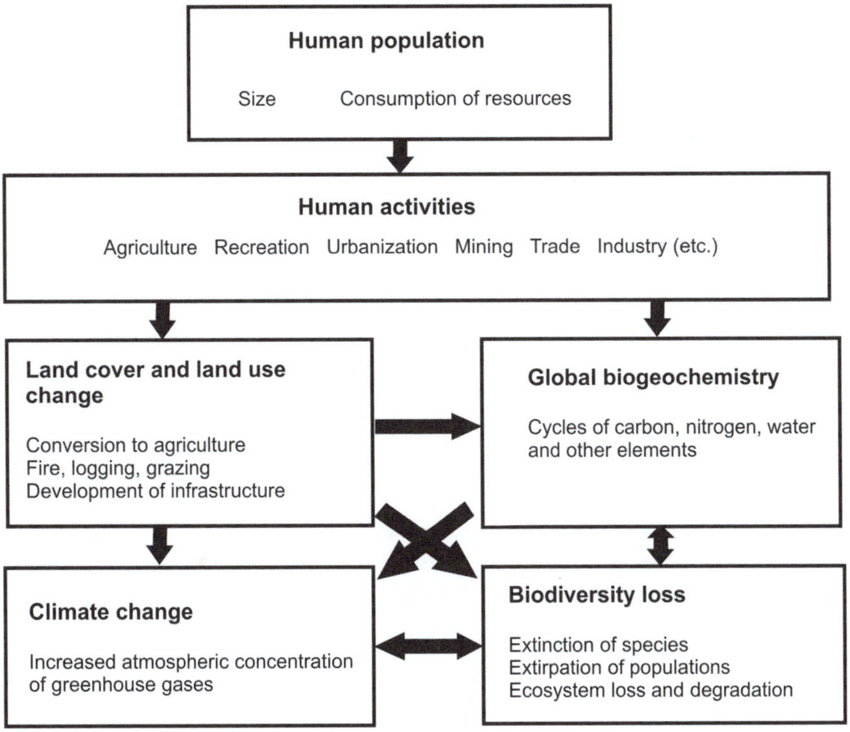

Human population
Size
Consumption of resources
Human activities
Agriculture
Recreation
Urbanization
Mining
Trade
Industry (etc.)
Land cover and land use change
Conversion to agriculture
Fire, logging, grazing
Development of infrastructure
Global biogeochemistry
Cycles of carbon, nitrogen, water and other elements
Climate change
Increased atmospheric concentration of greenhouse gases
Biodiversity loss
Extinction of species
Extirpation of populations
Ecosystem loss and degradation

FIGURE 2.7 Conceptual model of human impacts on the Earth system

Source: Based on information presented in Vitousek *et al.* (1997).

> ## Reflection point
>
> One of the reasons suggested for the recent collapse in the global financial system is that the mathematical models used by financial institutions were inadequate, because they are not sufficiently 'systems based' (Farmer *et al.*, 2012). While traditional economic models focus on standard statistical relationships, in reality, financial markets are heavily influenced by the social dynamics of human communities, including herd behaviour, emotional swings and political intervention. As a result, market behaviour is highly uncertain, unpredictable and prone to collapse, all of which are characteristics of complex systems.

See Arthur (1999), Bar-Yam (2003) and Holling (2001) for further details on complex systems.

2.3.3 Complex adaptive systems (CAS)

Complex adaptive systems (CAS) are a special type of complex system, in that they are adaptive, having the capacity to change and learn from experience. Examples of CAS include the stock market, ant colonies, ecosystems, the biosphere, the brain, the immune system, the developing embryo, and manufacturing businesses. In fact, this concept includes any human social group-based endeavour, such as political parties or communities, and including some large-scale online systems, such as social bookmarking and collaborative tagging systems.

Levin (2010) considered the relationship of complex adaptive systems to sustainability, and pointed out that:

- CAS are composed of agents (which can be individual organisms, people, or organisations), which interact locally in time and space based on information they use to respond to their environments.
- Macroscopic behaviours emerge from these local interactions and are not imposed or predetermined.
- At least some agents have the capacity to process information and modify (adapt) their behavioural strategies.
- CAS dynamics are often unpredictable and highly uncertain.

The main lesson in terms of sustainability that comes from the study of CAS is that unintended consequences of policy actions and local decisions are very common, even if the system is perfectly understood. Levin provides the example of cities, where about 50 per cent of the world's population now live. Urban areas occupy only 2 per cent of the Earth's surface, but import large amounts of resources and export large amounts of wastes. Understanding how urban infrastructure affects their dynamics is critical in terms of achieving a green economy (see Chapter 7). Because they are CAS, choices about the nature of infrastructure in urban areas can have unpredictable, unintended consequences.

Consider this insightful statement from Meadows (1999):

> The most stunning things that living and social systems can do is to change themselves utterly by creating whole new structures and behaviours. In biological systems that power is called evolution. In human society it's called technical advance or social revolution. In systems lingo, it's called self-organisation. Self-organisation means changing aspects of a system: adding completely new physical structures, such as brains or wings or computers; adding new negative or positive loops; making new rules. The ability to self-organise is the strongest form of system resilience.

Reflection point

The ability to self-organise is a key feature of CAS, and Meadows (1999) is right to emphasise this remarkable capacity of biological systems, including human social systems. Might this be a source of optimism, when considering development of the green economy? What does this kind of 'systems thinking' tell us about the way sustainability is most likely to be achieved in practice?

An illustration of a complex adaptive system is provided in Figure 2.8.

2.3.4 Chaotic systems

Chaos theory refers to the development of mathematical theory that has had a major impact on a wide range of fields over the past few decades. Chaos theory relates to the behaviour of dynamical systems that are highly sensitive to initial conditions (Gleick, 1987), an effect which is popularly referred to as the 'butterfly effect'. This name originates from the theoretical idea that a hurricane could result from a butterfly flapping its wings at a distant location, several weeks beforehand.

Chaotic systems are inherently unpredictable, and can display highly variable behaviour over time. This might look like 'random' variation, but one of the lessons from research into chaotic systems is that quite simple, deterministic mathematical formulae can lead to very complex outcomes. A good illustration of this is the discovery of fractals in the 1970s, which offered a mathematical understanding of complex patterns often found in nature, such as coastlines and clouds.

How does this relate to complex systems? Sensitivity to initial conditions means that a small perturbation of the current trajectory may lead to significantly different future behaviour. As a result, the future trajectory may be impossible to predict, even if the processes underlying the behaviour are relatively simple.

Are complex systems chaotic? Not necessarily; the two concepts relate to different phenomena, though they are sometimes presented as the same thing. Complexity is about how a large number of complicated and dynamic sets of relationships can generate patterns, whereas chaotic behaviour can be the result of a relatively small number of non–linear interactions. In a sense, chaotic systems can be regarded as a sub-set of complex systems; such systems may be complex in behaviour but are not necessarily complex in structure. Many real complex systems

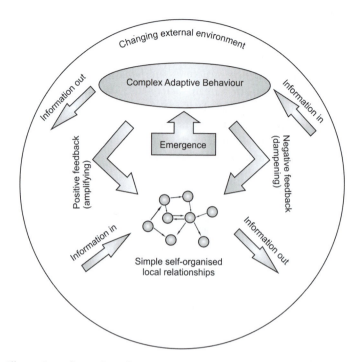

FIGURE 2.8   Illustration of complex adaptive systems, which could be used to model its dynamics
Source: Redrawn from:http://en.wikipedia.org/wiki/File:Complex-adaptive-system.jpg.

do not display behaviour that is genuinely chaotic; they can be highly stable over time. However, they do possess the potential for radical change.

2.4 Resilience and tipping points

2.4.1 Introduction

The word 'resilience' is increasingly being used in environmental policy and in political discourse. For example, environmental policy recently developed by the UK Government (HMG, 2011) refers to the need for resilience to climate change, and other forms of environmental change, while delivering benefits for people, business and biodiversity. Other national governments, and intergovernmental policy processes such as the Convention on Biological Diversity (CBD) and Intergovernmental Panel on Climate Change (IPCC), are also increasingly referring to resilience. But what is it? How might we know whether something is resilient or not? How might we measure it? And how does it relate to the concept of tipping points?

2.4.2 Definition of resilience

If we were to consult a dictionary, we might find resilience defined in terms of the ability of an object to return to its original form, after being compressed or stretched. In an environmental context, resilience might therefore be conceived as the ability of an ecological system to return to its initial state, after being changed in some way. The factors that could cause an ecosystem to alter are often called *pressures*, and include climate change, land-use change, pollution, development of infrastructure, etc. Many human activities associated with economic development could therefore be responsible for the alteration of an ecosystem. Consequently, the concept of resilience is crucial to the green economy. If an ecosystem was unable to recover after some kind of human activity, then this activity could be considered to be unsustainable.

However, it is important to note that different authors have defined resilience in different ways. This is a common problem in science, and particularly in interdisciplinary subjects – different researchers, or communities of researchers, may use a particular term in different ways to others.

In relation to resilience, this is examined in some detail by Gunderson (2000). He points out that many authors define the term resilience as the *time required* for a system to return to an equilibrium or steady state following a perturbation. This implies that the system exists, in the absence of perturbation, in a relatively stable condition. Hence the measure of resilience is how far the system has moved from that equilibrium and how quickly it returns to it. This definition actually originates from engineering, where the objective might be to design a structure – a bridge or a building, for example, for which only one stable state exists. If other states might exist, such as a building or bridge being reduced to a pile of components as a result of mechanical failure, they should be avoided by applying safeguards. Other fields such as physics and control system design use this same definition.

Alternatively, resilience can be defined as the magnitude of disturbance that can be absorbed before the system changes its structure. This has been referred to as 'ecological resilience', in contrast to 'engineering resilience'. This second type of resilience emphasises conditions far from any stable or equilibrium condition, where instabilities can potentially flip a system into another state (ibid.). The concept of ecological resilience is therefore based on the existence of multiple stable states in a system, and the tolerance of the system to perturbations that facilitate transitions among stable states. Hence, ecological resilience is defined by the magnitude of disturbance that a system can absorb before it changes into a different state.

What is clear from both of these definitions is that resilience is very much a *systems concept*. For example, Meadows (1999) suggests that the ability to self-organise is the strongest form of system resilience; a system that can evolve can survive almost any change, by changing itself. Similarly, Gunderson (2000) suggested that resilience is related to the self-organised behaviour of ecosystems, arising from the interactions between structure and process.

Reflection point

When policy-makers use the term 'resilience', which definition of the term do you think they are referring to?

2.4.3 Multiple stable states

The ecological concept of resilience depends on the presence of multiple stable states within ecological systems (Figure 2.9). What is the evidence that such multiple states occur in nature? And is there any evidence for transitions between them?

A good example is provided by transitions from grass-dominated to woody-dominated rangelands, which have been described for areas such as Zimbabwe and Australia (Gunderson, 2000; Hirota *et al.*, 2011) (Figure 2.9). In these cases the alternative states are described by dominant plant forms, such as grass or trees, and the disturbance is grazing pressure. Other examples include transitions from clear lakes to turbid ones, which differ in their plant and animal communities. Transitions can result from changes in light and temperature (Gunderson, 2000) (Figure 2.10).

Reflection point

Consider other ecosystems with which you are familiar. Can you identify multiple stable states in these systems?

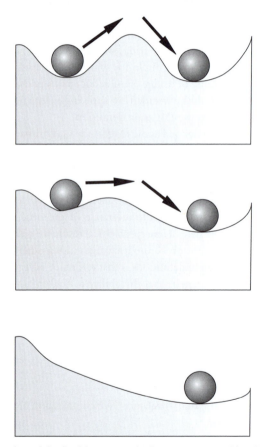

FIGURE 2.9 Conceptual model of stable states, which are represented by the cups or valleys in this diagram. The ball, representing the system, can potentially move from one valley to another, but comes to rest within an individual valley (or 'basin of attraction') until the system is perturbed in some way. The ability of the system to remain in a stable state may change as the shape of the domain changes, illustrated by the three slices in the diagram.

Source: Drawn from information presented in Beisner *et al.* (2003), Carpenter *et al.* (1999), Scheffer *et al.* (1993) and Gunderson (2000).

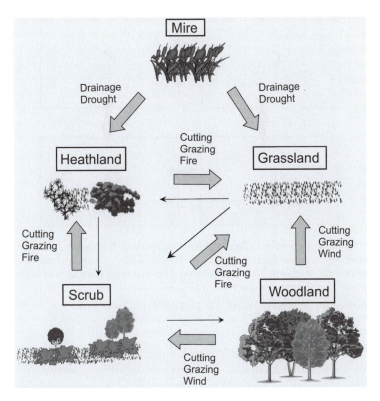

FIGURE 2.10 Transitions between different vegetation types in the New Forest National Park, in the UK, which can be caused by human disturbances (large arrows). Transitions can also occur through the ecological process of succession (small arrows). These kinds of transitions are common to many grazing-dominated ecosystems.

Source: Newton (2011), with permission from the copyright holder A. Newton.

Although the existence of multiple states is true for many ecosystem types (Brand, 2009; Hirota *et al.*, 2011), it is not true for all (Schroder *et al.*, 2005). Evidence shows that an alternative stable state is more likely in systems controlled by environmental adversity, e.g. deserts, Arctic tundra or savannahs (Brand, 2009).

2.4.4 The 'adaptive cycle' and resilience theory

One of the key thinkers on resilience is 'Buzz' Holling, who has played a major role in developing resilience theory. One of his principal contributions is the 'adaptive cycle' concept, which underpins much work on system dynamics and resilience (Holling, 2001; Gunderson and Holling, 2002) (Figure 2.11).

According to the theory of the adaptive cycle, dynamic systems such as ecosystems, societies, corporations and economies do not tend towards some stable or equilibrium condition. Instead, they pass through the following four characteristic phases: rapid growth and exploitation (r), conservation (K), collapse or release ('creative destruction', or Ω), and renewal or reorganisation (α). For example, imagine a growing forest stand (Holling, 2001; Gunderson and Holling, 2002). Over time, as it grows (r) the trees will get larger, and deadwood will

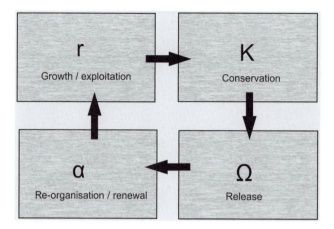

FIGURE 2.11 An illustration of the adaptive cycle concept, which includes four phases (r, K, Ω, α) and transitions between them (arrows). The transition from r to K is characterised by the relatively slow process of growth and accumulation. The transition from Ω to α represents a rapid phase of reorganisation, leading to renewal.

Source: Redrawn from ideas presented in Holling (2001) and Gunderson and Holling (2002).

accumulate. Once all of the trees have matured, it may be relatively stable for a period (K). However, after a time, such a lot of dead and living biomass accumulates that the risk of forest fire becomes very high. Such a fire could cause destruction of the forest stand. Once the forest stand has burned, killing all of the adult trees, the forest is able to regenerate, as tree seedlings are now able to establish on the burned area. In this way, the renewal of the forest can occur following a period of destruction.

The idea of the adaptive cycle has been highly influential and provides a leading example of 'systems thinking'. Carpenter *et al.* (2001) summarise one of the key features of this concept: that there may be long periods in a system with relatively little change, followed by a sudden transition. Such a transition may occur when the system undergoes a major shift or collapse.

Reflection point

Consider the transition to a green economy. According to Holling's ideas, this might only happen once the current global economic system has collapsed. Such a collapse might provide an opportunity for renewal. So, do you think that such a collapse is necessary for a transition to a green economy to occur?

2.4.5 Measuring resilience

As noted above, ecological resilience can be defined as the capacity of an ecosystem to resist disturbance and still maintain a specified state (Brand, 2009). But how can it be measured? Carpenter *et al.* (2005) recently noted that ecological resilience cannot be measured directly;

rather, it has to be estimated by using surrogates or indirect measures of resilience. These authors highlight four general approaches that have been used for this:

- *Stakeholder assessments*: Aspects of resilience are identified through consultation with stakeholders, or people or organisations familiar with the system of interest.
- *Model explorations*: Models (such as scenarios or computer simulation models) are used to explore the potential thresholds for change, and identify measurable aspects of the system that are related to resilience.
- *Historical profiling*: The history of the system is assessed to classify distinct dynamic regimes, and analyse events during the transitions. At these crucial times when resilience mattered, what changed and how?
- *Case study comparison*: Systems that have many similarities, but appear to be changing in different ways, can be examined to assess observable properties that may be related to resilience. What is different among systems that appear to have quite different resilience?

Reflection point

What do you think are the relative strengths and weaknesses of these different approaches? Which is best?

2.4.6 Tipping points

The concept of ecological resilience is based on the assumption that ecosystems can exist in alternative stable states, and can shift between them. For example, a coral reef can show an algae-dominated or a coral-dominated state, while savannahs may exhibit a grassy or woody state. Similarly, shallow lakes can exhibit two stable regimes with respect to nutrient load, namely, a clear-water regime with aquatic plants and a turbid regime without vegetation. If the lake is in the clear-water regime, an increase in the nutrient content will lead to a gradual rise in turbidity until the critical threshold for plant survival is reached. At this point, vegetation collapses and the lake shifts to the turbid regime. Ecological resilience corresponds to the distance of the current value of nutrient concentrations to the critical or threshold value at which change occurs. Thus, if the specific shallow lake had a very low nutrient content, the ecological resilience would be high (Brand, 2009). From this example, you can see that the lake ecosystem has undergone a transition from one state to another, because a threshold (in this case, relating to nutrient content and turbidity) has been reached.

Such 'tipping points' are now attracting a great deal of research interest (Lenton *et al.*, 2008; Scheffer *et al.*, 2012). Examples that have received recent attention include the potential collapse of the Atlantic thermohaline circulation (THC), the dieback of the Amazon rainforest, and the decay of the Greenland ice sheet. Such phenomena have been described as tipping points following the idea that, at a particular moment in time, a small change can have large, long-term consequences for a system (Lenton *et al.*, 2008). Some evidence suggests that we may be approaching a planetary-scale tipping point as a result of human influence (Barnosky *et al.*, 2012), though this is debated (Brook *et al.*, 2013).

2.4.7 Social-ecological systems

So far in this chapter, we have primarily focused on ecological processes and 'natural' ecosystems. However, it is also important to consider the human component of such systems. This has led to the concept of coupled or integrated 'social-ecological systems', of which humans are a part (Berkes *et al.*, 2008). This is a very valuable concept, which is central to the development of a green economy.

Progress has recently been made in understanding the complexity and behaviour of such systems. For example, Liu *et al.* (2007) profile six case studies from different parts of the world, indicating how coupled social-ecological systems display non-linear dynamics with reciprocal feedback loops, thresholds, time lags and effects of historical legacies on current conditions, as well as their resilience. Anderies *et al.* (2006) highlight the value of the resilience approach for an understanding of the dynamics of such systems, which could potentially guide interventions to improve their long-term performance. Key findings made to date suggest that social-ecological systems mainly demonstrate non-linear dynamics that result in multiple stable states, and that their dynamics tend to conform to linked adaptive cycles at multiple scales (Gunderson and Holling, 2002; Anderies *et al.*, 2006). However, these characteristics are not necessarily features of all social-ecological systems (Brand, 2009).

2.5 Critical loads and vulnerability

2.5.1 Introduction

A key issue for the green economy is how ecosystems might be affected by human activities, and how much disturbance they might be able to tolerate before shifting to another state. This issue can be considered from the perspective of *critical loads*. This is a concept that has been developed in the context of assessing the impacts of pollutants on ecosystems. A related concept is *vulnerability*: are some ecosystems more vulnerable than others to human disturbance? And if so, how might that vulnerability be measured, and potentially reduced?

First, it is helpful to consider the nature of environmental change. Such change can either be:

- *systemic* (i.e. changes operating at the global scale, through an impact on the Earth's system), e.g. industrial emissions of greenhouse gases, or ozone-depleting gases;
- *cumulative* (i.e. additive effects of individual local actions, 'snowballing' to have an effect at the global scale), e.g. deforestation, groundwater pollution.

Another key issue is the *scale* of the changes taking place, both in time and space. Many changes at the local scale can eventually produce changes at the global scale. Some changes have impacts of limited duration, others have changes that are very long-term.

There are many different forms of environmental change that are currently affecting the Earth, many of which result from human activities (Steffen *et al.*, 2004). These include:

- land cover and land-use change
- urban development
- air pollution

- acid rain
- global warming
- ozone depletion
- soil erosion
- deforestation
- desertification
- declining availability of water quality and problems with quantity
- soil contamination
- spread of invasive species
- loss of habitat and species.

Reflection point

You may be able to think of some additions to this list yourself. Note that some of these changes are connected; for example, climate change could lead to increased desertification in some areas.

2.5.2 Pollutant impacts on ecosystems

One of the most profound ways in which human activities impact on ecosystems is through the production and dispersal of pollutants. The processes by which these are dispersed at various scales are illustrated in Figures 2.12 and 2.13.

A valuable review of the impacts of pollutants on organisms and ecosystems is provided by Rhind (2009), who makes the following points:

- Pollutants, including synthetic organic materials and heavy metals, are known to adversely affect physiological systems in all animal species studied to date. While many individual chemicals can perturb normal functions, the combined actions of multiple pollutants are of particular concern because they can exert effects even when each individual chemical is present at concentrations too low to be individually effective.
- The biological effects of pollutants differ greatly between species, reflecting differences in the pattern of exposure, routes of uptake, metabolism following uptake, rates of accumulation and sensitivity of different organs.
- Although the production of pollutants by people has a long history, the nature and distribution of contaminants in the environment have changed rapidly in recent history as new compounds have been created. The Industrial Revolution concentrated people in cities and resulted in increased pollution of the air, as a result of the burning of fossil fuels, and of rivers, with organic pollutants in the form of sewage. These caused disease and illness in humans and killed fish and other wildlife in the rivers.
- The rate of release into our environment of known toxins has latterly declined in some areas, through use of improved sewage processing and legislation in Clean Air Acts. However, this has coincided with the development of completely novel organic substances used in the manufacture of a wide range of products including pesticides, plastics and fire retardants and the increased use of fossil fuels in transport and power generation. These new pollutants are generally invisible, present only at low concentrations, and do not exert

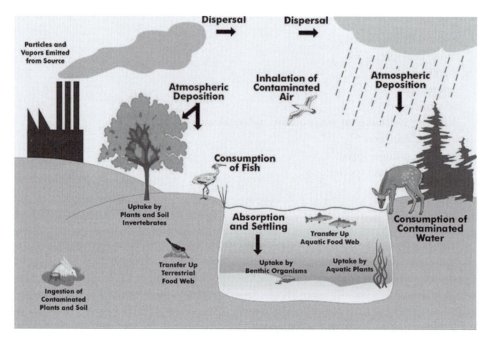

FIGURE 2.12 A conceptual model of how air pollutants are transferred within and between ecosystems

Source: Mitchell *et al.* (2004).

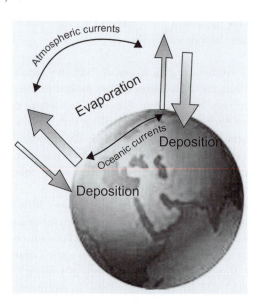

FIGURE 2.13 Processes influencing the global movement of pollutants. Long-distance atmospheric transport partly occurs because at low latitudes, evaporation of some pollutants exceeds deposition, whereas at high latitudes, the converse is true. Some chemicals move to higher latitudes by repeatedly evaporating and settling. The more volatile a chemical is, the further it travels before being deposited.

Source: Redrawn from information presented in Raven *et al.* (2008) and Wania and Mackay (1996).

acute effects on exposed animals or humans. However, their cumulative effects can be very profound.

- New chemicals of many classes, including halogenated organic compounds, phthalates, alkyl phenols and polycyclic aromatic hydrocarbons (PAHs) are now manufactured for use domestically and in industry and agriculture and inevitably are released into the environment. Some of these, labelled organic endocrine-disrupting compounds (EDCs), may affect the hormonal systems in animals, and have marked physiological effects. For example, there is currently concern about their impact on the reproductive ability and feminisation of fish, marine mammals and even people (e.g. see Colborn et al., 1993).
- The risks associated with certain classes of compounds differ considerably with the environmental context. For example, many EDCs are relatively insoluble in water and so many of the pollutants present in water are the more water-soluble substances, such as the steroid hormones associated with the human contraceptive pill. In terrestrial systems, other compounds bound to organic and mineral matter are more important (e.g. polychlorinated biphenyls (PCBs) and polybrominated diphenyl ethers (PBDEs)). Compounds also differ in their tendency to accumulate in the tissues of species extracting oxygen from air and water.

Another key issue is the fact that pollutants can be concentrated in the tissues of organisms, as a result of two processes:

- *bioaccumulation:* an increase in the concentration of a pollutant from the environment to the first organism in a food chain;
- *biomagnification:* an increase in the concentration of a pollutant from one link in a food chain to another.

A classic example is provided by the pesticide DDT (*d*ichloro, *d*iphenyl *t*richloroethane) (Figure 2.14), which has a half-life of 15 years, but can persist in the environment for

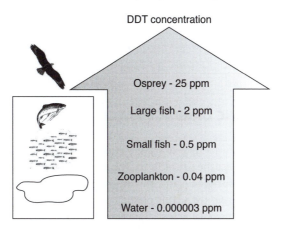

DDT concentration

Osprey - 25 ppm

Large fish - 2 ppm

Small fish - 0.5 ppm

Zooplankton - 0.04 ppm

Water - 0.000003 ppm

FIGURE 2.14   The example of the pesticide DDT, to illustrate the biomagnification and bioaccumulation of a pollutant

Source: Drawn from data provided in Ames (1966).

many decades. As the first of the modern pesticides, it was overused. By the 1960s, global problems with DDT and other pesticides were becoming so pervasive that they began to attract much attention, particularly as a result of the influential book, *Silent Spring* (1962) by Rachel Carson. The title of this book refers to a world in which all of the songbirds have been poisoned. Arguably, this book gave rise to the environmental movement.

A further key point is that when pollutants enter the Earth system, they may persist for many decades or even centuries (Figure 2.15). Many plastics, for example, are essentially immortal, as microorganisms are incapable of breaking them down; all that happens is that the particles get smaller through time as a result of abrasion (Box 2.1). Another example is provided by oil pollution. Few coastlines in the world remain uncontaminated by petroleum (crude oil) or oil products. Overall, human impacts on the oceans are now very widespread; Halpern *et al.* (2008) provide a useful recent review.

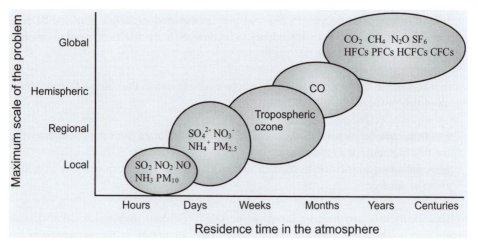

FIGURE 2.15   Residence time of some selected pollutants
Source: UNEP (2007).

BOX 2.1 THE PACIFIC GARBAGE PATCH

The Pacific Garbage Patch is a gyre of marine litter in the central North Pacific Ocean, estimated to be around twice the size of Texas. The patch is characterised by exceptionally high concentrations of suspended plastic and other debris that have been trapped by the currents of the North Pacific Gyre. This plastic could take hundreds of years to break down by abrasion and microbial action. Totalling an estimated 100 million tonnes of garbage, this is a remarkable example of the impact that humans are having even on oceanic areas remote from human habitation. Annual global consumption of plastic has reached approximately 110 million tonnes (Dautel, 2009).

2.5.3 Critical loads

How much pollution can an ecosystem tolerate? One way of addressing this question is through the concept of critical loads. A *critical load* is a quantitative estimate of exposure to one or more pollutants below which significant harmful effects on specified elements of the environment do not occur. This refers to deposition of pollutants from the air on the ground. A *critical level* refers to the gaseous concentration of a pollutant in the air, above which adverse impacts may occur (UNECE, 2013).

Critical loads are based on empirical evidence, such as observations from experiments and gradient studies (Lovett, 2013). Typically, critical loads are given as ranges (e.g. 10–20 kgN ha^{-1} yr^{-1}), which reflect variation in ecosystem response from place to place. An indication of the confidence in the critical loads is given by an uncertainty rating (e.g. 'reliable' or 'quite reliable'). Often, maps of critical loads are produced to support policy development and implementation. Similarly, the critical levels of air pollutants are defined by organisations such as the World Health Organization, in relation to human health.

> ### Reflection point
>
> Consider what kind of information you would need to identify a critical load of some pollutant. How would you obtain such information? How reliable do you think such information would be? Consequently, how certain can we be that critical loads and levels have been identified correctly?

In the UK, as in many other countries, critical loads and levels are used by regulatory agencies to assess the risk of impacts of plans and projects, such as an industrial installation or road scheme. This forms part of the 'environmental impact assessment' (EIA). Undertaking an EIA is an important method of reducing the environmental impact of development. Further details are provided by Glasson *et al.* (2005) and Noble (2009); see also Chapter 6.

2.6 Planetary boundaries and ecological footprint analysis

2.6.1 Introduction

There are other ways of considering the impact of human activities on the Earth system. This can be phrased as a simple question: what are the Earth's limits to environmental degradation? Or: how many people can the Earth support? In order to answer such questions, we need to consider further the impact of human activities on the environment, in relation to our understanding of the Earth system. Both of these can be considered as addressing issues of fundamental importance to the green economy.

2.6.2 Planetary boundaries

In 2009, the leading scientific journal *Nature* published a paper on the concept of planetary boundaries. In it, a group of Earth system and environmental scientists led by Johan Rockström of the Stockholm Resilience Centre estimated the boundaries for the biophysical processes that determine the Earth's capacity for self-regulation (Rockström *et al.*, 2009). The authors attempted to define sustainable limits for human existence, and suggested that these boundaries must not be crossed, if catastrophic environmental change is to be avoided.

This publication has already been very influential, and has generated a lot of debate. It is therefore worth considering how the problem is considered by Rockström *et al.* Their approach addresses the issue *holistically*, and examines *self-regulation*, with reference to *thresholds*, with the possibility of *non-linear changes*. These are all terms and concepts common to systems-based approaches to science, as noted earlier.

The research attempted to quantify the safe biophysical boundaries outside which, they believe, the Earth system cannot function in a stable state in which human civilisations can thrive. The scientists first identified the Earth system processes and potential biophysical thresholds, which, if crossed, could generate unacceptable environmental change for humanity. They then proposed the boundaries that should be respected in order to reduce the risk of crossing these thresholds.

The nine boundaries identified were:

1. climate change
2. stratospheric ozone
3. land-use change
4. freshwater use
5. biological diversity
6. ocean acidification
7. nitrogen and phosphorus inputs to the biosphere and oceans
8. aerosol loading
9. chemical pollution.

The study suggests that three of these boundaries (climate change, biological diversity and nitrogen input to the biosphere) may already have been transgressed (Figure 2.16). In addition, it emphasises that the boundaries are strongly connected – crossing one boundary may seriously threaten the ability to stay within safe levels of the others (see also Wijkman and Rockström, 2012).

An editorial in the same issue of *Nature* (Anon, 2009) raises further questions about the analyses presented by Rockström *et al.* (2009). Some of the points made include:

- The values chosen as boundaries by Rockström *et al.* are essentially arbitrary.
- There is, as yet, little scientific evidence to suggest that stabilising long-term concentrations of carbon dioxide at 350 parts per million is the right target for avoiding dangerous interference with the climate system.
- Similarly there is no consensus on the need to limit species extinctions at ten times the background rate, as the paper advises.
- Boundaries do not always apply globally, even for processes that regulate the entire planet. Local circumstances can ultimately determine how soon water shortages or biodiversity loss reach a critical threshold, for example.
- Some of the suggested limits may be easier to balance with ethical and economic issues than others. For example, although human influence on the nitrogen cycle may have damaging long-term consequences, the use of nitrogen to support agriculture has a major role in food production.

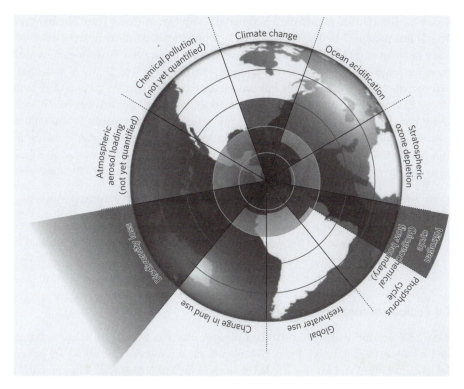

FIGURE 2.16   Planetary boundaries

Source: Rockström *et al.* (2009). Reprinted by permission from Macmillan Publishers Ltd: *Nature*, ©2009.

Reflection point

Do we understand the Earth system well enough to know the real limits to environmental degradation? And if we can define them, would doing so ultimately help or hinder efforts to protect the planet?

It is interesting to consider what would actually happen if such boundaries were crossed. Recently, there has been increasing concern about the rate of melting of the polar ice in the Arctic. This could have major implications, not only for the ecological processes influencing the Arctic Ocean and its associated wildlife, but for human access and exploitation of the area. Many companies and governments are now seeking to exploit resources in the Arctic that were previously inaccessible. Perhaps this represents a threshold, or even a tipping point in the Earth system.

2.6.3 Human appropriation of biomass production

Another way of considering human impact on the biosphere is to estimate how much of global biomass productivity is appropriated by people. This can be done by analysing net primary productivity (NPP), or the amount of biomass (or living material) produced each year by vegetation, then estimating how much of this is harvested and used by humans. This approach has attracted attention from a number of researchers in recent years. The most recent analysis is that presented by Haberl *et al.* (2007), who estimated human appropriation of net primary production (HANPP). Based on a combination of data and modelling, these authors provided an aggregate global HANPP value of 15.6 Pg C yr^{-1} or 23.8% of potential net primary productivity. In other words, humans are appropriating nearly a quarter of all biomass produced each year by ecosystems. This is a remarkable figure. As pointed out by the authors, HANPP not only reduces the amount of energy available to other species, it also influences biodiversity, water flows, carbon flows between vegetation and atmosphere, energy flows within food webs, and the provision of ecosystem services (ibid.). Appropriation of global biomass can therefore be seen to have a major impact on the functioning of the Earth system.

Reflection point

Is the current harvesting of the world's biomass production sustainable? How could you work out whether it is sustainable or not?

2.6.4 Ecological footprint analysis

'Ecological footprint' analysis is a standard measure that can be used to relate demand for natural resources to the planet's ability to replenish these resources. The results are presented as the amount of land and sea area needed to support human populations. The approach uses existing data to translate human demand on the environment into the area required for the production of food and other goods, together with the absorption of wastes (Ewing *et al.*, 2010). Results suggest that human demand may have exceeded the biosphere's regenerative capacity since the 1980s; humanity's load corresponded to 70 per cent of the capacity of the global biosphere in 1961, and grew to 120 per cent in 1999 (Wackernagel *et al.*, 2002).

It is important to note how these analyses are presented: as the number of earths that human society requires. This is a striking image, designed to generate media interest. The concept of the ecological footprint has been used by the environmental organisation World Wildlife Foundation (WWF), and forms part of the basis of their 'Living Planet' report, which is produced every two years. This report (WWF, 2010, 2012) makes the important point that human use of the biosphere is not equal in different parts of the planet; some countries have a much higher ecological footprint than others.

Suggested activity

Calculate your own environmental footprint, using on-line tools (e.g. http://footprint.wwf.org.uk/).

Reflection point

How accurate are measures of an ecological footprint? Consider the possible areas of uncertainty in such analyses. A recent critique of the concept is provided by Blomqvist *et al.* (2013).

2.7 Environmental limits to economic growth

2.7.1 Introduction

Could human impacts on the Earth system actually limit prospects for economic growth? This important question has been the focus of debate for more than 40 years.

2.7.2 The Limits to Growth (1972)

In 1972, Donella Meadows and co-authors produced a seminal book, entitled *The Limits to Growth* (Meadows *et al.*, 1972). This was commissioned by the influential think-tank, the Club of Rome, and presented models describing the consequences of a rapidly growing world population and finite resource supplies. This provides an example of the kind of 'systems model' that we briefly considered earlier. It also represents the first attempt to develop a model that linked the global economy with the environment. One of the main conclusions was that limited natural resources must limit human population and economic activity.

The global model presented in *The Limits to Growth* was constructed to estimate the future impact of continuous growth under a number of different assumptions (Cole, 1999). A 'standard' world model assumed that the physical, economic and social relationships that have historically governed the development of the world system would remain unchanged. The model assumed that population and industrial capital would continue to grow exponentially, leading to a similar growth in pollution and in demand for food and non-renewable resources. As the supply of both food and non-renewable resources was assumed to be fixed, unsurprisingly the model predicted economic collapse owing to depletion of non-renewable resources.

The book was enormously popular, and stimulated a great deal of debate (ibid.). However, it was also strongly criticised, for the following reasons:

- The model ('World3') focused on purely physical factors, a weakness recognised by Meadows *et al.*
- The assumptions of the model were questioned, particularly the assumption of finite limits to non-renewable resource stocks. No consideration was given to the possibility of such resources continuing to develop through new discoveries and recycling, which would have produced very different model outputs.

Some of the criticisms of this research stem from the fact that it was misunderstood. The model – as is commonly the case with systems models – was not intended to be predictive or for making detailed forecasts, but was to provide a means to better understand the behaviour of the world's economic system. Rather than provide exact predictions, the aim was to explore the behaviour of the system.

It is often claimed that Meadows *et al.* (1972) predicted that resources would be depleted and the world system would collapse by the end of the twentieth century. As this patently did not happen, the work has been widely discredited, and it has repeatedly been claimed that the model is flawed. However, these criticisms are not themselves correct, as this prediction was never actually made in the original book. The authors were also at pains to point out that it is possible to alter current trends and to establish a condition of ecological and economic stability that is sustainable far into the future.

The Limits to Growth can be seen as an early call for the transition to sustainability. The original work was subsequently updated by the authors (Meadows *et al.*, 2004). The authors still stood by their original conclusions, suggesting that human use of many essential resources and the generation of many kinds of pollutants have already surpassed rates that the Earth system can support. Meadows *et al.* (2004) suggest that economic decline is likely, unless measures are taken to limit consumption and population growth, and to increase the efficiency with which materials and energy are used.

But are these findings correct? In fact, few independent comparisons have been between the original model projections and what has actually happened since 1972. Such comparisons were undertaken by Turner (2008), who found that data describing trends over the past 30 years compare favourably with key features of the 'standard' model, which results in the collapse of the global system midway through the twenty-first century. The results also indicated the particular importance of understanding and controlling global pollution.

Atkisson (2010) further evaluates *The Limits to Growth*, and the impact that it had. He points out the main criticism of the book: that the authors underestimated some of the efficiency gains that have since occurred in industry. The original book predicted that oil, copper and several other critical resources would soon run out (see also Box 2.2); instead, most of these materials became cheaper and more widely available, owing to advances in recovery technology

---

BOX 2.2 PEAK OIL

It is easy to forget how dependent our modern economy is on petroleum (or crude oil); our economic growth in recent decades would have been impossible without it. Yet, this is a recent phenomenon: the world's first commercial oil well was drilled in 1853. Prior to that, whale oil was a major source of energy, with the result that whales were hunted near to extinction.

There is currently great concern that petroleum reserves might soon run out. More formally, 'peak oil' refers to the point in time when the maximum rate of global petroleum extraction is reached, after which the rate of production enters terminal decline. If this happens, then profound changes in our global economic system are inevitable. Petroleum therefore provides a prime example of a non-renewable resource that could act as a limit to economic growth. But will it? Contrasting perspectives on this question are provided by Bentley (2002), Maugeri (2004), Meng and Bentley (2008), Murray and King (2012) and Watkins (2006).

Recently there has been a rapid growth in the extraction of gas and oil from previously inaccessible shale reserves. Exploitation of such reserves has been made possible through new technologies, including horizontal drilling and multi-stage hydraulic fracturing (fracking). These developments have been highly controversial because of human health and environmental concerns (Howarth *et al.*, 2011). However, they are likely to have major impacts on the global economy and international geopolitics; for example, they may reinstate the United States as the largest oil producer in the world, eliminating their need for foreign imports (Hughes, 2013). Exploitation of shale oil may also have implications for the global oil price, and affect the transition to use of renewable energy (see Chapter 5). However, forecasts of increasing shale oil production may be overly optimistic, as the costs of exploitation are high.

and substitution by other sources. For example copper was long thought to be a critical limiting factor for industrial development, because of its use in telephone cabling. However, by the end of the twentieth century, most cables were fibre optic and made out of sand. According to Atkisson, the real legacy of *The Limits to Growth* is the way it raised awareness of the dynamics of the Earth system, and the possibility of collapse.

Reflection point

Do you believe that the global economy might collapse if a transition to a green economy is not achieved? If so, how would you know whether such a collapse was imminent?

2.7.3 The Simon–Ehrlich wager

Could non-renewable resources, such as minerals, present a limit to economic growth, as suggested by Meadows *et al.* (1972)? This was the focus of one of the best-known debates in environmentalism, namely a bet between Paul Ehrlich and Julian Simon. Ehrlich is a very eminent environmental scientist, who wrote in his well-known book, *The Population Bomb*, that hundreds of millions of people would starve to death in the 1970s from food shortages (Ehrlich, 1968). This was another alarming, best-selling book. To challenge Ehrlich's beliefs about impending scarcity of resources, Simon challenged him to a bet, based on the prices of five commodity metals: copper, chromium, nickel, tin and tungsten. Simon bet that their prices would decrease, whereas Ehrlich bet they would increase. Ehrlich ultimately lost the bet, for every one of the five commodities.

So why did Ehrlich get it wrong, and lose his bet? This is discussed by Davidson (2000), who notes that predictions of absolute limits to the size of the economy owing to resource exhaustion have repeatedly not been borne out. For example, despite over 150 years of predictions to the contrary, food production has consistently kept up with population growth (Brown, 1995). Predictions of economic limits imposed by limits in resources generally fail because they are based on the erroneous assumption that limits can be calculated according to current resource use and current resource stocks (Davidson, 2000). Most importantly, industrial production is often very flexible, substituting one input for another through advances in technology. As a result, the scale of economic activity is not likely to be limited by input constraints. This is despite the fact that quantities of specific resources may be limited and current levels of natural resource use have resulted in substantial environmental destruction.

For a recent discussion of the wager and its broader implications, see Sabin (2013).

Reflection point

Recently, concern has been growing about availability of 'rare earths', a group of minerals that are an essential component of many electronic components, including some of those used in renewable energy technologies. There are fears that supplies could soon collapse, placing our electronic industries (and therefore much of our economic activity) at risk (Crow, 2011). So, what do you predict will happen to the price of these minerals? Are you prepared to bet on this, as Ehrlich did?

2.7.4 Energetic limits to the economy

Another key concept relating to limits to economic growth focuses on thermodynamics. This approach has been developed by the well-known ecological economist Herman Daly, who has written a number of highly influential books (e.g. Daly, 1996, 1999). Building on work by Georgescu-Roegen (1971), Daly suggests that there may be limits to the economy based on thermodynamics and entropy, which cannot be avoided through substitution.

The idea rests on the fact that the Earth and the sun constitute a closed system. While the total amount of matter and energy in the system is fixed and constant, there is a continuous, irreversible decline in the level of entropy. In other words, according to the Second Law of Thermodynamics, available energy and matter are continuously and irrevocably degraded to an unavailable state. This could therefore be the ultimate regulator of economic activity. Based on the implications of the entropy law, Herman Daly advocates that unrestrained economic growth should be replaced by a steady (or stationary) state, defined as 'a constant stock of physical wealth (capital), and a constant stock of people (population)' (Daly, 1973, p. 15).

This is an interesting and challenging argument, which has had a major influence on green economic thinking. The issue of entropy was also explored by Kenneth Boulding in a classic paper (Boulding, 1966). He argued that the economy currently operates on a linear system: we take materials and energy in at one end and simply throw away so-called 'waste products' at the other end. The valuable energy and materials contained in these resources are often simply discarded into the environment, contributing towards increasing disorder. He argues that an economy that took the laws of thermodynamics seriously would be a circular economy, rather than a linear one.

> **Reflection point**
>
> The Second Law of Thermodynamics is used by Daly and others to argue that a sustainable economy is one that would be characterised by zero growth. Do you agree with this contention? How might entropy act as a limit to growth in practice?

While thermodynamic limits are theoretically absolute, Davidson (2000) suggests that they are meaningful only if the human economy has a chance of approaching the limit. What then is the thermodynamic limit to the global economy, and what is the size of the current global economy relative to those limits? Daly attempts to answer these questions by referring to an analysis by Vitousek et al. (1986) of human use of net primary productivity (NPP) (see Section 2.6.3). Vitousek et al. estimated that humans currently appropriate 25 per cent of potential total global NPP and 40 per cent of potential terrestrial NPP. Daly (1996) concluded that humans are therefore only 80 years away or less from appropriating the entire NPP, which he contends would be a 'biological disaster'.

Davidson (2000) provides a critique of this viewpoint, in which he notes:

- Human use of NPP is not an appropriate metric to assess possible entropy or thermodynamic limits, as it represents only a small fraction of the energy available on Earth.
- An entropy or thermodynamic limit to the economy implies that total human energy use is in danger of exceeding energy availability. Yet solar energy flow to Earth is many thousands of times greater than current global energy use.

- Unlike entropy, total NPP is not fixed and may be increased in agriculture. More important, other inputs can be substituted for the products of primary producers: direct solar energy can be used instead of firewood, and concrete or steel can be used instead of wood for building materials.

The issue of energetic limits to economic growth was recently examined further by Brown *et al.* (2011). The authors demonstrated a positive relationship between per capita energy use and per capita gross domestic product (GDP) both across nations and within nations over time. The authors conclude that an enormous increase in energy supply will be required to meet the demands of projected population growth and lift the developing world out of poverty, without jeopardising current standards of living in the most developed countries. Yet the possibilities for substantially increasing energy supplies are highly uncertain. It is possible that energy shortages could cause massive socio-economic disruption, providing one mechanism of how energy supply might limit economic growth in future.

2.7.5 Conclusions: are there environmental limits to growth or not?

The idea that there are environmental limits to economic growth has been very influential in terms of green economic thinking, and more broadly as a core concept of environmentalism. As a result, some observers believe that a green economy should be a zero growth economy (Jackson, 2009). But is this true?

According to Davidson (2000), despite the fact that human activities are causing environmental destruction at a scale and pace unprecedented in human history, biological or physical limits are seldom actually limiting to economic growth. Rather, the human economy is extremely adaptable and ways are found to adapt and continue to expand. Furthermore, in most cases, continued economic growth results not in ecological collapse, but rather in continuous environmental degradation without clear limit points.

2.8 Consumption

2.8.1 Introduction

If it is true that we are currently consuming more than the Earth can provide, as the ecological footprint analysis suggests, then the transition to a green economy will require a reduction in consumption. Similarly, natural resources that are finite and non-renewable will be exhausted more rapidly if rates of consumption are not reduced. But how do consumption patterns need to be changed, for sustainability to be achieved? And how might such changes be brought about? Such questions raise the need to identify the factors driving consumption patterns.

2.8.2 Current extent and trends in consumption

In 2011, the global human population passed 7 billion for the first time. Visualising this number is difficult. One way is to imagine yourself speaking aloud the name of everyone on Earth. If you were to spend just a single second speaking the name of each person, it would take you more than 220 years to say the name of all the 7 billion people who are alive today.

> ## Reflection point
>
> What does this mean in terms of consumption? Consider the numbers of animals killed for food worldwide in a single year: 52 billion chickens, 2.6 billion ducks, 1.3 billion pigs, 518 million sheep, and 292 million cows (FAO, 2013). Consider also the resources needed to feed these animals.

What are people consuming? And how are consumption patterns changing over time? A useful overview of global consumption patterns and trends is provided by the World Business Council for Sustainable Development (WBCSD, 2008), which makes the following points:

- On average, around 60 per cent of GDP is accounted for by consumer spending on goods and services. World GDP is projected to grow by 325 per cent between 2007 and 2050 as population growth is forecast to be accompanied by strong GDP growth.
- China's GDP is set to overtake that of the USA by 2025; India's GDP is expected to rival that of Japan at around the same time, and come close to that of the USA by 2050.
- The number of middle-class consumers worldwide is expected to triple by 2030, bringing almost 80 per cent of the world population into the middle-income bracket.
- Globalisation and economic integration are giving more consumers access to more products and services.
- Four billion people currently earn less than US$3,000 per year (the equivalent of US$3.35 per day). Low-income consumers have a combined spending power of approximately US$5 trillion.
- Food tends to dominate low-income household budgets. As incomes rise, the share spent on transportation and telecommunications grow rapidly. The process of economic development itself therefore leads to changing patterns of consumption.

Overall, these figures provide a striking impression of how rapidly the world is changing, not only in terms of population growth, but in economic development and therefore patterns of consumption. The growth of the middle class in rapidly developing countries such as India and China has major implications: greater wealth implies greater spending power, and therefore greater consumption (Liu and Diamond, 2005). But what will such people spend their money on?

> ## Reflection point
>
> Might it be true to say that the future development of a green economy will primarily be determined by what happens in India and China?

Suggested activity: count your stuff

We are all consumers. But why do we consume what we do? Try making a list of the things in your own home, or the room where you are sitting. Count how many things you possess. Consider where these things were made, and what resources were used to produce them. You might also like to think about how important all these objects are to you, and the degree to which they are essential. You might also consider why you bought them, and whether the environmental impact of producing each object influenced your purchasing decisions.

2.8.3 Research ideas about consumption

What research ideas and approaches have been developed by the international research community, in relation to consumption? This is an area that has received less research attention than you might think. However, certain ideas have received particular attention from researchers, some of which are summarised here.

I = PAT

Ehrlich and Holdren (1971) argued that environmental impacts (I) of the human population are the result of three variables: population (P); affluence (A); and technology (T), as follows:

$$I = P \times A \times T$$

This simple equation provides a framework for assessing the impacts of human population increase that consider other aspects than solely human numbers. The formula has been widely used, and has been further refined by various other researchers.

While the formula is conceptually useful, measuring the variables can be very challenging, especially the technology variable. There has also been considerable debate about the relative importance of the different parameters in the equation, for example the relative role of wealth and population numbers in causing environmental problems.

Holdren and Ehrlich (1974) stated the impact equation slightly differently, as:

Environmental degradation = population × consumption per person × damage per unit of consumption.

This emphasises the role of consumption, rather than solely wealth, in defining the extent of human impacts.

For an update on use of I = PAT, consult York *et al.* (2003), Dietz *et al.* (2007) and Waggoner and Ausubel (2002). Use of amended versions of I = PAT has suggested that through economic development, there may be reduction in the amount of consumption of energy or of goods per unit of GDP, a process called 'dematerialisation' (Ausubel and Waggoner, 2008).

Environmental Kuznets curves

Kuznets curves have attracted a great deal of attention from researchers in recent years, and continue to attract debate in the context of sustainability. They are often

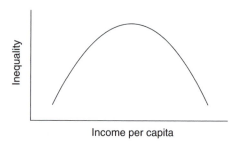

FIGURE 2.17 A Kuznets curve

Source: Wikimedia Commons, http://en.wikipedia.org/wiki/File:Kuznets_curve.png.

applied to areas of human impact other than consumption, typically production of pollutants and waste (which are of course related to consumption patterns and human lifestyles).

In its original form, a Kuznets curve is the graphical representation of Simon Kuznets's hypothesis, which states that economic inequality increases over time while a country is developing. After a certain mean income is attained, inequality then begins to decrease (Figure 2.17).

Kuznets curves have been explored in a broader context than purely environmental issues, in which their application has been highly controversial. The use of environmental Kuznets curves has usefully been reviewed by Stern (2004), who notes that according to an environmental Kuznets curve, in the early stages of economic growth degradation and pollution increase (Figure 2.18). However, beyond some level of per capita income, the trend reverses, suggesting that environmental impact is an inverted U-shaped function of per capita income. This implies that rather than being a threat to the environment, as many have claimed in the past, economic growth could be the means to eventual environmental improvement. It is for this reason that the hypothesis has attracted such a lot of interest.

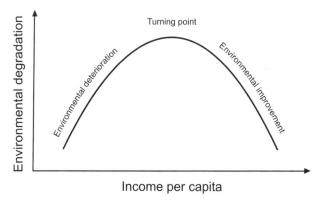

FIGURE 2.18 A typical environmental Kuznets curve

Source: Redrawn, based on information presented in Yandle *et al.* (2004).

Reflection point

Can you think of examples that might *support* the relationship described by the environmental Kuznets curve in Figure 2.18?

According to Stern (2004), the hypothesis does not have any theoretical basis; it is an empirical relationship, based on data. However, the statistical limitations of such data have often been overlooked in previous research, which is consequently analytically weak. Stern concludes that there is little evidence for a common inverted U-shaped pathway that countries follow as their income rises. Similarly, Copeland and Taylor (2004) found little evidence of a simple and predictable relationship between pollution and per capita income.

Stern (2004) therefore demonstrates the limitations of the environmental Kuznets curve approach, and you might therefore consider that the matter is now closed. But, of course, science does not necessarily proceed like that. What if Stern is wrong? Researchers are still testing whether the curve applies to particular situations, despite this paper.

For a test of the use of environmental Kuznets curves, see York *et al.* (2003) and Dietz *et al.* (2007).

2.8.4 Are we consuming too much?

A key question is this: are we consuming too much? Few researchers have actually addressed this question directly. You might consider why this is: in fact, the question is very difficult to answer. However, there has been a recent attempt to do so (Arrow *et al.*, 2004). This was undertaken as a collaborative venture between some ecologists and a group of economists interested in environmental issues.

What do these authors conclude? One finding is that there are places where the biggest problem is not that people are consuming too much, but that they are consuming too little. Consumption is obviously inadequate when people are dying of malnutrition. However, in developed countries, according to Arrow *et al.*, consumption may not be too high, as long as enough is invested to ensure that future generations enjoy standards of living that are at least as high as those currently enjoyed. The implication of this is that the key issue is not consumption *per se*, but how much is being invested in the poorest regions of the world. In a commentary on this research, Christensen (2005) highlights a key difference in opinion between economists and ecologists. Economists tend to believe that if we run out of some environmental resources, we will simply substitute one for another – as we did from horsepower to petroleum, for example. Ecologists, on the other hand, tend to believe that environmental resources are limited and some cannot be replaced.

Reflection point

Is it reasonable to suggest that the benefits that humans derive from ecosystems can be substituted? In other words, can they be replaced by an alternative? This question lies at the heart of what many environmentalists see as the problem with current economic thinking.

The paper by Arrow *et al.* (2004) sparked some additional debate in the scientific literature. Daly and his co-authors suggested that the research was limited, because it only considered consumption in relation to investment (Daly *et al.* 2007). This is not the same as asking whether the physical scale of total production is too large relative to the biosphere. Daly *et al.* (2007) cite ecological footprint analysis and the biodiversity crisis (see Chapter 4) as evidence that the consumption levels of the wealthy are currently excessive. Specifically, they suggest that the scale of the economy relative to the biosphere, which is currently left to the market, should be regulated by public policy. A response to the critique presented by Daly *et al.* (2007) was also published (Arrow *et al.*, 2007).

Reflection point

Here we have examined both sides of a debate. Who do you think is correct? How compelling is the evidence that consumption is excessive?

2.9 Common property resources and the 'tragedy of the commons'

2.9.1 Introduction

Why do people consume what they do? The answer depends on many factors: wealth, fashion, culture, etc. However, there is an additional factor that we have not so far considered: access to and ownership of the resource being consumed. In particular, what happens in terms of consumption when nobody actually owns the resource? Consideration of such 'common property' resources led to one of the most seminal papers on environmental science ever published: 'The tragedy of the commons'. Along with Rachel Carson's *Silent Spring*, this publication essentially launched the environmental movement in the 1960s. The issue is still topical today.

2.9.2 The tragedy of the commons

The original paper was written by Garrett Hardin, and was published in *Science* in 1968. Let us first consider the original paper (Hardin, 1968). Here the author focuses on the use of common land, or a pasture that is open to common use. He describes a pasture open to all, where each herdsman will try to keep as many cattle as possible on the commons. Each herdsman seeks to maximise his gain. The rational herdsman will conclude that the logical course for him to pursue is to add another animal to his herd. However, this same conclusion is reached by all other herdsmen sharing the commons. This gives rise to the tragedy. Each person is locked into a system that compels him to increase his herd without limit, which will result in environmental degradation that will negatively affect everyone. In Hardin's words: 'Freedom in a commons brings ruin to all.' Hardin goes on to say that examples of the tragedy of the commons are provided by the collapse of marine fisheries, and pollution of the environment.

In some ways, this paper paints a bleak picture, suggesting that over-exploitation of a natural resource is an inevitable consequence of human nature. But is this correct? This question has occupied many researchers over the past four decades (Box 2.3).

BOX 2.3 ELINOR OSTROM

When Elinor Ostrom was awarded the 2009 Nobel Memorial Prize in Economic Sciences, she became the first and only woman to win the Nobel Prize in this category. The subject of her research was economic governance, especially of common property resources. This is an issue of central importance to the green economy. Elinor's research provides a deeper understanding of the problem, and how it can potentially be addressed. Specifically, she showed how common resources such as forests, fisheries and grazing land can be managed successfully by the people who use them, without requiring interventions by governments or private companies. Some of her most important publications are Ostrom *et al.* (1999, 2007) and Ostrom (2007, 2009).

Reflection point

What are the implications if Hardin is correct? One implication is that natural resources should be converted into private property, through privatisation. However, this will inevitably cause injustice, as Hardin himself points out (Hardin, 1968). So, is he correct to say that 'injustice is preferable to total ruin'?

Another key point to make is the implication that the 'tragedy' would apply to any type of commons, not just grazing land, but any kind of common property resource. The concept has been explored in many different fields, including economics, evolutionary psychology, game theory, politics, taxation, and sociology. It can also perhaps be seen as an example of emergent behaviour, as it results from an outcome of interactions between individuals in a complex system.

Criticisms of Hardin's original paper are summarised briefly by Brekke *et al.* (2007), who note Hardin confuses open access and common property, which are different things. In fact, the use of many common properties is carefully regulated. This is particularly the case with grazing land, which was the principal example used by Hardin. For example, in countries such as the UK, traditional use of common land was often highly regulated, to ensure that only those people with formal 'commoners rights' were allowed to graze their animals. The same is true for many herding cultures today, in other parts of the world.

This is addressed by Fratkin (1997), who reviews the evidence for the tragedy of the commons in pastoral landscapes in different parts of the world. This paper provides a useful indication of the power and impact of Harding's idea, but also illustrates how it was misused. Some people began to see 'pastoral mismanagement' as a major cause of desertification, which contributed to the Sahara Desert moving farther south each year. Solutions were proposed to dismantle common property regimes, which were seen as key to the problem of environmental degradation. As a result, organisations such as the World Bank called for sweeping privatisation of land and commercialisation of livestock production, leading to widespread socio-economic upheaval. Subsequent research discovered that the southward advancement of desert had been exaggerated and that the extensive droughts of the 1970s and 1980s could be attributed to large climatic disruptions, rather than to unsustainable land use patterns (Fratkin, 1997).

> **Reflection point**
>
> This provides a powerful example of the misuse of science. The tragedy of the commons was used to justify an approach to economic development in Africa that was not only misplaced, but was highly damaging, leading to widespread negative social and environmental impacts. Why did some organisations use Hardin's paper to support a process of land privatisation?

> **Reflection point**
>
> Is anthropogenic climate change a tragedy of the commons? Some researchers think so; see Milinski *et al.* (2008) for an examination of this issue.

2.10 Human behaviour and the green economy

2.10.1 Introduction

In this chapter, we have examined the science underpinning the concepts of sustainability and the green economy. We have learned that humans can be considered as parts of coupled social-ecological systems, which extend to the global scale. In other words, our activities are intimately connected to the ecological processes on which we ultimately depend for our own survival. We have examined how our activities can affect ecological processes and systems, which can respond by changing in sudden and dramatic ways. We have noted that many environmental researchers believe that human society is currently operating in a way that is not environmentally sustainable, but when we try to define what actually *is* sustainable, the answers are often complex and highly uncertain. The truth is, we do not know for sure.

One thing that is clear, however, is that the Earth system is capable of sudden major shifts or transitions – it has demonstrated this capacity throughout its history. Furthermore, there is a great deal of evidence indicating that current human activities are having a profound effect on the biosphere and on other elements of the Earth system. It may be that the Earth system can withstand such impacts without affecting it substantially; in other words, it may be resilient. On the other hand, it may not. We may only discover that our activities are not sustainable, in that they lead to a major shift in the functioning of the Earth system, when it is too late to do anything about it. One of the key lessons from the research that we have examined is that the future is hard to predict, particularly when dealing with a social-ecological system as complex as the Earth's.

Given the current environmental impacts of human activities, you might consider it prudent – even essential – that we change our behaviour to reduce these impacts. This idea lies at the heart of thinking about the green economy; the transition to sustainability ultimately depends on changing human behaviour. In a sense, this offers hope: human behaviour is the one part of the Earth's social-ecological system that we might consider to be under our own control. This raises a fascinating question: how do we bring about a change in human behaviour? Moreover, how do we do this in an ethical and democratic way, which respects the rights and beliefs of every human individual on the planet?

Answering this question touches on many different research disciplines, including social science, ethology, anthropology and psychology. Understanding human behaviour is a highly active and rapidly developing research area. It is remarkable how little we still know about ourselves.

> **Reflection point**
>
> Consider yourself, your friends and family, and the people who live near you. Do you believe that your lifestyles are environmentally sustainable? If not, what would it take to convince the people whom you know to change to a more sustainable way of living? What would convince *you* to change your lifestyle?

2.10.2 Environmental psychology

The relationship of humans to nature or the environment, the preference of people for particular kinds of species or landscapes, the fear of particular species – these are all areas that are researched by psychologists, particularly environmental psychologists.

What do psychologists have to say about sustainability transitions? This is examined by Gifford (2011), who asks why more people do not engage in sustainable behaviour. The author identifies seven categories of psychological barriers that inhibit people from changing their behaviour: (1) limited cognition about the problem; (2) ideological worldviews that tend to preclude pro-environmental attitudes and behaviour; (3) comparisons with key other people; (4) sunk costs and behavioural momentum; (5) disbelief of experts and authorities; (6) perceived risks of change; and (7) positive but inadequate behaviour change.

Gifford examines the mismatch between human attitudes and behaviour. Just because a person is aware of an environmental problem, and even of the correct course of action that is needed to address the problem, does not guarantee that the person will change their behaviour accordingly. The reasons for this, according to Gifford, are partly the psychological barriers that he describes in his paper.

Some key points made by Gifford are:

- Humans are less rational than once believed. This is as true for thinking about climate change and other environmental issues as it is for other areas.
- Many environmental problems, such as climate change, are outside our immediate attention because they do not cause any immediate personal difficulties.
- Uncertainty reduces the frequency of pro-environmental behaviour. In other words, individuals tend to interpret any sign of uncertainty as sufficient reason to favour self-interest rather than that of the environment. For example, if the number of fish available in a lake is uncertain, people will tend to use this uncertainty to justify catching more fish. Similarly, uncertainty about climate change likely functions as a justification for inaction to address it.
- A recent study of over 3,000 respondents in 18 countries found that individuals in 15 of the countries believed that environmental conditions are worse in places other than their own (Gifford et al., 2009). This demonstrates that 'spatial discounting' of environmental problems occurs. If conditions are presumed to be worse elsewhere, individuals may be

expected to have less motivation to take action locally. This tendency occurs even in similar places, such as among inhabitants of English villages situated a few kilometres apart.

- Considerable evidence suggests that people underestimate personal risks, such as their likelihood of a heart attack, but also their environmental risks, for example, from radon exposure.
- Because climate change is a global problem, many individuals believe they can do nothing about it as individuals. This is the well-known 'collective action' problem.
- People routinely compare their actions with those of others and derive subjective and descriptive norms from their observations about what is the 'proper' course of action. For example, when homeowners were told the amount of energy that average members of their community used, they tended to decrease or increase their energy use accordingly (Schultz *et al.*, 2007).
- Most people could do more than they are doing, and in some pilot studies, almost everyone agrees that they could do more. Two major forms of this tendency are 'tokenism' and the 'rebound effect'. These refer to the fact that some actions are easier to undertake than others, and the fact that gains made can be diminished or erased by subsequent actions. For example, persons who buy fuel-efficient vehicles may drive further than they did when they owned less efficient vehicles.

Reflection point

The fact that people do not always behave rationally is now well established, but has major implications for the future of humanity. What implications do you think there might be of such irrational behaviour, in terms of developing the green economy?

These analyses indicate how psychological research can potentially inform the transition to a green economy. How might this be applied in practice? Consider the following points made by Swim *et al.* (2009):

- Mass media persuasion and information campaigns have often been ineffective in changing behaviour. Increasing knowledge about an issue often does not lead to a change in behaviour.
- However, providing immediate or frequent (e.g. daily) feedback on use of energy has yielded energy savings of 5–12 per cent in homes, often lasting 6 months or more (Fischer *et al.*, 2008). This kind of information is believed to be more effective than general information campaigns, because it is specific to the individual's situation and is conducive for learning how to achieve savings.
- Behavioural research suggests that the barriers to household behaviour change vary with the behaviour and the individual. The most effective interventions, therefore, are those that are tailored to the target individual or household.

The contribution that environmental psychology can make in understanding and promoting pro-environmental behaviour is reviewed by Steg and Vlek (2009).

Reflection point

Development of the green economy could be seen as requiring a tipping point in society, arising from changes in human behaviour. How might this be achieved? See Gladwell (2001) for some ideas!

Bibliography

Adams, J., Maslin, M. and Thomas, E. 1999. Sudden climate transitions during the Quaternary. *Progress in Physical Geography*, 23: 1–36.

Ames, P. L. 1966. DDT residues in the eggs of the osprey in the North-Eastern United States and their relation to nesting success. *Journal of Applied Ecology*, 3: 87–97.

Anderies, J. M., Walker, B. H. and Kinzig, A. P. 2006. Fifteen weddings and a funeral: case studies and resilience-based management. *Ecology and Society*, 11(1): 21. [Online]. Available at: http://www.ecologyandsociety.org/vol11/iss1/art21/.

Anon. 2009. Earth's boundaries? *Nature*, 461: 447–448.

Arrow, K. J., Dasgupta, P., Goulder, L., *et al.* 2004. Are we consuming too much? *Journal of Economic Perspectives*, 18: 147–172.

Arrow, K J., Daily, G., Dasgupta, P., *et al.* 2007. Consumption, investment, and future well-being: reply to Daly *et al. Conservation Biology*, 21: 1363–1365.

Arthur, W. B. 1999. Complexity and the economy. *Science*, 284: 107–109.

Atkisson, A. 2010. *Believing Cassandra: How to Be an Optimist in a Pessimist's World*, Earthscan, Oxford.

Ausubel, J. H. and Waggoner, P. E. 2008. Dematerialization: variety, caution, and persistence. *Proceedings of the National Academy of Sciences of the United States of America*, 105: 12774–12779.

Barnosky, A. D., Hadly, E. A., Bascompte, J., *et al.* 2012. Approaching a state shift in Earth's biosphere. *Nature*, 486: 52–58.

Bar-Yam, Y. 2003. *Dynamics of Complex Systems*, Westview Press, Boulder, CO.

Beisner, B. E., Haydon, D. T. and Cuddington, K. 2003. Stable states in ecology. *Frontiers in Ecology and the Environment*, 1(7): 376–382.

Bentley, R. W. 2002. Global oil and gas depletion: an overview. *Energy Policy*, 30, 189–205.

Berkes, F., Colding, J. and Folke, C. (eds) 2008. *Navigating Social-Ecological Systems: Building Resilience for Complexity and Change*, Cambridge University Press, Cambridge.

Blomqvist, L., Brook, B. W., Ellis, E. C., *et al.* 2013. The ecological footprint remains a misleading metric of global sustainability. *PLOS Biology*, 11(11): e1001702. doi:10.1371/journal.pbio.1001702.

Boulding, K. E. 1966. The economics of the coming spaceship Earth, in K. E. Boulding, and H. Jarrett (eds) *Environmental Quality in a Growing Economy: Essays from the Sixth RFF Forum*, Johns Hopkins University Press: Baltimore, MD.

Brand, F. 2009. Critical natural capital revisited: ecological resilience and sustainable development. *Ecological Economics*, 68: 605–612.

Brekke, K. A., Oksendal, B. and Stenseth, N. C. 2007. The effect of climate variations on the dynamics of pasture–livestock interactions under cooperative and noncooperative management. *Proceedings of the National Academy of Sciences of the United States of America*, 104: 14730–14734.

Brook, B. W., Ellis, E. C., Perring, M. P., *et al.* 2013. Does the terrestrial biosphere have planetary tipping points? *Trends in Ecology and Evolution*, 28(7): 396–401.

Brown, J. H., Burnside, W. R., Davidson, A. D., *et al.* 2011. Energetic limits to economic growth. *BioScience*, 61: 19–26.

Brown, L. R. 1995. *Who Will Feed China? Wake-up Call for a Small Planet*, Worldwatch Institute, New York.

Carpenter, S. R., Ludwig, D. and Brock, W. A. 1999. Management of eutrophication for lakes subject to potentially irreversible change. *Ecological Applications*, 9: 751–771.

Carpenter, S. R., Walker, B., Anderies, J. M. and Abel, N. 2001. From metaphor to measurement: resilience of what to what? *Ecosystems*, 4: 765–781.

Carpenter, S. R., Westley, F. and Turner, M. G. 2005. Surrogates for resilience of social-ecological systems. *Ecosystems*, 8: 941–944.

Carson, R. 1962. *Silent Spring*, Houghton Mifflin, Boston.

Christensen, J. 2005. Are we consuming too much? *Conservation in Practice*, 6: 64–70.

Colborn, T., vom Saal, F. S. and Soto, A. M. 1993. Developmental effects of endocrine-disrupting chemicals in wildlife and humans. *Environmental Health Perspectives*, 101(5): 378–384.

Cole, M. A. 1999. Limits to growth, sustainable development Kuznets curves: an examination of the environmental impact of economic development. *Sustainable Development*, 7: 87–97.

Copeland, B. R. and Taylor, M. S. 2004. Trade, growth, and the environment. *Journal of Economic Literature*, 42: 7–71.

Crow, J. M. 2011. 13 exotic elements we can't live without. *New Scientist*, 2817: 36–41.

Crutzen, P. J. 2002. Geology of mankind. *Nature*, 415: 23–25.

Daly, H. E. 1973. *Toward a Steady-State Economy*, W. H. Freeman, New York.

Daly, H. E. 1996. *Beyond Growth: The Economics of Sustainable Development*, Beacon Press, Boston.

Daly, H. E. 1999. *Ecological Economics and the Ecology of Economics: Essays in Criticism*, Edward Elgar, Cheltenham.

Daly, H. E., Czech, B., Trauger, D. L., *et al.* 2007. Are we consuming too much?: For what? *Conservation Biology*, 21: 1359–1362.

Dautel, S. L. 2009. Transoceanic trash: international and United States strategies for the Great Pacific Garbage Patch. *Golden Gate University Environmental Law Journal*, 3(1). Available at: http://digitalcommons.law.ggu.edu/gguelj/vol3/iss1/8.

Davidson, C. 2000. Economic growth and the environment: alternatives to the limits paradigm. *BioScience*, 50: 433–440.

de Vries, B. J. M. 2012. *Sustainability Science*, Cambridge University Press, Cambridge.

Dietz, T., Rosa, E. A. and York, R. 2007. Driving the human ecological footprint. *Frontiers in Ecology and the Environment*, 5: 13–18.

Ehrlich, P. R. 1968. *The Population Bomb*, Sierra Club/Ballantine Books, New York.

Ehrlich, P. R. and Holdren, J. P. 1971. Impact of population growth. *Science*, 171: 1212–1217.

Ewing, B., Reed, A., Galli, A., *et al.* 2010. *Calculation Methodology for the National Footprint Accounts, 2010 Edition*, Global Footprint Network, Oakland, CA.

Falkowski, P., Scholes, R. J., Boyle, E., *et al.* 2000. The global carbon cycle: a test of our knowledge of Earth as a system. *Science*, 290: 291–296.

FAO 2013. *FAOSTAT*, Food and Agriculture Organization of the United Nations: Rome. Available at: http://faostat3.fao.org/ (accessed 26 Sept. 2013).

Farmer, J. D., Gallegati, M., Hommes, C., *et al.* 2012. A complex systems approach to constructing better models for managing financial markets and the economy. *European Physical Journal Special Topics*, 214, 295–324.

Fischer, P., Greitemeyer, T. and Frey, D. 2008. Self-regulation and selective exposure: the impact of depleted self-regulation resources on confirmatory information processing. *Journal of Personality and Social Psychology*, 94: 382–395.

Fratkin, E. 1997. Pastoralism: governance and development issues. *Annual Review of Anthropology*, 26: 235–261.

Georgescu-Roegen, N. 1971. *The Entropy Law and the Economic Process*, Harvard University Press, Cambridge, MA.

Gifford, R. 2011. The dragons of inaction: psychological barriers that limit climate change mitigation and adaptation. *American Psychologist*, 66: 290–302.

Gifford, R., Scannell, L., Kormos, C., Smolova, L., Biel, A., Boncu, S., *et al.* 2009. Temporal pessimism and spatial optimism in environmental assessments: An 18-nation study. *Journal of Environmental Psychology*, 29: 1-12.

Gladwell, M. 2001. *The Tipping Point: How Little Things Can Make a Big Difference*, Abacus, New York.

Glasson, J., Therivel, R. and Chadwick, A. 2005. *Introduction to Environmental Assessment*, 3rd edn, Routledge, London.

Gleick, J. 1987. *Chaos: The Making of a New Science*, R. R. Donnelley & Sons Company, Harrisonburg, VA.

Grey, W. 1993. Anthropocentrism and deep ecology. *Australasian Journal of Philosophy*, 71: 463–475.

Gunderson, L. H. 2000. Ecological resilience: in theory and application. *Annual Review of Ecology and Systematics*, 31: 425–439.

Gunderson, L. H. and Holling, C. S. (eds) 2002. *Panarchy: Understanding Transformations in Human and Natural Systems*, Island Press, Washington, DC.

Haberl, H., Erb, K. H., Krausmann, F., *et al.* 2007. Quantifying and mapping the human appropriation of net primary production in Earth's terrestrial ecosystems. *Proceedings of the National Academy of Sciences of the United States of America*, 104: 12942–12945.

Halpern, B. S., Walbridge, S., Selkoe, K. A., *et al.* 2008. A global map of human impact on marine ecosystems. *Science*, 319: 948–952.

Hardin, G. 1968. The tragedy of the commons. *Science*, 162: 1243–1248.

Hirota, M., Holmgren, M., Van Nes, E. H. and Scheffer, M. 2011. Global resilience of tropical forest and savanna to critical transitions. *Science*, 334: 232–235.

HMG 2011. *The Natural Choice: Securing the Value of Nature*, The Stationery Office, Norwich.

Hoffman, P. F., Kaufman, A. J., Halverson, G. P. and Schrag, D. P. 1998. A neoproterozoic snowball Earth. *Science*, 281: 1342–1346.

Holdren, J. P. and Ehrlich, P. R. 1974. Human population and the global environment. *American Scientist*, 62.

Holling, C. S. 2001. Understanding the complexity of economic, ecological, and social systems. *Ecosystems*, 4: 390–405.

Howarth, R. W., Ingraffea, A. and Engelder, T. 2011. Should fracking stop? *Nature*, 477: 271–275.

Hughes, J. D. 2013. A reality check on the shale revolution. *Nature*, 494: 307–308.

IPCC 2001. *Climate Change 2001: Synthesis Report. A Contribution of Working Groups I, II, and III to the Third Assessment Report of the Intergovernmental Panel on Climate Change*, Cambridge University Press, Cambridge.

Jackson, T. 2009. *Prosperity Without Growth*, Earthscan, London.

Kates, R. W. (ed.) 2010. Readings in sustainability science and technology. CID Working Paper No. 213, Center for International Development, Harvard University, Cambridge, MA.

Kates, R. W., Clark, W. C., Corell, R., *et al.* 2001. Environment and development: sustainability science. *Science*, 292: 641–642.

Ladyman J., Lambert J. and Wiesner, K. 2013. What is a complex system? *European Journal for Philosophy of Science*, 3: 33–67.

Lenton, T. M., Held, H., Kriegler, E., *et al.* 2008. Tipping elements in the Earth's climate system. *Proceedings of the National Academy of Sciences of the United States of America*, 105: 1786–1793.

Levin, S. 2010. Complex adaptive systems and the challenge of sustainability, in S. A. Levin and W. C. Clark (eds) *Toward a Science of Sustainability: Report from Toward a Science of Sustainability Conference, Airlie Center, Warrenton, Virginia, November 29, 2009–December 2, 2009*, Center for Biocomplexity, Environmental Institute, Princeton University and Sustainability Science Program, Center for International Development, Harvard University, Princeton, NJ and Cambridge, MA.

Liu, J. G. and Diamond, J. 2005. China's environment in a globalizing world. *Nature*, 435: 1179–1186.

Liu, J. G., Dietz, T., Carpenter, S. R., *et al.* 2007. Complexity of coupled human and natural systems. *Science*, 317: 1513–1516.

Lovelock, J. 2006. *The Revenge of Gaia: Why the Earth Is Fighting Back – And How We Can Still Save Humanity*, Allen Lane, London.

Lovett, G. M. 2013. Critical issues for critical loads. *Proceedings of the National Academy of Sciences of the United States of America*, 110: 808–809.

McMichael, A. J., Butler, C. D. and Folke, C. 2003. New visions for addressing sustainability. *Science*, 302: 1919–1920.

Maugeri, L. 2004. Oil: never cry wolf: why the petroleum age is far from over. *Science*, 304: 1114–1115.

Meadows, D. 1999. *Leverage Points: Places to Intervene in a System*, The Sustainability Institute, Hartland, VT.

Meadows, D. H., Meadows, D. L., Randers, J. and Behrens, W. W. 1972. *The Limits to Growth*, Universe Books, New York.

Meadows, D. H., Randers, J. and Meadows, D. L. 2004. *The Limits to Growth: The 30-year Update*, Earthscan, London.

Meng, Q.Y. and Bentley, R.W. 2008. Global oil peaking: responding to the case for 'abundant supplies of oil'. *Energy*, 33: 1179–1184.

Milinski, M., Sommerfeld, R. D., Krambeck, H. J., Reed, F. A. and Marotzke, J. 2008. The collective-risk social dilemma and the prevention of simulated dangerous climate change. *Proceedings of the National Academy of Sciences of the United States of America*, 105: 2291–2294.

Miller, P. (2010) *Smart Swarm: Using Animal Behaviour to Change Our World*, Collins, London.

Mitchell, K. L., Smith, R. L. and Murphy, D. 2004. Part IV. Ecological risk assessment. *Air Toxics Risk Assessment Reference Library*, EPA's Office of Air Quality Planning and Standards, Research Triangle Park, NC.

Murray, J. and King, D. 2012. Oil's tipping point has passed. *Nature*, 481: 433–435.

NASA 1988. *Earth System Science: An Overview*, Earth System Sciences Committee, NASA Advisory Council, NASA, Washington, DC.

Newton, A. C. 2011. Social-ecological resilience and biodiversity conservation in a 900-year-old protected area. *Ecology and Society*, 16(4): 13. Available at: http://www.ecologyandsociety.org/vol16/iss4/art13/.

Noble, B. 2009. *Introduction to Environmental Impact Assessment: A Guide to Principles and Practice*, Oxford University Press, Oxford.

Ostrom, E. 2007. A diagnostic approach for going beyond panaceas. *Proceedings of the National Academy of Sciences of the United States of America*, 104: 15181–15187.

Ostrom, E. 2009. A general framework for analyzing sustainability of social-ecological systems. *Science*, 325: 419–422.

Ostrom, E., Burger, J., Field, C. B., *et al.* 1999. Sustainability: revisiting the commons: local lessons, global challenges. *Science*, 284: 278–282.

Ostrom, E., Janssen, M. A. and Anderies, J. M. 2007. Going beyond panaceas. *Proceedings of the National Academy of Sciences of the United States of America*, 104: 15176–15178.

Railsback, S. F. and Grimm, V. 2012. *Agent-Based and Individual-Based Modeling*, Princeton University Press, Princeton, NJ.

Raven, P. H., Berg, L. R. and Hassenzahl, D. M. 2008. *Environment*, 6th edn, John Wiley & Sons, Inc., Hoboken, NJ.

Reid, W. V., Chen, D., Goldfarb, L., *et al.* 2010. Earth system science for global sustainability: grand challenges. *Science*, 330: 916–917.

Rhind, S. M. 2009. Anthropogenic pollutants: a threat to ecosystem sustainability? *Philosophical Transactions of the Royal Society B: Biological Sciences*, 364: 3391–3401.

Rockström, J., Steffen, W., Noone, K., *et al.* 2009. A safe operating space for humanity. *Nature*, 461: 472–475.

Sabin, P. 2013. *The Bet: Paul Ehrlich, Julian Simon and Our Gamble over the Earth's Future*, Yale University Press, New Haven, CT.

Scheffer, M., Carpenter, S. R., Lenton, T. M., *et al.* 2012. Anticipating critical transitions. *Science*, 338: 344–348.

Scheffer, M., Hosper, S. H., Meijer, M. L., Moss, B., and Jeppesen, E. 1993. Alternative equilibria in shallow lakes. *Trends in Ecology and Evolution*, 8: 275–279.

Schroder, A., Persson, L. and De Roos, A. M. 2005. Direct experimental evidence for alternative stable states: a review. *Oikos*, 110: 3–19.

Schultz, P. W., Nolan, J. M., Cialdini, R. B., Goldstein, N. J. and Griskevicius, V. 2007. The constructive, destructive, and reconstructive power of social norms. *Psychological Science*, 18: 429–434.

Steffen, W., Sanderson, R. A., Tyson, P. D., *et al.* 2004. *Global Change and the Earth System: A Planet Under Pressure*, Springer, Berlin.

Steg, L. and Vlek, C. 2009. Encouraging pro-environmental behaviour: an integrative review and research. *Journal of Environmental Psychology*, 29: 309–317.

Stern, D. I. 2004. The rise and fall of the environmental Kuznets curve. *World Development*, 32: 1419–1439.

Swim, J. K., Clayton, S., Doherty, T., *et al.* 2009. *Psychology and Global Climate Change: Addressing a Multi-Faceted Phenomenon and Set of Challenges.* [Online]. Available at: www.apa.org (accessed 26 Sept. 2013).

Turner, G. 2008. A comparison of *The Limits to Growth* with thirty years of reality: socio-economics and the environment in discussion (SEED). CSIRO Working Paper Series Number 2008–09. June 2008.

Tyrell, T. 2013. *On Gaia: A Critical Investigation of the Relationship Between Life and Earth*, Princeton University Press, Princeton, NJ.

UNECE (United Nations Economic Commission for Europe) 2013. *ICP Modelling and Mapping: Critical Loads and Levels Approach.* Available at: www.unece.org/env/lrtap/WorkingGroups/wge/definitions. html.

UNEP 2007. EEA 1995: Europe's environment: the Dobris assessment. European Environment Agency, Copenhagen and Centre on Airborne Organics 1997: Fine particles in the atmosphere. 1997 Summer Symposium Report. MIT, Boston. *Global Environment Outlook: Environment for Development*, United Nations Environment Programme. Available at: www.unep.org/geo/geo4.asp.

United Nations 2012. *World Population Prospects: The 2012 Revision*, [Online]. United Nations, New York. Available at: http://esa.un.org/unpd/wpp/unpp/panel_population.htm (accessed 27 November 2013).

Vitousek, P. M., Ehrlich, P. R., Ehrlich, A. H. and Matson, P. A. 1986. Human appropriation of the products of photosynthesis. *BioScience*, 36: 368–373.

Vitousek, P. M., Mooney, H. A., Lubchenco, J. and Melillo, J. M. 1997. Human domination of Earth's ecosystems. *Science*, 277: 494–499.

Wackernagel, M., Schulz, N. B., Deumling, D., *et al.* 2002. Tracking the ecological overshoot of the human economy. *Proceedings of the National Academy of Sciences of the United States of America*, 99: 9266–9271.

Waggoner, P. E. and Ausubel, J. H. 2002. A framework for sustainability science: a renovated IPAT identity. *Proceedings of the National Academy of Sciences of the United States of America*, 99: 7860–7865.

Wania, F. and Mackay, D. (1996) Tracking the distribution of persistent organic pollutants. *Environmental Science and Technology*, 30(9): 390–396.

Watkins, G. C. 2006. Oil scarcity: what have the past three decades revealed? *Energy Policy*, 34: 508–514.

WBCSD 2008. *Sustainable Consumption Facts and Trends from a Business Perspective*, World Business Council for Sustainable Development (WBCSD), Geneva.

Wijkman, A. and Rockström, J. 2012. *Bankrupting Nature: Denying Our Planetary Boundaries*, Routledge, London.

WWF 2010. *Living Planet Report*, WWF, Gland, Switzerland.

WWF 2012. *Living Planet Report*, WWF, Gland, Switzerland.

Yandle, B., Bhattarai, M. and Vijayaraghavan, M. 2004. Environmental Kuznets curves: a review of findings, methods, and policy implications. *PERC Research Study 02-1 Update*, April 2004.

York, R., Rosa, E. A. and Dietz, T. 2003. Footprints on the earth: the environmental consequences of modernity. *American Sociological Review*, 68: 279–300.

Zachos, J. C., Röhl, U., Schellenberg, S. A., *et al.* 2005. Rapid acidification of the ocean during the Paleocene-Eocene Thermal Maximum. *Science*, 308: 611–1615.

Zalasiewicz, J., Williams, M., Steffen, W. and Crutzen, P. 2010. The new world of the Anthropocene. *Environmental Science & Technology*, 44: 2228–2231.

3

CLIMATE CHANGE AND CARBON MANAGEMENT

3.1 Introduction

Increasing concern about the potential impacts of global climate change, attributable primarily to human activities, has placed the issue of carbon management at the top of the international policy agenda. This chapter examines the science underpinning climate change and how this might be addressed through adaptation and mitigation measures, based on an understanding of the global carbon cycle. The aim is to provide an introduction to climate science, together with a broad and integrated overview of carbon management approaches. Climate change is one of the main drivers for the green economy, and carbon management is one of its main elements.

3.2 Global carbon cycle and carbon modelling

3.2.1 Carbon and the greenhouse effect

The carbon cycle plays a key role in regulating the Earth's climate by controlling the carbon dioxide (CO_2) concentration in the atmosphere. CO_2 is important because it contributes to the greenhouse effect, a process by which the atmosphere traps some of the Sun's thermal radiation, which warms the Earth.

Around 30 per cent of the solar energy that reaches the top of the Earth's atmosphere is reflected back to space, mainly by clouds and small particles in the atmosphere called 'aerosols'. The remaining 60 per cent is absorbed primarily by the Earth's surface and to a lesser extent by the atmosphere. To balance the incoming energy the Earth needs to radiate the same amount of energy back out into space. Because the Earth is much colder than the sun, the Earth radiates at much longer wavelengths compared to the incoming solar energy (primarily in the infrared part of the spectrum). Much of this thermal radiation is absorbed by water vapour (H_2O), CO_2, ozone, methane (CH_4) and nitrous oxide (N_2O) and reradiated back to Earth, warming the Earth's surface and the lower atmosphere. Atmospheric constituents that absorb long-wave radiation and hence contribute to the greenhouse effect are known as greenhouse gases (GHGs). Water vapour is the most important greenhouse gas; however, human activities have only a small direct influence on its amount in the atmosphere because of its rapid turnover (Le Treut *et al.*, 2007).

In the past 420,000 years, pre-industrial CO_2 concentrations in the atmosphere oscillated between 180–280 parts per million by volume (ppmv). Recent studies have revealed that post-industrial atmospheric CO_2 concentrations are now 110 ppmv higher, and have risen at a rate of between 10 and possibly 100 times faster than at any other time in this period (e.g. Falkowski *et al.*, 2000; Le Quéré *et al.*, 2013). CO_2 increase plays a significant role in enhancing the greenhouse effect and it is believed to be the main cause of anthropogenic climate change. With CO_2 emissions set to rise further, major efforts are being made at an international scale to stabilise its atmospheric concentration (e.g. the United Nations Framework Convention on Climate Change (UNFCCC), 1992).

Slowing the increase of atmospheric CO_2 presents a major challenge to society and requires a thorough understanding of the carbon cycle. In fact, the rate of change in CO_2 that stays in the atmosphere depends not only on human activities, but also on biogeochemical and climatological processes and their interactions with the carbon cycle. An overview of the global carbon cycle is presented in the following sections.

3.2.2 Overview of the global carbon cycle

First, some definitions of key terms (Penman *et al.*, 2003):

*   *Carbon stock*: The quantity of carbon in a 'pool' (i.e. a reservoir containing carbon) at a specified time. At the global scale, this is usually expressed in petagram (Pg) or gigatonne (Gt) of carbon (C): 1 PgC = 1 GtC = 1×10^{15}gC. At the regional scale, teragram (Tg) is used: 1 TgC = 1×10^{12}gC.
*   *Carbon flux*: The transfer of carbon from one carbon pool to another in units of measurement of mass per unit of area and time (e.g. tonnes C ha^{-1} yr^{-1}).
*   *Source*: Any process or activity that releases a greenhouse gas, an aerosol or a precursor of a greenhouse gas into the atmosphere.
*   *Sink*: Any process, activity or mechanism that removes a greenhouse gas, an aerosol, or a precursor of a greenhouse gas from the atmosphere.
*   *Carbon budget*: The balance of the exchanges of carbon between carbon pools. The examination of the budget of a pool will provide information on whether it is acting as a source or a sink.
*   *Carbon sequestration*: The process of increasing the carbon content of a carbon pool other than the atmosphere.

The main components of the carbon cycle include the atmosphere, land, ocean and the Earth's crust. The Earth's crust is the largest carbon pool (~ 100,000,000 PgC), followed by the oceans (~38,000 PgC), the terrestrial biosphere (~ 2,000 PgC) and the atmosphere (~ 780 PgC) (Figure 3.1). Atmospheric CO_2 continuously exchanges with the ocean and terrestrial ecosystems and the rate of the exchanges determines the overall atmospheric CO_2 concentration (Falkowski *et al.*, 2000). The main carbon fluxes are described below.

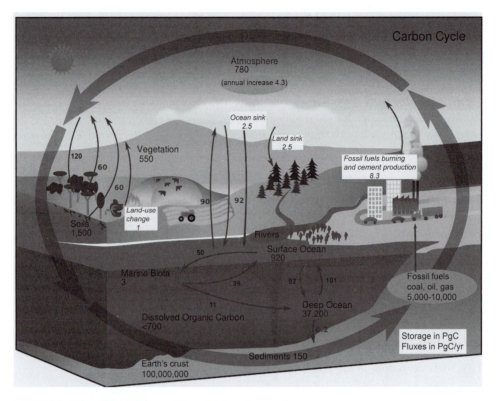

FIGURE 3.1 Simplified diagram of the global carbon cycle

Source: Modified from Wikimedia commons, http://commons.wikimedia.org/wiki/File:Carbon_cycle-cute_diagram. svg, based on information presented in Houghton (2007), Denman *et al.* (2007) and Le Quéré *et al.* (2013).

Carbon cycling in the ocean

Atmospheric CO_2 exchanges with oceanic CO_2 at the surface, through the process of diffusion. This exchange amounts to ~ 90 PgC yr^{-1} in each direction. Once in a dissolved form, CO_2 forms a carbonic acid (H_2CO_3) that reacts with carbonate anions (CO_3^{2-}) and water to form bicarbonate. While the formation of carbonate allows oceans to uptake a larger amount of CO_2 than would be possible if dissolved CO_2 remained in that form, this capacity is limited by the supply of mineral cations (positively charged molecules) from the slow weathering of coastal sediment. The concentration of total dissolved inorganic carbon (DIC) increases markedly in the ocean interior (from 725 PgC to 37,275 PgC) as a result of the combination of two processes: the 'solubility pump' and the 'biological pump' (Falkowski *et al.*, 2000).

   The 'solubility pump' is a process by which DIC is transported from the upper ocean to its interior. Sequestration of atmospheric CO_2 in the ocean interior depends on ocean circulation and mixing where cold dense waters, especially in the North Atlantic and Southern Ocean, sink to the deep ocean. These dissolve and capture carbon, until after an interval of decades to several hundred years, the water masses re-surface again. The 'biological pump' is a process that contributes to the absorption of atmospheric CO_2 in the ocean, where microscopic organisms called phytoplankton assimilate CO_2 through photosynthesis. The carbon is fixed in their biomass, of which 25 per cent sinks to the deep ocean, where it oxidises and adds to the dissolved carbon concentration. It is estimated that without phytoplankton, the atmospheric CO_2 concentration would be about 150 to 200 ppmv higher (ibid.).

Carbon cycling on land

CO_2 is removed from the atmosphere by photosynthesis of plants and stored in organic matter. The gross primary production (GPP) (total amount of organic carbon produced by photosynthesis) is estimated to be ~ 120 PgC yr^{-1}. Because some plants can live for hundreds of years, carbon is temporarily locked away and it is estimated that ~ 550 PgC is stored in plant structures at any given time. About half of the GPP is released back into the atmosphere through plant respiration. Virtually all of the remainder (~ 59 PgC yr^{-1}) joins the litter pool of organic matter in the soil, and is eventually returned to the atmosphere through soil decomposition. Some organic detritus has a short turnover time (< 10 years), while some is converted into modified soil carbon that has decadal to centennial turnover time. It is estimated that ~ 1500 PgC is stored in the organic matter of the world's soils at any given time (Houghton, 2007).

Today the global carbon cycle includes two important fluxes that stem from human activities. The most important of these is the combustion of fossil fuels (coal, oil and natural gas). These materials are the remains of organisms that once lived in oceans and lakes, and their transformation into fossil fuels took place over millions of years. Since the start of the Industrial Revolution these fuels have been extracted from the Earth's crust and combusted at increasing rates as a primary source of energy. The combustion of fossil fuels releases large amounts of CO_2 into the atmosphere (~8 PgC yr^{-1}), which alters the natural carbon cycle (Le Quéré et al., 2013).

Another human activity is land cover change, largely in the form of deforestation. As a result of human population increase and expansion of human settlements, large areas of native forests have been cleared and converted into agricultural and urban areas (see Chapter 4). Because terrestrial carbon storage occurs primarily in forests, the land cover changes have resulted into a net flux of carbon to the atmosphere. Although forests are regrowing in some places, where they can act as a sink of carbon, the net effect of land cover change at the global scale represents a flux of about 1.0 PgC yr^{-1} (ibid.).

Reflection point

The concept of carbon sinks is a really important one. Consider what would happen if any of the sinks mentioned here were somehow reduced in their capacity to absorb carbon. How might this happen in practice? Could this be affected by climate change, resulting in a positive feedback loop?

3.2.3 Measuring and modelling carbon

Measuring carbon stocks and fluxes at regional to continental scales is essential to evaluate the anthropogenic contributions to atmospheric CO_2. However, our current ability to account for the size and distribution of these stocks and fluxes is limited (e.g. Janssens *et al.*, 2003; Houghton, 2005; Le Quéré *et al.*, 2009). Current predictions of how the carbon cycle might evolve with changing climatic conditions are therefore uncertain (Friedlingstein *et al.*, 2006).

A range of measurement techniques are used at a variety of spatial and temporal scales, which are typically used in combination to improve the accuracy of carbon estimates. Assessing carbon stocks and fluxes is essential to develop optimal carbon management strategies (most often at regional to continental scales). It is also necessary to estimate carbon at a much finer scale to help define emission reductions or removals that can potentially be traded. The main techniques that are used to measure and predict carbon stocks and fluxes are described below.

Atmosphere-based carbon estimates

Atmosphere-based (also called 'top-down') approaches are based on the atmospheric concentrations of CO_2. Two main atmosphere-based methods have been used. The first uses the change in the atmospheric O_2/N_2 ratio as well as of $\delta^{13}C$ concentration to partition atmospheric sinks of carbon between land and ocean (Battle *et al.*, 2000). The second uses atmospheric transport models (also called 'inversion models'), together with variations in observed atmospheric CO_2 concentrations obtained through analysis of a network of flask air samples (Gurney *et al.*, 2002).

Vertical profiles of atmospheric CO_2 derived from aircraft samples have also been used to estimate regional carbon fluxes. This approach has been shown to give considerably different results from those obtained from most conventional inversion models (i.e. Gurney *et al.*, 2002). For example, Stephens *et al.* (2007), using air samples collected from aircraft at 12 locations worldwide, provided an estimate of the northern land uptake and tropical land emissions of -1.5 ± 0.6 and $+0.1 \pm 0.8$ PgC yr^{-1}, respectively. These values are noticeably different from the carbon fluxes of -2.4 ± 1.1 and $+1.8 \pm 1.7$ PgC yr^{-1}, respectively, reported by Gurney *et al.* (2002).

Land-based carbon estimates

Three main land-based (also called 'bottom-up') approaches have been used to estimate carbon fluxes at the regional scale. The first is based on analyses of carbon stock changes at repeated intervals, from which time-integrated carbon fluxes can be calculated. Such an approach includes comprehensive surveys of dissolved and particulate organic and inorganic carbon or tracers in the ocean (e.g. Sabine *et al.*, 2004); forest biomass inventories and models (e.g. Goodale *et al.*, 2002; Nabuurs *et al.*, 2003; Lewis *et al.*, 2009); soil carbon inventories and models (e.g. Bradley *et al.*, 2005; Falloon *et al.*, 2006); and vegetation- and biogeochemically based models such as LPJ, Orchidee and Biome-BGC (Jung *et al.*, 2007). The second approach is based on direct flux measurements of ocean CO_2 partial pressure (pCO_2) (e.g. Takahashi *et al.*, 2009) and ecosystem flux measurements via eddy covariance networks (www.fluxdata.org; e.g. Friend *et al.*, 2007; Baldocchi, 2008). The third method is obtained from estimates of land-use change and includes carbon sources mainly from deforestation and logging, and carbon sinks from ecosystem recovery, including both vegetation and soil (Houghton, 2003).

Remote sensing carbon estimates

Carbon stocks and fluxes have also been estimated using data produced from remote sensors, principally those borne on satellites. Several data products are available that can be related to carbon fluxes, including measures of gross primary production (GPP), net primary production (NPP), fraction of photosynthetically active radiation (FPAR) absorbed by the canopy of vegetation, the leaf area index (LAI), the surface reflectance, the surface temperature, the presence of fire, vegetation indices, aspects of the canopy structure and land cover and land cover change (e.g. Running *et al.*, 2004; Behrenfeld *et al.*, 2005; Hansen *et al.*, 2008; Hilker *et al.*, 2008; Goetz *et al.*, 2009).

Integrating atmosphere- and land-based carbon estimates

Bottom-up carbon measurements can potentially be integrated with top-down and satellite data to produce regional and continental carbon flux estimates (Davis, 2008). The first step towards integration is comparison of the estimates produced from different sources. However, this is not straightforward, because the time period, land area and set of biogeochemical fluxes for which the carbon budget is calculated do not necessarily correspond. In addition, carbon budgets derived from both top-down and bottom-up approaches have uncertainties that may be large (Denman *et al.*, 2007; Davis, 2008). For example, Pacala *et al.* (2001) applied both methods to the United States and showed that top-down and bottom-up estimates broadly agree, but the bottom-up estimates have a narrower range of uncertainty. However, they also concluded that this result was weakened by the large ranges of uncertainty for both methods.

Janssens *et al.* (2003) undertook a similar study for the European continent, using CO_2 measurements via an eddy covariance European network and satellite-based land cover classification. Results indicated that inverse atmospheric models report a mean uptake of carbon in the European terrestrial biosphere of 290 TgC yr^{-1} (range 80–560 TgC yr^{-1}), which contrasts with a much smaller sequestration rate of 111 TgC yr^{-1} ($\pm$279 TgC yr^{-1}) derived from land-based approaches. The gap between atmosphere- and land-based carbon estimates is reduced when correcting the atmospheric-based estimates for non-carbon dioxide carbon transfers (e.g. carbon monoxide, methane and other volatile organic compounds) that the atmospheric models do not take into account (see Figure 3.2, arrow A). In addition, there are CO_2 fluxes that are detected by the atmosphere-based method, but that bypass the terrestrial carbon pools (e.g. intercontinental trade in food and wood products) (see Figure 3.2, arrows B and C). Nevertheless, a difference of 70 TgC yr^{-1} between the two carbon estimates still remains, which can be attributed to carbon flows missing in either one or both methods, as well as the large uncertainty in both methods. Such variation in the results obtained with different approaches highlights the uncertainty that surrounds carbon measurement, and the technical difficulty of obtaining accurate measurements.

Efforts are ongoing to integrate carbon estimates derived from atmospheric, land-based and satellite data and to obtain a more comprehensive understanding of the carbon cycle (Davis, 2008; Ciais *et al.*, 2010).

3.2.4 The global carbon budget

Recent estimates of CO_2 fluxes to the global biosphere (the period 2002–2011) are reported in Le Quéré *et al.* (2013). As detailed in Table 3.1, the annual flux in CO_2 (4.3 ± 0.1 PgC yr^{-1})

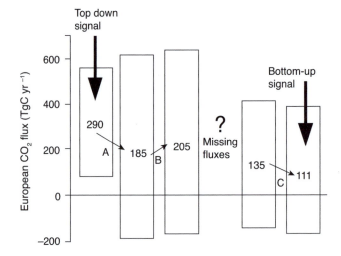

FIGURE 3.2   Carbon estimates in the European terrestrial biosphere obtained by different atmospheric transport models (top-down signal) and by integrated land-based approaches (bottom-up signal). Numbers give the mean carbon estimates and box sizes give an indication of their uncertainty.

Source: Based on information presented in Janssens *et al.* (2003).

Note: Arrow A: correction of the atmospheric signal for non-CO_2 carbon transfers; arrow B: correction of the atmospheric signal for the CO_2 fluxes bypassing the terrestrial carbon pools; arrow C: correction of the land signal for the carbon accumulation in the wood products pool.

is substantially smaller than the increment in anthropogenic emissions, owing to the combustion of fossil fuels and land-use change (8.3 ± 0.4 PgC yr^{-1} and 1.0 ± 0.5 PgC yr^{-1}, respectively). This is because natural sinks on land and in the ocean take up part of the anthropogenic CO_2, amounting to 5 PgC yr^{-1} (5 = (8.3 + 1) − 4.3)). Since estimates of the atmospheric CO_2 concentration are highly precise and fossil fuel emissions are tightly constrained by the growth in the world gross domestic product (GDP), and therefore have relatively small uncertainty, there is little doubt that without the land and ocean carbon sinks, the CO_2 concentration in the atmosphere would be increasing at nearly twice the rate that it is today (Deb Richter Jr and Houghton, 2011).

Table 3.1 Global carbon budget for the period 2002–2011

	PgC yr^{-1}
Emissions	
Emissions from fossil fuels combustion and cement production (E_{FF})	+ 8.3 ± 0.4
Net source from land-use change (E_{LUC})	+ 1.0 ± 0.5
Partitioning	
Storage in the atmosphere (G_{ATM})	− 4.3 ± 0.1
Ocean sink (S_{OCEAN})	− 2.5 ± 0.5
Residual terrestrial sink (S_{LAND})	− 2.5 ± 0.8

Source: Le Quéré *et al.* (2013).

Evidence from top-down and bottom-up approaches constrains the mean uptake rate for the ocean at 2.5 ± 0.5 PgC yr^{-1} (Le Quéré *et al.*, 2013), therefore the carbon sink on land can be calculated from the difference between all anthropogenic sources and all other known sinks as follows:

$$S_{LAND} = E_{FF} + E_{LUC} - (G_{ATM} + S_{OCEAN})$$

The uncertainty in S_{LAND} is estimated from the quadratic sum of the uncertainty in the right-hand terms, assuming the errors are not correlated.

The residual terrestrial sink calculated as above equals 2.5 ± 0.8 PgC yr^{-1} (Figure 3.3). However, scientists have only been able to account for a part of this carbon sequestered

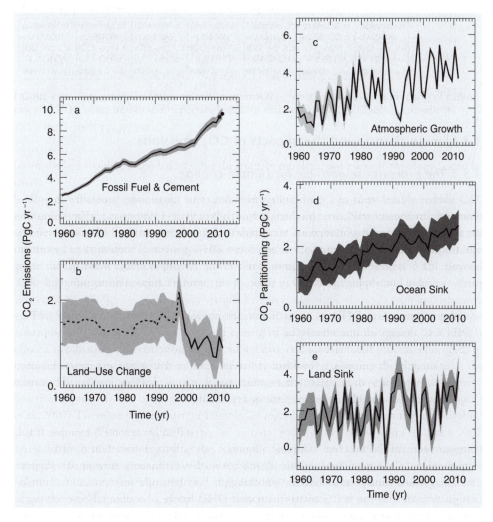

FIGURE 3.3 Component of the global carbon budget (in PgC yr^{-1}) and the uncertainty bounds (shaded) since 1960. (a) emissions from fossil fuels' combustion and cement production (E_{FF}); (b) net source from land-use change (E_{LUC}); (c) storage of CO_2 in the atmosphere (G_{ATM}); (d) ocean sink (S_{OCEAN}); (e) residual terrestrial sink (S_{LAND}).

Source: Le Quéré *et al.* (2013). Courtesy of the Global Carbon Project (www.globalcarbonproject.org).

(e.g. Goodale *et al.*, 2002); the remaining part of the carbon sink appears to be missing from the global carbon budget. This is sometimes referred to as the 'missing sink'. This may be explained by terrestrial carbon uptake by forests and other ecosystems being larger than can be accounted for, and is probably the result of land–use surface responses to climate variability. However, identification of the missing sink remains an area of active research.

> **Reflection point**
>
> While measurements are continuously improving, there is still large uncertainty associated with measurements of the carbon cycle, particularly in relation to estimating the effects of land-use change. This is important in the context of the green economy, because land-use change is one of the main elements of economic development, particularly in areas where the amount of agricultural land is expanding. Consider, therefore, whether clearance of forest for agriculture is ever likely to be environmentally sustainable, from the perspective of the global carbon cycle.

3.3 Climate change and the impacts of CO_2 emissions

3.3.1 The processes responsible for climate change

The anthropogenic input of CO_2 is widely believed to be largely responsible for the global warming that has recently been observed (Box 3.1). Petit *et al.* (1999) showed that throughout the four past glacial-interglacial cycles, atmospheric CO_2 concentrations have followed similar trends to those of air temperature. Crowley (2000) also suggests that there is close agreement between the temperature changes observed in the late twentieth century and the warming predicted from anthropogenic GHG increases. Is it therefore reasonable to infer that CO_2 emissions are now the most important cause of climate change?

What is climate change? The United Nations Framework Convention on Climate Change (UNFCCC) defines 'climate change' as:

> a change of climate which is attributed directly or indirectly to human activity that alters the composition of the global atmosphere and which is in addition to natural climate variability observed over comparable time periods.

The state of knowledge on climate change is periodically reported by the IPCC (Intergovernmental Panel on Climate Change) (www.ipcc.ch/index.htm). The latest assessment is 'Climate Change 2007 (AR4)', the IPCC Fourth Assessment Report. The Fifth Assessment Report (AR5) (see Box 3.1) will be completed in 2014. 'Climate change,' according to the IPCC, refers to any change in climate over time, whether owing to natural variability or as a result of human activity. Note that this definition differs from that of the UNFCCC.

Climate change is driven by changes to the energy balance of the Earth system. Many natural and anthropogenic processes can influence this. Factors that affect climate change are

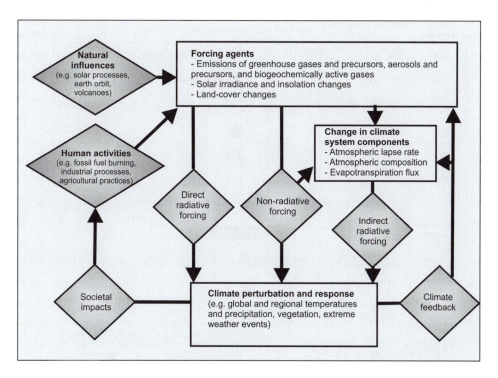

FIGURE 3.4 Conceptual framework of climate forcing, response and feedbacks under current climatic conditions

Source: Based on information presented in Forster *et al.* (2007) and Committee on Radiative Forcing Effects on Climate *et al.* (2005).

separated into *forcings* and *feedbacks* (Figure 3.4). Some definitions (Committee on Radiative Forcing Effects on Climate *et al.*, 2005):

- A *climate forcing* is an energy imbalance imposed on the climate system either externally or by human activities (i.e. solar energy output, volcanic emissions, anthropogenic emissions of GHGs, land use change), and it is usually expressed in watts per square metre (W m^{-2}). Climate forcings can be classified as radiative or nonradiative.
- *Radiative forcings* can be separated into *direct radiative forcings*, which affect the radiative budget of the Earth directly (e.g. added CO_2 absorbs and emits infrared radiation); and *indirect radiative forcings*, which create a radiative imbalance by first altering the climate system components that almost immediately lead to changes in radiative fluxes (e.g. the effect of aerosols on the precipitation efficiency of clouds). A radiative forcing (RF) can be related to the global mean equilibrium temperature change at the surface (ΔT_s) as follows: $\Delta T_s = \lambda$RF, where λ is the climate sensitivity parameter.
- *Nonradiative forcings* create an energy imbalance that does not involve radiation directly; an example is the increasing evapotranspiration flux resulting from agricultural irrigation.
- A *climate feedback* is an internal process that amplifies or restrains the climate response to an initial forcing.

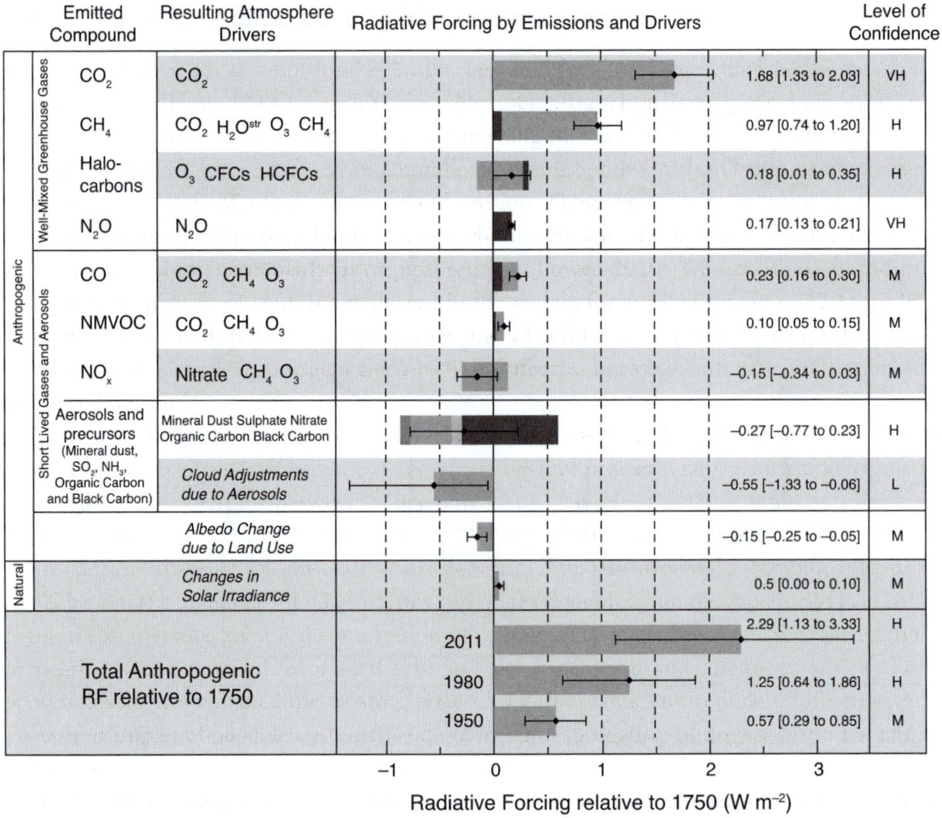
Emitted Compound
Resulting Atmosphere Drivers
Radiative Forcing by Emissions and Drivers
Level of Confidence
Anthropogenic
Well-Mixed Greenhouse Gases
CO2
CO2
1.68 [1.33 to 2.03]
VH
CH4
CO2 H2Ostr O3 CH4
0.97 [0.74 to 1.20]
H
Halo-carbons
O3 CFCs HCFCs
0.18 [0.01 to 0.35]
H
N2O
N2O
0.17 [0.13 to 0.21]
VH
Short Lived Gases and Aerosols
CO
CO2 CH4 O3
0.23 [0.16 to 0.30]
M
NMVOC
CO2 CH4 O3
0.10 [0.05 to 0.15]
M
NOx
Nitrate CH4 O3
−0.15 [−0.34 to 0.03]
M
Aerosols and precursors (Mineral dust, SO2, NH3, Organic Carbon and Black Carbon)
Mineral Dust Sulphate Nitrate Organic Carbon Black Carbon
−0.27 [−0.77 to 0.23]
H
Cloud Adjustments due to Aerosols
−0.55 [−1.33 to −0.06]
L
Albedo Change due to Land Use
−0.15 [−0.25 to −0.05]
M
Natural
Changes in Solar Irradiance
0.5 [0.00 to 0.10]
M
Total Anthropogenic RF relative to 1750
2011
2.29 [1.13 to 3.33]
H
1980
1.25 [0.64 to 1.86]
H
1950
0.57 [0.29 to 0.85]
M
−1
0
1
2
3
Radiative Forcing relative to 1750 (W m−2)

FIGURE 3.5 Summary of the main components of the radiative forcing (RFs) of climate change between 1750 and 2011 and their level of confidence (VH – very high, H – high, M – medium, L – low, VL – very low). Positive forcings lead to warming of climate and negative forcing lead to cooling.

Source: IPCC (2013), Figure SPM.5.

The main components of the radiative forcing of climate change between 1750 and 2011 are presented in Figure 3.5. Positive radiative forcings lead to warming of climate, and negative forcings lead to cooling. Of the long-lived greenhouse gases, CO_2 is the forcing agent with the highest radiative forcing (1.68 W m^{-2}), and it is therefore considered the main gas contributing to climate warming. Methane (CH_4) has the second largest positive radiative forcing (0.97 W m^{-2}).

Global average abundances of the major long-lived greenhouse gases (CO_2, CH_4, N_2O CFC-12 and CFC-11) have been increasing in recent decades (Figure 3.6). The growth rate of CO_2 has averaged about 1.68 ppm per year over the past 31 years (1979–2011). The CO_2 growth rate has increased over this period, averaging about 1.4 ppm per year before 1995 and 1.9 ppm per year thereafter. From 1999 to 2006, the CH_4 burden was about constant, but since 2007, globally averaged CH_4 has begun increasing again. Nitrous oxide continues to increase at a relatively uniform growth rate, while radiative forcing from the sum of observed CFC changes ceased increasing in about 2000 and is now declining. The latter is a response to decreased emissions related to the Montreal Protocol on substances that deplete the ozone layer (Butler, 2013).

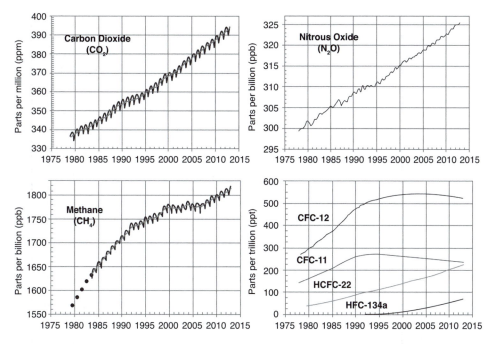

FIGURE 3.6   Global average abundances of the major long-lived greenhouse gases from the NOAA global air sampling network since the beginning of 1979. These gases account for about 96 per cent of the direct radiative forcing by long-lived greenhouse gases since 1750.

Source: Butler (2013); all modern data are from NOAA's Global Monitoring Division, with the exception of the methane data before 1983, which are annual averages from Etheridge *et al.* (1996), adjusted to the NOAA calibration scale referred to in Dlugokencky *et al.* (2005).

3.3.2 Main anthropogenic sources of CO₂ emissions influencing climate change

Fossil fuel combustion

A wide range of direct and indirect measurements confirm that the atmospheric mixing ratio of CO_2 has increased globally by about 110 ppm over the past 260 years, from a range of 275 to 285 ppm in the pre-industrial era (AD 1000–1750) to 391 ppm in 2011 (Forster *et al.*, 2007; Le Quéré *et al.*, 2013). The first continuous measurements of atmospheric CO_2 conducted by Charles David Keeling in 1958 represent the master time series documenting the changing composition of the atmosphere (Keeling, 1998). These data have iconic status in climate change science, as evidence of the effect of fossil fuel burning on the composition of the global atmosphere.

Carbon atoms occur with different atomic weights (with different numbers of neutrons in them), namely 14, 13 and 12, with ^{12}C making up around 98.9 per cent and ^{13}C around 1.1 per cent. ^{12}C and ^{13}C do not decay, whereas ^{14}C does so, with a half-life of 5,270 years. The CO_2 produced by burning fossil has a much lower $^{13}C/^{12}C$ ratio than normal atmospheric CO_2. If we added new CO_2 that had the same ratio as the rest of the CO_2 in the atmosphere, the total amount of CO_2 would increase, but the $^{13}C/^{12}C$ ratio would stay the same. So by adding anthropogenic CO_2 with a much lower $^{13}C/^{12}C$ ratio, we expect the data to show a decrease in this ratio over time. This is indeed what Keeling *et al.* (2005) observed. Further evidence that the increase in atmospheric CO_2 during the industrial era was caused by human activities was provided by Manning and Keeling (2006), who analysed the concentration of oxygen in the atmosphere (O_2). Burning fossil fuels consumes an average of 15 oxygen molecules for every 19 of CO_2, therefore by adding anthropogenic CO_2 we expect the overall concentration of O_2 to decline. Again, this is what was observed.

Today, the most extensive network of international air sampling sites is operated by the National Oceanic and Atmospheric Administration's Global Monitoring Division (NOAA/GMD; www.esrl.noaa.gov/gmd). Worldwide databases of CO_2 measurements are maintained by several organisations, including the Carbon Dioxide Information Analysis Center (CDIAC; http://cdiac.ornl.gov). CDIAC also provides global emissions data that are primarily based on energy data provided by the UN Statistics Division (http://unstats.un.org/unsd). Input data to calculate fossil fuel emissions are available for all countries with annual resolution; fossil fuel emissions have therefore relatively small uncertainty.

Land-use change

The second main source of CO_2 emissions is land-use change, primarily deforestation. As terrestrial carbon storage occurs primarily in forests, deforestation results in a net flux of carbon to the atmosphere. In contrast to fossil fuel emissions, CO_2 emissions from land-use change are more difficult to calculate, as much of the underlying data is not available on an annual basis and can only be estimated through the use of models.

Uncertainties arise primarily from two factors: (1) the availability of land-use data, especially with regards to the rate of deforestation; and (2) the availability of data on changes in carbon stocks resulting from land management, such as harvesting and burning (Houghton, 2003). Estimate of land-use change emissions are usually calculated using a book-keeping method that tracks the carbon stored in vegetation and soil for each hectare of land cultivated, harvested or reforested. The primary data for this model are the Food and Agricultural Organisation (FAO) Forest Resource Assessment (FRA) (www.fao.org/forestry/fra), and the FAO Statistics Division (http://faostat3.fao.org), which are based on countries' self-reporting data on changes in forest cover and management, cropland and pasture area. These data are published at intervals of five years. Satellite-based assessments and Dynamic Global Vegetation Models have recently been used to help quantify the uncertainties (Le Quéré *et al.*, 2013).

Because of the difficulties in calculating CO_2 fluxes from land-use change, different authors report different estimates. For example, values ranging from 0.9 to 2.2 PgC yr^{-1} were reported for the 1990s (Houghton, 2010) and 1.0 PgC yr^{-1} (± 0.5) was reported for 2002–2011, representing about 10 per cent of the total anthropogenic emission of carbon (Le Quéré *et al.*, 2013).

Reflection point

Despite the strong scientific consensus that human activities are largely responsible for recent climate change, many people are sceptical of this. What do you think the reasons for this might be?

BOX 3.1 IS CLIMATE CHANGE REALLY OCCURRING?

In 2013, the IPCC released its 5th Assessment Report, which was produced as a collaboration between many leading scientists. The report (IPCC, 2013) concluded that:

- Warming of the climate system is unequivocal, and many of the observed changes that have occurred since the 1950s are unprecedented over timescales of decades to millennia. Specifically, the atmosphere and ocean have warmed, the amounts of snow and ice have diminished, sea level has risen, and the concentrations of greenhouse gases have increased.
- Each of the last three decades has been successively warmer at the Earth's surface than any preceding decade since the 1850s.
- Ocean warming dominates the increase in energy stored in the climate system, accounting for more than 90 per cent of the energy accumulated between 1971 and 2010. It is *virtually certain* that the upper ocean (0–700 m) warmed from 1971 to 2010.
- Over the last two decades, the Greenland and Antarctic ice sheets have been losing mass, glaciers have continued to shrink almost worldwide, and Arctic sea ice and Northern Hemisphere spring snow cover have continued to decrease in extent.
- The rate of sea level rise since the mid-nineteenth century has been larger than the mean rate during the previous two millennia. Over the period 1901–2010, global mean sea level rose by 0.19 m.
- Human influence on the climate system is clear. Human influence has been detected in the warming of the atmosphere and the ocean, in changes in the global water cycle, in reductions in snow and ice, in global mean sea level rise, and in changes in some climate extremes. It is *extremely likely* (i.e. 95–100 per cent likelihood) that human influence has been the dominant cause of the observed warming since the mid-twentieth century.

The IPCC report provides an authoritative compilation of scientific evidence about climate change. But how representative is it of scientific opinion? A number of studies have examined this question, for example:

- Oreskes (2004) surveyed abstracts of 928 scientific papers relating to climate change, and found that none of them disagreed with the scientific consensus.
- Anderegg *et al.* (2010) examined 1,372 climate researchers and their publication and citation data, and showed that 97–98 per cent of the climate researchers most actively publishing in the field agree with the IPCC's position on anthropogenic climate change.

3.3.3 Main impacts of climate change

Anthropogenic climate change is predicted (and is already observed in some regions) to severely affect freshwater resources and their management; ecosystems; food, fibre and forest products; coastal systems and low-lying areas; industry; settlement; society and human health (Parry *et al.*, 2007). Documenting such impacts is currently a major research activity.

Impacts of recent climate change vary greatly according to the observed change in surface and atmospheric climate considered. These observed changes can be grouped into:

- *changes in means*: temperature, precipitation, sea-level rise;
- *changes in extremes*: tropical cyclones, storm surge, extreme rainfall, riverine floods, heatwaves or cold waves and droughts.

Rosenzweig *et al.* (2007) provide a synthesis of the significant observed changes resulting from climate change, in both physical and biological systems. The results show an agreement between the regions of significant warming across the globe and the locations of significant observed changes, including increases in water runoff, floods, droughts, shoreline erosion, changes in bird populations, migratory patterns, timing of Spring events, polewards tree range shifts, and increases of vector-borne diseases (Figure 3.7).

Walther *et al.* (2002) review the impacts of 30 years of warming on biological systems, focusing on: (1) the phenology of organisms; (2) the range and distribution of species; (3) the composition of communities; and (4) the dynamics of ecosystems. The authors highlight many examples where species distribution patterns have changed. For example, in North America and Europe at least 39 species of butterfly have shifted further north owing to increased warming. Zooplankton and other fish communities have increased in abundance owing to increased ocean temperatures, tree-lines are shifting to higher altitudes in Alpine regions, and plants and invertebrates are moving north owing to water availability in Antarctica. In 1998, over 16 per cent of the world's coral reef died owing to sea temperature rises. The described changes in phenology, species distributions and population dynamics are happening at a high rate, which may limit the potential for adaptation and increase the risk of extinction of many species. Global warming is also influencing the spread of diseases, such as an increased spread of mosquito-borne diseases in Asia, East Africa and Latin America.

Barnett *et al.* (2005) review the impacts of warming on water resources. The authors suggest that a modest increase in near-surface air temperature will lead to serious regional water shortages, as a result of less snow accumulation in the Winter and earlier peak stream-flow in the Spring. This could affect much of the industrialised world.

> **Reflection point**
>
> One way or another, sooner or later, climate change is going to affect you individually. Do you agree with that statement? How might climate change affect you personally?

3.4 Climate change policy

Policy-makers have been faced with a considerable challenge in developing international policies to address the problem of climate change. There are three main difficulties:

1. *The debate regarding the causes of global warming*, and the uncertainty about the severity and timescale of the impacts of climate change.
2. *The economic implications of climate change.* The global economy is built upon the production of GHGs from energy, transport, industrial and agricultural sources, and any action to change this threatens to slow down economic development.

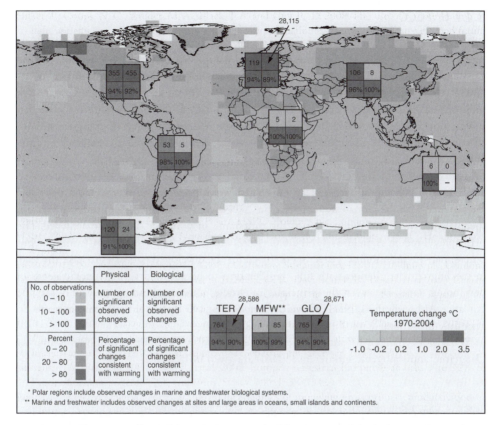

FIGURE 3.7 Changes in physical systems (snow, ice and frozen ground; hydrology; and coastal processes) and biological systems (terrestrial, marine and freshwater biological systems) and surface air temperature over the period 1970–2004. Data series are from about 75 studies and contain more than 29,000 data series, of which about 28,000 are from European studies. White areas do not contain sufficient observational climate data to estimate a temperature trend. The 2 × 2 boxes show the total number of data series with significant changes (top row) and the percentage of those consistent with warming (bottom row) for (1) continental regions: North America, Latin America, Europe, Africa, Asia, Australia and New Zealand, and Polar Regions; and (2) the global scale.

Source: Rosenzweig *et al.* (2007), Figure 1.9.
Notes: Terrestrial (TER), Marine and Freshwater (MFW), and Global (GLO).

3. *Political complexity*. Tackling the impacts of climate change requires a complex international response, addressing sectors as diverse as transportation, deforestation, energy generation, conservation of natural resources, economic growth, and personal liberties. It therefore crosses the sectoral boundaries that usually dominate international environmental regulation (Bell and McGillivray, 2008).

Climate change has been one of the fastest moving areas of international policy (Lefevere, 2009). This provides a key part of the context within which the green economy is developing. Selected key initiatives are considered below.

3.4.1 UNFCCC

Efforts to tackle climate change have been developed through international legal mechanisms since 1992. At that time, the United Nations Conference on Environment and Development (UNCED) in Rio, building on the scientific evidence presented in the first IPCC report, established an agreement on global warming called 'the UN Framework Convention on Climate Change' (UNFCCC). The nature of the Convention meant that it was not a comprehensive 'law of the atmosphere', but an overall framework with specific measures assisting its implementation to be added in subsequent Conferences of the Parties (CoPs).

The objective of the UNFCCC is expressed as 'the stabilization of greenhouse gas concentrations in the atmosphere at a level that would prevent dangerous anthropogenic interference with the climate system' (Article 2; UNFCCC, 1992). The Convention does not specify what that level might be, nor the timeframe in which it should be achieved. The principles listed in Article 3 (UNFCCC, 1992) introduce the concept of 'common but differentiated responsibility', reflecting the need for the developed countries to 'take the lead' in tackling climate change, with full consideration to be afforded to the specific needs of developing states. However, the principles in Article 3 are not binding; they only provide guidance. Although the UNFCCC has been signed by 195 Parties, this commits them to do very little or nothing at all (Fitzroy and Papyrakis, 2009).

What does 'dangerous anthropogenic interference' mean? Some proposed values of 'dangerous anthropogenic interference' (DAI) are given in Table 3.2.

Table 3.2 Example of numerical values of 'dangerous anthropogenic interference'

Vulnerability	*Global mean limit*	*Reference*
Shutdown of thermohaline circulation	3 °C in 100 years	O'Neill and Oppenheimer (2002)
Disintegration of West Antarctic ice sheet	2–4 °C, <550 ppm CO_2	Oppenheimer and Alley (2005)
Disintegration of Greenland ice sheet	1 °C	Hansen (2005)
Widespread bleaching of coral reefs	>1 °C	Smith *et al.* (2001), O'Neill and Oppenheimer (2002)
Broad ecosystem impacts with limited adaptive capacity (many examples)	1–2 °C	Leemans and Eickhout (2004), Hare (2003), Smith *et al.* (2001)
Large increase in numbers of people at risk of water shortage in vulnerable regions	450–650 ppm CO_2	Parry *et al.* (2001)
Increasingly adverse impacts, most economic sectors	>3–4 °C	Hitz and Smith (2004)

Source: Based on information presented in Oppenheimer and Petsonk (2005).
Notes: References are those which present a direct link to UNFCCC Article 2 or 'dangerous' climate change, rather than underlying physical or ecological studies. Vulnerabilities are also referred to as a 'reason for concern' in IPCC terms.

Reflection point

Can you see any problem with measuring these vulnerabilities? For example, how certain are the models predicting the disintegration of the West Antarctic ice sheet? Can you see any problem with using the bleaching of corals as a global limit?

3.4.2 The Kyoto Protocol

The Kyoto Protocol provides specific obligations that were left undefined in the UNFCCC. The Protocol sets up legally binding targets and timetables for a list of industrialised countries and the European Community to reduce specific GHG emissions. The Protocol entered into force in February 2005. Its first commitment period started in 2008 and ended in 2012. During this period, the Protocol was ratified by 193 Parties (UNFCCC, 2011a). The Kyoto Protocol was originally going to expire on 1 January 2013, but was then extended until 2020. During the second commitment period, Parties committed to reduce GHG emissions by at least 18 per cent below 1990 levels in the eight-year period from 2013 to 2020. However, the second phase only covers about 15 per cent of global emissions after Canada, Japan, New Zealand and Russia opted out (UN, 2012).

The Protocol tackles the emissions of six GHGs. These are carbon dioxide (CO_2), methane (CH_4), nitrous oxide (N_2O), for which Parties must use the year 1990 as baseline, and hydrofluorocarbons (HFCs), perfluorocarbons (PFCs), sulphur hexafluoride (SF_6) and nitrogen trifluoride (NF_3), for which Parties must use 1995 as the base year. Note that NF_3 was only added by the UNFCCC in the second Protocol compliance period.

The basket of gases considered in the Protocol meant that a common measure was needed to compare the effects of the emissions of the different gases, i.e. carbon dioxide equivalence. This was done using the concept of 'global warming potentials' (GWP). The GWP index is defined as the cumulative radiative forcing between the present and some chosen time horizon caused by a unit mass of gas emitted now, expressed relative to that of a unit mass of CO_2 (see Table 3.3).

The adequacy of the GWP index has been widely debated (e.g. O'Neill, 2000; Fuglestvedt et al., 2003). Academic criticism has focused on the assumptions made to calculate the GWPs (Forster et al., 2007). However, the GWP index has advantages in terms of political feasibility (Godal, 2003), and it still remains the metric used by the Parties to report on their emissions. GHGs other than CO_2 are expressed in terms of CO_2 equivalent (CO_2e) by multiplying the mass of the gas by its GWP.

According to the Protocol, Parties can meet their obligations either by reducing their emissions, and/or increasing GHG sequestration by sink options (i.e. activities that absorb GHGs from the atmosphere). The question of allowing Parties to use sink options to meet their targets was probably the most technically complex issue in the entire Kyoto negotiations (Grubb et al., 1999). This was due to the very high levels of scientific and technical uncertainty in measuring carbon sink uptake. Another issue was the definition of 'anthropogenic sink'. Eventually, reductions in emissions and removals by sinks 'resulting from direct human-induced land-use change and forestry activities, limited to afforestation, reforestation and deforestation since 1990' were allowed (Article 3(3); UN, 1998). Accounting on a wider range of 'additional human-induced activities related to changes in greenhouse gas emissions by sources and

Table 3.3 GHGs in the Kyoto Protocol and their global warming potentials (GWP) for a 100-year time horizon

Gas	Sources	Lifetime (years)	GWP-100
Carbon dioxide (CO_2)	Fossil fuel burning, cement, tropical deforestation	★	1
Methane (CH_4)	Natural wetlands, ruminant fermentation, fossil fuel production, rice paddies, landfills, biomass burning	12	21
Nitrous oxide (N_2O)	Fertilisers, fossil fuel burning, land conversion to agriculture	114	310
Hydrofluorocarbons (HFCs)	Industry, refrigerants	1.4–270, HFC134a (most common) is 14	140–11,700 HFC134a (most common) is 1300
Perfluorocarbons (PFCs)	Industry, aluminium, electronic and electrical industries, fire fighting, solvents	2,600–50,000	6,500–9,200
Sulphur hexafluoride (SF_6)	Electronic and electrical industries, insulation	3,200	23,900
Nitrogen trifluoride (NF_3)	Electronic industries (manufacture of semiconductors and LCD panels), some photovoltaic and chemical laser industries	740	17,200

Sources: Dale (1997) and Forster *et al.* (2007).

removals by sinks in the agricultural soils and the land-use change and forestry categories' was made voluntary (Article 3(4); UN, 1998).

Articles 3 and 4 left a number of technical issues to be resolved, including the precise meaning of words such as afforestation, reforestation and deforestation (ARD), 'direct human-induced' and 'human-induced' activities. As part of the technical advice, the IPCC was requested to produce a Special Report on land use, land-use change and forestry (LULUCF), which aimed to assist the Parties by providing scientific and technical information to illustrate how the main components of the global carbon cycle interact with the agricultural and forestry sectors, and what the implications of land use, land-use change and forestry activities are (Watson *et al.*, 2000).

The Kyoto Protocol established three innovative mechanisms, allowing Parties listed in Annex I to achieve their binding targets by undertaking, financing or purchasing emissions reductions generated outside their territories. These mechanisms are Joint Implementation (JI) (Article 6), the Clean Development Mechanism (CDM) (Article 12), and emissions trading (Article 17). These have had a significant impact on land use and economic development.

3.4.3 The Clean Development Mechanism (CDM)

The CDM enables Annex I Parties (i.e. industrialised countries) to establish project-based activities that reduce anthropogenic emissions in non-Annex I Parties (i.e. developing countries). The resultant 'Certified Emissions Reductions' (CERs) generated by such projects can be used by the Annex I Parties to meet part of their emissions targets. Article 12 states the dual purposes of the CDM to be:

> to assist Parties not included in Annex I in achieving sustainable development and in contribution to the ultimate objective of the Convention, and to assist Parties included in Annex I in achieving compliance with their quantified emission limitation and reduction commitments under Article 3.
>
> *(UN, 1998)*

From this, you can see that this is a mechanism that could potentially support the transition to a green economy.

How does this work in practice? The process is rather complex. The CDM project is commonly divided into two phases: the development phase, and the implementation phase. The development phase starts with the Designated National Authority (DNA) of the host developing country stating that the CDM project contributes to sustainable development. This is followed by a project design document (PDD) prepared by the project developer, which must demonstrate that emissions reductions are 'real, measurable and long-term' and 'additional', i.e. that the GHG emissions after project implementation are lower than would have occurred in the absence of the CDM project. After the project is registered, it is eligible to generate Certified Emissions Reductions (CERs). The implementation phase starts with the measurement of the GHG emissions from the project in order to determine the quantity of emission reductions attributable to the project. This is followed by periodic independent review by a Designated Operational Entity. If verification is satisfactory, a number of CERs are certified and issued, and are finally forwarded to the Parties and project participants involved (Olsen, 2007).

This simplified summary indicates the complex nature of the CDM project cycle. The World Bank has reported on the 'creaking' structure of the CDM, resulting in large numbers of projects awaiting validation and delays of over three years for the average project to make its way through the regulatory process and issue its first CERs (Kossoy and Ambrosi, 2010). As of October 2013, there were 7,322 registered CDM projects and 61 requesting registration. Projects details can be explored at: http://cdm.unfccc.int/Projects/projsearch.html.

In 2007, the CDM market accounted for transactions worth US\$7.4 billion, representing emission reductions of 551 million tonnes of CO_2 equivalent ($MtCO_2e$). In 2009, the CDM market fell to US\$2.7 billion, representing emission reductions of 211 $MtCO_2e$, a dramatic 62 per cent decline from 2007. The primary market for pre-2013 Kyoto offsets continued to decline in 2011 reflecting the end of the first Protocol compliance period. The CDM market fell to US\$990 million, representing emission reductions of 91 million tonnes of CO_2 equivalent ($MtCO_2e$) (Figure 3.8).

In 2011, the most important sectors described by the volumes of credits per year were renewable energy and energy efficiency. In terms of geographical distribution of registered CDM projects, the top country (measured by the annual volumes transacted) was China (88 per cent), followed by other Asian countries (6 per cent) and Africa (4 per cent) (Kossoy and Guigon, 2012).

The CDM mechanism represents a large market for GHG emission controls. However, it is not clear whether it can deliver the twofold objective of simultaneously delivering GHG

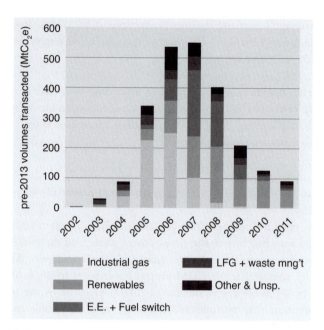

FIGURE 3.8 Pre-2013 primary CDM sectors, based on volumes purchased 2002–2011

Source: Kossoy and Guigon (2012).
Notes: E.E. = energy efficiency, LFG = Landfill Gas.

emission reduction and contributing to sustainable development. Subbarao and Lloyd (2011) indicate that large parts of CMD projects owned and operated by the private sector have been unsuccessful in providing environmental, economic, and social benefits to communities or regions.

3.4.4 Joint implementation (JI)

Joint implementation (JI) allows one Annex I Party to implement an emission-reducing project or a project that enhances removals by sinks of greenhouse gases in another Annex I party, and by doing so obtain emissions reduction units (ERUs) that will count towards meeting its own Kyoto target (Article 6; UN, 1998). As with the CDM mechanism, JI aims to offer Parties a flexible and cost-efficient way to fulfil part of their binding commitments, while the host Party benefits from foreign investment and technology transfer. The condition that a JI project must respect is that emission reductions have to be additional to what would have occurred in the absence of the project, and it must have approval of the Parties concerned. Compared to the CDM, JI transacts only a modest volume of CO_2 equivalent. In 2009, the JI market transacted US$339 million, representing emission reductions of 28 $MtCO_2e$ (Kossoy and Guigon, 2012).

3.4.5 International emission trading

Article 17 of the Kyoto Protocol provides a framework for Annex I Parties to 'participate in emissions trading for the purposes of fulfilling their commitments', providing that such trading is 'supplemental to domestic actions for the purpose of meeting quantified emission limitation and reduction commitments'. Parties that may otherwise not meet their targets are able to trade units (in tonnes of CO_2 equivalent) in the form of:

(i) Assigned Amount Units (AAUs) (i.e. units issued by Annex I Parties into their national registry up to their binding cap);
(ii) Removal Units (RMUs) (i.e. units issued by Parties in respect of net removals by sinks from LULUCF activities);
(iii) Certified Emission Reductions (CERs) (i.e. tradable units generated from CDM project activities); and
(iv) Emission Reduction Unit (ERUs) (i.e. tradable units generated by a JI project).

Thus, Article 17 created a new commodity in the form of emission reductions or removals. Since units are traded in CO_2 equivalent, this is typically referred to as 'trading in carbon'.

3.4.6 REDD

Tropical deforestation currently makes a major contribution to global GHG emissions. Recognising this, negotiators within the UNFCCC introduced a financial mechanism to Reduce carbon Emissions from Deforestation and forest Degradation (REDD) in developing countries (Miles and Kapos, 2008). At CoP 13 in Bali in 2007, Parties established indicative guidance for a pilot phase of REDD in the period to 2012 (Miles, 2010). Since then, progress has been made in developing national strategies, monitoring systems and social and environmental safeguards (UNFCCC, 2011b). Inclusion of enhancement of forest carbon stocks (for example through ecological restoration, see Chapter 4) led to the initiative being renamed as REDD+.

REDD+ includes the following activities (ibid.):

a   Reducing emissions from deforestation.
b   Reducing emissions from forest degradation.
c   Conservation of forest carbon stocks.
d   Sustainable management of forest.
e   Enhancement of forest carbon stocks.

Hence, under REDD+ developing countries undertaking forest restoration, afforestation and reforestation activities can qualify to receive funding under category (e). This therefore potentially provides an important funding mechanism to support the sustainable management of forests (see Chapter 7).

UNFCCC has requested countries undertake pilot work towards REDD+ on a voluntary basis. REDD+ funds for these activities have been made available to selected countries through the Forest Carbon Partnership Facility (FCPF; www.forestcarbonpartnership.org), the UN-REDD Programme (www.un-redd.org), and other bilateral agreements. Pilot projects are also being funded by NGOs and the private sector. By attracting money from the carbon market, REDD+ transactions had reached US$125 billion by 2008 and the REDD+ market was projected to reach over US$600 billion by 2013.

According to Stickler *et al.* (2009), developing countries undertaking REDD+ activities could potentially access a substantial amount of money from global stakeholders willing to pay to maintain carbon in tropical forests. However, regardless of its financial success and potential benefits, the approach has also been criticised (see Chapter 7).

3.5 Measuring and reporting GHGs

The UNFCCC requires Annex I and non-Annex I Parties to submit national communications covering all aspects of the UNFCCC implementation (Articles 4 and 12; UNFCCC, 1992). In addition, Annex I Parties need to submit annual inventories of anthropogenic GHG emissions by sources and removals by sinks. Annex I Parties also need to demonstrate compliance with the Kyoto's GHG reduction commitments (Article 3; UN, 1998). These requirements raise the question: how should GHG emissions be measured and reported?

GHG reduction commitments have led to development of standards for measuring emissions and reporting mechanisms. At the same time, many companies and non-commercial organisations are also increasingly interested in calculating and reporting their GHG emissions, to identify opportunities for cost and energy savings and to improve their reputation and brand value. Both of these aspects are considered below.

3.5.1 Measuring and reporting GHGs for the UNFCCC Parties

Parties regularly submit national communications to the UNFCCC, which contain information on: national circumstances; greenhouse gas inventory; policies and measures; projections of emissions and effects of policies; adaptation measures; financial resources and support for technologies; research and systematic observations; education, training and public awareness. This is followed by Annexes containing summary tables of GHG emission trends. A synthesis of the 5th national communications is provided by UNFCCC (2011c).

According to UNFCCC (2012), over the period 1990–2010, total aggregate GHG emissions/removals excluding land use, land-use change and forestry (LULUCF) for all Annex I Parties decreased by 8.9 per cent, while GHG emissions including LULUFC decreased by 14.6 per cent. For Annex I Parties with economies in transition (EIT), GHG emissions decreased by 39.2 per cent (excluding LULUFC) and by 52.6 per cent (including LULUCF). For Annex I non-EIT Parties, GHG emissions excluding LULUFC increased by 4.9 per cent and GHG emissions including LULUCF increased by 4.1 per cent (Figure 3.9).

With 195 Parties having to report GHG inventories, ensuring accuracy, consistency and comparability of the data reported is an issue of primary importance. In order to ensure quality and comparability of the data, the CoP has established guidelines that the Parties need to follow when reporting information to the UNFCCC Secretariat. Guidelines for the preparation of emissions inventories are based on the methodologies and reporting formats presented by the IPCC (Penman *et al.*, 2000; Penman *et al.*, 2003; Eggleston *et al.*, 2006).

Along with more complex modelling approaches, the 2006 Guidelines (Eggleston *et al.*, 2006) provide a simple method to measure GHG emissions:

Emissions = Activity Data (AD)* Emission Factors (EF)

For example, in the energy sector, fuel consumption would represent AD, and the mass of CO_2 emitted per unit of fuel consumed would be an EF. The IPCC default emission factors together with a variety of other emission factors and parameters have been compiled into the Emission Factor Database (www.ipcc-nggip.iges.or.jp/EFDB/main.php).

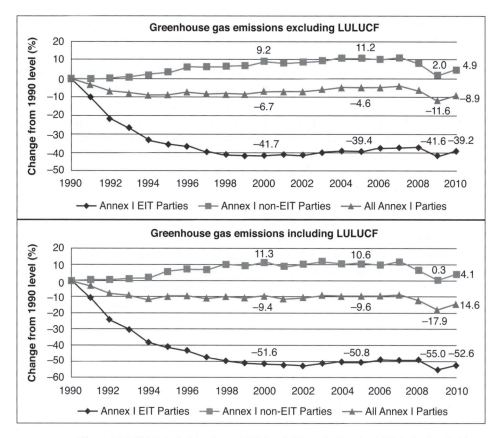

FIGURE 3.9 Change in GHG emissions from 1990 level (A) excluding and (B) including land use, land-use change and forestry (LULUCF) based on the 42 Annex I Parties.

Source: UNFCCC (2012).

Note: EIT = economies in transition

The Parties need to report GHG emissions by sources and removals by sinks using the 100-year global warming potential (GWP-100) values identified by the IPCC (Table 3.3). A national total is then calculated by summing up emissions and removals for each gas. For Annex I Parties, the UNFCCC also provides a mapping facility (http://maps.unfccc.int/di/map), which allows visualisation of GHG emissions by sector, by gas, and by year.

3.5.2 Measuring and reporting GHGs for businesses (carbon footprint)

Businesses and other organisations have become increasingly interested in measuring and reporting their GHG emissions, mainly in order to do the following:

- identify GHGs reduction opportunities (with the aim of saving energy and costs);
- report and participate publicly in voluntary GHG programmes (thereby improving their environmental reputation and brand value);
- participate in mandatory reporting programmes, such as the Carbon Reduction Commitment Energy Efficiency Scheme in the UK or the EU Emissions Trading Scheme;
- participate in GHG markets;

- show early voluntary action, rather than waiting to see if governments will make GHG reporting mandatory.

When accounting for their GHG emissions, most businesses use the expression 'carbon footprint'. The concept of the carbon footprint has become very popular among businesses, media and governments, in spite of the term lacking a widely accepted definition (Wiedmann and Minx, 2008). Carbon footprint mostly refers to the 'full amount of GHG emissions that are directly and indirectly caused by an activity or are accumulated over the life stages of a product' (Wiedmann, 2009). It can be estimated for many different functional units (from product to global) via different scales and using different methods (e.g. input-output models, Life-Cycle Assessment; see Chapter 5).

Most businesses follow the Greenhouse Gas (GHG) Protocol Initiative (www.ghgprotocol. org) to calculate their carbon footprint. The GHG Protocol was jointly convened in 1998 by the World Business Council for Sustainable Development (WBCSD) and the World Resources Institute (WRI). The GHG Protocol provides calculation tools for the seven Kyoto Protocol gases in the form of freely downloadable electronic spreadsheets with accompanying step-by-step guidance documents. It can be applied to many industries and businesses worldwide, regardless of their sector. Several separate business activities or operations can be audited, and all audited elements are converted into emissions. The default emission factors are averages based on the most extensive data sets available and they are largely identical to those used by the IPCC (WBCSD and WRI, 2004). The GHG Protocol has three levels of detail: Scope 1 covers the direct emissions from sources under the control of the company; Scope 2 accounts for the indirect emissions from the purchase of electricity; and Scope 3 is an optional reporting category that accounts for other indirect emissions from the company's supply chain (Figure 3.10).

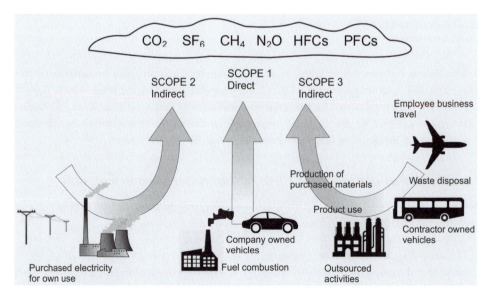

FIGURE 3.10 Overview of the GHG Protocol's scopes and emissions across a company's chain
Source: Redrawn from WBCSD and WRI (2004).

Reflection point

For a company to be genuinely sustainable, its supply chain also needs to be sustainable. In some sectors, companies are increasingly demanding high environmental and ethical standards from their suppliers, in response to consumer demand. Consider how pressure for a green economy can therefore potentially be transmitted along supply chains. Might an environmental tracking system such as that presented by the Environmental Investment Organisation (www.eio.org.uk) be part of the solution?

Numerous other carbon calculators (i.e. tools that estimate the carbon footprint) have been created by government agencies, NGOs, and private companies to promote GHG emission reduction through business/individual behaviour change, carbon offsetting and carbon mitigation measures.

Suggested activity

Search for and explore some of the many carbon calculators that are currently available online.

3.5.3 Carbon management plan (CMP)

A carbon management plan (CMP) is a document that identifies an organisation's strategy to reduce its carbon footprint. There is no single approach to developing a carbon plan. Rather, its content, structure and implementation vary between organisations. In many cases, the CMP is part of an existing environmental, energy management or sustainability strategy.

In some cases the CMP contains an organisation's commitment to become *carbon neutral*: i.e. to reduce the overall net climate impact of its operations to zero. This is usually achieved by reducing the organisation's GHG emissions, and/or by the purchase of carbon offsets (which are described below, Section 3.6). Some businesses decide to make a particular product, a service or an event carbon neutral (e.g. see Ben & Jerry's, DHL, Jamie Oliver's *American Roadtrip* TV series, Super Bowl). Others commit to make their entire business operation carbon neutral (e.g. HSBC, Vancity, Google, Dell, Swiss Re, Marks & Spencer).

According to (HEFCE, 2010a), an example format for a CMP could be as follows:

1. Executive summary
2. Introduction
3. Overview of strategy
4. Approach to carbon reduction and fit with strategic objectives
5. Carbon emissions data
6. Assessment against baseline and target
7. Financial and carbon options evaluation
8. Implementation plan
9. Governance and progress monitoring.

Some examples of carbon management plans are provided below.

Higher education institutions

The higher education sector in England has committed to meet targets for carbon emission reduction of 43 per cent by 2020 and 83 per cent by 2050 against a 2005 baseline. Higher Education institutions are each required to develop a carbon management plan and to report on progress towards the set targets (HEFCE, 2010b). Such organisations typically identify a list of carbon reduction projects in order to meet their targets, usually covering the following interventions (Edinburgh Napier University, 2009; De Montfort University, 2011):

1. Building energy and space management
2. Building fabric upgrade
3. Lights and electric appliances
4. Efficient energy supply
5. Behavioural change and new ways of working
6. Renewable energy.

Methods of reducing emissions through renewable energy and increased energy efficiency are considered further in Chapter 5.

Green corporations

Many companies are developing carbon management plans as part of their corporate environmental strategies. For example, Johnson & Johnson (www.jnj.com) is the world's largest medical devices and diagnostics company, with sales of US$24.6 billion in 2010. The Corporate Knights Research Group and Inflection Point Capital Management identified Johnson & Johnson as the second most sustainable corporation in the world in 2011, according to a global analysis based on ten environmental, social and governance performance indicators and a transparency indicator (www.global100.org).

In 2003, Johnson & Johnson adopted a 'Climate Friendly Energy Policy' aiming to reduce the company's GHG emissions by 7 per cent by 2010, using 1990 as a base year. This was addressed through five main pathways:

1. Energy efficiency improvements in all operations.
2. Cogeneration: on-site generation of electricity and recovery of the waste heat to potentially achieve overall efficiencies of more than 80 per cent.
3. On-site renewable energy that produces no CO_2 emissions.
4. Renewable electric purchases.
5. Carbon trading and sequestration.

Since 2003, the company has invested US$40 million each year in cogeneration and renewable energy capital projects, and since 2005 it has completed 80 energy reduction projects that will reduce the company's CO_2 emissions by more than 160,000 tCO_2 per year. In 2010, the company was recognised as owning the first commercial hybrid vehicle fleet in the industry.

As results of its carbon initiatives, the company exceeded its GHG reduction goal by 2010, and is currently targeting a further 20 per cent emission cut from its 2010 baseline by 2015, without the use of voluntary offsets.

A further example is provided by HSBC Holdings plc (www.hsbc.com; headquartered in London), which is one of the world's largest banking and financial services organisations, providing services to around 89 million customers. In 2005, HSBC become the first major bank to commit to carbon neutrality (i.e. to reduce the overall net CO_2 emissions of its worldwide operations to zero) through a carbon management plan including the following four steps:

- Measuring the carbon footprint.
- Reducing energy consumption.
- Buying green electricity.
- Offsetting remaining CO_2 emissions (HSBC, 2008).

During the last quarter of 2005, HSBC achieved neutrality by buying 170,000 tCO_2 of carbon offset credits produced from four offset projects:

- Renewable wind, offsetting 125,000 tCO_2 in New Zealand (Te Apiti wind farm), and validated by the Gold Standard (see Table 3.6 on p. 99).
- Waste-composting, offsetting 15,000 tCO_2 in Australia (Victoria), avoiding the production of CH_4 by composting waste using aerobic methods.
- Agriculture methane capture, offsetting 14,000 tCO_2 in Germany, reducing CH_4 emissions by 90 per cent by storing fresh manure in a biogas plant, which is then converted into renewable heat and electricity by a combined heat and power generation unit.
- Biomass co-generation, offsetting 16,000 tCO_2 in India, generating four megawatts of electricity from agricultural biomass for the production of liquid glucose and starch (HSBC, 2005).

Since 2005, the company has helped maintain its carbon neutral status by implementing a number of additional initiatives, including:

- Creation of a 'zero carbon' branch in New York, which utilises solar panels, a ground-source heat pump, 'intelligent' lighting systems and rainwater recycling.
- Installation of solar panels and solar thermal technology at a number of HSBC buildings.
- Installation of video conferencing technology and other energy-efficient IT devices.
- Sourcing of renewable energy produced from clean energy projects (primarily wind projects).
- Purchase of verified emission reductions (VERs) and certified emissions reductions (CERs) (HSBC, 2008).

Since 2012, HSBC has no longer been carbon neutral mainly because of the increased risks of double-counting (see Section 3.6.2); instead, the company invests an equivalent amount to that previously allocated to carbon neutrality programmes in an annual Eco-efficiency Fund (HSBC, 2013).

Green events

The Vancouver 2010 Olympic and Paralympic Winter Games were the first games in history to achieve carbon neutral status. The Vancouver Organizing Committee adopted a carbon management programme with a carbon neutral target based on four principles and strategies (Table 3.4).

Through their carbon management programme the 2010 Winter Games achieved an 18 per cent reduction in carbon emissions thanks to energy efficiency measures at its venues and associated sites. In addition, it offset the estimated direct emissions (118,000 tCO_2) from all operations over the seven-year period of the Games, including athlete travel and the torch relay, and it invited sponsors, partners and spectators to offset their emissions on a voluntary basis.

3.6 The compliance and voluntary carbon markets

The term 'carbon market' refers to the buying and selling of emissions permits that have either been issued by a regulatory body in the form of Assigned Amount Units (AAUs), or

Table 3.4 Overview of the Carbon Management Program for the 2010 Olympic Winter Games

What	*How*	
KNOW Carbon emissions generated by the 2010 Winter Games	Consult, inventory, forecast, measure and publicly report on direct and indirect emissions.	Released Carbon Emissions Forecasts in 2007 and 2009 (vancouver2010.com). Publicly reported on actual emissions in annual sustainability reports.
REDUCE Direct carbon footprint	Use green building and operating practices that emphasise energy and fuel efficiency, green procurement, waste reduction, renewable energy, smart fleet management and public transit. Create a baseline Business as Usual reference case against which to measure reductions achieved from the measures cited.	2009 Carbon Forecast projected a 15–18% reduction in carbon emissions over pre-existing performance benchmarks.
OFFSET Direct footprint	Invest in carbon reduction projects that showcase British Columbia leadership and innovation in clean technology and support the transition to a low-carbon economy.	Secured the first carbon offset sponsor of the Olympic Movement, Offsetters Clean Technology (www.offsetters.ca), to finance and deliver carbon reduction projects to offset the direct carbon footprint from the Games.
ENGAGE & INSPIRE 2010 partners, sponsors, participants and spectators to address indirect footprint	Voluntarily calculate, reduce and offset carbon emissions generated by their travel to and from the Games region.	With Offsetters, provided 'Carbon Partner Program' for interested partners and sponsors.

Source: VANOC (2010).

generated by GHG emission reductions projects in the form of Removal Units (RMUs), Certified Emission Reductions (CERs), or Emission Reduction Unit (ERUs) (see Section 3.4.5). Since units are expressed in CO_2 equivalent, these are referred to as 'carbon credits' and 'trading in carbon'. ICE Futures Europe (www.theice.com) is the leading market for CO_2 emissions.

Carbon trading mechanisms have been advocated as a powerful way to combat climate change (e.g. the Stern Review; Stern, 2006), and have been characterised by some success as well as great controversy. Carbon markets can be distinguished into two main major categories: the *compliance* (or *regulatory*) *market* and the *voluntary market*. Both are considered below.

3.6.1 The compliance carbon market ('cap-and-trade')

Three mechanisms are the basis for the international compliance carbon market: (1) the Clean Development Mechanism (CDM) (Article 12, Kyoto Protocol); (2) the Joint Implementation (JI) (Article 6, Kyoto Protocol) (see Section 3.4); and (3) international emissions trading (Article 17, Kyoto Protocol).

Under international emissions trading, transfers and acquisitions of AAUs, RMUs, CERs, and ERUs are recorded through registry systems, and an International Transaction Log verifies the registry transactions to ensure that these are consistent with the Kyoto Protocol rules (Figure 3.11). In addition to accounting for the Kyoto units, these registries 'settle' emissions trades by delivering units from the accounts of sellers to those of buyers, therefore creating the backbone infrastructure for the carbon market.

International emissions trading is linked to domestic and regional trading schemes, such as the European Union Emissions Trading System (EU ETS), which is the largest carbon trading scheme in operation (Table 3.5).

The EU ETS was established by the EC (EC, 2003). Although created before the Kyoto Protocol came into force, the EU ETS represents the keystone in the EU's attempts to comply

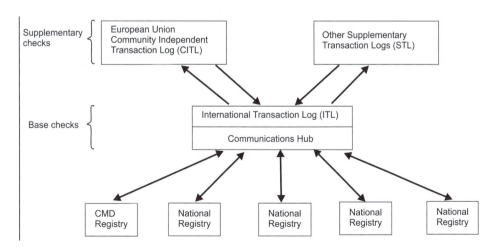

FIGURE 3.11 The Kyoto and EU registry systems

Source: UNFCCC (2013).

Table 3.5 Carbon market volumes and values in 2011

	Volume (Mt CO₂e)	Value (US$ million)
	Allowances market	
EUA (average price $18.8/tCO₂e)	7,853	147,848
AAU	47	318
RMU	4	12
NZU	27	351
RGGI	120	249
CCA	4	63
Others	26	40
Subtotal	8,081	148,881
	Forward (primary) project-based transactions	
pCER pre-2013	91	990
pERU	28	339
Voluntary market (average price $6.5/tCO₂e)	87	569
Subtotal	378	3,889

Source: Kossoy and Guigon (2012).
Notes: EUA = European Union Allowance, AAU = Assigned Amount Unit, RMU = Removal Unit, NZU = New Zealand Unit, RGGI = Regional Greenhouse Gas Initiative, CCA = California Carbon Allowance, pCER = primary Certified Emission Reduction, pERU = Emission Reduction Unit.

with the Kyoto commitments. The EU ETS carbon market functions on the 'cap-and-trade' principle as follows (Brohe *et al.*, 2009):

- Setting of a cap and a commitment period.
- Allocation of allowance (= emissions of rights).
- Monitoring and reporting.
- Implementation of a registry to track allowances.
- Reconciliation and penalties for non-compliance.

This means that there is a limit (or cap) on the allowable level of emissions that polluters can emit. Companies under this cap are required to hold a number of permits equivalent to their set emissions, and they can sell their spare permits to those who have exceeded their cap. Emission permits are traded (bought and sold) as carbon credits or shares in a similar way to any other financial market.

The EU ETS operates in 31 countries (27 EU countries plus Croatia, Iceland, Liechtenstein and Norway). It covers GHG emissions (CO_2, N_2O and PFCs) from more than 11,000 heavy energy-using installations in power generation and manufacturing industries, together with flights within the EU, Iceland, Liechtenstein and Norway. Altogether, the EU ETS accounts for 45 per cent of the 27 countries' total GHG emissions (EC, 2013).

The EC also established guidelines for the monitoring, reporting and verification of the companies' emissions. To determine emissions, companies can choose between: (1) a method based on calculations, using the formula 'CO_2 emissions = activity data ★ emission factors ★ oxidation factor'; or (2) a method based on continuous emission measurement systems approved by a competent authority (EC, 2007). Compared to the Kyoto Protocol accounting system (see Section 3.4.2), data uncertainties are fewer because it is easier to monitor emissions at the scale of a company than at a country level (Brohe *et al.*, 2009).

The Community Independent Transaction Log (CITL), a standardised database system established in January 2005, records the issue, transfer and cancellation of the EU allowances that take place in the Community and national registries. Since 2008, the CITL has been complemented by the ITL (Figure 3.11), which manages the exchange of AAUs and other Kyoto units.

Outside Europe, other state governments have developed their own regulatory emissions trading schemes. These include the Regional Greenhouse Gas Initiative in the United States (RGGI; www.rggi.org) and the Clean Energy Future Package in Australia (www. cleanenergyfuture.gov.au), which from 1 July 2015 would allow Australian businesses to use EU allowances to help cover their emissions.

Despite its apparent success, the 'cap-and-trade' system has been marked by controversy. Lohmann (2006), for example, argued that 'global warming requires a more radical solution: nothing less than a reorganisation of society and technology that will leave most remaining fossil fuels safely underground' and that 'carbon trading can't do this'. Carbon trading rewards the heaviest polluters and allows them to buy cheap offsets from abroad (frequently, these are developed countries). According to Gilbertson and Reyes (2009), carbon trading has had a 'disastrous track record' since its adoption. During the first phase of the EU ETS (2005–2007), most Member States over-allocated emissions permits, creating an excess of supply over demand. Once verified, this led to a crash in the market. At the end of the first phase, polluters had been permitted to emit 2.1 per cent more CO_2 than they actually emitted. The over-allocation problem has been repeated during the second phase of the EU ETS (2008–2012) owing to the ability of the Member States to trade a large volume of emissions for offset credits from outside Europe. The over-allocation problem has also been exacerbated by the current global financial crisis. Leonard (2009) identifies three 'devils' in the cap-and-trade system: free permits, offsetting, and distraction.

3.6.2 The voluntary carbon market (carbon offsets: carbon standards and verification)

Unlike the compliance market, the voluntary market does not depend on compulsory GHG reductions to generate demand. The market is fragmented and lacks uniformity, transparency and the standard verification and registration of carbon credits with a central body. As a result, it has been subjected to a great deal of criticism from environmentalists, buyers and some companies. However, some feel that it has important advantages over the compliance market, including the flexibility, innovation and lower transaction cost of its carbon products. The voluntary carbon market can also support specific types of projects such as forest protection projects that are currently not approved within the CDM mechanism. Many NGOs also support the voluntary market because they see it as an important tool to educate the public about climate change, and to encourage them to participate in addressing it (Bayon *et al.*, 2007a).

The principle on which the voluntary carbon market is based is relatively simple. An offset retailer usually estimates a business or individual's carbon footprint (see Section 3.5.2). The retailer then proposes to the business or individual to offset part of its carbon footprint, by buying carbon offset credits generated by verified GHG emissions reductions obtained from an offset project (Figure 3.12).

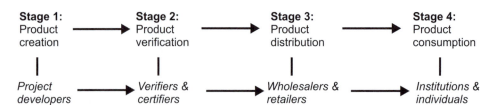

FIGURE 3.12   Simplified model of the voluntary carbon market

Source: Bayon *et al.* (2007a), Figure 2.1, with permission from Taylor & Francis.

Fundamental to the quality of carbon offsets is their ability to demonstrate a number of key features (usually abbreviated to 'VALID'). These are:

- **V**erifiability: there is a rigorous auditing process assuring that the offset project's emissions reductions are valid (before the project starts) and verified (after the project has been implemented).
- **A**dditionality: the project must be additional to a business-as-usual scenario and there must be assurance that it would not have happened without the incentives from the offset market. This feature is one of the most important things to look for when assessing the quality of the carbon offsets and it has proven to be quite difficult to determine this in practice (Bayon *et al.*, 2007b). The best assessments of additionality rely on a series of tests.
- **L**eakage: this refers to a situation where a GHG reduction in one region indirectly drives an increase in emissions elsewhere. This issue is of particular concern for forestry projects.
- **I**mpermanence: the project must ensure GHG mitigation over the stated time period. This is especially important for forestry projects in which risks such as fires, logging, and diseases would cause the release of some or all of the sequestered carbon back into the atmosphere, therefore affecting the delivery of the carbon credits.
- **D**ouble-counting: GHG reductions must only be claimed once. Because offsets are an intangible commodity, it is fundamental that the GHG reductions that the project represents have a clear unique ownership. Publicly available offset registries can help resolve this issue.

Although the exact size of the voluntary carbon market is not known, in 2012, the Ecosystem Marketplace (www.ecosystemmarketplace.com) reported a market volume totalling 101 Mt CO_2e (US$516 million). Based on 87 survey respondents, the market volume has been projected to reach US$2.3 billion by 2020 (Peters-Stanley and Yin, 2013). The carbon credits in 2012 came primarily from renewable energy (34 per cent) and forestry and land use activities (32 per cent), including REDD projects, undertaken in developing countries (China and India) and the USA.

Projects to avoid deforestation have great potential to create carbon credits and strengthen the contribution to sustainable development. For all types of projects, community participation and the alignment with development priorities of local people are critical. It is also essential to find the balance between better regulation through best practice guidelines, and keeping the overhead costs low to allow innovation and access to the market for small-scale projects that specifically benefit the poor. Buyers can play an important role by demanding projects with high standards, transparency, and success in ensuring benefits for local communities.

Table 3.6 Summary of the major certification standards available for the voluntary carbon market

Standards' name and website	Details
Verified Carbon Standard (VCS; www.v-c-s.org)	The VCS aims to provide a basic quality threshold for all carbon credits on the voluntary market. It looks to ensure that offset credits are 'real, measurable, permanent, additional and independently verified'.
Climate, Community and Biodiversity Standard (CCB; www.climate-standards.org/ccb-standards)	The CCB Standard was created to support land management projects that simultaneously sequester GHG, support the sustainable development of the local communities, and conserve biodiversity.
Gold Standard (www.cdmgoldstandard.org)	The Gold Standard is the global benchmark certification for high quality carbon reductions projects in both the compliance and the voluntary markets. Gold Standard projects demonstrate real and permanent GHG reductions, adhere to the strictest standards on additionality and support the sustainable development of local communities.

However, if the price for carbon on the voluntary market is low, it can be difficult to compete with other land uses with larger immediate financial gains (Chapple, 2008).

Most market players believe that if the projected voluntary carbon volumes are to be achieved, it will be essential to formalise and streamline the voluntary market (Bayon *et al.*, 2007a). Currently several attempts are underway to make the voluntary carbon market more 'investor-friendly' and to help purchasers judge the quality of carbon offsets. Most project developers finance the verification of their GHG emissions reductions before selling them to either retailers or end-consumers by using third-party verifiers, who can certify the credits being sold with a recognised set of standards (Table 3.6). Offset credits verified by a third party are often referred to as Verified Emissions Reductions (VERs) to distinguish them from the CERs originating from CMD projects. Over 200 retailers currently offer offset credits, and independent guides have been produced to help consumers make more informed offset purchases (e.g. David Suzuki Foundation, 2009).

Reflection point

To what extent do you believe that carbon markets can address the problem of climate change?

3.7 Adaptation and mitigation measures

The UN Framework Convention on Climate Change (UNFCCC; see Section 3.4.1) identifies two policy responses to climate change: *adaptation* to the impacts of climate change, and *mitigation* of climate change by reducing anthropogenic GHG emissions and enhancing carbon sinks (Article 4: UNFCCC, 1992).

The IPCC uses the following definitions (Klein *et al.*, 2007):

- *Adaptation*: adjustment in natural or human systems in response to actual or expected climatic stimuli or their effects, which moderates harm or exploits beneficial opportunities.

- *Mitigation*: an anthropogenic intervention to reduce the sources or enhance the sinks of greenhouse gases.

Adaptation and mitigation can be complementary, substitutable or independent from each other and have very different timescales. The benefits of mitigation carried out today will accrue in several decades because of the long lifetime of GHGs in the atmosphere, whereas many adaptation measures would have immediate benefits (i.e. avoided damage) by reducing vulnerability to climate change. Both adaptation and mitigation depend on the capacity of societies to implement climate change policies and are intimately related to the green economy (ibid.).

3.7.1 Adaptation strategies

Adaptation to climate change refers to adjustments that reduce vulnerability or enhance resilience to observed or expected changes in climate and associated extreme weather events. Adaptation occurs in physical, ecological and human systems. Biological adaptation is only reactive, whereas human adaptation can be both anticipatory and reactive. From a temporal perspective, adaptation practices can be divided into three main groups:

- responses to current variability;
- responses to observed medium- and long-term trends in climate;
- anticipatory responses to model-based scenario of long-term climate change (Adger *et al.*, 2007).

A large number of adaptation measures have been put in place in the past 20 years in different parts of the world, especially to adapt to the current climate variability (Adger *et al.*, 2007, Hallegatte, 2009). Table 3.7 lists various examples of adaptation practices that have been undertaken by a range of actors, including national and local governments, private sector organisations, local communities and individuals. Such measures include anticipatory and reactive measures typically undertaken in response to multiple climate risks, as part of existing processes or programmes such as drought relief, water resource management and livelihood improvement. They include a combination of technologies, institutional and behavioural responses, and the design of climate resilient infrastructure.

Estimates of adaptation costs and benefits are currently limited in availability. Adaptation costs are usually expressed in monetary terms, while most benefits are quantified in non-monetary terms (i.e. changes in welfare of citizens, proportion of population exposed to risk). Many of the adaptation studies focus on sea-level rise, agriculture, energy demand, water resources management and transportation infrastructure in the United States and in the OECD (i.e. Organisation for Economic Co-operation and Development) countries. These studies show that many adaptation practices can be implemented at relatively low cost. However, comprehensive estimates of both costs and benefits of adaptation are currently lacking (Adger *et al.*, 2007).

Adaptation is regarded as a necessary measure to tackle climate change, owing to the warming already 'loaded' into the climate system (Adger *et al.*, 2007; Van Vuuren *et al.*, 2008). However, adaptive capacity (i.e. the ability or potential of a system to respond successfully to climate change) is not evenly distributed across or within societies. Across societies, adaptive

Table 3.7 Examples of adaptation practices by region relative to present climate risks

Region/ Country	Climate-related stress	Adaptation practices	Source
AFRICA			
Egypt	Sea-level rise	Adoption of National Climate Change Action Plan integrating climate change concerns into national policies; adoption of Law 4/94 requiring Environmental Impact Assessment (EIA) for project approval and regulating setback distances for coastal infrastructure; installation of hard structures in areas vulnerable to coastal erosion	El Raey (2004)
Botswana	Drought	National government programmes to re-create employment options after drought; capacity building of local authorities; assistance to small subsistence farmers to increase crop production	FAO (2004)
ASIA AND OCEANIA			
Bangladesh	Sea-level rise; salt-water intrusion	Consideration of climate change in the National Water Management Plan; building of flow regulators in coastal embankments; use of alternative crops and low-technology water filters	OECD (2003)
The Philippines	Sea-level rise; storm surges	Capacity building for shoreline defence system design; introduction of participatory risk assessment; provision of grants to strengthen coastal resilience and rehabilitation of infrastructures; construction of cyclone-resistant housing units; retrofit of buildings to improved hazard standards; review of building codes; reforestation of mangroves	Lasco *et al.* (2006)
AMERICAS			
Canada	(1) Permafrost melt; change in ice cover (2) Extreme temperatures	(1) Changes in livelihood practices by the Inuit, including: change of hunt locations; diversification of hunted species; use of Global Positioning Systems (GPS) technology; encouragement of food sharing. (2) Implementation of heat health alert plans in Toronto, which include measures such as: opening of designated cooling centres at public locations; information to the public through local media; distribution of bottled water through the Red Cross to vulnerable people; operation of a heat information line to answer heat-related questions; availability of an emergency medical service vehicle with specially trained staff and medical equipment.	(1) Ford and Smit (2004) (2) Mehdi (2006)

(Continued)

Table 3.7 (Continued)

Region/ Country	Climate-related stress	Adaptation practices	Source
Mexico and Argentina	Drought	Adjustment of planting dates and crop variety (e.g., inclusion of drought-resistant plants such as agave and aloe); accumulation of commodity stocks as economic reserve; spatially separated plots for cropping and grazing to diversify exposures; diversification of income by adding livestock operations; set-up/provision of crop insurance; creation of local financial pools (as alternative to commercial crop insurance)	Wehbe *et al.* (2006)
EUROPE			
Austria, France, Switzerland	Upward shift of natural snow–reliability line; glacier melt	Artificial snow-making; grooming of ski slopes; moving ski areas to higher altitudes and glaciers; use of white plastic sheets as protection against glacier melt; diversification of tourism revenues (e.g. all-year tourism)	Austrian Federal Government (2006); Direction du Tourisme (2002)
United Kingdom	Floods; sea-level rise	Coastal realignment converting arable farmland into salt marsh and grassland to provide sustainable sea defences; maintenance and operation of the Thames Barrier through the Thames Estuary 2100 project that addresses flooding linked to the impacts of climate change; provision of guidance to policy-makers, chief executives, and Parliament on climate change and the insurance sector (developed by the Association of British Insurers)	DEFRA (2006)

Source: Modified from Adger *et al.* (2007), Table 17.1.

capacity is influenced by a combination of biophysical conditions (i.e. soil quality, groundwater availability), socio-economic conditions (i.e. institutions and governance structure, social networks, economic resources) and technological capacity (i.e. availability of irrigation). Evidence suggests that there are substantial limits and barriers to climate change adaptation, especially in vulnerable nations and communities. Barriers include physical and ecological limits, as some natural systems may not be able to adapt to the rate and magnitude of climate change without altering their functions and integrity. In addition there are technological, financial, cognitive and behavioural and social and cultural constraints. New planning processes, such as the development of National Adaptation Programmes of Action (NAPAs) in the least-developed countries, are attempting to overcome these barriers (Adger *et al.*, 2007).

3.7.2 Mitigation strategies

A range of policies on climate change, energy security and sustainable development have been effective in reducing GHG emissions in different sectors in many countries (EC, 2010).

Overall emissions of Annex I Parties in 2010 were 8.9 per cent lower than the base year (see Figure 3.9). Several mitigation technologies and practices are currently commercially available that cover seven main sectors, i.e. the energy supply sector, including carbon capture and storage; transport and associated infrastructures; the residential, commercial and service sectors; the industrial sector, including internal recycling and the reuse of industrial wastes; the agricultural sector, including land-use carbon sequestration; the forestry sector, including afforestation, reforestation and forest management; and the waste management; post-consumer recycling and reuse sectors (see Chapters 5 and 7). A wide variety of national policies and instruments are also available to governments to promote mitigation action. However, the scale of such measures has not been large enough to offset the global growth in emissions. It is projected that without additional policies and behavioural changes, global GHG emissions will continue to grow over coming decades (Rogner *et al.*, 2007).

A Special Report on Emissions Scenarios (SRES) has been developed by the IPCC that describes four different narrative storylines of how the future might unfold. These cover a wide range of the main demographic, economic and technological driving forces influencing GHG emissions (Figure 3.13 and Figure 3.14). The storylines assume no implementation of the UNFCCC or the emissions targets of the Kyoto Protocol, thus they form a baseline against which different mitigation strategies options can be compared (Nakicenovic and Swart, 2000).

The concept of mitigation potential is used to assess the degree of GHG reduction that could be achieved by a mitigation option for a given cost per tonne of CO_2 equivalent

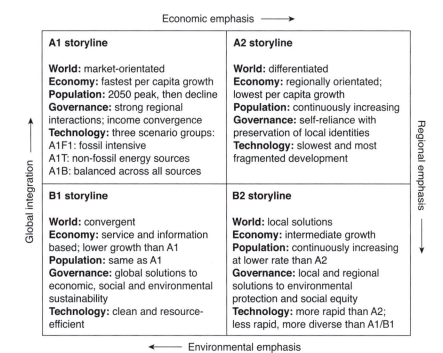

FIGURE 3.13 Summary of characteristics of the four Special Report on Emissions Scenarios (SRES) storylines

Source: Carter *et al.* (2007), Figure 2.5.

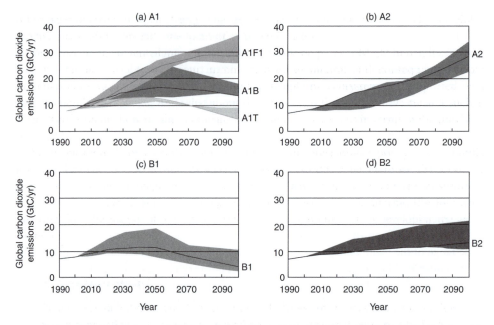

FIGURE 3.14 Total global annual CO_2 emissions from all sources from 1990–2100 for the Special Report on Emissions Scenarios. Each emission band shows the range of scenarios within each group.

Source: Nakicenovic and Swart (2000), Figure 3.

Note: Solid and dashed lines represent an illustrative scenario.

emission avoided or reduced over a given period, compared with an emission baseline (such as SRES or a reference case). Mitigation potential is usually differentiated in terms of 'market potential', 'economic potential' or 'technical potential' (Halsnæs *et al.*, 2007):

- *Market potential* is potential based on private costs and discount rates, which might be expected to occur under forecast market conditions, including policies and measures currently in place. A zero social cost of carbon and no additional mitigation policies are assumed.
- *Economic potential* takes into account social costs and benefits for particular carbon prices and social discount rates, assuming that market efficiency is improved by policies, and measures and barriers are removed.
- *Technical potential* is the amount by which it is possible to reduce GHG emissions by implementing a technology or practice that has already been demonstrated. There is no specific reference to costs, but only to practical constraints.

Pacala and Socolow (2004) demonstrate that we already possess 15 different strategies with the technical potential to stabilise worldwide GHG emission at today's emission rate. The authors divided these technologies into three categories: (1) energy efficiency and conservation; (2) decarbonisation of electricity and fuel shift (including renewables); and (3) forest and agricultural soils management. They conclude that each technology offers the potential to provide one 'wedge' (i.e. 1 GtC y^{-1} of reduced CO_2 emissions in 50 years), and that, since only

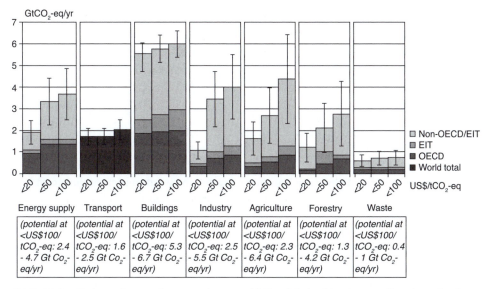

FIGURE 3.15 Estimated sectoral economic potential for global mitigation as a function of carbon price in 2030, compared to the respective baselines assumed in the IPCC sector assessments

Source: IPCC (2007), Figure SPM.6.

seven wedges would be needed to solve the climate problem, not every technology has to be used.

Energy efficiency options for new and existing buildings can considerably reduce CO$_2$ emissions with net economic benefit in the short to medium term. New energy infrastructures and new industrial facilities can also make a significant contribution. Agriculture and forestry practices can considerably reduce GHG emissions at medium cost, whereas transport and waste management practices provide lower direct mitigation benefits (Figure 3.15). Beyond 2030, high mitigation potential is projected to occur in the energy supply and industry sectors (Fisher *et al.*, 2007).

The objective of the UNFCCC is the stabilisation of GHG concentrations in the atmosphere. Choices about the scale and timing of adaptation and mitigation to achieve a chosen stabilisation concentration require an iterative risk management process. This needs to consider several key issues such as the uncertainty involved in assessing the climate risks, the costs and benefits of avoided climate change damages, the inertia in the climate system, equity (i.e. distribution of costs of adaptation and mitigation), and sustainable development (Rogner *et al.*, 2007). There are gaps in current knowledge regarding the scale and timing of mitigation that is required (Fisher *et al.*, 2007).

A debate is underway regarding the economic feasibility and cost of different mitigation strategies. To provide a quantitative basis for this discussion, McKinsey & Company (http://solutions.mckinsey.com/climatedesk/), supported by ten leading companies and organisations across the world, produced a global GHG abatement database that provides an evaluation of the costs of more than 200 GHG mitigation strategies. Results show that there is sufficient potential to stabilise GHG atmospheric concentration at 400 ppm by 2030 (McKinsey & Company 2010), which according to the IPCC (e.g. Fisher *et al.*, 2007) would result in a mean increase of global mean temperature of just below 2°C. Relative to projected business–as–usual

GHG emissions of 66 $GtCO_2e$ in 2030, McKinsey & Company's study identifies a mitigation potential of 38 $GtCO_2e$ (58 per cent) through technical mitigation strategies costing below €80 per tCO_2. These analyses showed that mitigation would deliver a net economic benefit to society.

However, to capture their full potential in 2030, mitigation strategies would need to be aggressively and promptly pursued. For example, a 10-year delay in their implementation would reduce by half the mitigation potential in 2030. From the financial point of view, the total up-front investment needed would be €860 billion annually, corresponding to 5–6 per cent on top of business-as-usual investments.

Other studies, notably the Stern Review (Stern, 2006), have similarly concluded that there is sufficient potential to stabilise GHG emissions to avoid the worst impacts of climate change, and that the benefits of strong and prompt action far outweigh the economic cost of not acting.

3.8 Trade-offs between carbon storage and other ecosystem services

Parties who have ratified the UNFCCC need to take measures to mitigate climate change by limiting their anthropogenic GHG emissions and/or protecting and increasing their carbon sinks and reservoirs (Article 4: UNFCCC, 1992). Agriculture and forestry activities can effectively protect and increase the terrestrial carbon sink, and have therefore become an integral part of the mitigation strategies to offset the global growth in GHG emissions.

In addition to their carbon storage and sequestration service, many agricultural and forestry mitigation measures can have positive or negative effects on the provision of other ecosystem services, or other benefits provided by ecosystems to people (see Chapter 4). Negative effects can result in trade-offs, which may be defined as 'a choice that involves losing one quality or service (of an ecosystem) in return for gaining another quality or service' (TEEB, 2010). Addressing trade-offs between ecosystem services is necessary for the successful implementation of mitigation measures (Nabuurs *et al.*, 2007; Smith *et al.*, 2007).

3.8.1 Trade-offs of forestry mitigation measures

Forests provide numerous important services to people, including provision of timber, food, medicines and fuelwood, water protection and regulation of the hydrological cycle, as well as recreational, cultural and aesthetic values (see Chapter 4). The relationship between carbon stock/sequestration and other ecosystem services can vary in many different ways, from mutually beneficial to mutually exclusive. For example, forest plantations can contribute significantly to carbon sequestration, but they may also lead to loss of grazing land and biodiversity if they replace biologically rich native grassland. Therefore, developing forestry mitigation strategies often requires complex analysis of trade-offs between carbon storage/ sequestration and other ecosystem services (Nabuurs *et al.*, 2007).

While the benefits of forest mitigation measures are global, co-benefits (and costs) tend to be local, therefore analyses of trade-offs need to be undertaken at the local scale (ibid.). The relationships between carbon stocks and biodiversity are not well understood at local and regional scales (Midgley *et al.*, 2010). Data are also lacking on the relationships between carbon stocks and other ecosystem services (Naidoo *et al.*, 2008).

An example of trade-offs between carbon and other ecosystem services is offered by Anderson *et al.* (2009). The authors present national-scale estimates of the spatial covariance between four ecosystem services (carbon stock, biodiversity, annual income from agriculture, and recreational value) using Britain as a case study. They show that areas important for carbon storage support low biodiversity and low agricultural value, whereas there is no strong relationship between carbon and recreation. In contrast, in a landscape studied in southern England, Newton *et al.* (2012) found only weak relationships between carbon storage and other ecosystem services assessed. Potential trade-offs between ecosystem services were indicated by significant negative correlations observed between crop value and flood risk mitigation, aesthetic value and cultural value, but not carbon storage.

Market approaches, including cost-benefit analyses, have recently been used to explore trade-offs between ecosystem services provided by different management options. For example, Birch *et al.* (2010) show a net increase in carbon sequestration, non-timber forest products, timber and tourism and a decrease in livestock production as a result of forest restoration in Latin America. However, spatial variation in the net social benefit for the combined ecosystem services was recorded within each study area, demonstrating the importance of spatial analysis to identify areas of trade-offs and 'win-win' outcomes for both carbon sequestration and support for local livelihoods (Figure 3.16).

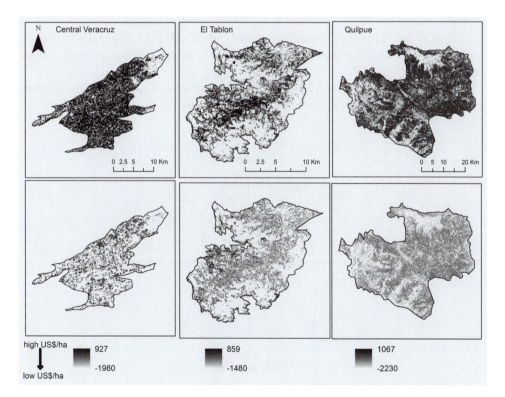

FIGURE 3.16 Maps of net social benefit (US$ ha^{-1}) for the combined ecosystem services (20 years, 5 per cent discount rate) for three study areas under two restoration scenarios: (above) passive restoration; and (below) active restoration

Source: Redrawn from data presented in Birch *et al.* (2010).

3.8.2 Trade-offs of agricultural mitigation measures

Agricultural activities account for 12–14 per cent of global anthropogenic GHG emissions. These include CH_4 and N_2O emissions from livestock production, energy-intensive inorganic fertiliser production, flooded rice paddies and burning of crop residues. Agricultural soils store less carbon than their counterparts in natural ecosystems because carbon losses occur through the removal of biomass, tillage, drainage and erosion. These exceed carbon gains (Lal, 2010). Further, agriculture is responsible for large carbon emissions through land conversion from forests to crop lands, particularly in tropical regions (Power, 2010). West et al. (2010) indicate that for every hectare of land that is cleared in the tropics for agriculture, up to 120 tons ha^{-1} of carbon is released, which is nearly twice that of temperate regions. With food demand expected to rise, there is an urgent need to find synergies between carbon sequestration and food production.

Virtually all agro-ecosystems involve trade-offs between the provision of food and other ecosystem services. The extent to which agricultural mitigation measures result in trade-offs or in synergies between ecosystem services is often both system- and location specific (Smith et al., 2007). According to Power (2010), agricultural practices such as conservation tillage, crop diversification, legume intensification and biological control (see Chapter 7) can reduce GHG emissions and increase yields by up to 79 per cent. Lal (2010) suggests that measures such as the restoration of degraded and desertified soils, the management of peatlands and restoration of wetlands, and the protection and enhancement of forest ecosystems all can enhance the existing terrestrial carbon sink and reduce GHG emissions. Further examples of possible trade-offs and synergies of mitigation options are summarised in Table 3.8.

Trade-offs between ecosystem services can be illustrated with radar diagrams, in which the condition of each ecosystem service provided by a land use is depicted along each axis (Figure 3.17).

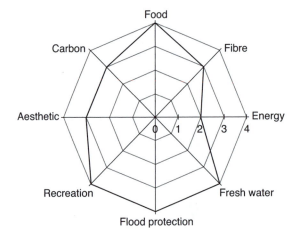

FIGURE 3.17 A radar diagram for comparing trade-offs between ecosystem services

Source: Redrawn from data presented in Newton *et al.* (2012), for an individual river catchment.

Table 3.8 Summary of possible trade-offs and synergies of agricultural mitigation measures

Measure	Examples	Food security	Water quality	Soil quality	Air quality	Biodiversity	Energy conservation	Aesthetic/amenity value
Cropland management	Nutrient management	-/+	+	+	+		+	
	Tillage/residue management	+	+/-	+		+	+	
	Water management (irrigation, drainage)	+	+/-	+/-			-	
	Agro-forestry	+/-	+/-	+		+	+	
	Set-aside, land-use change	-	+	+	+	+	+	+
Grazing land management/pasture improvement	Grazing intensity	+/-		+		+	+	+
	Nutrient management	+/-	+	+		+	-	+/-
	Fire management	+		+	+	+/-		+/-
Management of organic soils	Avoid drainage of/restore wetlands	-	+	+		+	+	+
Restoration of degraded lands	Erosion control, organic amendments, nutrient amendments	+	+	+		+	+	+
Livestock management	Improved feeding practices	+		+/-				
Manure/biosolid management	Improved storage and handling	+	+/-	+	+/-			
	Anaerobic digestion				+		+	
	More efficient use as nutrient source	+	+	+	+		+	
Bioenergy	Energy crops, solid, liquid, biogas, residues	-				-	+	

Source: Smith et al. (2007), Table 8.12.

Reflection point

Identifying trade-offs and synergies is a key issue when integrating carbon sequestration into landscape planning, management and decision-making. How do you think trade-offs might be addressed in practice?

Bibliography

Adger, W. N., Agrawala, S., Mirza, M. M. Q., *et al.* 2007. Assessment of adaptation practices, options, constraints and capacity, in M. L. Parry, O. F. Canziani, J. P. Palutikof, *et al.* (eds) *Climate Change 2007: Impacts, Adaptation and Vulnerability. Contribution of Working Group II to the Fourth Assessment Report of the Intergovernmental Panel on Climate Change.* Cambridge University Press: Cambridge.

Anderegg, W. R. L., Prall, J. W., Harold, J. and Schneider, S. H. 2010. Expert credibility in climate change. *Proceedings of the National Academy of Sciences of the United States of America*, 107: 12107–12109.

Anderson, B. J., Armsworth, P. R., Eigenbrod, F., *et al.* 2009. Spatial covariance between biodiversity and other ecosystem service priorities. *Journal of Applied Ecology*, 46: 888–896.

Austrian Federal Government 2006 *Fourth National Communication of the Austrian Federal Government, in Compliance with the Obligations under the United Nations Framework Convention on Climate Change (Federal Law Gazette No. 414/1994), According to Decisions 11/CP.4 and 4/CP.5 of the Conference of the Parties*, Federal Ministry of Agriculture, Forestry, Environment and Water Management, Vienna.

Baldocchi, D. 2008. Turner Review No. 15. 'Breathing' of the terrestrial biosphere: lessons learned from a global network of carbon dioxide flux measurement systems. *Australian Journal of Botany*, 56: 1–26.

Barnett, T. P., Adam, J. C. and Lettenmaier, D. P. 2005. Potential impacts of a warming climate on water availability in snow-dominated regions. *Nature*, 438: 303–309.

Battle, M., Bender, M. L., Tans, P. P., *et al.* 2000. Global carbon sinks and their variability inferred from atmospheric O_2 and $\delta^{13}C$. *Science*, 287: 2467–2470.

Bayon, R., Hawn, A. and Hamilton, K. 2007a. *Voluntary Carbon Markets: An International Business Guide to What They Are and How They Work*, Earthscan, London.

Bayon, R., Hawn, A. and Hamilton, K. 2007b. Understanding supply and demand in the voluntary carbon market, in *Voluntary Carbon Markets: An International Business Guide to What They Are and How They Work*. Earthscan: London.

Behrenfeld, M. J., Boss, E., Siegel, D. A. and Shea, D. M. 2005. Carbon-based ocean productivity and phytoplankton physiology from space. *Global Biogeochemical Cycles*, 19: 1–14.

Bell, S. and McGillivray, D. 2008. Climate change and air quality. *Environmental Law*, 7th edn, Oxford University Press: Oxford.

Birch, J. C., Newton, A. C., Aquino, C. A., *et al.* 2010. Cost-effectiveness of dryland forest restoration evaluated by spatial analysis of ecosystem services. *Proceedings of the National Academy of Sciences of the United States of America*, 107: 21925–21930.

Bradley, R. I., Milne, R., Bell, J., *et al.* 2005. A soil carbon and land use database for the United Kingdom. *Soil Use and Management*, 21: 363–369.

Brohe, A., Eyre, N. and Howarth, N. 2009. *Carbon Markets: An International Business Guide*, Earthscan, London.

Butler, J. H. 2013. *The NOAA Annual Greenhouse Gas Index (AGGI)*. [Online]. NOAA: Earth System Research Laboratory, Boulder, CO, USA. Available at: www.esrl.noaa.gov/gmd/aggi/aggi.html (accessed 30 Nov. 2013).

Carter, T. R., Jones, R. N., Lu, X., *et al.* 2007. New assessment methods and the characterisation of future conditions, in M.L. Parry, O.F. Canziani, J.P. Palutikof, *et al.* (eds) *Climate Change 2007: Impacts, Adaptation and Vulnerability. Contribution of Working Group II to the Fourth Assessment Report of the Intergovernmental Panel on Climate Change.* Cambridge University Press: Cambridge.

Chapple, A. 2008. *Making the Voluntary Carbon Market Work for the Poor*, Forum for the Future, London.

Ciais, P., Canadell, J. G., Luyssaert, S., *et al*. 2010. Can we reconcile atmospheric estimates of the Northern terrestrial carbon sink with land-based accounting? *Current Opinion in Environmental Sustainability*, 2: 225–230.

Committee on Radiative Forcing Effects on Climate, Climate Research Committee and National Research Council 2005. *Radiative Forcing of Climate Change: Expanding the Concept and Addressing Uncertainties*, National Academies Press, Washington, DC.

Crowley, T. J. 2000. Causes of climate change over the past 1000 years. *Science*, 289: 270–277.

Dale, V. H. 1997. The relationship between land-use change and climate change. *Ecological Applications*, 7: 753–769.

David Suzuki Foundation 2009. *Purchasing Carbon Offsets: A Guide for Canadian Consumers, Businesses, and Organizations*, David Suzuki Foundation and Pembina Institute, Vancouver, BC.

Davis, K. J. 2008. Integrating field measurements with flux tower and remote sensing data, in C. M. Hoover (ed.) *Field Measurements for Forest Carbon Monitoring: A Landscape-Scale Approach*. Springer, New York.

Deb Richter Jr., D. and Houghton, R. A. 2011. Gross CO_2 fluxes from land-use change: Implications for reducing global emissions and increasing sinks. *Carbon Management*, 2: 41–47.

DEFRA 2006. *The UK's Fourth National Communication under the United Nations Framework Convention on Climate Change*, United Kingdom Department for Environment, Food and Rural Affairs, London.

De Montfort University 2011. *De Montfort University Carbon Management Plan. February 2011* [Online]. Available at: www.dmu.ac.uk/about-dmu/dmu-estate/energy/carbon-management.aspx (accessed 11 Oct. 2013).

Denman, K. L., Brasseur, G., Chidthaisong, A., *et al*. 2007. Couplings between changes in the climate system and biogeochemistry, in S. Solomon, D. Qin, M. Manning, *et al*. (eds) *Climate Change 2007: The Physical Science Basis. Contribution of Working Group I to the Fourth Assessment Report of the Intergovernmental Panel on Climate Change*. Cambridge University Press: Cambridge.

Direction du Tourisme 2002. *Les chiffres clés du tourisme de montagne en France*, 3rd edn, Service d'Etudes et d'Aménagement touristique de la montagne, Paris.

Dlugokencky, E. J., Myers, R. C., Lang, P. M., *et al*. 2005. Conversion of NOAA atmospheric dry air CH_4 mole fractions to a gravimetrically prepared standard scale. *Journal of Geophysical Research-Atmospheres*, 110.

EC 2003. *Directive 2003/87/EC. Official Journal of the European Union L 275/32* [Online]. Available at: http://eur-lex.europa.eu/en/index.htm (accessed 11 Oct. 2013).

EC 2007. *Decision 2007/589/EC. Official Journal of the European Union L 229/1* [Online]. Available at: http://eur-lex.europa.eu/en/index.htm (accessed 1 Oct. 2013).

EC 2010. *Report from the Commission: Progress Towards Achieving the Kyoto Objectives. SEC(2010) 1204* [Online]. Available at: http://eur-lex.europa.eu/en/index.htm (accessed 11 Oct. 2013).

EC 2013. *The EU Emissions Trading System (EU ETS)* [Online]. Available at: http://ec.europa.eu/clima/policies/ets/index_en.htm (accessed 11 Oct. 2013).

Edinburgh Napier University 2009. *Edinburgh Napier University. Carbon Management Programme. Carbon Management Plan 2008–2013* [Online]. Available at: http://staff.napier.ac.uk/services/facilities/sustainability/managementprogrammes/Pages/CarbonManagement.aspx (accessed 11 Oct. 2013).

Eggleston, H. S., Buendia, L., Miwa, K., *et al*. (eds) 2006. *2006 IPCC Guidelines for National Greenhouse Gas Inventories*, IGES: Japan.

El Raey, A. 2004. *Adaptation to Climate Change for Sustainable Development in the Coastal Zone of Egypt. ENV/EPOC/GF/SD/RD(2004)1/FINAL*, OECD, Paris.

Etheridge, D. M., Steele, L. P., Langenfelds, R. L., *et al*. 1996. Natural and anthropogenic changes in atmospheric CO_2 over the last 1000 years from air in Antarctic ice and firn. *Journal of Geophysical Research: Atmospheres*, 101: 4115–4128.

Falkowski, P., Scholes, R. J., Boyle, E., *et al*. 2000. The global carbon cycle: a test of our knowledge of earth as a system. *Science*, 290: 291–296.

Falloon, P., Smith, P., Bradley, R. I., *et al.* 2006. RothCUK – a dynamic modelling system for estimating changes in soil C from mineral soils at 1-km resolution in the UK. *Soil Use and Management*, 22: 274–288.

FAO 2004. Drought impact mitigation and prevention in the Limpopo River Basin: a situation analysis. Land and Water Discussion Paper 4, FAO, Rome.

Fisher, B. S., Nakicenovic, N., Alfsen, K., *et al.* 2007. Issues related to mitigation in the long term context, in B. Metz, O. R. Davidson, P. R. Bosch, *et al.* (eds) *Climate Change 2007: Mitigation. Contribution of Working Group III to the Fourth Assessment Report of the Intergovernmental Panel on Climate Change.* Cambridge University Press: Cambridge.

Fitzroy, F. and Papyrakis, E. 2009. *Introduction to Climate Change Economics and Policy*. Earthscan: London.

Ford, J. and Smit, B. 2004. A framework for assessing the vulnerability of communities in the Canadian Arctic to risks associated with climate change. *Arctic*, 57: 389–400.

Forster, P., Ramaswamy, V., Artaxo, P., *et al.* 2007. Changes in atmospheric constituents and in radiative forcing, in S. Solomon, D. Qin, M. Manning, *et al.* (eds) *Climate Change 2007: The Physical Science Basis. Contribution of Working Group I to the Fourth Assessment Report of the Intergovernmental Panel on Climate Change.* Cambridge University Press: Cambridge.

Friedlingstein, P., Cox, P., Betts, R., *et al.* 2006. Climate-carbon cycle feedback analysis: results from the (CMIP)-M-4 model intercomparison. *Journal of Climate*, 19: 3337–3353.

Friend, A. D., Arneth, A., Kiang, N. Y., *et al.* 2007. FLUXNET and modelling the global carbon cycle. *Global Change Biology*, 13: 610–633.

Fuglestvedt, J. S., Berntsen, T. K., Godal, O., *et al.* 2003. Metrics of climate change: assessing radiative forcing and emission indices. *Climatic Change*, 58: 267–331.

Gilbertson, T. and Reyes, O. 2009. Carbon trading: how it works and why it fails. *Critical Currents*, 7.

Godal, O. 2003. The IPCC's assessment of multidisciplinary issues: the case of greenhouse gas indices. An editorial essay. *Climatic Change*, 58: 243–249.

Goetz, S. J., Baccini, A., Laporte, N. T., *et al.* 2009. Mapping and monitoring carbon stocks with satellite observations: a comparison of methods. *Carbon Balance and Management*, 4: 2 doi: 10.1186/1750-0680-4-2.

Goodale, C. L., Apps, M. J., Birdsey, R. A., *et al.* 2002. Forest carbon sinks in the Northern Hemisphere. *Ecological Applications*, 12: 891–899.

Grubb, M., Brack, D. and Vrolijk, C. 1999. *The Kyoto Protocol: A Guide And Assessment*, Royal Institute of International Affairs and Earthscan, London.

Gurney, K. R., Law, R. M., Denning, A. S., *et al.* 2002. Towards robust regional estimates of CO_2 sources and sinks using atmospheric transport models. *Nature*, 415: 626–630.

Hallegatte, S. 2009. Strategies to adapt to an uncertain climate change. *Global Environmental Change*, 19: 240–247.

Halsnæs, K., Shukla, P., Ahuja, D., *et al.* (eds) *Climate Change 2007: Mitigation. Contribution of Working Group III to the Fourth Assessment Report of the Intergovernmental Panel on Climate Change.* Cambridge University Press: Cambridge.

Hansen, J. E. 2005. A slippery slope: how much global warming constitutes "dangerous anthropogenic interference"? *Climatic Change,* 68: 269–279.

Hansen, M. C., Stehman, S. V., Potapov, P. V., *et al.* 2008. Humid tropical forest clearing from 2000 to 2005 quantified by using multitemporal and multiresolution remotely sensed data. *Proceedings of the National Academy of Sciences of the United States of America*, 105: 9439–9444.

Hare, W. 2003. *Assessment of Knowledge on Impacts of Climate Change – Contribution to the Specification of Article 2 of the UNFCCC: Impacts on Ecosystems, Food Production, Water and Socio-Economic Systems,* Wissenschaftlicher Beirat der Bundesregierung Globale Umweltveränderungen, Berlin.

HEFCE 2010a. *Carbon Management Strategies and Plans. A Guide to Good Practice* [Online]. Available at: www.hefce.ac.uk/pubs/hefce/2010/10_02/ (accessed 11 Oct. 2013).

HEFCE 2010b. *Carbon Reduction Target and Strategy for Higher Education in England* [Online]. Available at: www.hefce.ac.uk/pubs/hefce/2010/10_01/ (accessed 11 Oct. 2013).

Hilker, T., Coops, N. C., Wulder, M. A., Black, T. A. and Guy, R. D. 2008. The use of remote sensing in light use efficiency based models of gross primary production: a review of current status and future requirements. *Science of the Total Environment*, 404: 411–423.

Hitz, S. and Smith, J. 2004. Estimating global impacts from climate change. *Global Environmental Change: Human and Policy Dimensions,* 14: 201–218.

Houghton, R. A. 2003. Revised estimates of the annual net flux of carbon to the atmosphere from changes in land use and land management 1850–2000. *Tellus, Series B-Chemical and Physical Meteorology*, 55: 378–390.

Houghton, R. A. 2005. Aboveground forest biomass and the global carbon balance. *Global Change Biology*, 11: 945–958.

Houghton, R. A. 2007. Balancing the global carbon budget. *Annual Review of Earth and Planetary Sciences*, 35: 313–347.

Houghton, R. A. 2010. How well do we know the flux of CO_2 from land-use change? *Tellus, Series B: Chemical and Physical Meteorology*, 62: 337–351.

HSBC 2005. *HSBC Carbon Neutral Pilot Project*, HSBC Holdings plc, London.

HSBC 2008. *HSBC and Carbon Neutrality*, Group Corporate Sustainability, HSBC Holdings plc, London.

HSBC 2013. *Sustainability Report 2012*, Global Corporate Sustainability, HSBC Holdings plc, London.

IPCC 2007. Summary for policymakers, in B. Metz, O. R. Davidson, P. R. Bosch, *et al.* (eds) *Climate Change 2007: Mitigation. Contribution of Working Group III to the Fourth Assessment Report of the Intergovernmental Panel on Climate Change.* Cambridge University Press: Cambridge.

IPCC 2013. *Working Group I Contribution to the IPCC Fifth Assessment Report Climate Change 2013: The Physical Science Basis. Summary for Policymakers* [Online]. Available at: www.climatechange2013.org/images/uploads/WGIAR5-SPM_Approved27Sep2013.pdf (accessed 10 Oct. 2013).

Janssens, I. A., Freibauer, A., Ciais, P., *et al.* 2003. Europe's terrestrial biosphere absorbs 7 to 12% of European anthropogenic CO_2 emissions. *Science*, 300: 1538–1542.

Jung, M., Vetter, M., Herold, M., *et al.* 2007. Uncertainties of modeling gross primary productivity over Europe: a systematic study on the effects of using different drivers and terrestrial biosphere models. *Global Biogeochemical Cycles*, 21, GB4021, doi: 10.1029/2006GB002915.

Keeling, C. D. 1998. Rewards and penalties of monitoring the earth. *Annual Review of Energy and the Environment*, 23: 25–82.

Keeling, C. D., Bollenbacher, A. F. and Whorf, T. P. 2005. Monthly atmospheric $^{13}C/^{12}C$ isotopic ratios for 10 SIO stations, in *Trends: A Compendium of Data on Global Change.* Carbon Dioxide Information Analysis Center: Oak Ridge National Laboratory, U.S. Department of Energy, Oak Ridge, TN.

Klein, R. J. T., Huq, S., Denton, F., *et al.* 2007. Inter-relationships between adaptation and mitigation, in M. L. Parry, O. F. Canziani, J. P. Palutiko, *et al.* (eds) *Climate Change 2007: Impacts, Adaptation and Vulnerability. Contribution of Working Group II to the Fourth Assessment Report of the Intergovernmental Panel on Climate Change.* Cambridge University Press: Cambridge.

Kossoy, A. and Ambrosi, P. 2010. *State and Trends of the Carbon Market 2010*, World Bank, Washington, DC.

Kossoy, A. and Guigon, P. 2012. *State and Trends of the Carbon Market 2012*, World Bank, Washington, DC.

Lal, R. 2010. Managing soils and ecosystems for mitigating anthropogenic carbon emissions and advancing global food security. *BioScience*, 60: 708–721.

Lasco, R., Cruz, R., Pulhin, J. and Pulhin, F. 2006. Tradeoff analysis of adaptation strategies for natural resources, water resources and local institutions in the Philippines. AIACC Working Paper No. 32, International START Secretariat, Washington, DC.

Leemans, R. and Eickhout, B. 2004. Another reason for concern: regional and global impacts on ecosystems for different levels of climate change. *Global Environmental Change: Human and Policy Dimensions,* 14: 219–228.

Lefevere, J. 2009. A climate of change: an analysis of progress in EU and international climate change policy, in J. Scott. (ed.) *Environmental Protection: European Law and Governance.* Oxford University Press: Oxford.

Leonard, A. 2009. *The Story of Cap and Trade* [Online]. Available at: http://storyofstuff.org/blog/movies/story-of-cap-and-trade/ (accessed 11 Oct. 2013).

Le Quéré, C., Andres, R. J., Boden, T., *et al.* 2013. The global carbon budget 1959–2011. *Earth System Science Data*, 5: 165–185.

Le Quéré, C., Raupach, M. R., Canadell, J. G., *et al.* 2009. Trends in the sources and sinks of carbon dioxide. *Nature Geoscience*, 2: 831–836.

Le Treut, H., Somerville, R., Cubasch, U., *et al.* 2007. Historical overview of climate change, in S. Solomon, D. Qin, M. Manning, *et al.* (eds) *Climate Change 2007: The Physical Science Basis. Contribution of Working Group I to the Fourth Assessment Report of the Intergovernmental Panel on Climate Change.* Cambridge University Press: Cambridge.

Lewis, S. L., Lopez-Gonzalez, G., Sonké, B., *et al.* 2009. Increasing carbon storage in intact African tropical forests. *Nature*, 457: 1003–1006.

Lohmann, L. 2006. A licence to carry on polluting? *New Scientist*, 2580: 18–19.

McKinsey & Company 2010. *Impact of the Financial Crisis on Carbon Economics. Version 2.1 of the Global Greenhouse Gas Abatement Cost Curve.* [Online]. Available at: http://ww1.mckinsey.com/clientservice/sustainability/pdf/Impact_Financial_Crisis_Carbon_Economics_GHGcostcurveV2.1.pdf (accessed 11 Oct. 2013).

Manning, A. C. and Keeling, R. F. 2006. Global oceanic and land biotic carbon sinks from the Scripps atmospheric oxygen flask sampling network. *Tellus, Series B: Chemical and Physical Meteorology*, 58: 95–116.

Mehdi, B. 2006. *Adapting to Climate Change: An Introduction for Canadian Municipalities*, Occasional Paper, Canadian Climate Impacts and Adaptation Research Network (C-CIARN), Ottawa.

Midgley, G. F., Bond, W. J., Kapos, V., *et al.* 2010. Terrestrial carbon stocks and biodiversity: key knowledge gaps and some policy implications. *Current Opinion in Environmental Sustainability*, 2: 264–270.

Miles, L. 2010. *Implications of the REDD Negotiations for Forest Restoration*, UNEP World Conservation Monitoring Centre, Cambridge.

Miles, L. and Kapos, V. 2008. Reducing greenhouse gas emissions from deforestation and forest degradation: global land-use implications. *Science*, 320: 1454–1455.

Nabuurs, G.-J., Schelhaas, M.-J., Mohren, G. M. J. and Field, C. B. 2003. Temporal evolution of the European forest sector carbon sink from 1950 to 1999. *Global Change Biology*, 9: 152–160.

Nabuurs, G.-J., Masera, O., Andrasko, K., *et al.* 2007. Forestry, in B. Metz, O. R. Davidson, P. R. Bosch, *et al.* (eds) *Climate Change 2007: Mitigation. Contribution of Working Group III to the Fourth Assessment Report of the Intergovernmental Panel on Climate Change.* Cambridge University Press: Cambridge.

Naidoo, R., Balmford, A., Costanza, R., *et al.* 2008. Global mapping of ecosystem services and conservation priorities. *Proceedings of the National Academy of Sciences of the United States of America*, 105: 9495–9500.

Nakicenovic, N. and Swart, R. (eds) 2000. *Emissions Scenarios. A Special Report of Working Group III of the Intergovernmental Panel on Climate Change*, Cambridge University Press: Cambridge.

Newton, A. C., Hodder, K., Cantarello, E., *et al.* 2012. Cost–benefit analysis of ecological networks assessed through spatial analysis of ecosystem services. *Journal of Applied Ecology*, 49: 571–580.

OECD 2003. *Development and Climate Change in Bangladesh: Focus on Coastal Flooding and the Sundarbans*, *COM/ENV/EPOC/DCD/DAC(2003)3/FINAL.* OECD, Paris.

Olsen, K. H. 2007. The clean development mechanism's contribution to sustainable development: a review of the literature. *Climatic Change*, 84: 59–73.

O'Neill, B. C. 2000. The jury is still out on global warming potentials. *Climatic Change*, 44: 427–443.

O'Neill, B. C. and Oppenheimer, M. 2002. Climate change: dangerous climate impacts and the Kyoto Protocol. *Science,* 296: 1971–1972.

Oppenheimer, M. and Alley, R. B. 2005. Ice sheets, global warming, and Article 2 of the UNFCCC. *Climatic Change,* 68, 257–267.

Oppenheimer, M. and Petsonk, A. 2005. Article 2 of the UNFCCC: historical origins, recent interpretations. *Climatic Change*, 73: 195–226.

Oreskes, N. 2004. Beyond the ivory tower: the scientific consensus on climate change. *Science*, 306: 1686.

Pacala, S., Hurtt, G. C., Baker, D., *et al.* 2001. Consistent land- and atmosphere-based US carbon sink estimates. *Science*, 292: 2316–2320.

Pacala, S. and Socolow, R. 2004. Stabilization wedges: solving the climate problem for the next 50 years with current technologies. *Science*, 305: 968–972.

Parry, M., Arnell, N., McMichael, T., *et al.* 2001. Millions at risk: defining critical climate change threats and targets. *Global Environmental Change: Human and Policy Dimensions,* 11: 181–183.

Parry, M. L., Canziani, O. F., Palutikof, J. P., *et al.* 2007. *Climate Change 2007: Impacts, Adaptation and Vulnerability. Contribution of Working Group II to the Fourth Assessment Report of the Intergovernmental Panel on Climate Change*, Cambridge University Press, Cambridge.

Penman, J., Gytarsky, M., Hiraish, I. T., *et al.* (eds) 2003. *Good Practice Guidance for Land Use, Land-Use Change and Forestry* IPCC/IGES: Japan.

Penman, J., Kruger, D., Galbally, I., *et al.* (eds) 2000. *Good Practice Guidance and Uncertainty Management in National Greenhouse Gas Inventories*, IPCC/OECD/IEA/IGES: Japan.

Peters-Stanley, M. and Yin, D. 2013. *Maneuvering the Mosaic: State of the Voluntary Carbon Markets 2013. A Report by Ecosystem Marketplace & Bloomberg New Energy Finance.* [Online]. Available at: www.forest-trends.org (accessed 11 Oct. 2013).

Petit, J. R., Jouzel, J., Raynaud, D., *et al.* 1999. Climate and atmospheric history of the past 420,000 years from the Vostok ice core, Antarctica. *Nature*, 399: 429–436.

Power, A. G. 2010. Ecosystem services and agriculture: tradeoffs and synergies. *Philosophical Transactions of the Royal Society B: Biological Sciences*, 365: 2959–2971.

Rogner, H.-H., Zhou, D., Bradley, R., *et al.* 2007. Introduction, in B. Metz, O. R. Davidson, P. R. Bosch, *et al.* (eds) *Climate Change 2007: Mitigation. Contribution of Working Group III to the Fourth Assessment Report of the Intergovernmental Panel on Climate Change.* Cambridge University Press: Cambridge.

Rosenzweig, C., Casassa, G., Karoly, D. J., *et al.* 2007. Assessment of observed changes and responses in natural and managed systems, in M. L. Parry, O. F. Canziani, J. P. Palutikof, *et al.* (eds) *Climate Change 2007: Impacts, Adaptation and Vulnerability. Contribution of Working Group II to the Fourth Assessment Report of the Intergovernmental Panel on Climate Change.* Cambridge University Press: Cambridge.

Running, S. W., Nemani, R. R., Heinsch, F. A., *et al.* 2004. A continuous satellite-derived measure of global terrestrial primary production. *BioScience*, 54: 547–560.

Sabine, C. L., Feely, R. A., Gruber, N., *et al.* 2004. The oceanic sink for anthropogenic CO_2. *Science*, 305: 367–371.

Smith, J. B., Schellnhuber, H.-J. and Mirza, M. Q. 2001. Vulnerability to climate change and reasons for concern: a synthesis, in J.J. McCarthy, O. F. Canziani, N. A. Leary, *et al.* (eds) *Climate Change 2001: Impacts, Adaptation and Vulnerability, Contribution of Working Group II to the Third Assessment Report of the Intergovernmental Panel on Climate Change*, Cambridge University Press, Cambridge.

Smith, P., Martino, D., Cai, Z., *et al.* (eds) 2007. *Climate Change 2007: Mitigation. Contribution of Working Group III to the Fourth Assessment Report of the Intergovernmental Panel on Climate Change.* Cambridge University Press: Cambridge.

Stephens, B. B., Gurney, K. R., Tans, P. P., *et al.* 2007. Weak northern and strong tropical land carbon uptake from vertical profiles of atmospheric CO_2. *Science*, 316: 1732–1735.

Stern, N. 2006. *The Economics of Climate Change*, Cambridge University Press, Cambridge.

Stickler, C. M., Nepstad, D. C., Coe, M. T., *et al.* 2009. The potential ecological costs and cobenefits of REDD: a critical review and case study from the Amazon region. *Global Change Biology*, 15: 2803–2824.

Subbarao, S. and Lloyd, B. 2011. Can the Clean Development Mechanism (CDM) deliver? *Energy Policy*, 39: 1600–1611.

Takahashi, T., Sutherland, S. C., Wanninkhof, R., *et al.* 2009. Climatological mean and decadal change in surface ocean pCO_2, and net sea-air CO_2 flux over the global oceans. *Deep-Sea Research Part II: Topical Studies in Oceanography*, 56: 554–577.

TEEB 2010. *The Economics of Ecosystems and Biodiversity: Mainstreaming the Economics of Nature: A Synthesis of the Approach, Conclusions and Recommendations of TEEB* [Online]. Available at: www.teebweb.org/

publication/mainstreaming-the-economics-of-nature-a-synthesis-of-the-approach-conclusions-and-recommendations-of-teeb/ (accessed 11 Oct. 2013).

UN 1998. *Kyoto Protocol to the United Nations Framework Convention on Climate Change* [Online]. Available at: http://unfccc.int/essential_background/kyoto_protocol/background/items/1351.php (accessed 10 Oct. 2013).

UN 2012. *Doha Amendement to the Kyoto Protocol* [Online]. Available at: http://treaties.un.org/doc/Treaties/2012/12/20121217%2011-40%20AM/CN.718.2012.pdf (accessed 11 Oct. 2013).

UNFCCC 1992. *United Nations Framework Convention on Climate Change* [Online]. Available at: http://unfccc.int/essential_background/convention/background/items/2853.php (accessed 9 Oct. 2013).

UNFCCC 2011a. *Status of Ratification of the Kyoto Protocol* [Online]. Available at: http://unfccc.int/kyoto_protocol/status_of_ratification/items/2613.php (accessed 10 Oct. 2013).

UNFCCC 2011b. *Report of the Conference of the Parties on its Sixteenth Session, Held in Cancun from 29 November to 10 December 2010. Addendum. Part Two: Action Taken by the Conference of the Parties at its Fifteenth Session* [Online]. Available at: http://unfccc.int/meetings/cop_16/items/5571.php (accessed 10 Oct. 2013).

UNFCCC 2011c. *Compilation and Synthesis of Fifth National Communications. Executive Summary. FCCC/SBI/2011/INF.1* [Online]. Available at: http://unfccc.int/national_reports/annex_i_natcom/compilation_and_synthesis_reports/items/2736.php (accessed 10 Oct. 2013).

UNFCCC 2012. *National Greenhouse Gas Inventory Data for the Period 1990–2010. Note by the Secretariat. FCCC/SBI/2012/31* [Online]. Available at: http://unfccc.int/ghg_data/ghg_data_unfccc/items/4146.php (accessed 10 Oct. 2013).

UNFCCC 2013. *Registry Systems under the Kyoto Protocol* [Online]. Available at: http://unfccc.int/kyoto_protocol/registry_systems/items/2723.php (accessed 23 July 2013).

VANOC 2010. *Vancouver 2010 Sustainability Report 2009–10. Environmental Stewardship and Impact Reduction* [Online]. Available at: www.olympic.org/Documents/Games_Vancouver_2010/VANOC_Sustainability_Report-EN.pdf (accessed 11 Oct. 2013).

Van Vuuren, D. P., Meinshausen, M., Plattner, G. K., *et al.* 2008. Temperature increase of 21st century mitigation scenarios. *Proceedings of the National Academy of Sciences Directive 2003/87/EC.*

Walther, G. R., Post, E., Convey, P., *et al.* 2002. Ecological responses to recent climate change. *Nature*, 416: 389–395.

Watson, R. T., Noble, I. R., Bolin, B., *et al.* 2000. *Land Use, Land-Use Change, and Forestry: An IPCC Special Report*, Cambridge University Press, Cambridge.

WBCSD and WRI 2004. *The Greenhouse Gas Protocol. A Corporate Accounting and Reporting Standard*, World Business Council on Sustainable Development (WBCSD) and World Resources Institute (WRI), Washington, DC.

Wehbe, M., Eakin, H., Seiler, R., *et al.* 2006. Local perspectives on adaptation to climate change: lessons from Mexico and Argentina. AIACC Working Paper 39, International START Secretariat, Washington, DC.

West, P. C., Gibbs, H. K., Monfreda, C., *et al.* 2010. Trading carbon for food: global comparison of carbon stocks vs. crop yields on agricultural land. *Proceedings of the National Academy of Sciences of the United States of America*, 107: 19645–19648.

Wiedmann, T. 2009. Editorial: carbon footprint and input-output analysis – an introduction. *Economic Systems Research*, 21: 175–186.

Wiedmann, T. and Minx, J. 2008. A definition of 'carbon footprint', in C. C. Pertsova (ed.) *Ecological Economics Research Trends*. Nova Science Publishers: Hauppauge, NY.

4

BIODIVERSITY AND ECOSYSTEM SERVICES

4.1 Introduction

One of the fundamental principles underpinning the green economy is that economic activities should not unduly damage the environment. But what do we mean by 'the environment'? Generally, when people use that term they are referring to the environment in which people live, which includes both living and non-living components. The living component is comprised of a multitude of plant, animal and microbial species, which form highly complex interacting communities, collectively referred to as biological diversity or 'biodiversity'. There is great concern that we are currently experiencing a global biodiversity crisis, characterised by an exceptionally high rate of biodiversity loss, caused by human activities. Potentially, this could have major implications for the future of life on Earth, including human society. This is because human life depends on a number of ecological benefits, or 'ecosystem services', provided by biodiversity. There is a risk that the provision of such services could be undermined, or somehow fail, as a result of the biodiversity crisis.

This raises a number of questions, including: what are the ecosystem services on which humans depend? What is the relationship between provision of these services and biodiversity? Is there really a 'biodiversity crisis', and if so, how might development of the green economy help address it? This chapter examines the answers to these questions.

4.1.1 Definition of key terms

'Biodiversity' is unfortunately a term that has been defined in a variety of ways by different authors, often leading to confusion about precisely what is being discussed (DeLong, 1996). It is important to bear this in mind when reading material on the subject. The word 'biodiversity' is a shortened form of 'biological diversity'. Although the latter term has been in use since the 1960s, the shortened form was coined only in the 1980s (Wilson and Peter, 1988). Many authors interpret biodiversity as species richness, or the number of species occurring in an area, but the concept is often defined more broadly than that. For example, Gaston and Spicer (2004) define biodiversity as 'variation of life at all levels of biological organization'; others interpret the term more simply as 'the variety of life' (DeLong, 1996).

The nearest thing to a formal definition of 'biological diversity' is that employed by the Convention on Biological Diversity (www.cbd.int), where it is taken to mean:

> the variability among living organisms from all sources including, *inter alia*, terrestrial, marine and other aquatic ecosystems and the ecological complexes of which they are part; this includes diversity within species, between species and of ecosystems.

It is important to note here the inclusion of variation at the genetic level and that of ecosystems, as well as species. This implies a much broader interpretation than simply species richness. It can therefore be helpful to remember that biodiversity, as typically defined in policy, has three main components:

1. *Genetic diversity*, namely, all the different genes contained in all the living species, including individual plants, animals, fungi and microorganisms.
2. *Species diversity*, namely, all the different species, as well as the differences within and between different species.
3. *Ecosystem diversity*, namely, all the different habitats, biological communities and ecological processes, as well as variation within individual ecosystems.

Noss (1990) goes further, by suggesting that biodiversity is not simply the number of things in a defined area, whether they are genes, species, or ecosystems, but includes the major structural components and functional processes at different levels of organisation. This highlights the need to consider the structure and function of biological communities, as well as species composition, to fully characterise biodiversity. This is of particular relevance to the concept of ecosystem services, which we will explore later in this chapter.

Reflection point

Some commentators are concerned by use of the term 'biodiversity', because many people do not readily understand what it means. For example, in a recent survey when members of the public were asked what they thought what biodiversity was, the most common answer was 'a kind of washing powder' (BBC, 2010). This suggests that public understanding of the term is still limited, despite rapid growth in use of the term in international media in recent years.

Another key term is *ecosystem*. This can be defined as a system involving the interactions between a community of living organisms in a particular area and its non-living environment. It is important to consider what is implied by this definition. The characteristics of systems, including complex adaptive systems, were examined in Chapter 2. A complex system is composed of interconnected parts that exhibit one or more 'emergent' properties, which are not obvious from the properties of the individual parts. A 'system' is therefore a dynamic and complex whole, interacting as a structured functional unit; energy, material and information flow among the different elements that compose the system. Systems often have processes that tend towards equilibrium (through regulation), but systems can also exhibit oscillating, chaotic, or exponential behaviour. The ecosystem concept therefore has its origins in the field of *cybernetics*, which is the study of regulatory systems. One of the implications of this concept is that it leads to a greater focus on the behaviour of the complete system rather than its individual components, such as individual species or organisms.

> **Reflection point**
>
> Inclusion of ecosystems within the definition of biodiversity implies that the non-living component of ecosystems, such as rocks, minerals and energy, also forms part of biodiversity. Does this make sense to you? Where would you draw the boundaries of an ecosystem?

4.1.2 Policy context

During the past 20 years, there has been a great deal of policy activity focusing on biodiversity at the global scale, specifically in the wake of UNCED held at Rio de Janeiro in 1992. This launched the Convention on Biological Diversity (CBD), the first intergovernmental process to focus explicitly on biodiversity. However, there are other international Conventions that are relevant to biodiversity, at least in part. The key Conventions are:

- Convention on Biological Diversity (CBD) (www.cbd.int);
- Convention on International Trade in Endangered Species (CITES) (www.cites.org);
- United Nations Framework Convention on Climate Change (UNFCCC) (http://unfccc.int/2860.php);
- The Ramsar Convention (www.ramsar.org);
- The Convention on Migratory Species (CMS) (www.cms.int);
- United Nations Convention to Combat Desertification (UNCCD) (www.unccd.int).

> **Suggested activity**
>
> Explore the websites of these different Conventions. How do they differ in terms of objectives, scope, and the number of countries (Parties) that have ratified them? What are the key specific issues, themes or actions, which are currently the focus of attention of these Conventions?

At present, efforts are underway to create a new intergovernmental initiative, namely the Intergovernmental Panel on Biodiversity and Ecosystem Services (www.ipbes.net). This is intended to operate in a similar way to how the Intergovernmental Panel on Climate Change (IPCC) operates for climate change (www.ipcc.ch), and will bring together scientific information to support policy processes such as the Conventions.

4.1.3 How many species are there on Earth?

If species richness is one measure of biodiversity, then a logical question is: how many species are there? This is a surprisingly difficult question to answer with any precision. There are two main reasons for this. First, many species have simply not been discovered yet. New species are being discovered and described all the time, even in better-documented groups such as mammals. Our level of knowledge of some of the most diverse groups, such as insects or fungi, is very poor; current evidence suggests that many thousands, if not millions of species still await discovery. This is particularly emphasised by the fact that those regions of the world that appear to be richest in species for such groups, namely the tropics, are also the least surveyed. A second major reason is the problem of taxonomy. Once a new species has been collected and identified as something new to science, it has to be accurately described, named and its details published, and specimens must be archived in a suitable location such as a museum or herbarium. The number of people with the specialist skills required to undertake this task is very limited, and as a result, many species remain undescribed even once they have been collected.

It is difficult to appreciate just how poor our current knowledge of biodiversity actually is. To explore this in greater depth, consider the species occurring in the world's oceans. During the past decade, a major initiative was undertaken to increase knowledge about marine biodiversity, through the *Census of Marine Life* (www.coml.org). This represented an unprecedented international project, which produced some remarkable discoveries, including 1,200 new marine species, with another 5,000 or more awaiting formal description. Recent estimates suggest that perhaps another million species remain to be discovered in the deep pelagic (Webb *et al.*, 2010).

A similar lack of knowledge exists for other highly species-rich ecosystem types such as tropical forests. Given this, any estimate of the total number of species is likely to be highly uncertain. Producing such an estimate has long been the subject of scientific debate; a recent attempt to do so is presented by Mora *et al.* (2011), who provide a figure of around 8.7 million species (Table 4.1). This suggests that only about 14 per cent of species have been described to date.

Table 4.1 The number of species in different groups that have been described (catalogued) and the number of species that are predicted to occur

Species	Earth		± SE	Ocean		± SE
	catalogued	Predicted		catalogued	Predicted	
Eukaryotes						
Animalia	953,434	7,770,000	958,000	171,082	2,150,000	145,000
Chromista	13,033	27,500	30,500	4,859	7,400	9,640
Fungi	43,271	611,000	297,000	1,097	5,320	11,100
Plantae	215,644	298,000	8,200	8,600	16,600	9,130
Protozoa	8,118	36,400	6,690	8,118	36,400	6,690
Total	1,233,500	8,740,000	1,300,000	193,756	2,210,000	182,000
Prokaryotes						
Archaea	502	455	160	1	1	0
Bacteria	10,358	9,680	3,470	652	1,320	436
Total	10,860	10,100	3,630	653	1,320	436
Grand total	1,244,360	8,750,000	1,300,000	194,409	2,210,000	182,000

Source: From Mora *et al.* (2011).

As noted by Mora *et al.* (2011), current catalogues of species are biased towards species that are relatively conspicuous, with large geographical ranges, body sizes, and abundances. Consequently, the majority of species that remain to be discovered are likely to be small-ranged and perhaps concentrated in less explored areas such as the deep sea and soil. The importance of insects to the overall diversity of animal species is very clear.

It is also worth considering the number of prokaryote species that exist. The term 'prokaryotes' refers to two taxonomic domains: the bacteria and the archaea, the latter being recognised as recently as 1990. The number of prokaryote species is considered by Curtis *et al.* (2002), who provide an estimate based on statistical analysis of variation in DNA and RNA sequences. These authors conclude that a tonne of soil could contain 4×10^6 different taxa. These estimates for microbial diversity in soils are astonishingly high, and emphasise that documenting or understanding this diversity represents a true frontier of knowledge.

Recent analyses of genetic diversity measured at the level of DNA and RNA sequences have transformed our understanding of life on Earth. Such analyses show that variation in prokaryotes is far higher than in eukaryotes (Figure 4.1). This is consistent with the widely held view that the prokaryotes were the first living organisms on planet Earth, from which all other organisms evolved.

4.2 Global biodiversity crisis

4.2.1 Introduction

Many commentators believe that we are currently experiencing a mass extinction event, comparable with those that have occurred several times in previous geological eras. The previous mass extinction events, which are indicated by the fossil record, were the result of

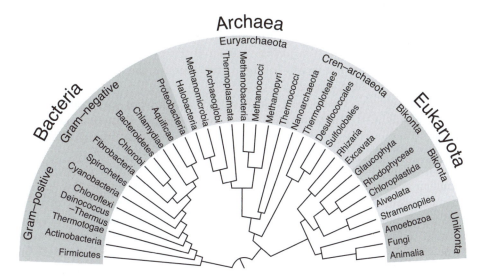

FIGURE 4.1 Phylogenetic tree, based on molecular sequence data, illustrating the higher genetic diversity in prokaryotes than in eukaryotes

Source: Wikimedia commons, http://en.wikipedia.org/wiki/File:Phylogenetic_Tree_of_Life.png.

natural catastrophic events such as meteorite collisions and large-scale volcanism. In contrast, the current mass extinction – often referred to as the 'sixth extinction' – is the result of human activities. The implications could be profound, not only for the future evolution of life on this planet, but also for human society.

But is it true? Is there a global biodiversity crisis? Are we really experiencing a mass extinction event, comparable to those documented in the geological past? And if so, what are the implications for human life?

4.2.2 Numbers of extinct species

How many species have actually become extinct in recent years? This is a surprisingly difficult question to answer. Part of this difficulty stems from the uncertainty about how many species actually exist, as was explored above. Many species have either not been discovered or described yet, and therefore some species may become extinct before anyone is aware of their existence. Estimating the number of such species represents a challenge. Even for species that are relatively well known, in that they have been scientifically described and may even be the subject of major conservation concern, information on their current status is often lacking. For example, a recent conservation assessment of the great apes (including gorillas, chimpanzees and bonobos) highlighted the fact that even for these most charismatic of animals, the number of individuals remaining is not accurately known (Caldecott and Miles, 2005).

For this reason, definitive statements regarding whether or not a species is actually extinct are often difficult to make. Statements regarding the status of a species may more accurately represent the current state of knowledge than its actual status. This is illustrated by the fact that species that were once believed to have been extinct are quite often rediscovered. This has been termed the 'Lazarus effect' by Keith and Burgman (2004), who found that the majority of species listed as extinct during the 20-year history of conservation lists in Australia have subsequently been rediscovered. A recent example is provided by the Ivory Billed Woodpecker, which was believed to have become extinct in North America some time in the 1940s. Following a major five-year survey, Fitzpatrick et al. (2005) presented evidence suggesting that the species had been rediscovered – though the claim remains controversial (e.g. see Sibley et al., 2006).

The most definitive resource on which species have recently gone extinct is that provided by CREO ('The Committee on Recently Extinct Organisms' http://creo.amnh.org). Their database lists some 92 mammal species that have been documented as having become extinct since AD 1500. However, some estimates of recent extinctions are much higher, particularly for diverse groups such as insects. For example, the Millennium Ecosystem Assessment (MEA) (2005a) estimated that humans have increased species extinction rates by as much as 1,000 times the background rates that were typical over Earth's history. Many species may be on the brink of extinction. For example, Thomas et al. (2004) estimated that 15–37 per cent of species in the areas they sampled may be at risk of extinction from climate change. However, such estimates are highly uncertain. As a consequence, some authors – most notably Lomborg (2001) – have suggested that reports of an extinction crisis have been exaggerated. Pimm (2002) provides a response to such arguments.

4.2.3 A palaeoecological view

Is the Earth currently experiencing a sixth mass extinction event, or not? To answer this question, it is relevant to compare the current situation against previous mass extinction events that are discernible in the fossil record. Barnosky *et al.* (2011) present a recent review using this approach. First, they present information about previous mass extinctions (Table 4.2).

These authors then present a careful evaluation of the evidence regarding both recent extinctions and those in the geological past, paying particular attention to the limitations of available data and the consequent uncertainty associated with any conclusions drawn. These authors conclude that the recent loss of species is dramatic and serious, but does not yet qualify as a mass extinction, comparable to those that have occurred in the geological past. However, many species are currently threatened with extinction as a result of human activity, and if these

Table 4.2 Summary of previous mass extinction events, based on fossil evidence

Event	*Proposed causes*
The Ordovician event ended ~443 Myr ago; within 3.3 to 1.9 Myr 57 per cent of genera were lost, an estimated 86 per cent of species	Onset of alternating glacial and interglacial episodes; repeated marine transgressions and regressions. Uplift and weathering of the Appalachians affecting atmospheric and ocean chemistry. Sequestration of CO_2.
The Devonian event ended ~359 Myr ago; within 29 to 2 Myr 35 per cent of genera were lost, an estimated 75 per cent of species	Global cooling (followed by global warming), possibly tied to the diversification of land plants, with associated weathering, paedogenesis, and the drawdown of global CO_2. Evidence for widespread deep-water anoxia and the spread of anoxic waters by transgressions. Possible bolide impact.
The Permian event ended ~251 Myr ago; within 2.8 Myr to 160 Kyr 56 per cent of genera were lost, an estimated 96 per cent of species	Siberian volcanism. Global warming. Spread of deep marine anoxic waters. Elevated H_2S and CO_2 concentrations in both marine and terrestrial realms. Ocean acidification. Possible bolide impact.
The Triassic event ended ~200 Myr ago; within 8.3 Myr to 600 Kyr 47 per cent of genera were lost, an estimated 80 per cent of species	Activity in the Central Atlantic Magmatic Province (CAMP) thought to have elevated atmospheric CO_2 concentrations, which increased global temperatures and led to a calcification crisis in the world oceans
The Cretaceous event ended ~65 Myr ago; within 2.5 Myr to less than a year 40 per cent of genera were lost, an estimated 76 per cent of species	A bolide impact in the Yucatán is thought to have led to a global cataclysm and caused rapid cooling. Preceding the impact, biota may have been declining owing to a variety of causes: Deccan volcanism contemporaneous with global warming; tectonic uplift accelerating erosion, potentially contributing to ocean eutrophication and anoxic episodes.

Source: Adapted by permission from Macmillan Publishers Ltd: *Nature*, Barnosky *et al.* (2011), ©2011.
Note: Myr, millions of years; Kyr, thousands of years

were to be lost in the near future, the Earth could experience a mass extinction that has previously been seen only five times in about 540 million years.

Evidence of recent major declines in species are provided by Boyce *et al.* (2010) for phytoplankton, Christensen *et al.* (2003) for fish, Stuart *et al.* (2004) and Pounds *et al.* (2006) for amphibians, Schipper *et al.* (2008) for mammals, Sekercioğlu *et al.* (2004) for birds, and Butchart *et al.* (2010) for a range of different organisms.

4.2.4 Assessing extinction risk

How is extinction risk assessed? The IUCN (International Union for Conservation of Nature) Red List of Threatened Species™ (www.redlist.org) is widely recognised to be the most authoritative global assessment of the extinction risk of species (Lamoreux *et al.*, 2003; Rodrigues *et al.*, 2006). Although principally designed to evaluate the extinction risk of individual species throughout their ranges, increasingly the IUCN criteria are also being used to develop regional, national and local lists of threatened species. In addition, recent efforts have focused on the use of the Red List to develop an indicator to monitor global biodiversity loss (Butchart *et al.*, 2010), and to assess the status of ecosystems.

Ideally, application of the criteria involves reference to high quality data, but in practice such data are often lacking. This reflects the poor state of knowledge of the status and distribution of many species. As a result, there are frequently uncertainties associated with the Red Listing process (IUCN, 2001). It is also important to note how Red List assessments are conducted in practice: typically by volunteer groups of specialists, who make an expert judgement based on the best evidence available.

4.3 Ecosystem collapse

4.3.1 Introduction

If biodiversity is currently being lost at a high rate, what might the implications of this be for ecosystems? Could they somehow collapse, or cease to function? If so, what would this mean for people?

There is increasing concern that many ecosystems, or even the Earth system as a whole, may be approaching a 'tipping point' (see Chapter 2) (Figure 4.2). A tipping point can be defined as a critical threshold at which a small perturbation can alter the state or development of a system. In other words, they are points at which systems can undergo rapid and substantial change. Some ecosystems can display a variety of different stable states, and can change relatively rapidly from one state to another (Chapter 2). In some cases, such transitions can be permanent and very profound; ecosystems may essentially 'collapse'.

The following statements summarise the current condition of the world's ecosystems (SCBD, 2010):

- Natural habitats in most parts of the world are declining in extent and integrity. Tropical forests, mangroves, freshwater wetlands, sea ice habitats, salt marshes, coral reefs, seagrass beds and shellfish reefs are all showing serious declines.
- Extensive fragmentation and degradation of forests, rivers and other ecosystems have also led to loss of biodiversity and ecosystem services.

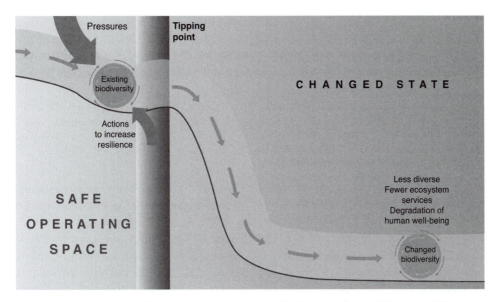

FIGURE 4.2 Explanation of tipping point. Pressures on biodiversity, depicted here as a rolling stone, can push ecosystems beyond what might be termed their safe operating space. Once they enter the danger zone – the vertical bar in this diagram – they are in danger of crossing a threshold which tips them into an alternative state. The arrow shows that actions to increase the resilience of ecosystems, including the conservation of biodiversity, are critical to prevent the tipping point being reached.

Source: Secretariat of the Convention on Biological Diversity (SCBD, 2010).

- Crop and livestock genetic diversity continues to decline in agricultural systems.
- The five principal pressures directly driving biodiversity loss are habitat change, overexploitation, pollution, invasive alien species and climate change. All of these are either constant or are increasing in intensity.

Note the use of the term 'natural habitats' here, rather than ecosystems. 'Habitat' generally refers to the environment in which species live. Note also the suggestion that such habitats are declining, both in terms of their extent (area) and their 'integrity', which refers to their ecological condition, such as their spatial connectivity or level of pollution.

What about ecosystem collapse? The following are potential examples (SCBD, 2010):

- Coral reefs are at particular risk of collapse, as a result of the bleaching impact of warmer water associated with climate change, elevated nutrient concentrations from pollution, over-fishing, sediment deposition arising from inland deforestation, and other pressures. As a result, coral reefs can increasingly become algae-dominated.
- Fish stocks are also at risk. Stocks assessed since 1977 have experienced an 11 per cent decline in total biomass globally. The average maximum size of fish caught declined by 22 per cent since 1959 globally for all assessed communities. There is also an increasing trend of stock collapses over time, with 14 per cent of assessed stocks having collapsed by 2007. In some ocean fisheries, larger predators have been caught preferentially in such numbers that their stocks do not recover. There has also been a tendency for catches to

become dominated by smaller fish and invertebrates, a phenomenon known as 'fishing down the food web'.

•   The collapse of large predator species in the oceans, triggered by over-exploitation, can lead to a shift towards the dominance of less desirable, more resilient species such as jellyfish. Marine ecosystems under such a shift become much less able to provide the quantity and quality of food needed by people. Such changes could prove to be long-lasting and difficult to reverse, even with significant reduction in fishing pressure.

4.3.2 Examples of ecosystem collapse

Much of the evidence for ecosystem collapse is derived from studies of marine ecosystems. The best-known examples are the widespread collapses in fish populations that have resulted primarily from over-fishing, as noted above. One of the most striking examples of a fishery collapse is the case of Atlantic cod in Canada (Figure 4.3). Hutchings and Reynolds (2004) note that in the early 1960s, the northern cod stock numbered almost two billion breeding individuals and comprised 75–80 per cent of Canada's cod. Over the past three generations, northern cod have declined by 97 per cent. The primary cause was over-exploitation. These authors note that rapid declines threaten the persistence of many marine fish, in addition to cod. Data from more than 230 populations reveal a median reduction of 83 per cent in breeding population size from known historic numbers. Few populations recover rapidly; most exhibit little or no change in abundance up to 15 years after a collapse. Reductions in fishing pressure, though clearly necessary, are often insufficient to ensure recovery.

This lack of recovery once fishing has stopped highlights a problem that animal populations often face when they reach very low densities: they may be unable to recover, because individuals find it difficult to find mates. This is what is referred to as the 'Allee effect', which is a form of positive feedback loop. Such processes are poorly understood in many animal species.

Jackson et al. (2001) analysed palaeoecological, archaeological and historical data in an attempt to estimate historical population sizes of many fish species prior to human impact. Their results were very striking, indicating the massive changes in coastal ecosystems that have often resulted from human disturbance. Ecological extinction of entire trophic levels makes ecosystems more vulnerable to other natural and human disturbances, such as nutrient loading and eutrophication, hypoxia, disease, storms, and climate change. Such pressures can interact, which can magnify the effects of individual disturbances. Examples include the increase of eutrophication, hypoxia, outbreaks of toxic blooms and disease that followed the destruction of oyster reefs by mechanical harvesting of oysters. Other examples are outbreaks of seagrass-wasting disease owing to the removal of green turtles (Jackson et al., 2001).

When populations of animals decline because of over-fishing, this can have knock-on effects on many other species in the community. This can lead to rapid transitions in the community – examples of tipping points. The effects of over-fishing may not immediately be apparent until some threshold has been passed. This can occur because of ecological *redundancy* – in other words, the ecological role of one species might be replaced by another, after it has become extinct. The effect of some factor such as over-fishing on the functioning of the ecosystem may not be observable until that species has also become extinct.

Coral reefs provide another example of ecosystems undergoing rapid change. In many parts of the world, coral reefs are in serious decline; an estimated 30 per cent are already

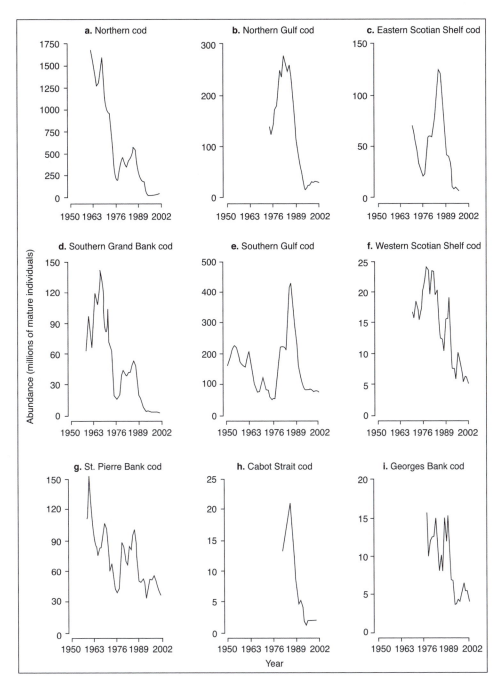

FIGURE 4.3 Collapse of Atlantic cod stocks in Canada. The stocks are (a) northern cod; (b) northern Gulf of St. Lawrence cod; (c) eastern Scotian Shelf cod; (d) southern Grand Bank cod; (e) Southern Gulf of St. Lawrence cod; (f) western Scotian Shelf and Bay of Fundy cod; (g) St. Pierre Bank cod; (h) Cabot Strait cod; and (i) Georges Bank cod (Canadian portion).

Source: Hutchings and Reynolds (2004), Figure 4. © 2004 by the American Institute of Biological Science. Published by the University of California Press. Reproduced here with permission.

severely damaged, and close to 60 per cent may be lost by 2030 (Hughes *et al.*, 2003). The main causes have been the direct and indirect effects of over-fishing and pollution from agriculture and land development, which have caused massive and accelerating decreases in abundance of coral reef species, and widespread changes in reef ecosystems, over the past two centuries (Hughes *et al.*, 2003). But do such changes represent an example of ecosystem collapse? Mumby *et al.* (2007) described reefs in which the decline of one species (sea urchin) led to parrot fishes becoming the main animals keeping algae in check through their grazing activities. Over-fishing of parrot fishes would therefore lead to dominance of the reef by algae – a major transition in reef structure and composition. This provides an example of a tipping point, leading to an ecosystem collapse that could be difficult to reverse.

Concern has also been expressed that the rainforests of the Amazon may also be at risk of collapse. Some models predict that Amazon forest may largely be replaced by savannah-like vegetation by the end of the twenty-first century, as a result of climate change (Malhi *et al.*, 2008, 2009). This process could be exacerbated by increasing demand for biofuels and agricultural crops, and by positive feedbacks between fire, drought and deforestation (Nepstad *et al.*, 2008). Field studies have indicated a decline in forest biomass as a result of recent drought events, which may be associated with climate change (Phillips *et al.*, 2009).

4.3.3 Extinction cascades

The extinction or loss of species can potentially have knock-on effects on other species, leading to 'extinction (or 'trophic') cascades'. No species exists in isolation; rather, each species is a member of a 'food web', which links species through their feeding relationships (Figure 4.4). At the base of the food web or food chain are plants (such as phytoplankton in the case of Figure 4.4). Animal species occurring along the food chain occur at different trophic levels; for example, herbivores or 'primary consumers' eat plants, whereas 'secondary consumers' eat herbivores. At the top of the food chain are the 'top predators' (such as the toothed whales in Figure 4.4), which are always less numerous than lower trophic levels, because energy is dissipated at each trophic level.

From this brief consideration of the ecological structure of communities, it is immediately obvious that loss of one or more species could have profound implications for other species, which could potentially be influenced by their position in the food web. Bascompte and Stouffer (2009) provide a recent review of recent research into this process, and conclude that:

- The structure of ecological communities generally appears able to withstand the loss of species at random, but may be sensitive to the loss of species that consume a wide range of other species.
- The disassembly of ecological communities leads to thresholds whereupon the system can collapse. The consequences of species extinction become amplified and self-reinforcing as more and more species are extirpated.

Montoya *et al.* (2006) highlight the difficulty of identifying simple rules regarding the potential impact of species loss on ecological communities. However, these authors note that extinction cascades can potentially occur when a top predator either declines or goes extinct. In marine

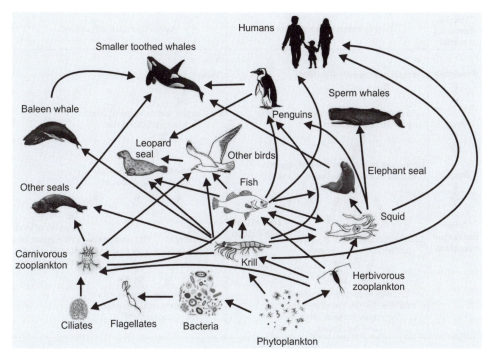

FIGURE 4.4 Simplified diagram of a food web, depicting feeding relationships, based on the Antarctic Ocean

Note: Not to scale.

ecosystems, particular concern has focused on the decline and extinction of shark species, which are heavily exploited. For example, as catch rates of large sharks, such as blacktip sharks, declined during research surveys along the east coast of the United States, cownose rays began to increase (Heithaus *et al.*, 2008). This eventually led to declines in catches of North Carolina bay scallops.

In general, fewer examples are available for terrestrial than for marine and fresh water ecosystems (Pace *et al.*, 1999). A good example is provided by the extirpation and eventual reintroduction of wolves to Yellowstone National Park in the USA, as described by Ripple and Beschta (2004). Here, extirpation of the grey wolf – a keystone predator in this ecosystem – is most likely the over-riding cause of the precipitous decline in the recruitment of three tree species, namely aspen, cottonwood, and willow. This is directly linked to the loss of beaver and the decline in food availability for other animal species (Figure 4.5).

The extent to which top predators structure communities and ecosystems has long been the subject of scientific interest. Research by Terborgh *et al.* (2001) in Venezuela provides a classic study. A set of predator-free islands created by a hydroelectric impoundment showed that when predators of vertebrates were absent, densities of rodents, howler monkeys, iguanas, and leaf-cutter ants were 10 to 100 times greater than on the nearby mainland, suggesting that predators normally limit their populations. The densities of seedlings and saplings of canopy trees were severely reduced on herbivore-affected islands, providing evidence of a trophic cascade.

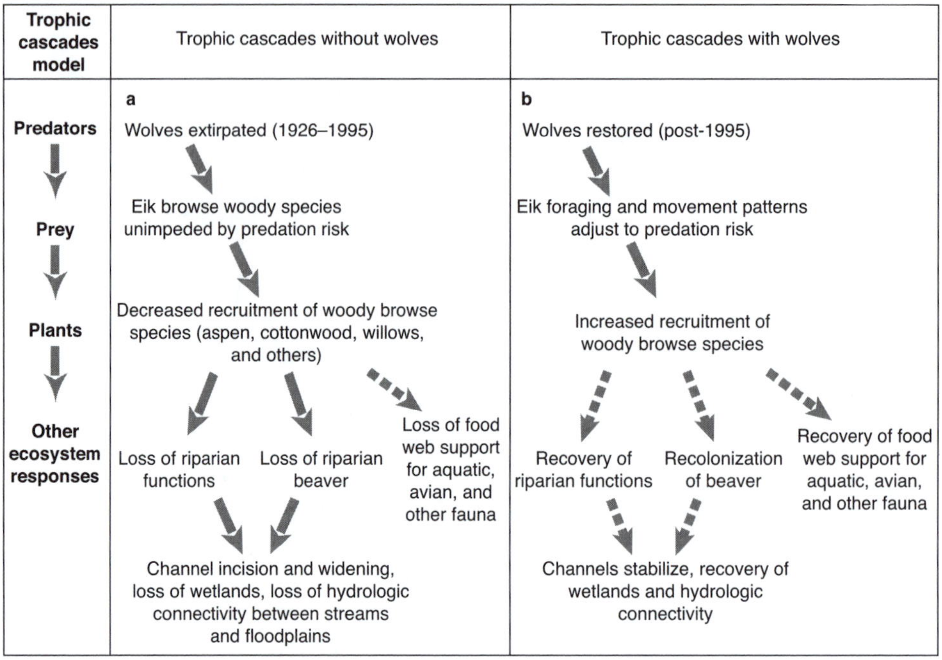

Trophic cascades model	Trophic cascades without wolves	Trophic cascades with wolves
Predators ↓	**a** Wolves extirpated (1926–1995)	**b** Wolves restored (post-1995)
Prey ↓	Eik browse woody species unimpeded by predation risk	Eik foraging and movement patterns adjust to predation risk
Plants ↓	Decreased recruitment of woody browse species (aspen, cottonwood, willows, and others)	Increased recruitment of woody browse species
Other ecosystem responses	Loss of riparian functions Loss of riparian beaver Loss of food web support for aquatic, avian, and other fauna	Recovery of riparian functions Recolonization of beaver Recovery of food web support for aquatic, avian, and other fauna
	Channel incision and widening, loss of wetlands, loss of hydrologic connectivity between streams and floodplains	Channels stabilize, recovery of wetlands and hydrologic connectivity

FIGURE 4.5 Trophic interactions owing to predation risk and selected ecosystem responses to (a) wolf extirpation (1926–1995); and (b) wolf recovery (post-1995) for northern ecosystems of Yellowstone National Park. Solid arrows indicate documented responses; dashed arrows indicate predicted or inferred responses.

Source: Ripple and Beschta (2004), Figure 5. © 2004 by the American Institute of Biological Science. Published by the University of California Press. Reproduced here with permission.

Reflection point

All species are part of complex food webs. At the same time, many species are consumed by people for food. How many species might therefore be incorporated within the food webs that include humans?

4.4 Biodiversity and ecosystem function

4.4.1 Introduction

If species are declining or are being lost, then what might the implications be for the functioning of ecosystems? And what do we really mean by 'ecosystem function'?

4.4.2 Defining ecosystem function

A definition is provided by Naeem *et al.* (1999):

> Ecosystem functioning reflects the collective life activities of plants, animals, and microbes and the effects these activities – feeding, growing, moving, excreting waste, etc. – have on

the physical and chemical conditions of their environment. A functioning ecosystem is one that exhibits biological and chemical activities characteristic for its type.

Ecologists generally consider two compartments of ecosystems, namely, biotic and abiotic. The biotic compartment refers to the community of species present, which can be divided functionally into plant producers, consumers that feed on these producers and on each other, and decomposers (Figure 4.6). The abiotic compartment consists of organic and inorganic nutrient pools (Naeem *et al.*, 1999). Energy and materials move between these two compartments, as well as into and out of the system. Ecosystem processes are quantified by measuring rates of these movements (e.g. plant production, decomposition, nutrient leaching or other measures of material production, transport or loss).

Ecosystem function is therefore taken to refer both to sizes of compartments (e.g. pools of materials such as carbon or organic matter) and rates of processes (e.g. fluxes of materials and energy among compartments) in an ecosystem. It is important to note the variety of different processes that account for the movement of energy and different materials through ecosystems. For example, the cycling of carbon through an ecosystem is dependent on the processes of photosynthesis, respiration and decomposition. Energy is captured by plants through the process of photosynthesis, and is then transferred through ecosystems through the processes of consumption and decomposition. The flow of materials such as water and mineral nutrients (nitrogen, phosphorus, etc.) is similarly governed by a variety of different ecosystem processes. In this way, biodiversity – or the biosphere – can be seen to play a major role in the Earth's biogeochemical processes (see Chapter 2).

The relationship of biodiversity and ecosystem processes to environmental change, and the potential impacts on human society, are illustrated in Figure 4.7.

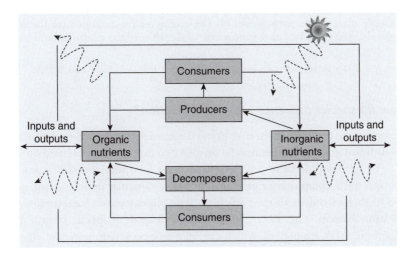

FIGURE 4.6 Basic ecosystem functioning. Producers acquire energy through photosynthesis and take up inorganic nutrients to produce living biomass, forming the food base for consumer species such as herbivores and their predators. Mortality leads to accumulation of organic nutrients that are transformed by decomposers into living biomass, forming the food base for consumers. Decomposers and consumers contribute to formation of inorganic nutrients by mineralisation, completing the cycling of nutrients between organic and inorganic forms. Energy flows (wavy, dashed lines) begin with acquisition by producers and end in loss owing to the respiration activities of all organisms.

Source: Redrawn from Naeem *et al.* (1999).

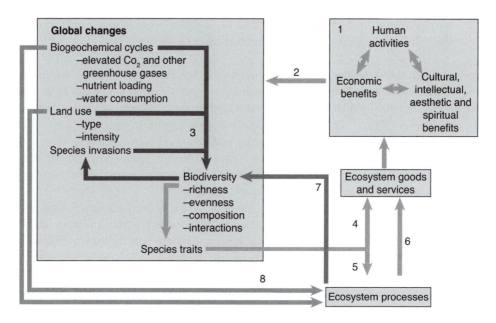

FIGURE 4.7 Relationship between biodiversity, ecosystem processes and human activities. Human activities that are motivated by economic, cultural, intellectual, aesthetic and spiritual goals (1) are now causing environmental and ecological changes of global significance (2). By a variety of mechanisms, these global changes contribute to changing biodiversity, for example, by causing biodiversity loss or species invasions. Changes in biodiversity, through changes in species composition and associated functional traits, can have direct consequences for ecosystem services, and as a result, human economic and social activities (4). In addition, changes in biodiversity can influence ecosystem processes (5). Altered ecosystem processes can thereby influence ecosystem services that benefit humanity (6) and feed back to further alter biodiversity (7). Global changes may also directly affect ecosystem processes (8). Depending on the circumstances, the direct effects of global change may be either stronger or weaker than effects mediated by changes in diversity.

Source: Chapin *et al.* (2000). Reprinted by permission from Macmillan Publishers Ltd: *Nature*, ©2000.

4.4.3 How do species influence ecosystem function?

Groups of species that perform similar roles in an ecosystem process are referred to as 'functional types' or 'functional groups'. Species may be divided into functional types based on what they consume or by their trophic status (i.e. their place in the food web); in other words, whether they are producers, decomposers or predators. Within a particular trophic group, species can be divided further according to their life history or physiological characteristics, or other biological traits (Naeem *et al.*, 1999). The number and kinds of species present determine which organismal traits are present, which can influence ecosystem processes. Species traits may affect energy and material fluxes directly or may alter abiotic conditions that regulate the rates of ecological processes (Chapin *et al.*, 2000).

Any decline or loss of species could therefore change the functioning of the ecosystem of which they are a part, because of the change in functional traits. The introduction of a new species to an area (such as an invasive or exotic species) can have a similar effect. Chapin *et al.* (2000) provide some real-world examples to illustrate this, including reduction in river flow due to invasion of deep-rooted desert trees; increased fire frequency resulting from grass invasion that destroys native trees and shrubs in Hawaii; and insulation of soils by mosses in Arctic tundra, contributing to conditions that allow for permafrost.

Naeem *et al.* (1999) note that the species composition of a community is important, because species vary in their contributions to ecosystem functioning. The fact that some species matter more than others is recognised by concepts such as 'keystone species' and 'ecosystem engineers'. For example, the eating behaviour of moose (*Alces alces*) greatly reduces soil nitrogen content, which can affect the regeneration of tree species. Similarly, through their feeding and dam-building, beavers can alter soil fertility and forest dynamics, whereas termites can similarly play a major role in the nutrient cycling of grasslands.

> ### Reflection point
>
> It is important to note here the concept of 'keystone' species – named after the keystone in a stone bridge, without which the bridge would collapse. It is widely recognised that some species have a particularly important role in ecosystems or ecological communities. Many palm species, for example, are considered to be keystone species in tropical rainforests, because they provide food for a large number of other organisms. What does this imply in terms of the potential impacts of loss of such species?

4.4.4 Species richness and ecosystem function

If species have an influence on ecosystem function, then one might predict that there should be some form of relationship between species richness and ecosystem function. In other words, ecosystem processes should alter if the number of species in an area either decreases or increases. But what is the precise nature of this relationship? This question has been the focus of a great deal of research attention over the past three decades.

Early research considered how the relationship might look if plotted on a simple graph, with ecosystem process on the 'y' axis and species richness on the 'x' axis. A range of different relationships have been suggested by different researchers, as illustrated in Figure 4.8.

> ### Reflection point
>
> Inspect the graphs on Figure 4.8. Which of them do you think is correct? Or can you think of an alternative to these?

These different hypotheses are described by Lawton (1994). The *redundant species* hypothesis suggests that there is a minimal diversity necessary for proper ecosystem functioning (for example, keystone species), but beyond that, most species are redundant in their roles. This hypothesis has been highly controversial, because conservationists do not like to accept that many species may have little functional importance. However, Naeem (1998) points out that in engineering, 'redundancy' is something that is positively valued. For example, a building might typically be designed with redundancy in mind, so that if one supporting structure failed, another might take over its role. In this respect, functional redundancy might confer resilience on ecosystems. One species might compensate for the loss of another of the same functional type.

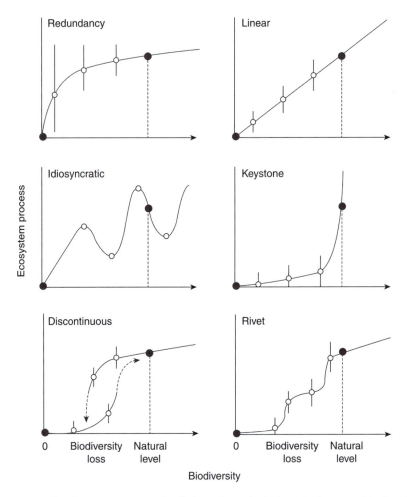

FIGURE 4.8 Graphical representations of early hypothetical relationships between biodiversity and ecosystem processes. Note that in this context, 'biodiversity' has generally been interpreted as 'species richness'.

Source: Naeem *et al.* (2002), by permission of Oxford University Press.

An alternative view is the *rivet* hypothesis (developed by Paul Ehrlich), which suggests that all species make a contribution to ecosystem performance. This likens species to rivets holding together a complex machine, and postulates that functioning will be impaired as its rivets (or species) are lost (Lawton, 1994). This provides a striking image of an ecosystem acting like an aeroplane, which might continually lose rivets until it reaches some key threshold, or tipping point, beyond which it suddenly collapses.

Reflection point

Do you think that a machine such as an aeroplane provides an appropriate metaphor for an ecosystem? (See Larson, 2011, for a discussion of such metaphors.)

A third view, the *idiosyncratic response*, suggests that ecosystem function changes when diversity changes, but the magnitude and direction of change are unpredictable, because the roles of individual species are complex and varied (Lawton, 1994). Alternatively, species richness may be linearly related, or may not be related at all to function (not illustrated in Figure 4.8).

These different hypotheses are now generally deemed too simple to represent the actual situation in nature. However, the underlying question – what is the relationship between biodiversity and ecosystem function? – continues to be the subject of much debate (Loreau *et al.*, 2001; Duffy, 2009). There are essentially two different points of view, as detailed by Wardle *et al.* (2000). One is of the view that there are clear, causative relationships between diversity and ecosystem functioning, particularly above ground. The alternative view is that ecosystem properties are not necessarily driven by species diversity *per se*, but by the key functional attributes or traits of the dominant species present and the composition of functional types. This might seem like a rather limited reason for a major controversy, but the implications are profound. In the latter view, ecosystem function would be predicted to be much less affected by species loss than in the former view, unless those species of particular functional importance – the keystone species – were eliminated. In the latter view, species identity matters: the consequences of species loss will depend on which species actually become extinct, and what their functional roles are.

Hooper *et al.* (2005) provided a review of both sides of the debate, and concluded that:

- Species' functional characteristics strongly influence ecosystem properties.
- Alteration of the entire group of species in ecosystems via species invasions and extinctions caused by human activities has altered ecosystem functioning that may be difficult, expensive, or impossible to reverse, or to fix with technological solutions.
- The effects of species loss or changes in composition differ among ecosystem types and the ecological properties concerned.
- Some ecosystem properties are initially insensitive to species loss because ecosystems may have multiple species that carry out similar functional roles, or because some species may contribute relatively little to ecosystem properties.
- More species are needed to ensure a stable supply of ecosystem services as spatial and temporal variability increases.

Similarly, Loreau *et al.* (2001) concluded that there is consensus that at least some minimum number of species is essential for ecosystem functioning, and that a larger number of species is probably essential for maintaining the stability of ecosystem processes in changing environments. More recently, Hooper *et al.* (2012) have further shown, through a suite of meta-analyses of published data, that the effects of species loss on productivity and decomposition of ecosystems are of comparable magnitude to the effects of many other global environmental changes.

4.5 Ecosystem services

4.5.1 Introduction

Any economic activity that results in the extinction of species can be considered to be unsustainable, because extinction is irreversible – it really is 'for ever'. In this, it differs from other types of environmental change. This irreversibility is one of the reasons why the global biodiversity crisis is currently the focus of so much concern.

But what are the potential impacts of biodiversity loss on people? Might humanity, in some way, be doomed as a result of an imminent mass extinction and consequent collapse of ecosystems? Or can the benefits provided to people by ecosystems be supported by a reduced number of species? And what about the ecosystems that people have created, such as agricultural systems: how do they compare with 'natural' ecosystems in terms of the provision of benefits?

Such questions have recently come to the fore in international policy and scientific research. The concept of 'ecosystem services' is central to this issue. Here we first examine the origins of the concept, then explore how it has risen to its current position of importance. We then evaluate its strengths and weaknesses, by considering the following question: does the analysis of ecosystem services provide a sound basis for developing the green economy?

> ## Reflection point
>
> Before exploring the historical development of ecosystem services as a concept, it is worth conducting a brief 'thought experiment', following that described by Daily (1997). Imagine that you were setting out to live on Mars. Let us imagine that the climate of Mars was similar to that of Earth, and the atmosphere was breathable. Which species would you need to take with you from Earth in order to sustain you in your new home? The striking fact is that we do not know which – or even how many – other species are needed to support human life.

4.5.2 Origins and definition of the concept

While the idea that natural ecosystems play a role in supporting human society has a long ancestry, it is only in recent years that ecosystem services have explicitly been recognised as a concept. A growth in the awareness of the importance of ecosystem function to human life can be dated to the environmental movement that began in the 1960s. The term 'environmental services' first appeared in print in 1970, and 'ecosystem services' in 1981 (Mooney and Ehrlich, 1997). From this point onwards, two questions have been paramount: how the loss of biodiversity will affect ecosystem services, and whether it is possible to develop and deploy substitutes for these services through the development of technology (ibid.).

Ecosystem services can be defined simply as 'the benefits provided to human society by ecosystems'. Daily *et al.* (1997) highlighted that:

- Ecosystem services are essential to civilisation.
- Ecosystem services operate on such a grand scale and in such intricate and little-explored ways that most could not be replaced by technology.
- Human activities are already impairing the flow of ecosystem services on a large scale.
- If current trends continue, humanity will dramatically alter virtually all of Earth's remaining natural ecosystems within a few decades.

Note here the emphasis on 'natural ecosystems' – in other words, ecosystems not resulting from human activity. The origins of the concept therefore lie in an environmentalist agenda: to prevent the loss and degradation of nature. Note also the key argument being made here: that ecosystems such as natural forests are being lost through conversion to other land uses, because the value of the ecosystem services that they provide is not being adequately appreciated or valued. Addressing this problem lies at the heart of much of the recent emphasis on ecosystem services, and places it at the heart of approaches to 'green accounting'.

It is important to note the separation between ecosystem 'goods' and 'services'. Ecosystem goods can be considered as the tangible, material products that are produced by ecosystems, whereas ecosystem 'services' are referred to as intangible processes and functions. However, the distinction between goods and services is unclear in the scientific literature; often, the term 'ecosystem services' is used in a way that includes both goods and services. Here, we will employ this broader definition of 'services', to include goods.

Also note the related concept of 'natural capital'. This term originates in economics, and essentially extends the traditional economic capital (manufactured means of production) to the natural environment. Natural capital can therefore be viewed as the stock of natural ecosystems that yield a flow of ecosystem services into the future. A forest may therefore be viewed as a form of natural capital, which can provide a flow of many different ecosystem services (e.g. carbon storage, timber production, water flow regulation) on a sustainable basis.

Reflection point

Do you think that human-created ecosystems, such as agro-ecosystems, should be considered as part of 'natural capital'?

Interest in ecosystem services has grown rapidly in the past decade. This can partly be attributed to the activities of the Millennium Ecosystem Assessment (MEA). The MEA was a major international environmental assessment initiative, which examined the consequences of ecosystem change for human well-being. The objective was to provide a state-of-the-art scientific appraisal of the condition and trends in the world's ecosystems and the services they provide.

Suggested activity

Download the reports available on the MEA website (www.unep.org/maweb/en/index. aspx), and explore their content. You might find the synthesis reports a particularly useful and digestible summary of its main findings.

The definition of ecosystem services employed by the MEA is as follows (Millennium Ecosystem Assessment, 2005b):

> Ecosystem services are the benefits people obtain from ecosystems. These include provisioning services such as food and water; regulating services such as regulation of

floods, drought, land degradation, and disease; supporting services such as soil formation and nutrient cycling; and cultural services such as recreational, spiritual, religious and other nonmaterial benefits.

The MEA identified four different groups of ecosystem services: provisioning, regulating, cultural and supporting. 'Supporting' services support the provision of the other groups of service. Provision of ecosystem services can affect human livelihoods, which the MEA addressed through the concept of 'human well-being', which was defined as the basic material for a good life, freedom of choice and action, health, good social relations, and security (ibid.).

> **Reflection point**
>
> Do you think that this definition captures what you would consider as your own well-being? Consider also how difficult this concept is to measure.

The MEA presented a major scientific challenge, requiring analysis of the effects and interactions of multiple global drivers, differing spatial extents and turnover times of key ecological and social processes, as well as the connections between individual actions, institutional responses, and ecological changes across these scales (Carpenter *et al.*, 2009) (Figures 4.9 and 4.10).

The main findings of the MEA (2005b) were as follows:

*   Over the past 50 years, humans have changed ecosystems more rapidly and extensively than in any comparable period of time in human history, largely to meet rapidly growing demands for food, fresh water, timber, fibre and fuel. This has resulted in a substantial and largely irreversible loss in the diversity of life on Earth.
*   The changes that have been made to ecosystems have contributed to substantial net gains in human well-being and economic development, but these gains have been achieved at growing costs in the form of the degradation of many ecosystem services, increased risks of nonlinear changes, and the exacerbation of poverty for some groups of people.
*   Human actions are depleting Earth's natural capital, putting such strain on the environment that the ability of the planet's ecosystems to sustain future generations can no longer be taken for granted.
*   Reversing the degradation of ecosystems while meeting increasing demands for services will involve significant changes in policies, institutions and practices that are not currently underway. Many options exist to conserve or enhance specific ecosystem services in ways that reduce negative trade-offs or that provide positive synergies with other ecosystem services.
*   Some losses of ecosystem services were related to a mismatch between the scales at which ecosystem processes operate, and the scales at which institutions were effective. In other cases, factors such as governance and feedback control mechanisms, prices and property rights were found to operate at scales similar to those of ecosystem services. However, the assessment found that coordinated stewardship

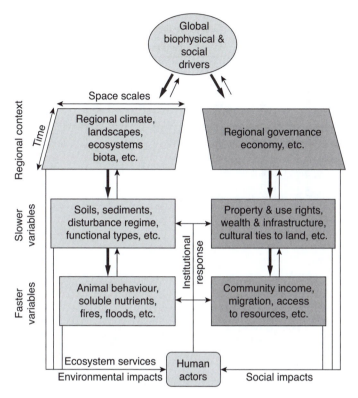

FIGURE 4.9   Illustration of a conceptual framework for integrated analysis of coupled social-ecological systems, highlighting the key issues of scales of both space and time, social-ecological interactions, dynamics of individual actors, and institutional responses

Source: Carpenter *et al.* (2009) modified from Chapin *et al.* (2006). Copyright (2006) National Academy of Sciences, USA.

of ecosystem services across multiple scales is difficult to achieve in practice (Carpenter *et al.*, 2009) (Figure 4.10).

The impact of the MEA was initially slow to take effect, but it has now undoubtedly left a major legacy in terms of both policy and scientific research (Diaz *et al.*, 2006; Carpenter *et al.*, 2009; Raudsepp-Hearne *et al.*, 2010). Many countries, including recently the UK (http://uknea.unep-wcmc.org/), have since undertaken their own national ecosystem assessments. Many national and international policy initiatives have been developed focusing on ecosystem services, as illustrated by the development of IPBES and the activities of the CBD.

Reflection point

Here we have focused on ecosystem services as the benefits provided by ecosystems to people. But can you think of any examples of the converse – situations where ecosystems might provide *disbenefits* or *disservices* to people?

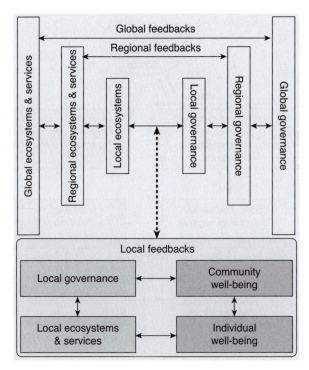

FIGURE 4.10   Links between governance and ecosystem services at multiple scales, and their relationship with human well-being

Source: Carpenter *et al.* (2009).

4.6 Valuing nature

4.6.1 Introduction

The concept of ecosystem services has been developed because decisions relating to economic development, such as those relating to land use, usually do not consider the economic value of the services provided by ecosystems. As a result, decisions are continually being made that lead to the loss and degradation of natural ecosystems, such as conversion of tropical forest to agricultural land. If the true value of ecosystems were recognised, it can be argued, then much greater emphasis would be placed on their conservation. In addition, the costs of finished goods and services might more accurately reflect the true environmental costs of their production.

A critical element of this logic is the economic valuation of ecosystem services. In order to factor ecosystem services into economic decision–making, an estimate of their economic value is required, in monetary units. This might sound like a straightforward proposition, but it is an area fraught with difficulty. Furthermore, the very idea of putting an economic value on nature is highly controversial, and is rejected strongly by some people. This debate is very active at present. The issue is also central to the green economy.

4.6.2 Valuing the world's ecosystem services

One of the most influential publications on this topic is that by Costanza *et al.* (1997), entitled 'The value of the world's ecosystem services and natural capital'. This was the first systematic attempt to provide an estimate of the value of the world's ecosystem services. Costanza *et al.* estimated the current economic value of 17 ecosystem services, for the entire biosphere, to be in the range of US$16–54 trillion per year, with an average of US$33 trillion per year. Most of this value is not captured in economic markets.

> **Reflection point**
>
> Costanza *et al.* (1997) note that these ecosystem services are not currently factored into economic decision-making; they are essentially being obtained for free. Consider why this is. Remember that many are common property resources, and therefore potentially subject to the 'tragedy of the commons' (see Chapter 2). Consider also not only the total value, but the range of values given – why is there such a high degree of uncertainty?

The figures presented by Costanza *et al.* (1997) are now out of date; the global economy has since grown (despite the recent economic crisis), as have levels of debt. One point is worth highlighting, however: the most valuable service identified by these authors, accounting for more than half of total value, was soil formation.

The results of this study were highly controversial, and generated a good deal of debate (e.g. see Pimm, 1997). For example, the journal *Ecological Economics* published a special forum on the topic in 1998 (Vol. 25, pp. 1–142). In this context, it is pertinent to consider the methods used by Costanza *et al.* (1997), which were primarily based on attempts to estimate the 'willingness-to-pay' of individuals for ecosystem services.

> **Reflection point**
>
> The 'willingness to pay' (WTP) technique is widely used by ecological economists. The methods can be used to measure either a consumer's hypothetical or actual willingness to pay, and do so either by direct or indirect measurement methods. One approach, for example, is to estimate the value of the WTP through a choice experiment, by presenting a potential customer with alternatives. Consider the strengths and weaknesses of this approach. Note also that WTP is constrained by an individual's wealth. Can you think of any other problems with the technique?

Costanza *et al.* (1997) also used supply and demand curves, which are used in much economic analysis (Figure 4.11; see also Chapter 1). As noted by these authors, demand curves for ecosystem services are very difficult, if not impossible, to estimate in practice. Also, as ecosystem services cannot readily be increased or decreased by actions of the economic system, their supply curves might be considered nearly vertical. Another important issue is the concept of 'substitution'. Economic analyses are often based on the assumption that one product or service can be substituted by another – for example, furniture made out of plastic might substitute for furniture made out of wood, leading to a decline in the demand for timber. Many ecosystem services cannot be substituted, however.

The MEA provides a number of examples of the valuation of ecosystem services in different countries, while highlighting the importance of considering their intrinsic value as well as their financial value. Intrinsic value can be defined as 'the value of something in and for itself, irrespective of its utility for someone else' (MEA, 2005c). The development of methods for assessing intrinsic value, and incorporating them in decision-making, remains a major challenge.

Analysis of the case studies considered by MEA (ibid.) suggested that the total economic value associated with managing ecosystems more sustainably is often higher than the value associated with the conversion of the ecosystem through farming, clear-cut logging, or other intensive uses. Some studies have found that the benefit of managing the ecosystem more sustainably can exceed that of converting the ecosystem, even when the monetary benefits would favour conversion or unsustainable management. However, relatively few such studies have been completed to date; evidence on this issue is therefore lacking.

The MEA (ibid.) also highlighted that market failures associated with ecosystem services can lead to greater conversion of ecosystems than is economically justified. 'Market failure' refers to a situation where the distribution of goods and services by a free market is not 'efficient', in economic terms. For example, the distribution of resources might be unfair, leading to inequality. Alternatively, economic activity might lead to costs imposed on a third party (for example, pollution emitted by a factory); such costs are termed 'negative externalities'. In such a case, prices in a competitive market would not reflect the full costs of producing or consuming a product or service. This is why the market is said to have 'failed'.

Reflection point

Why do you think the lack of economic valuation of ecosystem services might lead to market failure, as is widely believed?

While a wide range of methods are used to value ecosystem services (Box 4.1; Daily, 1997, Kumar, 2010), many studies employ a version of the total economic value (TEV) framework (Figure 4.12) (Pearce and Turner, 1990; Pearce and Moran, 1994).

One of the problems of the framework developed by the MEA was the risk of double-counting. For example, 'supporting services', such as nutrient cycling could support the production of other types of service, such as food crops. This could potentially lead the contribution of a particular service being counted twice. For this reason, Fisher *et al.* (2008) devised an alternative framework, which clearly separates out final services, or benefits, from what they term 'intermediate services'. These are the ecosystem processes (or functions) on which services depend (Figure 4.13). This provides a basis for a more robust valuation of ecosystem services.

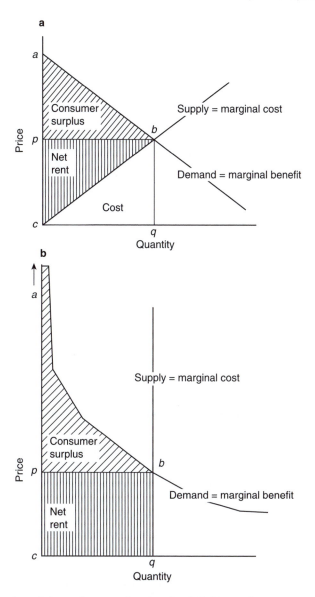

FIGURE 4.11 Supply and demand curves, showing the definitions of cost, net rent and consumer surplus for normal goods (a) and some essential ecosystem services (b).

Source: Costanza *et al.* (1997). Reprinted by permission from Macmillan Publishers Ltd: *Nature*, ©1997.

Fisher *et al.* (2008) also point out the importance of the concept of *marginality* for valuing ecosystem services. In other words, it is the changes in the provision of ecosystem services that are important to policy, not the value of the total stocks of natural capital. Progress with analysing such 'marginal changes' has come about through another recent initiative, The Economics of Ecosystems and Biodiversity (TEEB). This is a major collaborative project focusing on the valuation of ecosystem services (Kumar, 2010).

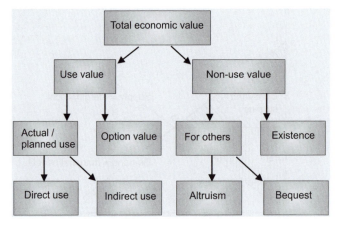

FIGURE 4.12   Overview of the 'total economic value' framework. *Direct use* may be either consumptive, which refers to the use of resources extracted from the ecosystem (such as food or timber), or non-consumptive, which is the use of services without extraction (such as recreation or amenity). An *option value* refers to the value that people place on having the option to use a resource in the future, even if they are not current users. *Bequest value* refers to the value that the ecosystem resource will be passed on to future generations, and *altruistic value* is the value attached to the service being available to others in the current generation. *Existence value* is the value associated with existence of the resource, even if the individual has no actual or planned use of it.

Source: After DEFRA (2007) and Balmford *et al.* (2008).

BOX 4.1 METHODS OF VALUING ECOSYSTEM SERVICES

Valuation methods fall broadly into two main types (after DEFRA, 2007):

1. *Economic valuation* focuses on expressing values of the environment in monetary terms. The main types of economic valuation methods available for estimating public preferences for changes in ecosystem services are:
    a. *Revealed preference* methods, which rely on market data regarding individuals' preferences for marketable services, and include market prices, hedonic pricing and the travel cost method.
    b. *Stated preference* methods use questionnaires to elicit individuals' preferences for a given change in a natural resource or environmental attribute. The main options in this approach are contingent valuation and choice modelling.
2. *Non-economic valuation* approaches express values in units other than money. Examples include qualitative semi-structured surveys, and group discussions.

Suggested activity

The website of TEEB (www.teebweb.org) provides access to a number of reports and other materials that are of relevance to this topic, which you are encouraged to explore.

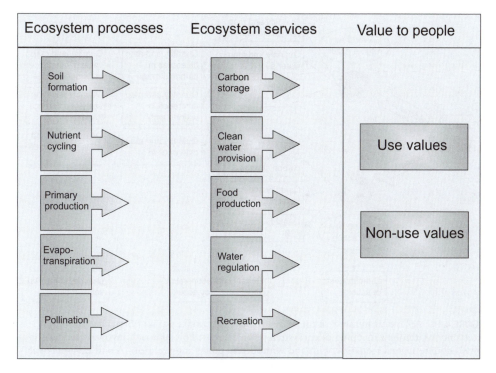

FIGURE 4.13 Stylised relationships among representative ecosystem processes, final ecosystems services, and different values to people as incorporated in the 'total economic value' framework

Source: Adapted from Fisher *et al.* (2008) and UK National Ecosystem Assessment (2011).

As part of the TEEB initiative, Balmford *et al.* (2008, 2011) presented a framework for analysing the marginal costs and benefits of different policy interventions or management actions, in a robust way (Figure 4.14). This focuses on the mapping of ecosystem services, recognising the value of spatial data for supporting land management decisions.

With contributions such as those of Fisher *et al.* (2008) and Balmford *et al.* (2011), improved approaches for the valuation of ecosystem services are being developed. Nevertheless, any attempt to estimate such values will necessarily be subject to a high degree of uncertainty, simply because many values are difficult to value with precision, particularly when they lie outside financial markets. This should be borne in mind when considering any information relating to ecosystem services.

4.6.3 Should we place an economic value on nature?

The economic valuation of ecosystem services – essentially, the economic valuation of nature – is itself a very controversial topic. Should it be done at all? Does it even represent the 'ultimate triumph of the neoliberal agenda', as some commentators have suggested (Monbiot, 2011)?

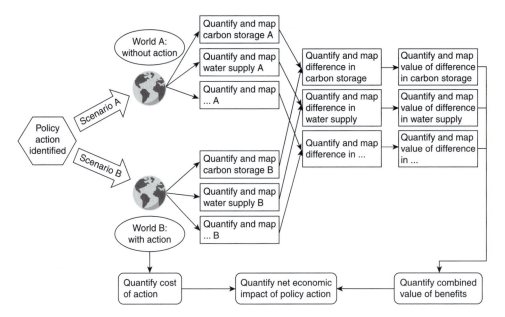

FIGURE 4.14 Analytical framework for estimating the marginal costs and benefits of policy interventions, through mapping of ecosystem service values. The approach involves comparison of two counterfactual scenarios, with and without the policy intervention (A and B, respectively). Ecosystem services are mapped for each scenario, and the marginal costs and benefits derived by calculating the difference between the two scenarios.

Source: After Balmford *et al.* (2008).

In an influential study, Balmford *et al.* (2002) reviewed more than 300 case studies providing estimates of the marginal values of services delivered by ecosystems when relatively intact, and when converted to typical forms of human use. This evidence showed that natural ecosystems generate significant economic benefits, which exceed those obtained from habitat conversion. These authors estimated that the overall benefit: cost ratio of an effective global program for biodiversity conservation is at least 100:1.

Other authors have similarly highlighted the importance of valuing nature, in order to both increase investments in biodiversity conservation and support human well-being (Bockstael *et al.*, 2000; Daily *et al.*, 2000; Daily *et al.*, 2009). However, others have argued against this approach. For example, McCauley (2006) identifies a number of risks associated with placing an economic value on nature, and suggests that nature has an intrinsic value that makes it priceless, and this is reason enough to protect it. Similarly, Rull (2010) suggests that the adoption of market perspectives to manage biodiversity could accelerate its loss, as not all species are required to meet human needs. If environmental decisions are fundamentally framed as questions of economic welfare, it can be argued that 'public officials and the public itself will opt nearly every time for whatever policy promises more economic growth, more production, and more jobs' (Sagoff, 2012).

Reflection point

Do you think that people should attempt to place an economic value on nature, or not? What are the potential risks of either doing so, or conversely, of not doing so?

4.7 Impacts of biodiversity loss

4.7.1 Introduction

What are the actual or likely consequences of biodiversity loss, and other forms of environmental change, for the provision of ecosystem services? Given that biodiversity loss is primarily caused by human actions related to different forms of economic activity, understanding the answer to this question is highly relevant to developing the green economy. Analyses based on scenarios and models suggest that future changes could be profound (Millennium Ecosystem Assessment, 2005a; Schroter *et al.*, 2005; Pereira *et al.*, 2010). Some specific examples are considered below.

4.7.2 A theoretical example

Few researchers have explicitly examined what the implications of biodiversity loss for provision of ecosystem services might be. One example is provided by Dobson *et al.* (2006), who concluded that:

*   Because different ecosystem services tend to be provided by species at different trophic levels, and because food webs will tend first to thin and then to collapse from top to bottom, we would expect to see a predictable sequential loss of ecosystem services as ecosystems become degraded by anthropogenic activities.
*   Ecosystem services provided by species at high trophic levels will disappear before those provided by species at the bottom of the food chain.

Reflection point

The implications of this research are profound. At present, conservation action is primarily focused on charismatic species, such as wolves, lions and tigers, which are mostly of higher trophic levels (in other words, they are at a higher position in a food web). Some people have argued (e.g. Thompson, 2010) that this emphasis is misplaced, and that conservation action should instead prioritise those species that play a major functional role in ecosystems, such as fungi and bacteria. Yet the conclusions of Dobson *et al.* (2006) are that species of high trophic levels *should* be the focus of conservation efforts. What do you think?

The study by Dobson *et al.* (2006) was based on an analytical model rather than empirical evidence. So, what empirical evidence is available of such impacts of biodiversity loss? Let us explore a few examples.

4.7.3 Birds

Sekercioğlu *et al.* (2004) investigated the potential ecological consequences of avian declines, by developing a database of the status and functional roles of birds together with a model for forecasting change. These authors showed that a quarter or more of frugivorous and omnivorous species, and one-third or more of herbivorous, piscivorous, and scavenger species, are currently at risk of extinction. By 2100, these authors estimate that 6–14 per cent of all bird species will be extinct, and 7–25 per cent will be functionally extinct. Important ecosystem processes, particularly decomposition, pollination, and seed dispersal, will likely decline as a result. Also, declines in pollination and seed dispersal as a result of bird extinctions may lead to extinctions of dependent plant species.

4.7.4 Bees

Concern about widespread declines in bees and other insect pollinators has grown significantly in recent years. According to UNEP (2010), out of some 100 crop species that provide 90 per cent of food worldwide, 71 are bee-pollinated. In Europe, 84 per cent of the 264 crop species are animal pollinated and 4,000 vegetable varieties depend on pollination by bees. Overall, the contribution of pollinators to the production of crops used directly for human food has been estimated at €153 billion globally, which is about 9.5 per cent of the total value of human food production worldwide.

Are pollinators declining in number? A dramatic decline has been recorded in the number of honey-producing bee colonies in the USA and Europe in recent decades, which is often attributed to 'colony collapse disorder' (CCD). The reasons for the collapse of colonies are complex and are poorly understood, but the introduction of parasitic mites has been one contributory factor. Unknown infectious agents or disease may be another. Although dramatic, CCD currently accounts for about 7 per cent of losses in the USA and even less in Europe; the loss of queen bees seems to be a much more common cause of declines in bee colonies, accounting for about 25 per cent (UNEP, 2010).

It is important to note that most commercial honey production employs domesticated bees, which are usually non-native species or strains. In that sense, declines in honeybee colonies could perhaps be considered equivalent to declines in other domesticated animals, such as the death of cattle caused by rinderpest. On the other hand, populations of wild pollinators are also declining rapidly. For example, in the UK, 71 per cent of butterfly species have decreased and 3.4 per cent became extinct over the past 20 years (ibid.).

4.7.5 Ocean ecosystems

The potential impact of biodiversity loss in marine ecosystems on the provision of ecosystem services was explored by Worm *et al.* (2006), who projected the global collapse of all taxa currently fished by the mid-twenty-first century. These authors also suggested that the elimination of locally adapted populations and species will impair the ability of marine ecosystems to feed a growing human population, and also undermine their stability and recovery potential. The results of this study were criticised, however, for the statistical methods used (see Holker *et al.*, 2007).

4.7.6 Forests

A recent study examined the relationship between tree species richness and provision of multiple ecosystem services across a scale of 400,000 km^2 (Gamfeldt *et al.*, 2013). The authors concluded that tree species richness in production forests showed positive to positively hump-shaped relationships with multiple ecosystem services, including production of tree biomass, soil carbon storage, berry production and game production potential. This highlights the need to maintain multiple tree species in production forests.

4.8 Response options: sustainable use and protected areas

4.8.1 Introduction

Great progress has been made in recent decades in terms of changing attitudes towards the value of biodiversity, and in terms of taking practical steps towards addressing the causes of biodiversity loss. The fact that such efforts have only been partially successful, though, highlights the enormity of the challenge.

Essentially, there are three main approaches to biodiversity conservation: (1) protection, through designation of some form of protected area; (2) sustainable use, including the sustainable harvesting of wildlife; and (3) ecological restoration. Here we consider these approaches specifically in relation to the provision of ecosystem services, which provides a mechanism for exploring the value of nature to people. First, we will briefly consider what some leading researchers have said about approaches to biodiversity conservation.

4.8.2 Can we defy nature's end?

Over a decade ago, a paper with the provocative title 'Can we defy nature's end?' was published, as a collaborative venture between a number of eminent conservation scientists (Pimm *et al.*, 2001). Overall, the authors concluded that preventing extinctions is practical, but requires innovative measures. The principal recommendation focused on the need for enforceable protection of remaining natural ecosystems. The authors then considered whether protecting biodiversity is economically possible, indicating that a global reserve network covering ~15 per cent of each continent might cost ~US$30 billion annually. Although this is a sizeable sum, it is 1/1000th the value of the ecosystem services provided by Costanza *et al.* (1997).

In addition to increasing biodiversity protection, for example through parks and reserves, the authors also considered actions designed to address the economic factors responsible for biodiversity loss. These include tax savings, transferable development rights, and mitigation credits to private, public or indigenous landowners to secure economic benefits from biodiversity and ecosystem services. They also suggested amending policies, to reduce so-called 'perverse subsidies', which are a major cause of biodiversity loss (Myers and Kent, 2001). These governmental measures maintain resource prices for producers and consumers below market levels, thereby encouraging resource over-exploitation and associated environmental problems. Estimates of the total value of perverse subsidies vary between US$950 billion (van Beers and de Moor, 1999) and US$1450 billion per year globally (Myers, 1998).

Many other researchers have similarly considered how best to prevent biodiversity loss. Their conclusions are not always the same. For example, Ehrlich and Pringle (2008) highlight 'seven strategies that, if implemented soundly and scaled up dramatically, would preserve a substantial portion of global biodiversity'. These are:

- actions to stabilise the human population and reduce its material consumption;
- the deployment of endowment funds and other strategies to ensure the efficacy and permanence of conservation areas;
- steps to make human-dominated landscapes hospitable to biodiversity;
- measures to account for the economic costs of habitat degradation;
- the ecological reclamation of degraded lands and repatriation of extirpated species;
- the education and empowerment of people in the rural tropics;
- the fundamental transformation of human attitudes to nature.

The authors point out that the science and technologies needed to implement this strategy already exist; the remaining challenges are largely social, political and economic.

4.8.3 Ecosystem approaches

Chapin *et al.* (2010) take a rather different approach to biodiversity conservation, which is very much grounded in 'systems thinking' concepts (see Chapter 2). Their approach focuses on what they refer to as 'ecosystem stewardship', which is described as an 'action-oriented framework intended to foster the social-ecological sustainability of a rapidly changing planet'. This approach has particular relevance to the green economy, given its primary focus on sustainability and maintenance of ecosystem services. The approach focuses on three strategies, namely, (1) reducing the magnitude of, and exposure and sensitivity to, known stresses; (2) focusing on proactive policies that shape change; and (3) avoiding or escaping unsustainable social-ecological traps. Ecosystem stewardship integrates three broadly overlapping sustainability approaches: (1) reducing vulnerability to expected changes; (2) fostering resilience to sustain desirable conditions in the face of perturbations and uncertainty; and (3) transforming from undesirable trajectories when opportunities emerge.

The shift to 'ecosystem stewardship' advocated by these authors focuses on maintaining multiple ecosystem services, rather than exploitation of individual species. The focus on vulnerability, resilience, transformation and adaptive capacity, and also the concept of considering human communities and the environment as parts of integrated social-ecological systems, is very much based on the concepts that were explored in Chapter 2. The focus is on maintenance of entire social-ecological systems, and the provision of ecosystem services, rather than biodiversity *per se*. How might this be achieved in practice? Some recommendations suggested by Chapin *et al.* (2010) are listed below:

- Maintain a diversity of options.
- Subsidise innovations that foster socio-economic novelty and diversity.
- Renew the functional diversity of degraded systems.
- Prioritise conservation of biodiversity hotspots and pathways that enable species to adjust to rapid environmental change.

- Sustain a diversity of cultures, languages and knowledge systems that provide multiple approaches to meeting societal goals.
- Enhance social learning to facilitate adaptation.
- Broaden the problem definition and knowledge co-production by engaging multiple disciplinary perspectives and knowledge systems.
- Use scenarios and simulations to explore consequences of alternative policy options.
- Develop transparent information systems and mapping tools that contribute to developing trust among decision-makers and stakeholders, and build support for action.
- Adapt governance to implement potential solutions.

Reflection point

Note the emphasis here on maintaining diversity to maintain adaptability and resilience of entire systems. Note also how this approach explicitly recognises environmental change, and seeks to identify ways of adapting to such change, rather than resist or prevent it.

An example of ecosystem-based management in practice is provided by Olsson *et al.* (2008) for the Great Barrier Reef in Australia, and Lester *et al.* (2010) provide a further marine example focusing on the US West Coast.

4.8.4 Protected areas

It is generally recognised that the establishment of protected areas provides the most effective method of conserving biodiversity, and this is reflected in the central role that they play in most national conservation strategies. A protected area is defined by the IUCN (Dudley, 2008) as: 'A clearly defined geographical space, recognised, dedicated and managed, through legal or other effective means, to achieve the long-term conservation of nature with associated ecosystem services and cultural values.'

The term 'protected area' refers to a wide range of different designations, some of the best known of which include *national park, nature reserve, wilderness area, wildlife management area* and *landscape protected area* (ibid.). Protected areas may be managed with a wide range of different approaches, ranging from sites with a high degree of protection from which people are largely excluded, through areas where the emphasis is on conservation but visitors are welcome, to less restrictive approaches where conservation is integrated with some form of sustainable resource extraction, such as the hunting of wildlife (Stolton and Dudley, 2010).

Chape *et al.* (2005) provide an overview of the global network of protected areas. These authors highlight how the number of protected areas has increased over time, a trend that is still continuing today. The protected areas that have been designated represent around 12 per cent of the Earth's terrestrial surface. Parties to the CBD recently committed themselves to raise this figure to 17 per cent by 2020. This is a powerful indication of the extent to which the current biodiversity crisis is being recognised globally, and provides an important example of the increasing efforts that are being undertaken to address the problem. However, as noted by Chape *et al.*, many protected areas are not fully effective in conserving biodiversity. Also some ecosystem types, such as marine systems, remain relatively unprotected.

The main threats to protected areas are summarised by Carey *et al.* (2000) as:

- Individual elements removed from the protected area without alteration to the overall structure (e.g. animal species used as bushmeat, exotic plants or over-fishing of specific species).
- Overall impoverishment of the ecology of the protected area (e.g. through encroachment, long-term air pollution damage or persistent poaching pressure).
- Major conversion and degradation (e.g. through the removal of vegetation cover, constructing roads through the protected area, major settlements or mining).
- Isolation of protected areas (e.g. through major conversion of surrounding land).

In the context of the green economy, a key issue is the extent to which people benefit from protected areas. The concept of ecosystem services has only recently been considered in relation to the planning and management of protected areas. However, as pointed out by Dudley (2008), it is possible to identify a range of benefits to people that might be provided by a protected area, including opportunities for recreation and the health benefits that these provide, the genetic potential of wild species, provision of water, and aesthetic, cultural or spiritual values. On the other hand, protected areas can also provide 'dis-benefits' to people, for example by limiting or preventing their traditional land-use activities. In the past, many people have been forcibly removed from protected areas, and those human communities living within such areas may be negatively affected by the activities of wildlife (for example, through losses of crops). Such conflicts have led to the development of a new paradigm for protected areas, in which meeting the needs of local people is a central objective (Phillips, 2003). Features of this new paradigm include management for socio–economic objectives as well as biodiversity conservation, as illustrated by the development of community-based and collaborative approaches to protected areas management (Lockwood *et al.*, 2006).

4.8.5 Sustainable use of species

Many individual species are being harvested unsustainably, which is a major cause of biodiversity loss. If species could be harvested sustainably, then potentially such natural resources could be considered as part of the green economy. How, then, can sustainable use of species be achieved in practice?

First, it is important to note that this is a highly controversial subject. Many people do not believe that hunting or killing of wildlife is justifiable, on ethical grounds. On the other hand, it is important to note just how widespread such hunting is. This is exemplified by what has been termed the 'bushmeat' crisis, which refers to the unsustainable harvesting of wildlife for human consumption. This is widely recognised to be a major cause of biodiversity loss, particularly in parts of Africa (Milner-Gulland and Bennett, 2003). Another related issue is the trade in wildlife (including wildlife parts).

Suggested activity

Search for information on the bushmeat crisis on the internet, for example, by exploring the following links:

- http://www.bushmeat.org
- http://www.bushmeatcrisisafrica.com
- http://bushmeat.net
- http://www.janegoodall.ca/chimps-issues-bushmeat-crisis.php

Analysis of the wildlife trade is the focus of TRAFFIC (www.traffic.org), a non-governmental organisation. The World Wildlife Fund (WWF) is also working to address the threat of the illegal wildlife trade (WWF, 2013). According to TRAFFIC (2013), the wildlife trade currently involves hundreds of millions of individual plants and animals from tens of thousands of species, with timber and seafood being the most important categories both in terms of volume and value. The Food and Agriculture Organization (FAO) statistics suggest that around US$100 billion of fish and US$200 billion timber are currently traded annually. In 2009, TRAFFIC estimated the value of legal imports of wildlife products to be over US$323 billion globally. The size of the illegal wildlife trade is difficult to estimate with precision, but is considered to be around US$8–10 billion per year, with the illegal timber trade amounting to around US$7 billion per year. The value of illegal and unregulated fisheries may be more than twice that.

Addressing the illegal wildlife trade would require issues of governance and law to be addressed, as explored in Chapter 6. The scientific principles on which sustainable harvesting can be based are relatively well established, particularly for economically valuable resources such as fisheries (Milner-Gulland and Mace, 1998). Commonly, these principles are based on the use of bio-economic models (e.g. Ling and Milner-Gulland, 2006). However, there has been a widespread failure to apply these principles to the management of wild resources (Milner-Gulland and Mace, 1998; Ludwig, 2001).

Although the maximum sustainable yield (MSY) concept has traditionally been used to identify sustainable approaches to the harvesting of species, this approach is now being extended towards more integrated, systems models, which include a human component. The effective use of such models is dependent on accurate data on variables such as the size of the stock of the species, its reproductive ability, and the amount being harvested. Accurate information on such variables is often difficult to obtain, particularly for relatively elusive species (such as fish) or when a large number of people are involved in harvesting activities. As a result, such models are often associated with a high degree of uncertainty.

4.9 Response options: ecological restoration

4.9.1 Introduction

The green economy is based on the idea of avoiding environmental degradation. Such degradation has occurred very widely as a result of human activities, including urban expansion, agricultural intensification, mining and harvesting of species. Are there approaches that not only can prevent further environmental degradation, but can also facilitate some form of ecological recovery?

Ecological restoration aims to achieve precisely this. In the context of the green economy, ecological restoration can increase the natural capital on which the economy is built. Restoration has grown rapidly over the past few decades, both in terms of a scientific discipline and in terms of environmental management practice. Billions of dollars are now being invested in restoration actions throughout the world (Goldstein *et al.*, 2008), supported by international policy commitments such as the CBD (Normile, 2010). Consequently, ecological restoration is now making a significant contribution to sustainable development (Nellemann and Corcoran, 2010). Many environmental organisations and community groups are actively engaged in ecological restoration projects, but increasingly restoration actions are also being undertaken by other organisations, including governments and large companies.

Ecological restoration can involve the recovery or reintroduction of populations of individual species. However, the focus here is on restoration of ecosystems or ecological communities.

4.9.2 Aims and approaches

The term 'ecological restoration' has been defined in many different ways by different authors, and definitions have changed over time as the principles and practice of restoration have evolved. A widely used definition is provided by the Society of Ecological Restoration (SER, 2004): 'Ecological restoration is the process of assisting the recovery of an ecosystem that has been degraded, damaged, or destroyed.'

A number of related terms are widely used in the literature. *Rehabilitation* emphasises ecosystem recovery, without including the re-establishment of some pre-existing state as a management goal. *Reclamation* generally refers to the environmental improvement of mined lands, and may incorporate soil stabilisation and aesthetic improvement. In this case, there may be less emphasis on restoring the original biodiversity present at a degraded site, and greater emphasis on restoring productivity or soil stabilisation.

SER (2004) provides further information on the principles of ecological restoration. The attributes listed below provide a basis for determining when restoration has been accomplished (ibid.):

1. The restored ecosystem contains a characteristic assemblage of the species that occur in the reference (i.e. undegraded) ecosystem, and that provide appropriate community structure.
2. The restored ecosystem consists of indigenous species to the greatest practicable extent. In restored cultural ecosystems, allowances can be made for exotic domesticated species and for non-invasive ruderal and agricultural species, which presumably co-evolved with them.
3. All functional groups necessary for the continued development and/or stability of the restored ecosystem are represented or, if they are not, the missing groups have the potential to colonise by natural means.

4. The physical environment of the restored ecosystem is capable of sustaining reproducing populations of the species necessary for its continued stability or development along the desired trajectory.
5. The restored ecosystem apparently functions normally for its ecological stage of development, and signs of dysfunction are absent.
6. The restored ecosystem is suitably integrated into a larger ecological matrix or landscape, with which it interacts through abiotic and biotic flows and exchanges.
7. Potential threats to the health and integrity of the restored ecosystem from the surrounding landscape have been eliminated or reduced as much as possible.
8. The restored ecosystem is sufficiently resilient to endure the normal periodic stress events in the local environment that serve to maintain the integrity of the ecosystem.

Reflection point

These attributes provide a useful set of principles of ecological restoration. However, it is important to note that they are just one set of proposals – other perspectives might differ. For example, is the near-exclusive focus on indigenous or native species that is proposed here necessarily appropriate?

Suggested activity

The SER website (www.ser.org) provides a great deal of information on the topic, which is well worth exploring. This includes a useful primer on ecological restoration, and details of practical restoration projects in different parts of the world.

Different approaches to restoration vary in terms of their relative cost, their benefits to biodiversity and their potential impact on provision of ecological services, such as water regulation and nutrient cycling. In general, the preferred method is to allow the ecosystem to recover naturally through a process of succession, a process referred to as 'passive restoration'. For such successional recovery to occur, the following conditions must be met (Lamb and Gilmour, 2003):

*   *The disturbing agent or agents must be removed*. If disturbances such as fire, timber harvesting or grazing continue, succession is interrupted and recovery is unlikely.
*   *Plants and animals must remain at the site* or in the region as a source of new colonists, and must be able to move across the landscape and recolonise the degraded area. The more distant these source populations are, the slower the recolonisation process. Potentially, connecting habitat fragments can increase the rate of the recovery process. This is an argument for planning restoration at the landscape scale, and for the development of 'ecological networks' in which ecosystems are connected spatially.

- *Soils at the site must remain reasonably intact.* If severe erosion has taken place or if fertility has been depleted, the soils may no longer be suitable for the original species, and other species (perhaps not native to the area) may come to dominate.
- *Weed species, invasive exotic species or animal pests must be excluded or controlled* if the original community is to be re-established successfully.

An alternative to passive restoration is offered by 'active restoration' approaches, which involve the introduction of species to an area, for example, through tree planting. Such approaches may be preferred where the site is so degraded that passive approaches are unlikely to succeed.

4.9.3 Outcomes of ecological restoration

Evidence suggests that ecological restoration can be effective in enhancing both biodiversity and provision of ecosystem services (Rey Benayas *et al.*, 2009; Birch *et al.*, 2010; Bullock *et al.*, 2011). Nellemann and Corcoran (2010) highlight how ecological restoration can contribute to improved water supply, health and wastewater management, food security, disaster prevention and mitigation, and climate change mitigation. An example is given of the Golden Horn Estuary, in the centre of Istanbul, Turkey, where over 40 years of uncontrolled industrial and urban growth caused major damage to local water resources. The major components of rehabilitation, which took place over two decades, included: (1) demolition and relocation of industries and homes along the shore; (2) creation of wastewater infrastructure; (3) removal of anoxic sludge from the estuary; (4) removal of a floating bridge that impeded circulation; and (5) creation of cultural and social facilities. These efforts were largely successful in revitalising the area through dramatic water quality improvements. This provides a prime example of how ecological rehabilitation can be successfully achieved in spite of inadequate management funds, institutions, policies and legal structure.

Suggested activity

There are many successful examples of ecological restoration available on the internet; you are encouraged to explore these resources. Some examples are listed below:

- New York City Watershed, USA and Chesapeake Bay, USA (www.esa.org/ecoservices/wate/body.wate.case.case.html).
- The restoration of the Florida Everglades, one of the largest ecological restoration projects in the world (www.evergladesplan.org).
- Oostvaardersplassen in the Netherlands, one of the best-known examples of habitat restoration at the landscape scale, in the largest freshwater wetland in NW Europe (www.staatsbosbeheer.nl/english/oostvaardersplassen.aspx).
- The Great Fen project, eastern England (www.greatfen.org.uk).
- The Carrifran Wildwood Project, Scotland (www.carrifran.org.uk).
- Trees for Life, Scotland (www.treesforlife.org.uk).
- Auroville, India (www.auroville.org/environment/env_introduction.htm).
- Greening Australia (www.greeningaustralia.org.au).

4.10 Linking with the green economy

4.10.1 Introduction

This section briefly considers how biodiversity and ecosystem services can be integrated with the green economy.

4.10.2 How much does conservation cost?

What are the costs of establishing and managing protected areas? A number of researchers have examined this question. For example, James *et al.* (2001) estimated that an annual total of US$6 billion is spent on management of the global protected area network. Some 88 per cent of this is spent in developed countries. These authors note that protected areas can impose significant opportunity costs on local communities, especially in developing countries. These can result from the loss of access to resources or development opportunities when a protected area is established. James *et al.* therefore suggested that direct financial compensation should be provided to address the opportunity costs associated with reserves. These authors provided a total cost estimate for a comprehensive global biodiversity conservation programme to be approximately US$317 billion annually.

The issue of conservation costs was further considered by Balmford *et al.* (2003), who found that the annual costs of effective field-based conservation vary enormously, from <US$0.1 to >US$1,000,000 per km^2. Corresponding measures of conservation benefit are limited but show opposing global trends, being higher in less developed parts of the world. More recently, McCarthy *et al.* (2012) estimated the cost of reducing the extinction risk of all globally threatened bird species (by ≥1 IUCN Red List category) to be US$0.875–1.23 billion annually over the next decade. These authors also estimated that protecting and effectively managing all terrestrial sites of global avian conservation significance (11,731 Important Bird Areas) would cost US$65.1 billion annually.

4.10.3 How can the costs of conservation be met?

The issue of who should pay for conservation, and how these costs might be met, is explored by Balmford and Whitten (2003). These authors first identify three potential groups of stakeholders:

- local people, living in or near the area targeted by a conservation intervention such as a park;
- the national community, which includes locally based commercial elites but consists mainly of more distant stakeholders;
- the global community of concerned individuals, businesses, non-governmental organisations (NGOs), governments and inter-governmental organisations.

These authors then consider who benefits from conservation, in relation to five classes of benefits, namely:

1. sustainable consumption of conserved resources for food, timber and other fibres, and medicines;
2. nature-based tourism;

3. localised ecosystem services such as regulation of water supply, prevention and reduction of storm and flood damage, and erosion and sedimentation control;
4. more widely dispersed ecosystem services such as nutrient and climate regulation and carbon storage; and
5. option, existence and bequest values.

Who should pay for these benefits? Balmford and Whitten suggest the greatest contribution to meeting the currently unmet costs of tropical conservation should come from the global community, followed by national and then local stakeholders. They then suggest three main methods of achieving this in practice, through:

* increased individual donations;
* bringing the market to bear;
* expanding direct contributions from governments.

The second of these could partly be achieved through the extension of existing markets, by consumers choosing to invest in environmentally responsible companies or paying premium prices for certified products that have been sustainably harvested (e.g. Forest Stewardship Council, Marine Stewardship Council, Marine Aquarium Council, etc.). Other market-based initiatives involve creating entirely new markets through which beneficiaries pay producers for the provision of ecosystem services (see Section 4.10.4).

4.10.4 Integrating conservation with sustainable development

Traditional approaches to implementation of protected areas have often led to negative impacts on local people (Kilbane Gockel and Gray, 2009). Latterly, conservation approaches have increasingly focused on integrating biodiversity conservation with sustainable development approaches. The integrated conservation and development project (ICDP) approach became particularly popular for working with communities in or around protected areas. Principally funded by both international conservation and development organisations, such projects were viewed as a way to incorporate models of sustainable development into conservation (ibid.). Critiques of this approach have identified widespread failure, as a result of a lack of monitoring and evaluation, uncertain financial sustainability and low benefit generation (Wells *et al.*, 2004). Mistry *et al.* (2010) suggest that such problems could potentially be overcome by 'a more integrative, holistic and adaptive approach to project development, monitoring and evaluation', explicitly referring to the concept of coupled social-ecological systems explored in Chapter 2.

Reflection point

How do you think a 'systems approach' might help integrate biodiversity conservation with sustainable development?

4.10.5 Payments for Ecosystem Services (PES)

Payments for Ecosystem Services (PES) represent a relatively new approach, which is attracting increasing attention as a potential mechanism to finance biodiversity conservation.

In principle, the concept of a PES scheme is simple: the users of a particular ecosystem service should pay those responsible for producing it. A good example is provided by the provision of water for the city of New York by landowners in the Catskills Mountains (see www. nycwatershed.org). A PES scheme has also been introduced in the Florida Everglades (Bohlen *et al.*, 2009).

In recent years, hundreds of new PES initiatives have been introduced in different parts of the world (Tallis *et al.*, 2008). For example Costa Rica, Mexico, and China have introduced large-scale programmes that give direct payments to landowners for undertaking specific land use practices that could increase the provision of hydrological services, biodiversity conservation, erosion prevention, carbon sequestration, or scenic beauty (Jack *et al.*, 2008; Liu *et al.*, 2008). The effectiveness of such schemes depends on providing environmental benefits at relatively low cost. Such costs do not only include direct implementation costs, but also the transaction costs of the programme (such as those involved in contract negotiation) and the 'opportunity costs', which are the value of the alternative productive uses of the resource that have been foregone (Jack *et al.*, 2008). The cost-effectiveness of PES depends crucially on programme design (Engel *et al.*, 2008).

A wide variety of different PES schemes have been developed, which differ in the type and scale of ecosystem services included, the payment source, the type of activity paid for, the performance measures used, and the amounts paid. Engel *et al.* (2008) highlight an important distinction between user-financed PES, in which the buyers are the users of the ecosystem services, and government-financed PES, in which the buyers are others (typically the government) acting on behalf of service users. From the perspective of recipients, PES acts like an environmental subsidy, as the payments are aimed at supporting increases in environmentally beneficial activities.

How effective are PES schemes? Research on this aspect is lacking, though the available evidence suggests that different PES schemes have produced a wide variety of results. Particular concerns relate to whether the benefits of such programs will continue once the payments end. One of the advantages of PES schemes is that they address the fact that biodiversity conservation is often not 'win–win': rather, activities that are desirable from a conservation point of view are often unattractive to farmers, loggers, fishers and others who use ecosystems directly (Wunder *et al.*, 2008). The idea of providing compensation to those who provide ecosystem services should, in theory, be a more efficient way of achieving biodiversity conservation. However, in practice, the potential benefits of PES schemes have not always been realised. One key finding is that user-financed programmes tend to be better targeted, are more closely tailored to local conditions and needs, and have better monitoring than government-financed programmes (ibid.).

Suggested activity

There are now very many PES schemes in operation. You might like to explore the following links, which profile some examples and initiatives:

- Ecosystem Marketplace: http://www.ecosystemmarketplace.com
- IIED: http://www.iied.org/markets-payments-for-environmental-services
- Katoomba Group: http://www.katoombagroup.org/

Note that the REDD$^+$ initiative, which focuses on actions to support carbon storage, is a further example of a PES scheme (in fact, it is the largest in existence) (see Chapter 3).

Reflection point

What do you think would be needed to ensure that a PES scheme is successful?

Bibliography

Balmford, A., Bruner, A., Cooper, P., *et al.* 2002. Economic reasons for conserving wild nature. *Science*, 297: 950–953.

Balmford, A., Fisher, B., Green, R. E., *et al.* 2011. Bringing ecosystem services into the real world: an operational framework for assessing the economic consequences of losing wild nature. *Environmental & Resource Economics*, 48: 161–175.

Balmford, A., Gaston, K. J., Blyth, S., *et al.* 2003. Global variation in terrestrial conservation costs, conservation benefits, and unmet conservation needs. *Proceedings of the National Academy of Sciences of the United States of America*, 100: 1046–1050.

Balmford, A., Rodrigues, A. S. L., Walpole, M., *et al.* 2008. *The Economics of Ecosystems and Biodiversity: Scoping the Science*, European Commission (contract: ENV/070307/2007/486089/ETU/B2), Cambridge.

Balmford, A. and Whitten, T. 2003. Who should pay for tropical conservation, and how could the costs be met? *Oryx*, 37: 238–250.

Barnosky, A. D., Matzke, N., Tomiya, S., *et al.* 2011. Has the Earth's sixth mass extinction already arrived? *Nature*, 471: 51–57.

Bascompte, J. and Stouffer, D. B. 2009. The assembly and disassembly of ecological networks. *Philosophical Transactions of the Royal Society B: Biological Sciences*, 364: 1781–1787.

BBC 2010. Biodiversity – a kind of washing powder? *BBC News Science & Environment*, 16 October 2010. [Online]. Available at: www.bbc.co.uk/news/science-environment-11546289 (accessed 19 Nov. 2013).

Benayas, J. M. R., Newton, A. C., Diaz, A. and Bullock, J. M. 2009. Enhancement of biodiversity and ecosystem services by ecological restoration: a meta-analysis. *Science*, 325: 1121–1124.

Birch, J. C., Newton, A. C., Aquino, C. A., *et al.* 2010. Cost-effectiveness of dryland forest restoration evaluated by spatial analysis of ecosystem services. *Proceedings of the National Academy of Sciences of the United States of America*, 107: 21925–21930.

Bockstael, N. E., Freeman, A. M., Kopp, R. J., Portney, P. R. and Smith, V. K. 2000. On measuring economic values for nature. *Environmental Science & Technology*, 34: 1384–1389.

Bohlen, P. J., Lynch, S., Shabman, L., *et al.* 2009. Paying for environmental services from agricultural lands: an example from the northern Everglades. *Frontiers in Ecology and the Environment*, 7: 46–55.

Boyce, D. G., Lewis, M. R. and Worm, B. 2010. Global phytoplankton decline over the past century. *Nature*, 466: 591–596.

Bullock, J. M., Aronson, J., Newton, A. C., *et al.* 2011. Restoration of ecosystem services and biodiversity: conflicts and opportunities. *Trends in Ecology & Evolution*, 26: 541–549.

Butchart, S. H. M., Walpole, M., Collen, B., *et al.* 2010. Global biodiversity: indicators of recent declines. *Science*, 328: 1164–1168.

Caldecott, J. and Miles, L. (eds) 2005. *World Atlas of Great Apes and Their Conservation*, University of California Press: Berkeley, CA.

Carey, C., Dudley, N. and Stolton, S. 2000. *Squandering Paradise?*, WWF International, Gland, Switzerland.

Carpenter, S. R., Mooney, H. A., Agard, J., *et al.* 2009. Science for managing ecosystem services: beyond the Millennium Ecosystem Assessment. *Proceedings of the National Academy of Sciences of the United States of America*, 106: 1305–1312.

Chape, S., Harrison, J., Spalding, M. and Lysenko, I. 2005. Measuring the extent and effectiveness of protected areas as an indicator for meeting global biodiversity targets. *Philosophical Transactions of the Royal Society B: Biological Sciences*, 360: 443–455.

Chapin, F. S., Carpenter, S. R., Kofinas, G. P., et al. 2010. Ecosystem stewardship: sustainability strategies for a rapidly changing planet. *Trends in Ecology & Evolution*, 25: 241–249.

Chapin, F. S., Lovecraft, A. L., Zavaleta, E. S., et al. 2006. Policy strategies to address sustainability of Alaskan boreal forests in response to a directionally changing climate. *Proceedings of the National Academy of Sciences of the United States of America*, 103: 16637–16643.

Chapin, F. S., Zavaleta, E. S., Eviner, V. T., et al. 2000. Consequences of changing biodiversity. *Nature*, 405: 234–242.

Christensen, V., Guenette, S., Heymans, J. J., et al. 2003. Hundred-year decline of North Atlantic predatory fishes. *Fish and Fisheries*, 4: 1–24.

Costanza, R., d'Arge, R., de Groot, R., et al. 1997. The value of the world's ecosystem services and natural capital. *Nature*, 387: 253–260.

Curtis, T. P., Sloan, W. T. and Scannell, J. W. 2002. Estimating prokaryotic diversity and its limits. *Proceedings of the National Academy of Sciences of the United States of America*, 99: 10494–10499.

Daily, G. C. 1997. Introduction: What are ecosystem services? in G. C. Daily (ed.) *Nature's Services: Societal Dependence on Natural Ecosystems.* Island Press, Washington, DC.

Daily, G. C., Ehrlich, P. R. and Alexander, S. 1997. Ecosystem services: benefits supplied to human societies by natural ecosystems. *Issues in Ecology*, 2.

Daily, G. C., Polasky, S., Goldstein, J., et al. 2009. Ecosystem services in decision making: time to deliver. *Frontiers in Ecology and the Environment*, 7: 21–28.

Daily, G. C., Soderqvist, T., Aniyar, S., et al.. 2000. Ecology: the value of nature and the nature of value. *Science*, 289: 395–396.

DEFRA 2007. *An Introductory Guide to Valuing Ecosystem Services*, Department for Environment, Food and Rural Affairs (DEFRA), London.

DeLong, D. C. 1996. Defining biodiversity. *Wildlife Society Bulletin*, 24: 738–749.

Diaz, S., Fargione, J., Chapin, F. S. and Tilman, D. 2006. Biodiversity loss threatens human well-being. *Plos Biology*, 4: 1300–1305.

Dobson, A., Lodge, D., Alder, J., et al. 2006. Habitat loss, trophic collapse, and the decline of ecosystem services. *Ecology*, 87: 1915–1924.

Dudley, N. (ed.) 2008. *Guidelines for Applying Protected Area Management Categories*, IUCN: Gland, Switzerland.

Duffy, J. E. 2009. Why biodiversity is important to the functioning of real-world ecosystems. *Frontiers in Ecology and the Environment*, 7: 437–444.

Ehrlich, P. R. and Pringle, R. M. 2008. Where does biodiversity go from here? A grim business-as-usual forecast and a hopeful portfolio of partial solutions. *Proceedings of the National Academy of Sciences of the United States of America*, 105: 11579–11586.

Engel, S., Pagiola, S. and Wunder, S. 2008. Designing payments for environmental services in theory and practice: an overview of the issues. *Ecological Economics*, 65: 663–674.

Fisher, B., Turner, K., Zylstra, M., et al. 2008. Ecosystem services and economic theory: integration for policy-relevant research. *Ecological Applications*, 18: 2050–2067.

Fitzpatrick, J. W., Lammertink, M., Luneau, M. D., et al. 2005. Ivory-billed woodpecker (*Campephilus principalis*) persists in continental North America. *Science*, 308: 1460–1462.

Gamfeldt, L., Snall, T., Bagchi, R., et al. 2013. Higher levels of multiple ecosystem services are found in forests with more tree species. *Nature Communications*, 4: 1340 doi: 10.1038/ncomms2328.

Gaston, K. J. and Spicer, J. I. 2004. *Biodiversity: An Introduction*, Blackwell Science, Malden, MA.

Goldstein, J. H., Pejchar, L. and Daily, G. C. 2008. Using return-on-investment to guide restoration: a case study from Hawaii. *Conservation Letters*, 1: 236–243.

Heithaus, M. R., Frid, A., Wirsing, A. J. and Worm, B. 2008. Predicting ecological consequences of marine top predator declines. *Trends in Ecology & Evolution*, 23: 202–210.

Holker, F., Beare, D., Dorner, H., et al. 2007. Comment on 'Impacts of biodiversity loss on ocean ecosystem services'. *Science*, 316: 1285–1285.

Hooper, D. U., Adair, E. C., Cardinale, B. J., *et al.* 2012. A global synthesis reveals biodiversity loss as a major driver of ecosystem change. *Nature*, 486: 105–109.

Hooper, D. U., Chapin, F. S., Ewel, J. J., *et al.* 2005. Effects of biodiversity on ecosystem functioning: a consensus of current knowledge. *Ecological Monographs*, 75: 3–35.

Hughes, T. P., Baird, A. H., Bellwood, D. R., *et al.* 2003. Climate change, human impacts, and the resilience of coral reefs. *Science*, 301: 929–933.

Hutchings, J. A. and Reynolds, J. D. 2004. Marine fish population collapses: consequences for recovery and extinction risk. *BioScience*, 54: 297–309.

IUCN 2001. *IUCN Red List Categories and Criteria. Version 3.1. IUCN Species Survival Commission*, IUCN, Gland, Switzerland.

Jack, B. K., Kousky, C. and Sims, K. R. E. 2008. Designing payments for ecosystem services: lessons from previous experience with incentive-based mechanisms. *Proceedings of the National Academy of Sciences of the United States of America*, 105: 9465–9470.

Jackson, J. B. C., Kirby, M. X., Berger, W. H., *et al.* 2001. Historical overfishing and the recent collapse of coastal ecosystems. *Science*, 293: 629–638.

James, A., Gaston, K. J. and Balmford, A. 2001. Can we afford to conserve biodiversity? *BioScience*, 51: 43–52.

Keith, D. A. and Burgman, M. A. 2004. The Lazarus effect: can the dynamics of extinct species lists tell us anything about the status of biodiversity? *Biological Conservation*, 117: 41–48.

Kilbane Gockel, C. and Gray, L. C. 2009. Integrating conservation and development in the Peruvian Amazon. *Ecology and Society*, 14(2): 11. [Online]. Available at: www.ecologyandsociety.org/vol14/iss2/art11/.

Kumar, P. (ed.) 2010. *The Economics of Ecosystems and Biodiversity. Ecological and Economic Foundations*, Earthscan, London.

Lamb, D. and Gilmour, D. 2003. *Rehabilitation and Restoration of Degraded Forests*, IUCN and WWF, Gland, Switzerland.

Lamoreux, J., Akcakaya, H. R., Bennun, L., *et al.* 2003. Value of the IUCN Red List. *Trends in Ecology & Evolution*, 18: 214–215.

Larson, B. 2011. *Metaphors for Environmental Sustainability: Re-defining our Relationship with Nature*, Yale University Press, New Haven, CT.

Lawton, J. H. 1994. What do species do in ecosystems? *Oikos*, 71: 367–374.

Lester, S. E., McLeod, K. L., Tallis, H., *et al.* 2010. Science in support of ecosystem-based management for the US West Coast and beyond. *Biological Conservation*, 143: 576–587.

Ling, S. and Milner-Gulland, E. J. 2006. Assessment of the sustainability of bushmeat hunting based on dynamic bioeconomic models. *Conservation Biology*, 20: 1294–1299.

Liu, J., Li, S., Ouyang, Z., Tam, C. and Chen, X. 2008. Ecological and socioeconomic effects of China's policies for ecosystem services. *Proceedings of the National Academy of Sciences of the United States of America*, 105, 9489–9494.

Lockwood, M., Worboys, G. and Kothari, A. (eds) 2006. *Managing Protected Areas: A Global Guide*, Earthscan: London.

Lomborg, B. 2001. *The Skeptical Environmentalist*, Cambridge University Press, Cambridge.

Loreau, M., Naeem, S., Inchausti, P., *et al.* 2001. Ecology: biodiversity and ecosystem functioning: current knowledge and future challenges. *Science*, 294: 804–808.

Ludwig, D. 2001. Can we exploit sustainably? In J. D. Reynolds, G. M. Mace, K. H. Redford and J. G. Robinson (eds) *Conservation of Exploited Species*. Cambridge University Press: Cambridge.

McCarthy, D. P., Donald, P. F., Scharlemann, J. P. W., *et al.* 2012. Financial costs of meeting global biodiversity conservation targets: current spending and unmet Needs. *Science*, 338: 946–949.

McCauley, D. J. 2006. Selling out on nature. *Nature*, 443: 27–28.

Malhi, Y., Aragao, L. E. O. C., Galbraith, D., *et al.* 2009. Exploring the likelihood and mechanism of a climate-change-induced dieback of the Amazon rainforest. *Proceedings of the National Academy of Sciences of the United States of America*, 106: 20610–20615.

Malhi, Y., Roberts, J. T., Betts, R. A., *et al.* 2008. Climate change, deforestation, and the fate of the Amazon. *Science*, 319: 169–172.

Millennium Ecosystem Assessment 2005a. *Ecosystems and Human Well-being: Biodiversity Synthesis*, Island Press, Washington, DC.

Millennium Ecosystem Assessment 2005b. *Ecosystems and Human Well-being: Current State and Trends*, Vol. 1, Island Press, Washington, DC.

Millennium Ecosystem Assessment 2005c. *Ecosystems and Human Well-being: Synthesis*, Island Press, Washington, DC.

Milner-Gulland, E. J. and Bennett, E. L. 2003. Wild meat: the bigger picture. *Trends in Ecology & Evolution*, 18: 351–357.

Milner-Gulland, E. J. and Mace, R. 1998. *Conservation of Biological Resources*, Blackwell Science, Oxford.

Mistry, J., Berardi, A., Simpson, M., Davis, O. and Haynes, L. 2010. Using a systems viability approach to evaluate integrated conservation and development projects: assessing the impact of the North Rupununi Adaptive Management Process, Guyana. *Geographical Journal*, 176: 241–252.

Monbiot, G. 2011. The true value of nature is not a number with a pound sign in front. *The Guardian*, 6 June 2011. [Online]. Available at: www.theguardian.com/commentisfree/2011/jun/06/monetisation-natural-world-definitive-neoliberal-triumph (accessed 22 Nov. 2013).

Montoya, J. M., Pimm, S. L. and Sole, R. V. 2006. Ecological networks and their fragility. *Nature*, 442: 259–264.

Mooney, H. A. and Ehrlich, P. R. 1997. Ecosystem services: a fragmentary history. in G. C. Daily (ed.) *Nature's Services: Societal Dependence on Natural Ecosystems*. Island Press, Washington, DC.

Mora, C., Tittensor, D. P., Adl, S., *et al.* 2011. How many species are there on earth and in the ocean? *Plos Biology*, 9: e1001127.

Mumby, P. J., Hastings, A. and Edwards, H. J. 2007. Thresholds and the resilience of Caribbean coral reefs. *Nature*, 450: 98–101.

Myers, N. 1998. Lifting the veil on perverse subsidies. *Nature*, 392: 327–328.

Myers, N. and Kent, J. 2001. *Perverse Subsidies: How Tax Dollars Can Undercut Both the Environment and the Economy*, Island Press, Washington, DC.

Naeem, S. 1998. Species redundancy and ecosystem reliability. *Conservation Biology*, 12: 39–45.

Naeem, S., Chapin, T., Costanza, R., *et al.* 1999. Biodiversity and ecosystem functioning: maintaining natural life support processes. *Issues in Ecology*, 4.

Naeem, S., Loreau, M. and Inchausti, P. 2002. Biodiversity and ecosystem functioning: the emergence of a synthetic ecological framework, in S. Naeem, M. Loreau, and P. Inchausti (eds) *Biodiversity and Ecosystem Functioning: Synthesis and Perspectives*. Oxford University Press: Oxford.

Nellemann, C. and Corcoran, E. (eds) 2010. *Dead Planet, Living Planet: Biodiversity and Ecosystem Restoration for Sustainable Development*, United Nations Environment Programme and GRID-Arendal, Arendal, Norway.

Nepstad, D. C., Stickler, C. M., Soares, B. and Merry, F. 2008. Interactions among Amazon land use, forests and climate: prospects for a near-term forest tipping point. *Philosophical Transactions of the Royal Society B: Biological Sciences*, 363: 1737–1746.

Normile, D. 2010. U.N. Biodiversity Summit yields welcome and unexpected progress. *Science*, 330: 742–743.

Noss, R. F. 1990. Indicators for monitoring biodiversity: a hierarchical approach. *Conservation Biology*, 4: 355–364.

Olsson, P., Folke, C. and Hughes, T. P. 2008. Navigating the transition to ecosystem-based management of the Great Barrier Reef, Australia. *Proceedings of the National Academy of Sciences of the United States of America*, 105: 9489–9494.

Pace, M. L., Cole, J. J., Carpenter, S. R. and Kitchell, J. F. 1999. Trophic cascades revealed in diverse ecosystems. *Trends in Ecology & Evolution*, 14: 483–488.

Pearce, D. W. and Moran, D. 1994. *The Economic Value of Biodiversity*, Earthscan, London.

Pearce, D. W. and Turner, R. K. 1990. *Economics of Natural Resources and the Environment*, Johns Hopkins University Press, Baltimore, MD.

Pereira, H. M., Leadley, P. W., Proenca, V., *et al.* 2010. Scenarios for global biodiversity in the 21st century. *Science*, 330: 1496–1501.

Phillips, A. 2003. Turning ideas on their head: the new paradigm for protected areas. *The George Wright Forum*, 20: 8–32.

Phillips, O. L., Aragao, L. E. O. C., Lewis, S. L., *et al.* 2009. Drought sensitivity of the Amazon rainforest. *Science*, 323: 1344–1347.

Pimm, S. L. 1997. The value of everything. *Nature*, 387: 231–232.

Pimm, S. L. 2002. The Dodo went extinct (and other ecological myths). *Annals of the Missouri Botanical Garden*, 89: 190–198.

Pimm, S. L., Ayres, M., Balmford, A., *et al.* 2001. Can we defy nature's end? *Science*, 293: 2207–2208.

Pounds, J. A., Bustamante, M. R., Coloma, L. A., *et al.* 2006. Widespread amphibian extinctions from epidemic disease driven by global warming. *Nature*, 439: 161–167.

Raudsepp-Hearne, C., Peterson, G. D., Tengo, M., *et al.* 2010. Untangling the environmentalist's paradox: why is human well-being increasing as ecosystem services degrade? *BioScience*, 60: 576–589.

Ripple, W. J. and Beschta, R. L. 2004. Wolves and the ecology of fear: can predation risk structure ecosystems? *BioScience*, 54: 755–766.

Rodrigues, A. S. L., Pilgrim, J. D., Lamoreux, J. F., *et al.* 2006. The value of the IUCN Red List for conservation. *Trends in Ecology & Evolution*, 21: 71–76.

Rull, V. 2010. The candid approach. *Embo Reports*, 11: 14–17.

Sagoff, M. 2012. The rise and fall of ecological economics. *Breakthrough Journal*, Winter.

SCBD 2010. *Global Biodiversity Outlook 3*, Secretariat of the Convention on Biological Diversity (SCBD), Montréal, Canada.

Schipper, J., Chanson, J. S., Chiozza, F., *et al.* 2008. The status of the world's land and marine mammals: diversity, threat, and knowledge. *Science*, 322: 225–230.

Schroter, D., Cramer, W., Leemans, R., *et al.* 2005. Ecosystem service supply and vulnerability to global change in Europe. *Science*, 310: 1333–1337.

Sekercioğlu, C. H., Daily, G. C. and Ehrlich, P. R. 2004. Ecosystem consequences of bird declines. *Proceedings of the National Academy of Sciences of the United States of America*, 101: 18042–18047.

SER 2004. The SER International Primer on Ecological Restoration. *Society for Ecological Restoration (SER) International Science and Policy Working Group*, 2 October 2004. [Online]. Available at: www.ser.org/resources/resources-detail-view/ser-international-primer-on-ecological-restoration (accessed 22 Nov. 2013).

Sibley, D. A., Bevier, L. R., Patten, M. A. and Elphick, C. S. 2006. Comment on 'ivory-billed woodpecker (*Campephilus principalis*) persists in continental North America'. *Science*, 311.

Stolton, S. and Dudley, N. (eds) 2010. *Arguments for Protected Areas: Multiple Benefits for Conservation and Use*. Routledge, London.

Stuart, S. N., Chanson, J. S., Cox, N. A., *et al.* 2004. Status and trends of amphibian declines and extinctions worldwide. *Science*, 306: 1783–1786.

Tallis, H., Kareiva, P., Marvier, M. and Chang, A. 2008. An ecosystem services framework to support both practical conservation and economic development. *Proceedings of the National Academy of Sciences of the United States of America*, 105: 9457–9464.

Terborgh, J., Lopez, L., Nunez, P., *et al.* 2001. Ecological meltdown in predator-free forest fragments. *Science*, 294: 1923–1926.

Thomas, C. D., Cameron, A., Green, R. E., *et al.* 2004. Extinction risk from climate change. *Nature*, 427: 145–148.

Thompson, K. 2010. *Do We Need Pandas?: The Uncomfortable Truth About Biodiversity*, Green Books, Dartington.

TRAFFIC 2013. *Wildlife Trade: What Is It?* [Online]. TRAFFIC: Cambridge. Available at: www.traffic.org/trade/ (accessed 22 Nov. 2013).

UK National Ecosystem Assessment 2011. *The UK National Ecosystem Assessment: Technical Report*, UNEP-WCMC, Cambridge.

UNEP 2010. *UNEP Emerging Issues: Global Honey Bee Colony Disorder and Other Threats to Insect Pollinators*, UNEP, Nairobi, Kenya.

van Beers, C. P. and de Moor, A. P. G. 1999. *Addicted to Subsidies*, Institute for Research on Public Expenditure, The Hague.

Wardle, D. A., Huston, M. A., Grime, J. P., *et al.* 2000. Biodiversity and ecosystem function: an issue in ecology. *Bulletin of the Ecological Society of America*, 81: 235–239.

Webb, T. J., Vanden Berghe, E. and O'Dor, R. 2010. Biodiversity's big wet secret: the global distribution of marine biological records reveals chronic under-exploration of the deep pelagic ocean. *Plos One*, 5: e10223.

Wells, M. P., McShane, T. O., Dublin, H. T., *et al.* 2004. The future of integrated conservation and development projects: building on what works, in T. O. McShane and M. P. Wells (eds) *Getting Biodiversity Projects to Work. Towards More Effective Conservation and Development.* Columbia University Press, New York.

Wilson, E. O. and Peter, F. M. (eds) 1988. *BioDiversity*, National Academy Press, Washington, DC.

Worm, B., Barbier, E. B., Beaumont, N., *et al.* 2006. Impacts of biodiversity loss on ocean ecosystem services. *Science*, 314: 787–790.

Wunder, S., Engel, S. and Pagiola, S. 2008. Taking stock: a comparative analysis of payments for environmental services programs in developed and developing countries. *Ecological Economics*, 65: 834–852.

WWF 2013. *Unsustainable and Illegal Wildlife Trade*, [Online]. WWF International, Gland, Switzerland. Available at: wwf.panda.org/about_our_earth/species/problems/illegal_trade/ (accessed 22 Nov. 2013).

5

GREEN TECHNOLOGY
AND RENEWABLE ENERGY

5.1 Introduction

Development of the green economy will need technologies that are more efficient in the use of energy and other resources, and that minimise the generation of harmful pollutants (UNDESA, 2011). Such green technology is often considered to be 'environmentally friendly', by minimising the negative environmental impacts that can arise through production processes and the supply chain. The creation of technology that is applied either to conventional processes to make them more environmentally friendly, or to substitute for existing processes, is being widely pursued. For example, IBM recently developed 'Project Big Green' in which they committed to spend US$1 billion annually to research ways to make computing more environmentally friendly. This was predicted to yield average savings of 42 per cent for information technology enterprises (Hasper, 2009).

The term 'green technology' can be defined as the practical application of scientific knowledge that is designed to reduce or reverse the negative effects of human activities on the environment. Other related terms are environmentally sound technology, environmental technology, low carbon technology and clean technology.

Green technology covers a wide range of different production and consumption technologies, including (UNESCAP, 2012):

- *environmental technologies* for environmental monitoring and assessment, pollution prevention and control, and remediation and restoration technologies designed to improve the condition of ecosystems;
- *monitoring and assessment technologies* used to measure and track the condition of the environment, including the release of materials of a harmful nature;
- *prevention technologies* that avoid the production of environmentally hazardous substances or alter human activities in ways that minimise damage to the environment;
- *control technologies* that render hazardous substances harmless before they enter the environment.

In addition, green technology encompasses production and deployment systems, and organisational and managerial procedures.

The goals that inform development of green technology include (Green Technology, 2013):

- *Sustainability*: meeting the present needs without compromising the ability of future generations to meet their own needs.
- *'Cradle to cradle' design*: ending the 'cradle to grave' cycle of manufactured products, by creating products that can be fully reclaimed or re-used.
- *Source reduction*: reducing waste and pollution by changing patterns of production and consumption.
- *Innovation*: developing alternatives to technologies that have been demonstrated to damage human health and the environment.
- *Viability:* creating economically viable activity around technologies and products that benefit the environment.

This chapter examines a range of different green technologies, including those associated with renewable energy, which can potentially contribute to the development of the green economy. Key questions relate to the relative cost–effectiveness of different technologies, the factors influencing their development and deployment, and the extent to which they can genuinely be considered 'green'.

5.2 Types of renewable energy

Fossil and nuclear fuels (see Box 5.1) are often described as *non-renewable* energy sources. This is because the quantities in which they are available, though potentially very large, are finite. By contrast, *renewable* sources are replenished at the same rate as they are used (Sorensen, 2010). The prime renewable energy resources are the sun, gravity and the Earth's rotation (Quaschning, 2009).

BOX 5.1 SHOULD NUCLEAR ENERGY BE CONSIDERED AS GREEN TECHNOLOGY?

Nuclear energy is based on harnessing the energy that is released when the nuclei of heavy elements, most commonly uranium-235 and plutonium-239, are split during fission. The products of the fission collide with water in a reactor, generating heat that is used to raise high-pressure steam, which then turns steam turbines to generate electricity. The nuclear life-cycle starts with mining uranium that is then transported to a processing facility. Here the uranium is enriched, manufactured into metal fuel rods and delivered to the reactors. After 18–24 months of use, the uranium's energy is consumed, and the spent uranium is reprocessed or delivered to a final storage for geological disposition. Reprocessing significantly extends the lifetime of a given mass of uranium (Hecht, 2009).

How green is nuclear power? A major advantage is that the operation of a nuclear power plant results in no emissions of CO_2 or other GHGs. In this sense, nuclear power can be considered as a 'green technology', and this is one of the reasons why countries keen to reduce their carbon emissions are considering further investment in this source of energy (Adamantiades and Kessides, 2009; von Hippel *et al.*, 2012). However, when GHG emissions resulting from uranium mining, enrichment, transport, waste disposal as well as construction and decommissioning of reactors are considered, they can be significant. For example, in a meta-analysis of 103 life-cycle studies of nuclear energy, Sovacool (2010) concluded that renewable technologies are two to seven times more effective than nuclear power plants on a per kWh basis at mitigating climate change. In contrast, Rogner (2010) indicates that a nuclear reactor has lifetime GHG emissions comparable with the best forms of renewable energy generation.

5.2.1 Biomass energy

Plants are able to create biomass in the form of carbohydrates through the process of photosynthesis. Use of plant biomass as fuel was the dominant form of energy for most of human history, and is still a major source of energy for many of the world's developing nations. With the emergence of fossil fuels in the eighteenth century, the use of biomass has declined, but with rising oil prices and growing concerns about climate change, biomass energy is experiencing a renaissance (Quaschning, 2009).

Today, the largest potential for biomass energy exists for wood and wood products. Waste from agriculture and forestry are also important. Another modern source of bioenergy is biofuel produced by fermenting organic matter in special energy plants. However, crops cultivated for biofuel production compete with food crops for land, and there is therefore considerable controversy over their large-scale application. For example, Escobar *et al.* (2009) note that the production of biofuels may have serious environmental impacts, such as the use of large amounts of water, deforestation, reduced food production and increased soil degradation. Searchinger *et al.* (2008) suggested that farmers worldwide would increase conversion of forest and grassland to new cropland, to replace loss of agricultural land diverted to biofuels. This would result in a substantial net increase in GHG emissions resulting from biofuel production from corn in the USA.

Tilman *et al.* (2009) suggest that biofuels should possess the following characteristics, in order to be considered 'green': they should not compete with food crops; they should not lead to destruction of ecosystems; and they should offer GHG reductions. These criteria could be expanded to include the maximisation of social benefits (Rist *et al.*, 2009) and the minimisation of negative environmental and health impacts from the by-products of biofuel generation (Biksey and Wu, 2009). Disagreement exists over whether perennial agricultural crops are most likely to meet these criteria, as opposed to trees or microalgae (Duffy *et al.*, 2009; Kauppi and Laura, 2009). This dispute could potentially be settled by a comprehensive Life Cycle Analysis of each fuel source (Escobar *et al.*, 2009) (see Section 5.9).

Biomass for heat and electricity

Owing to the low energy density of biomass compared to fossil fuels, solid biomass is largely used for heating as opposed to electricity generation. Wood available in different processed forms (i.e. round wood, firewood, wood briquettes and wood pellets) is the main biomass fuel used for heating. A characteristic of firewood is that, unlike coal, three-quarters or more of the wood energy is in the form of volatile matter. This means that the design of any fireplace or heat plant needs to ensure that these vapours burn and do not escape through the chimney. This explains why open fireplaces usually reach only 20–30 per cent efficiency, whereas modern firewood boilers and large heat plants can reach efficiencies of more than 90 per cent (Quaschning, 2009).

Biomass can also be used with natural gas or with coal in power plants that exclusively generate electricity, and in heat power plants that generate both heat and electricity, which is referred to as cogeneration.

Biofuels

Liquid and gaseous biofuels are more versatile than wood as they are easier to transport, handle and burn cleanly. In addition to generating heat and power, liquid biofuels can replace petrol and diesel in the transport sector. Conventional (also referred to as first-generation) biofuels include bio-oil, biodiesel, bioethanol and biogas (ibid.).

Bio-oil (also called *vegetable oil*) is the easiest biofuel to produce. Seeds of over 1,000 plant species can be used in the production of bio-oil, through seed pressing or extraction processes. The most popular plants used are rapeseed, soya and palm. Vegetable oils have energy content similar to that of diesel (37–39 GJ t^{-1}) and can be burned in diesel engines when the latter are adapted and converted.

Biodiesel is produced by transesterification, a chemical reaction between feedstock oil and methanol in the presence of a catalyst. This produces fatty acid methyl ester (FAME), commonly known as biodiesel. The process also produces glycerol, a highly valuable substance with a variety of cosmetic and industrial uses. Biodiesel is becoming more popular as the price of conventional fuel rises, and as it offers the potential to use waste oils from cooking that otherwise would be discarded. Also, oil crops such as *Miscanthus* spp., switchgrass (*Panicum virgatum*) and *Jatropha* spp. are increasingly being grown on a commercial scale in order to produce biodiesel (da Costa *et al.*, 2010; EBTP, 2013). Diesel engines can be run on biodiesel without any problem if the fuel is used in small quantities mixed with diesel.

Bioethanol can be produced from any biological feedstock that has sufficient amounts of sugar content, or materials that can be converted to sugar. It is the largest biofuel contributor and is regarded as a replacement for petrol. It can be used in a petrol engine up to a 15:85 blend ratio (E15) of bioethanol to petrol without any need for engine modification (RFA, 2013a). Bioethanol use is widespread in Brazil, where the mandatory blend is 25 per cent bioethanol and 75 per cent petrol (E25), which has led to great success of bioethanol in the country (da Costa *et al.*, 2010). Bioethanol is also widely used as a fuel additive in the United States, Canada and Europe (RFA, 2013b).

Biogas is produced by the anaerobic digestion of organic material such as manure, sewage, municipal solid waste and energy crops. The more digestible the organic material, the higher the biogas production. With cow dung, the gas yield is around 60 cubic metres per tonne, whereas with maize silage, yields of at least 200 cubic metres per tonne can be achieved (SEAI, 2013). To produce biogas the organic material is fed into a purpose-built digester where it is broken down by anaerobic microorganisms. The decomposition process produces a biogas consisting of 50–75 per cent methane, 25–45 per cent carbon dioxide, water, and traces of other gases (e.g. ammonia and sulphur hydrogen), and a nutrient-rich digestate that can be used a fertiliser. The biogas is stored in a tank and can be used in combustion engines to generate electricity and heat, or upgraded to natural gas-quality biomethane to be fed into the gas grid or used as clean fuel for transport (NNFCC, 2013) (Figure 5.1).

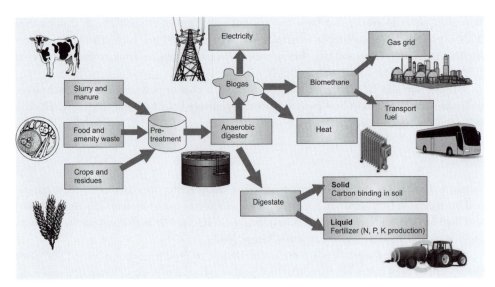

FIGURE 5.1   Schematic diagram of the anaerobic digestion process for the production of biogas

Source: Based on information presented in Møller *et al.* (2009), DEFRA (2011), NNFCC (2013).

Reflection point

Second- and third-generation biofuels (also known as advanced biofuels) such as cellulosic ethanol, biomethanol and algae-derived fuels are often regarded as sustainable biofuels, as they are derived from non-edible biomass. What do you think are the additional energy inputs required for growing, harvesting and processing of these advanced biofuels?

5.2.2 Hydroelectric energy

Hydroelectricity is a well-established renewable energy, which has been used by humanity for many centuries. It currently supplies about 16 per cent of total electricity generated worldwide (IEA, 2013b), involving structures ranging from small 'run of the river' water wheels to colossal dams with a capacity of thousands of megawatts (MW). The world's largest producers of hydroelectricity are China, Brazil and Canada. Norway and Brazil use hydroelectricity for nearly all (95.3 per cent and 80.6 per cent, respectively) of their electricity generation (ibid.).

   For any hydropower scheme, there are two critical success factors: the effective head of water, and rainfall. The head provides the water with significant gravitational potential energy, which can be used. Sufficient rainfall is needed to replenish the water and keep the system working. Historically, hydropower systems involved placing a water wheel in a running river. The water caused the wheel to turn, and this kinetic energy could be used to do mechanical work such as grinding corn. In the modern era, however, large-scale hydropower has developed.

By damming large rivers and creating vast reservoirs, water can be stored and then released downstream on demand, with the water turning turbine generators and producing electricity (Ramage, 2012).

A major advantage of large hydropower dams is their ability to store energy. Unlike most other renewable energy sources, which suffer from intermittency of supply, hydropower can hold water until energy is needed and then release it on demand, reaching peak generating capacity in a matter of seconds. For this reason, governments are keen to explore the potential for using hydropower to cover peaks in demand. Hydropower can also help overcome the intermittency of other renewable sources by using the electricity generated by such sources to pump water from a lower altitude to a higher altitude. This pumped storage of water at a higher altitude would then provide an electricity supply on demand.

An issue with large hydroelectric installations is their physical size. The land requirement of large hydropower dams is very high (50 km^2 per 100 MW installed, according to Jacobson (2009)), and involves dramatic changes to local ecosystems and human communities, often changing them irrevocably by flooding (New and Xie, 2008). For example, the Three Gorges Dam in China, which is the largest hydropower dam in the world, resulted in extensive flooding of fields, forests and whole towns, and involved the relocation of over a million people (Wu *et al.* 2003). The huge body of water that was created by this dam is causing significant ecological changes, and an increased risk of landslides owing to the weight of water (Stone, 2011). The dam has caused huge controversy and has highlighted the importance of assessing all environmental impacts before embarking on a hydropower scheme (McCartney, 2009).

Key advantages of hydropower include its flexibility and storage capacity, price stability, contribution to fresh water storage, low emissions of GHGs and lack of pollutants (Kaygusuz, 2009). However, hydropower developments may have far-reaching social, environmental and economic consequences. While a number of different measures have been developed to ameliorate the negative impacts of dams, relatively few studies have been conducted to evaluate their effectiveness. In many cases, such measures may fail for technical or socio–economic reasons. There is therefore a need to improve environmental practices in the operation of both new and existing dams (McCartney, 2009).

The controversy surrounding large dams was examined in detail by the World Commission on Dams (2000). A hydropower sustainability assessment protocol was launched in 2011 to provide a consistent and globally applicable methodology to assess the sustainability of hydropower projects (www.hydrosustainability.org).

5.2.3 Solar energy

The global amount of solar energy incident on the Earth is about 5.4 million EJ yr^{-1}. The capture of even 1 per cent of this energy would meet the world's energy demands. The issue with direct uses of solar energy is thus not one of availability, but of the technical issue of converting it to forms that are economically viable for human use (Turkenburg *et al.*, 2012).

Solar energy is strongest near the Equator and the Tropics. Because of the curved surface of the Earth, when the sun is overhead at the Equator, sunlight is more direct and more concentrated than at the poles. The poles receive the same amount of light compared with the Equator, but this is spread across a larger area, reducing intensity (Boyle, 2012). The solar radiation energy received on a given surface area in a given time is commonly expressed as average irradiance (or insolation) in watts per square metre ($W\ m^{-2}$) or kilowatt hours per square metre per day ($kWh\ m^{-2}\ day^{-1}$). The annual average irradiance is approximately $170\ W\ m^{-2}$; highest values of $300\ W\ m^{-2}$ can be found in the Red Sea area. Typical values are about $200\ W\ m^{-2}$ in Australia and $105\ W\ m^{-2}$ in the United Kingdom (WEC, 2013a).

Solar photovoltaics

The most important direct method of generating electricity from solar energy is photovoltaic (PV) cells. PV cells consist of a junction between two thin layers of dissimilar semiconducting materials that are electrically charged, known as 'p' (positive)-doped silicon and 'n' (negative)-doped silicon. When photons of light fall within the p–n junction, they can transfer their energy to some of the electrons in the material, so 'promoting' them to a higher level of energy. The net effect of this is the production of electrical energy (Boyle, 2012).

Practical applications of solar energy require high voltages. Therefore, many cells are interconnected together to form solar modules (also called *solar panels*), and arrays of solar modules are combined into solar power plants.

One of the major advantages of solar PV technology is its operating simplicity. There are no moving parts, and PV modules require very little maintenance, while offering a good rate of production if sited correctly. However, solar PV is currently a very expensive form of renewable energy. This is because high efficiency PV cells are normally manufactured using processes that are slow, require highly skilled operators and are labour-intensive. Also, the storage of sunlight (necessary to deal with the intermittent irradiance of the sun) is costly (Quaschning, 2009). However, developments in PV technology are occurring rapidly (Parida *et al.*, 2011), and it is expected that the price of PVs will drop significantly over the next decade, increasing its economic viability.

One way to improve the economics of a PV system is using concentrated photovoltaic (CPV) systems. This technology uses mirrors or reflective lenses to focus (concentrate) sunlight on a small area of the PV cell, thus reducing the need for multiple PV modules across a dispersed area (Quaschning, 2009).

Grid-connected PV systems can be integrated into buildings, either on a roof or in a building façade, where the electricity produced is for use at the point of generation. In this instance, the electricity generated supplements energy use of the building, with any shortfall in supply met by the existing grid infrastructure. Any excess capacity can be exported to the grid, an option that has become popular with the introduction of favourable payment rates for electricity supplied by some governments (Boyle, 2012). The alternative form of grid-connected solar energy production is a system designed solely for electricity export. These 'solar farms' operate in much the same way as a conventional power plant, with electricity sent for distribution and utilisation via the grid network.

Currently, owing to the high cost of making solar panels, widespread use of solar energy is largely confined to more affluent nations that have implemented policies specific to solar energy. However, as the technology develops and reduces in price, solar PV systems are expected to increase their global market share (BCC Research, 2012). Countries that have adopted appropriate policy measures for the penetration of renewable energy into energy generation have achieved some success. Examples are the feed-in tariffs adopted in Germany (see Box 5.2) and Spain, which guarantee a premium for the renewable electricity delivered to the grid, and the Renewables Portfolio Standard in the United States, which encourage electricity supply companies to produce a specified share of their electricity from renewable energy (Solangi *et al.*, 2011).

Solar thermal systems

Solar thermal systems convert solar radiation into heat. The simplest form of solar heating involves passing a fluid through pipes. The sun heats up the pipes, and consequently the fluid within. This heated fluid then flows to a heat exchanger, normally a water tank, and the heat is transferred to another fluid for use in various applications such as hot water and/or radiator space heating. The cooled fluid then flows back to the solar panel to be heated again, and the cycle continues. In countries with a sunny climate, this kind of system can meet the hot water and heating demands of a family (Quaschning, 2009).

Although less expensive than solar PV systems, solar thermal systems are often more expensive than conventional fossil fuel plants. As the technology matures, however, this is expected to change (Swanson, 2009). In terms of world market, China dominates the solar thermal market, where it is often one of the least expensive alternatives for providing hot water. Within the EU, Germany is the country with the most installed capacity, as a result of policy measures introduced to support renewable energy (see Box 5.2).

Ways to increase solar efficiency are being explored with concentrated solar power (CSP) technology, which uses a similar mechanism to that of CPV. Sunlight is concentrated by mirrors or lenses to heat a fluid in a collector at high temperature. The heated fluid then passes through a heat engine where a portion of the heat is converted into electricity. CSP technology

BOX 5.2 GREEN ENERGY IN GERMANY

Germany has developed ambitious plans for an energy transition (*Energiewende*), with the aim of generating at least 35 per cent of its electricity from green sources by 2020, rising to more than 80 per cent by 2050. Currently, renewable energy meets more than 25 per cent of the country's gross electricity needs. To achieve the higher targets, Germany is currently investing >€1.5 billion per year in energy research, while aiming to build more storage systems for renewable energy, as well as extending the electricity grid to incorporate remote wind turbines and small-scale PV installations. Owners of solar panels and wind turbines are able to sell their electricity to the grid at a fixed price, which is higher than that of the open market. The total costs of the plan are expected to exceed €1 trillion, which are being met by consumers, who currently pay some of the highest electricity prices in Europe. Other elements of the plan include the use of power-to-gas (P2G) plants, which use electricity to create methane out of water and CO_2. The methane provides a means of storing energy, and can be burned in power plants to generate electricity, or used as heating or potentially as a vehicle fuel. Germany also aims to have one million battery-powered cars in use by 2020. At the same time, use of smart-grid meters is being explored to help households reduce their energy consumption.

Source: based on Schiermeier (2013).

has demonstrated the highest solar-to-electric conversion efficiency; however, it is still a relatively immature technology and is relatively expensive to implement (WEC, 2013a). CSP plants also require a continuous supply of water, which could place a significant strain on water resources in arid areas (Tsoutsos et al., 2005).

Another issue with solar energy, both PV and thermal systems, is their visual impact. Current planning permission laws in many countries limit the exploitation of building-integrated PV and solar heating systems owing to regulations regarding visual appearance of the built environment. Other potential negative impacts of solar energy systems include the need for large areas of land for large-scale installations (Turkenburg et al., 2012). The production of current generation PVs is also relatively energy-intensive and requires large quantities of bulk materials, including small quantities of scarce materials (such as indium, tellurium and silver) and cadmium terruride, which is toxic (Tsoutsos et al., 2005). Large photovoltaic recycling initiatives such PV Cycle (www.pvcycle.org) and new research and development into low cost and commonly available materials could solve some of these sustainability issues.

> ## Reflection point
>
> North Africa has a lot of sunshine, whereas Europe has a high demand for energy. Do you think it would be feasible to send the solar energy from Africa to Europe? What problems would need to be overcome? See Clery (2010) for more on this visionary idea.

5.2.4 Wind energy

Solar radiation warms different regions of the atmosphere to differing extents, most at the Equator and least at the poles. Since air masses tend to move from warmer to cooler regions, this causes major air circulations or winds around the world. This wind energy can be harnessed by wind turbines to produce electricity. In addition to the main global wind currents, there are also local wind patterns in areas near the coast (so-called sea breezes) and near mountains (mountain-valley winds) (Taylor, 2012).

A wind turbine uses kinetic energy from wind to drive rotor blades. The spinning rotor blades in turn move a generator, creating electricity that can be exported for use or stored in another energy form.

The power contained in the wind, P_{wind}, is proportional to two parameters: (1) the area through which the wind is passing, A (m^2); and (2) the cube of the wind speed, v (ms^{-1}). This is why the average wind speed of an area is critical when assessing the potential of a wind turbine site. Note that the power contained in the wind is different from the power that can be extracted. Wind power extraction operates under certain constraints. In simple terms, this means that even an ideal wind turbine, operating at optimum conditions, can only ever extract 59.3 per cent of the available power in the wind. This percentage value is often referred to as the *Betz limit* (Taylor, 2012).

The largest supply of wind energy is over the open seas where there are no obstacles slowing the wind down. Over land the wind loses power owing to the effects of rough terrain. However, offshore wind energy is more expensive than onshore wind energy, requiring far more complex foundations in addition to expensive materials to combat the negative effects of salty sea water. Currently, it is only with the aid of government subsidies that this form of energy generation is feasible, but it is expected that as the industry grows and costs reduce, offshore wind energy generation will become cost competitive in the near future (EWEA, 2009).

Over the past ten years, global cumulative installed wind capacity has risen tenfold and high annual grow rates continue to be anticipated as a result of increasing wind power uptake in emerging economies (GWEC, 2013). According to the Global Wind Energy Council (GWEC), at the end of 2012, 282 GW of wind power was installed worldwide. The countries with the most installed cumulative wind capacity were China (75 GW), the USA (60 GW), Germany (31 GW) and Spain (23 GW).

Denmark is currently the country with the highest penetration of wind power in electricity consumption (27 per cent), with high values also recorded in Portugal (17 per cent), Spain (16 per cent), the Republic of Ireland (13 per cent) and Germany (11 per cent) (EWEA, 2013). Wind energy currently meets 7 per cent of the EU's gross electricity consumption from an installed capacity of 106 GW (ibid.), and it is forecast to meet 16 per cent of EU electricity demand by 2020 (EWEA, 2011). Wind energy technology is also improving. The cost per kWh of wind power was halved between 1980 and 2000, and its reliability, efficiency, level of turbine noise, and grid stability greatly improved over the same period (UNDESA, 2011).

According to Archer and Jacobson (2005), the costs of land-based wind energy without subsidy can be similar to those of a new coal-fired power plant when the annual-average wind speed at 80 m altitude is at least 6.9 ms^{-1} (15.4 miles per hour). The wind power available over such locations is about 72 TW, which corresponds to almost five times the world's primary energy consumption. Therefore, wind energy could potentially meet all of the world's energy needs. However, this would require about half the area of the state of Alaska and clearly shows that land availability is a major obstacle to wind power development (Jacobson and Archer, 2012).

Other major barriers to land-based wind energy are the intermittent nature of the source (similarly to solar energy), and public opposition (MacKay, 2008). In addition, wind power can have a significant environmental impact. For example, it has been shown that wind energy facilities can lead to significant mortality of bats (Kunz *et al.*, 2007) and birds (Saidur *et al.*, 2011). Wind turbines may also be a significant source of noise pollution, and have a substantial visual impact on both landscapes and seascapes.

Reflection point

There is a great deal of debate about wind energy. In some countries, large amounts of public money are being spent on installation of wind turbines, in the form of incentives provided to energy companies. These incentives are typically recouped through taxation, such as 'green taxes' on fossil fuels. Do you think that such incentives should be provided to energy companies? Is there a risk that wind turbines are being installed in situations where they are unlikely to be cost effective?

5.2.5 Wave energy

Wave power captures the energy from the motion of ocean waves, which is generated by wind passing over stretches of water. As wind is derived from solar energy, wave power may be considered as a stored, concentrated form of solar energy (Duckers, 2012).

The precise mechanisms involved in the interaction between the wind and the surface of the sea are complex. In essence, in an idealised ocean wave, the power (kW m^{-1}) is approximately equal to the square of the wave height (m) multiplied by the wave period (s) (the time required for a wave crest to form another crest). In general, larger waves contain more energy per metre of crest length than smaller waves (ibid.).

The World Energy Council reported that economically exploitable wave energy varies from 140–750 TWh yr^{-1} for current designs of devices when fully mature and could rise as high as 2000 TWh yr^{-1}, if all the potential improvements to existing devices were realised (WEC, 2010b). For comparison, global electricity production in 2011 was 22,126 TWh (IEA, 2013b).

Large amounts of energy could be generated in any country with coastline appropriate for the use of wave energy. The highest concentration of wave power can be found in the western coasts of America, Europe, Southern Africa and Australia and New Zealand (Figure 5.2). However, harvesting this energy is difficult and a wide range of wave energy conversion devices have been developed, indicating that wave energy is currently an immature technology (WEC, 2013a).

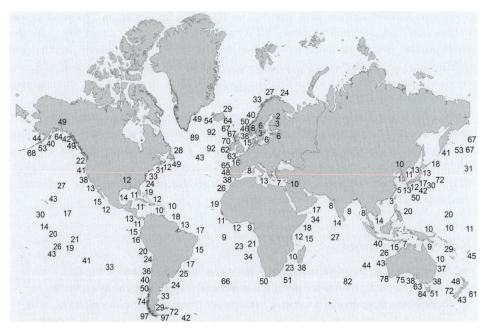

FIGURE 5.2 Average annual wave power level as kW m^{-1} of wave front. Any area with yearly average of over 15kW m^{-1} has the potential to generate energy at competitive prices.

Source: Duckers (2012), Figure 8.8, with permission from Oxford University Press, and ESRI (2013).

Wave energy conversion devices can be classified under three main types (Quaschning, 2009):

- *Point absorber systems* consist of a buoy that floats at or near the surface of the water and follows the movement of waves. Energy is generated by reacting these movements against some kind of resistance, which is used to drive electric generators.
- *Oscillating water column systems* comprise a partially submerged structure forming an air chamber in which the air is compressed by the oscillating water column. The compressed air escapes through an opening above the water column and powers a turbine and generator.
- *Attenuator/contouring systems* are elongated floating devices that extend parallel to the wave direction. As the incoming wave rides along the device, it generates movements within the device that are used to power a generator.

Wave power technology is currently immature and generating costs are high. Yet wave energy generation devices are considered among the most environmentally benign of energy technologies as they have little potential for chemical pollution, little visual impact and low noise generation (Duckers, 2012). However, given the low number of wave power projects, environmental impacts on marine life and coastal erosion are not yet fully understood (Thorpe, 1999).

5.2.6 Tidal energy

Tidal energy is the result of the interaction of the gravitational pull of the moon, and to a lesser extent the sun, on the world's oceans. Schemes that harness tidal energy rely on the regular rise and fall of the tides that occur approximately every 12.5 hours. Tidal power availability is very site-specific. As Figure 5.3 indicates, there are many places in the world with exceptionally large tidal ranges that would be appropriate for large tidal power schemes. Sites of particular interest include the Bay of Fundy in Canada, the Severn Estuary between England and Wales, and northern France (Elliott, 2012). The world's first large-scale, grid-connected tidal energy farm is at La Rance in France, which become operational in 1966 with a capacity of 240 MW (0.012 per cent of the power demand of France) (WEC, 2010b).

There are two main different approaches to the harnessing of tidal energy. The first is to exploit the cyclic rise and fall of the sea level through barrage methods as well as tidal lagoons. The second approach is to exploit local tidal currents beneath the sea surface in a similar way to wind power (Elliott, 2012).

A *tidal barrage* works by blocking off an area such as an estuary, trapping the water between the land and a barrage wall. Once built, water flows in and out of the tidal basin (the area behind the barrage wall) on high and low tides, turning gated turbines and generating electricity. In the simplest type of tidal barrage, the water is allowed to fill up the basin during the flood tide. At high tide, the gates are closed and the water is retained behind the barrage. At low tide, when the water outside the barrage has fallen sufficiently, the water is released through the gated turbines. The advantage of this scheme, as with all tidal power schemes, is that it guarantees electricity generation at least twice a day, and as an additional benefit it can also act as an energy storage, much like a hydroelectric dam.

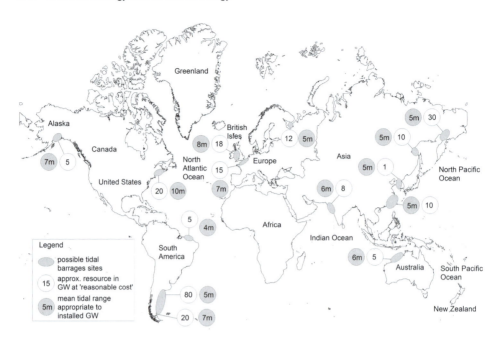

FIGURE 5.3 Locations appropriate for tidal barrages

Source: Elliott (1996), modified from Baker (1991), with permission from Oxford University Press and The Institution of Engineering and Technology (www.theiet.org), and ESRI (2013).
Note: GW: gigawatts.

A *tidal lagoon* works in same manner as a barrage, holding water at high tide and emptying that water at low tide through hydroelectric turbines. The difference is that a lagoon can be constructed in shallow water, avoiding the environmental impacts associated with tidal barrages that block off and alter the shoreline. This makes it an attractive alternative to estuarial barrages (ibid.).

Tidal stream technology uses the oscillating ocean currents caused by the gravitational attraction between the Earth and the Moon. In this case, the energy is harnessed by constructing what resembles a wind farm, but under water. The movement of the water causes the turbine blades to turn, generating electricity (ibid.). Major advantages of this technology are that it has wider applicability and is potentially cheaper, and the turbine rotors lie below the water surface. This makes the technology more acceptable to many of those who object to renewable energy installations on aesthetic grounds.

Tidal energy exploitation is still costly and immature (Bahaj, 2013; WEC, 2013a). Designs are not yet fully developed and eventual impacts on marine ecosystems are not fully understood. Potentially, tidal barrages could cause significant ecological impacts, particularly on bird feeding areas when they are constructed in coastal estuaries or bays (Frid *et al.*, 2012). Both tidal and wave energy generation devices are likely to pose less direct risk to birds than wind turbines, because of their lower profiles, but conversely they may pose the threat of underwater collision. In addition, they may indirectly impact marine birds by altering oceanographic processes and food availability, with implications for trophic cascades (Grecian *et al.*, 2010; Langton *et al.*, 2011). However, they could also have positive impacts on food provision for marine birds.

Reflection point

The UK has one of the best potential sites for a tidal energy plant, in the Severn Estuary. A hypothetical scheme for the Severn Estuary has been at the centre of discussions since 1925 when the first official feasibility study was commissioned. If built, its capacity would be around 17 TWh y^{-1} (Elliott, 2012) and could provide the equivalent of 4.9 per cent of UK electricity consumption. Why do you think this scheme has never been built? Do you think that the likely environmental impact associated with such a development might be acceptable to the general public?

5.2.7 Geothermal energy

Geothermal energy is derived from the natural heat of the Earth, which mainly originates from the decay of naturally long-lived radioactive elements. The amount of heat flowing through the Earth's surface is 10^{21} J yr^{-1}, which is tiny in comparison with the massive 5.4 x 10^{24} J yr^{-1} solar heating of the Earth, but is comparable with the value of worldwide primary energy consumption (524 x 10^{18} J yr^{-1} in 2012; BP, 2013). The main advantage of geothermal heating and electricity generation systems is that they are available 24 hours per day, all year round. Therefore, unlike most other renewable sources, geothermal energy can provide base-load power generation. However, only a fraction of the very large reserves of geothermal energy can be utilised. So far utilisation has been mainly limited to places where the Earth's heat flow is sufficiently concentrated in the form of steam and hot water, and is available in shallow rocks. These places are those situated around the Pacific 'Ring of Fire', or along tectonic plate margins where volcanoes and earthquakes are concentrated (Figure 5.4). Iceland provides a notable example (Garnish and Brown, 2012).

In general, geothermal resources below 150 °C are used directly to provide heating, cooling and domestic hot water for homes and commercial buildings; resources above 150 °C are used to generate electricity in geothermal plants. Both systems are described below.

Direct-use geothermal systems

Direct-use geothermal systems make direct use of underground hot thermal water. Typically they include a production well and circulation pumps, a heat exchanger, networks of underground pipes, and a reinjection well to discharge the cooled water. Peak-load and back-up boilers (usually fossil fuel-fired) are also usually connected to cover heat peaks and to supply heat in case of supply problems (Quaschning, 2009).

Geothermal plants

Geothermal plants include three main types, *dry steam* and *flash steam* systems that operate where geothermal resources temperatures are 180–370 °C or higher, and *binary systems* used when the resource temperature is 120–180 °C (Jacobson, 2009). In both dry and flash steam plants, two boreholes are drilled: the production well for the steam (in the case of dry steam) or steam/brine (in the case of flash steam) to flow up; and the injection well for the condensed water to return to the ground. The pressure of the vapour rising up powers a turbine that drives

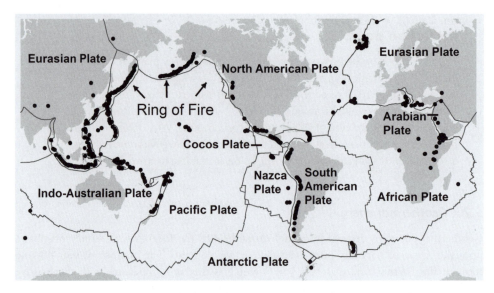

FIGURE 5.4 World map showing the lithospheric plate margins where geothermal resources are most accessible for electricity generation. Dots represent active volcanoes.

Source: USGS and ESRI (2011a, 2011b), and ESRI (2013).

a generator to produce electricity. About 70 per cent of the steam recondenses and the rest is released to the air, together with some CO_2 and other non-condensable gases. In binary systems the water rising up the production well is kept in an enclosed pipe and heats a fluid with a low boiling point such as iso-butane, which is vaporised and used to drive the turbine. Binary systems produce virtually no emissions of CO_2 or other GHGs (Jacobson, 2009).

The total installed capacity from worldwide geothermal power plants in 2010 was 10.7 GW and generated 67.2 TWh yr^{-1} of electricity (Bertani, 2010). For comparison, global electricity production in 2011 was 22,126 TWh (IEA, 2013b). An increase of about 20 per cent (approx. 350 MW yr^{-1}) was achieved in the period 2005–2010. Worldwide, half of the geothermal generating capacity is concentrated in the USA and the Philippines, with Indonesia, Mexico, Italy and Iceland accounting for the majority of the remainder (Bertani, 2010).

Geothermal energy is already making a locally useful contribution to world energy supplies and its global technical potential is enormous. The International Energy Agency (IEA) estimates that geothermal electricity generation could reach 1,400 TWh per year, i.e. around 3.5 per cent of global electricity production (IEA, 2011a).

A new technology called *hot dry rock* (HDR) or *enhanced geothermal systems* (EGS) has also been developed to make use of the hot dry rock resources that store vast amounts of energy in the Earth's crust, which are currently inaccessible by conventional technology. According to Bertani (2010), the scale-up of EGS technology would make it possible to produce up to 8.3 per cent of the total world electricity production by 2050. However, the technology is currently immature and costly. Central to the scale-up of geothermal development is the question of resource ownership or rights, which complicates the financing of projects (Garnish and Brown, 2012).

Geothermal energy is generally accepted as being relatively environmentally benign. However, it is not completely free of impacts on the environment. In Turkey, for example, geothermal waters are highly mineralised with elevated concentrations of arsenic, boron, cadmium and lead, resulting in scaling and corrosion. Geothermal discharges can result in contamination of soil and waterways. Potential incidents such as spillage, leakage and drainage failures may lead to water pollution (Baba and Ármannsson, 2006). Other negative environmental impacts include air pollution from steam production; increased risk of landslides and soil erosion; and ecosystem loss or damage during construction of infrastructure (Phillips, 2010).

Reflection point

Alongside biomass, geothermal energy is the only other renewable energy that requires careful extraction to avoid depletion. Do you think geothermal energy is currently extracted at a rate faster than it is replenished from the Earth? If so, what do you think are the implications? Can geothermal energy be truly considered as renewable energy?

Nuclear energy

The main problem with nuclear energy is waste produced by nuclear reactors, which can be highly radioactive and must be disposed of very carefully. This may require large exclusion zones that must be in place for hundreds of years to allow the waste to decay sufficiently to become 'safe' again (von Hippel et al., 2012). Major concerns also include the environmental damage from uranium mining (Rogner, 2010), and the risk of nuclear accidents, which can be devastating for the environment and all living creatures, including people (Møller and Mousseau, 2011). Many consider that contamination by toxic by-products and the potential risks of nuclear energy disqualify nuclear energy from ever being considered 'green' (Pampel, 2011) (see Box 5.1). Nuclear weapon proliferation is also an ongoing concern (von Hippel et al., 2012).

Currently, nuclear energy production is confined to a few nations, predominantly in the developed world (ibid.). Will it ever play a significant role at the global scale? Although public acceptance of nuclear power was growing (Adamantiades and Kessides, 2009), this was reversed by the Fukushima nuclear disaster in Japan that occurred in 2011 (Pampel, 2011). This disaster had major impacts on policy; for example, Germany committed itself to phasing out nuclear energy as a result, Italians voted against a restart of the nuclear power programme and Japan responded with a new policy that emphasises renewable sources. However, despite the recent accidents and growing public opposition, nuclear power is back on the agenda of many countries as it has predictable long-term generation costs, it can enhance energy security and can help achieve GHG emission targets. The strongest expansion in nuclear power is expected in China, India, the Republic of Korea and the Russian Federation (WEC, 2013a).

Reflection point

If alternative energy sources fail to deliver sufficient energy to satisfy demand, do you think that governments would be justified to bring forward new plans for nuclear plants? Or are the risks too high?

5.3 Cost-effectiveness of renewable energy

5.3.1 Financial cost of renewable energy

The cost of energy is 'a measure of the minimum amount for which the producer must sell energy in order for its production to make a profit' (Everett, 2003). Note the distinction between cost and price. In simple terms, price = cost + profit. It is important to remember that there are different ways of estimating costs, therefore it is important to understand the different assumptions and methods that are used to estimate costs, and be critical when costs are taken out of context.

The most common way to express the cost of renewable energy is in terms of levelised cost of energy (LCOE). This represents the total life-cycle cost (in pence or other unit of currency) of producing a unit of power (in kilowatt-hour or joule) using a specific technology (WEC, 2013b). The levelised cost includes capital costs, fuel costs, fixed and variable operations and maintenance costs. It also includes a capacity factor that represents the theoretical fraction of the annual energy output that the technology would produce if operated at rated capacity for a full year (NREL, 2013).

The capacity factor has a significant impact on the calculation of the LCOE. Unlike electricity from fossil fuel systems that operate 75 per cent of the time, the amount of electricity that can be generated by a solar PV installation or a wind turbine, for example, depends on the environmental characteristics (i.e. hours of sun, wind speed) of the place where the technology is installed. If net investment costs are the same, the electricity costs decrease with higher specific yields of solar radiation (for solar PV) and full-load hours (for wind turbines) (IPCC, 2011).

Another critical parameter in the calculation of the LCOE is the discount rate. This rate takes into account the time value of money. In practice, a pound in the future is worth less than a pound today. Discounting is a financial mechanism that takes account of such changes in value. However, the choice of which discount rate is appropriate for assessing the cost-effectiveness of energy investments is a matter of intense debate (Walker, 1996). In essence, if all other values remain the same, the higher the discount rate, the lower is the LCOE (IPCC, 2011). Great uncertainties arise, especially when estimating the future capital costs, operations and maintenance expenditures (which are mostly dependent on progress in technology and creation of the infrastructure) and fuel costs (which could increase as a result of government energy policies). Scenarios of different price trajectories are commonly used to reflect uncertainty.

Whenever comparing the cost of energy from different power sources, it is therefore important to consider the assumptions on which the cost estimates are based. Very different values can be produced by making different assumptions, which partly explains why the issue of the relative costs of different energy sources has been so controversial. The US National Renewable Energy Laboratory offers a LCOE calculator (www.nrel.gov/analysis/tech_lcoe.html) that allows analysis of the effect of the different factors influencing the LCOE.

The Special Report on Renewable Energy Sources and Climate Change Mitigation produced by the IPCC (2011) presents a comparison of the levelised cost of energy from renewable energy sources with recent non-renewable energy costs (Figure 5.5).

Figure 5.5 shows that ranges of LCOE are wide and depend on a number of factors, including technology characteristics and regional variations in cost and performance

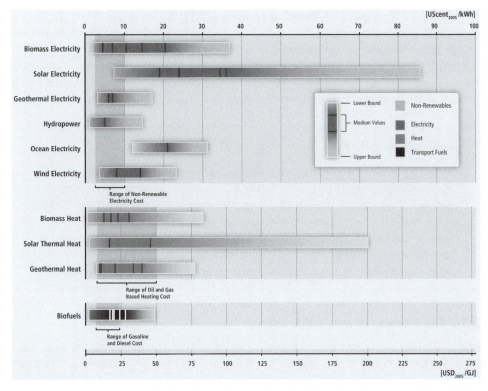

FIGURE 5.5 Range in recent levelised cost of energy (LCOE) for selected commercially available renewables in comparison to recent non-renewable energy costs. Technology sub-categories and discount rates (3–10 per cent) are aggregated in this figure. The lower range and upper range of the LCOE for each renewable technology are based on a combination of the most favourable and least favourable input values, respectively (US cent = 0.01 US$).

Source: IPCC (2011), Figure SPM.5.

(in addition to the capital factor and discount rate mentioned above). Many renewable technologies have a higher LCOE than existing energy prices. However, in certain settings, renewables can provide competitive energy services, especially in regions with favourable resource conditions or lack of infrastructure (e.g. solar thermal in rural China) (Quaschning, 2009).

In most regions of the world, the cost of energy from renewable sources is often not yet competitive. However, this might change, as renewable energy costs are brought down through technological development and market penetration. The highest projected declines in LCOE are expected for solar PV (from 15–70 to 3–13 US cent kWh^{-1}), solar thermal electricity (from 10–30 to 5–15 US cent kWh^{-1}), wave energy (from 15–85 to 8–30 US cent kWh^{-1}), bioethanol (from 11–45 to 6–30 US cent kWh^{-1}) and offshore wind (from 7–25 to 5–15 US cent kWh^{-1}) (Turkenburg *et al.*, 2012).

Another critical issue with the LCOE is illustrated by the fact that there is no agreement on what should or should not be included in the 'real' cost of electricity. Some argue that social costs (i.e. health costs owing to air pollution or disasters), environmental costs (i.e. biodiversity loss, water and soil pollution) and climate change costs (see Chapter 3) should be included (i.e. Sovacool, 2008; Brown and Sovacool, 2011). Jacobson and Masters (2001), for example, demonstrate that the inclusion of health and environmental costs would double the energy price from a new coal power plant if they were incorporated into the real cost of electricity. Other studies (i.e. Walker, 1996; Sundqvist, 2004; Streimikiene *et al.*, 2009; Sakulniyomporn *et al.*, 2011) suggest that the costs of negative externalities associated with current electricity production can surpass the direct cost of energy, sometimes many times over.

Reflection point

According to the International Energy Agency, fossil-fuel consumption subsidies worldwide amounted to US$523 billion in 2011, with oil products representing over half of the total. By comparison, renewable-energy subsidies were only US$88 billion in 2011. However, this value is expected to reach US$240 billion by 2035 (IEA, 2012a). Do you think governments should remove or substantially reduce subsidies to fossil fuels in order to promote renewable energy? What would this mean for people living in fuel poverty? Are there any better policy tools available?

5.3.2 Effectiveness of renewable energy

Can renewable energy meet the world's future energy needs? Annual renewable energy flows are abundant and exceed even the highest future energy estimate (1740 EJ yr^{-1} in 2100, according to Moriarty and Honnery, 2012) by orders of magnitude (Table 5.1). While the available renewable energy flows far exceed global energy needs, the technical challenge to capture these for human use lies in developing and scaling up adequate technologies to manage their lower energy density, greater intermittency and patchiness compared to solid and liquid fossil fuel (Kerr, 2010).

Several studies provide estimates of the technical potential of renewable energy, ignoring economic and socio-political limits. As presented in Table 5.1, published estimates of renewable

Table 5.1 Renewable energy flow and technical potential

Renewable Energy Source	Technical potential (EJ yr^{-1})			Annual flow (EJ yr^{-1})
	MacKay (2008)*	IPCC (2011)	GEA (2012)	Rogner et al. (2012)
Geothermal energy	63	130–1420	810–1545	1500
Solar energy	370	1575–50,000	62,000–280,000	3,900,000
Wind energy	189	85–580	1250–2250	110,000
Biomass energy	284	50–500	160–270	2200
Hydropower	29	50–52	50–60	200
Ocean energy	6.5	7–331	3240–10,500	1,000,000
TOTAL	941	1900–52,800	76,500–294,500	> 4,900,000

Source: After MacKay (2008), IPCC (2011), GEA (2012).

Notes: These figures ignore any social or political constraints. For example, according to MacKay (2008), the harnessing of 284 EJ of biofuels would require the use of all of the world's cropland, which is clearly not feasible.

* MacKay's values in this table are based on MacKay (2008) assuming a world population of six billion people and a conversion of 1 kWh = 3.6 x 10^{-12}EJ.

energy span an enormous range, except for hydropower. Upper and lower values can vary by one and sometimes two orders of magnitude. Renewable energy technical potentials are a direct function of the performance characteristics of their respective conversion technologies, as well as of factors such as geographic location and orientation, terrain, supply density, distance to markets or availability of land and water (Rogner *et al.*, 2012). Estimates tend to vary depending on the assumptions made to calculate each of these factors. Despite the wide range, estimated values (Table 5.1) indicate that to satisfy the current global energy consumption ($524 \times EJ \ yr^{-1}$ in 2012; BP, 2013), a mixture of renewable energy with at least some form of solar energy will need to be harnessed.

Technical limits of renewables are based on power densities of the technologies (i.e. energy flux per unit of horizontal surface), their conversion efficiencies and their deployment potential (UNDESA, 2011). Solar power reaches spatial power densities that are two orders of magnitude higher than for wind. Solar power can in principle reach power densities commensurate with demand densities in individual houses, but in large cities, the needs of industry and high-rise buildings require higher power densities than solar could offer. In contrast, wind power or biomass, with power densities less than $0.5 \ Wm^{-2}$, require very large areas of land and power infrastructure to provide power to urban areas (ibid.). In fact, the energy demand footprint for large parts of Europe is larger than what could be provided with non-solar renewables (MacKay, 2008).

So, how much of the world energy needs could renewables supply in coming decades? A variety of energy scenarios have been constructed to explore the various possible energy patterns in the future, and in particular the role that renewables might play in them. The assumptions of scenario creators can vary greatly, leading to differing projections (Everett and Boyle, 2012).

Conventional energy scenarios are published every two years by the International Energy Agency in its Energy Technology Perspectives (ETP). The ETP 2012 presents a 2 °C scenario (2DS) that sets the target of cutting energy-related CO_2 emissions by more than half by 2050 (compared with 2009) and ensuring that they continue to fall thereafter. This is in line with an emissions trajectory that recent climate science research indicates would give an 80 per cent chance of limiting average global temperature increase to 2 °C. In the 2DS scenario, world energy use continues to grow and renewables reach a share of 57 per cent in the generation mix by 2050 (IEA, 2012b).

The International Institute for Applied Systems Analysis (IIASA)'s Global Energy Assessment (GEA) also explores possible transformational pathways of the future global energy system (Riahi *et al.*, 2012). In addition to limiting climate change, GEA also considers meeting three additional sustainability objectives: (1) providing almost universal access to affordable clean cooking and electricity for the poor; (2) limiting air pollution and health damages from energy use; and (3) improving energy security throughout the world. Commonalities across all pathways include (ibid.):

- a strong growth in renewables beginning immediately and reaching 165–650 EJ of primary energy by 2050 (equivalent to shares in primary energy of at least 60–80 per cent);
- an increasing requirement for storage technologies to support system integration of intermittent wind and solar;
- a growth in bioenergy in the medium term to 80–140 EJ by 2050 (including extensive use of agricultural residues and second-generation biofuels);

- fossil carbon capture and storage (CCS, see Section 5.8) as an optional bridging or transitional technology in the medium term;
- increasing contribution of biomass with CCS in the long term;
- feasible phase-out of nuclear energy.

Probably the most ambitious renewable target of all is that proposed by Delucchi and Jacobson (2011) and Jacobson and Delucchi (2011). Their research demonstrates that a world powered by solar and wind is feasible, but in order to provide a stable power supply, geothermal and tidal energy would need to be generated, with hydroelectric power available to fill any gaps (Table 5.2). Further measures would be required to achieve a 100 per cent renewable global energy solution. These include demand-response management, better weather forecasting for planning, interconnecting energy generators over wide regions, onsite electricity storage, excess power utilisation to produce hydrogen for flexible transportation and heat uses, and electric power storage in electric-vehicle batteries (Delucchi and Jacobson, 2011). Other optimistic studies reaching similar conclusions are those produced by WWF (2011) and Greenpeace (2012).

Jacobson and Delucchi (2011), WWF (2011) and Greenpeace (2012) all suggest that the barriers to complete a global renewable conversion are primarily social and political, rather than technological or economic, though many renewable options continue to be relatively expensive (UNDESA, 2011). Unpriced externalities, together with higher up-front costs and technical and market risks, have a major influence on the cost-effectiveness of renewable energy. Externalities can make it difficult for renewables to compete in today's market, in which negative environmental and social impacts of traditional energy sources are not reflected in the market price of energy (Brown and Sovacool, 2011).

According to the IEA (2012b), achieving a renewables share in the generation mix of 57 per cent by 2050 would require US$36 trillion (35 per cent) more in investments than today. According to the GEA pathways (Riahi et al., 2012), global energy-related investments would need to increase to between US$1.7 trillion and US$2.2 trillion annually, compared with about US$1.3 trillion in annual investment today. WWF (2011) and Greenpeace (2012) also acknowledge that implementing their renewable-intensive future

Table 5.2 Number of green technology plants or devices required to meet the world energy demand (1.8 TW), including their footprint and spacing areas

Energy technology	Percentage of 2030 demand met by plant/device	Number of plants/ devices needed	Footprint and spacing area (% of global land area)
Wind turbine	50	3.8 million	1.17
CSP	20	49,000	0.192
Solar PV plant	14	40,000	0.097
Roof PV system	6	1.7 billion	0.042
Hydroelectric plant	4	900	0.407
Geothermal plant	4	5350	0.0013
Wave device	1	720,000	0.00026
Tidal turbine	1	490,000	0.000098
Total	100	> 1.7 billion	1.9

Source: derived from Jacobson and Delucchi (2011).

world energy scenarios would entail high up-front investments (1–2 per cent of global GDP), but conclude that the long-term costs for energy supply would be lower, leading to a positive cash flow by 2050.

In addition to the issue of cost-effectiveness, other widespread barriers to the deployment of renewable energy have been identified. The IEA (2011b), for example, classifies the barriers to renewable energy into seven main categories (Figure 5.6).

No study has analysed the environmental and social costs that a renewable-intensive future world would entail. Renewables appear more 'green' than fossil fuel and nuclear energy as they are essentially inexhaustible and their use usually involve lower life-cycle GHG emissions and other pollutants and fewer health hazards (Boyle *et al.*, 2012). However, they can also have environmental and social impacts (Table 5.3). These impacts should be considered on a case-specific basis if a comprehensive cost-benefit assessment is required.

Realising the multiple benefits of a renewable-intensive future world requires a holistic and integrated approach that addresses a diverse set of objectives simultaneously. While technically possible, the task remains extremely ambitious and will require rapid introduction of policies and fundamental political changes that lead to concerted and coordinated efforts to integrate global concerns, such as climate change, into local and national policy priorities such as health and pollution, access to clean energy, and energy security (Riahi *et al.*, 2012).

In most regions of the world, policy measures are still required to ensure rapid deployment of many renewable sources (IPCC, 2011). Key policy elements include (IEA, 2011b; Everett and Boyle, 2012):

- Publicity and education, ensuring that potential users are fully informed of the latest technologies.
- Research and development support for new renewable technologies, enhancing the performance of nascent technologies so they can meet the demands of initial adopters.

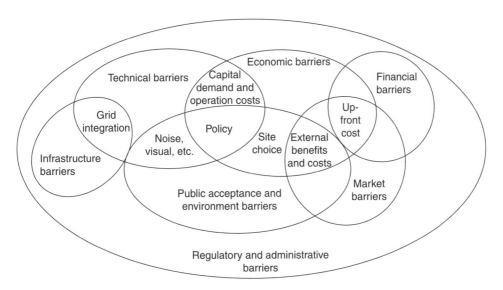

FIGURE 5.6 Barriers to renewable energy development as classified by the IEA

Source: IEA (2011b), Figure 3.1, ©OECD/IEA 2011.

Table 5.3 Main environmental and social effects of renewable energy types

Renewable energy type	Environmental and social impacts
Biomass	Competition with other biomass uses (especially food production) for fertile land and water; loss of existing uses for biomass wastes; biodiversity loss, destruction of ecosystems.
Hydroelectric	Loss of homes and livelihoods for those displaced; changes in the river's physical, chemical, biological and ecosystem characteristics; inundation of farmland or natural forest; possible increases in micro-seismicity and slope instability; increased downstream erosion; coastal land retreat and declining soil fertility from loss of sediment deposition; greenhouse gas emissions from submerged biomass.
Solar	Pollution from PV production depending on the cell type; depletion of scarce materials, competition for fresh water and land-use change for large-scale installations.
Wind	Bird and bat deaths; noise and vibration pollution for nearby residents; adverse effects on visual amenity; possible adverse effects on benthic, fisheries and marine life from offshore wind energy.
Wave and tidal	Loss of bird feeding areas when tidal barrages are constructed at coastal estuaries or bays; disruption to marine ecosystems from need to pump vast amounts of seawater; possible adverse effects on marine mammals from wave and current energy devices, and electromagnetic fields; loss of access to space for competing users.
Geothermal	Ground subsidence; increase in micro-seismicity; potential air pollution and contamination of soil and waterways, land use impacts of natural features.

Source: Adapted from Moriarty and Honnery (2012).

- Government targets for renewables.
- Legislation and regulation, such as standards and codes for the use of renewable energy in buildings.
- Financial mechanisms, including capital grants, tax incentives for companies taking up renewables; obligations on electricity suppliers to obtain a certain proportion of their electricity from renewables; renewable energy feed-in tariffs and incentives aimed at generating additional revenues.

In addition, the IEA (2011b) suggests the following policy mechanisms to accelerate the diffusion of renewables in developing countries: risk insurance, loan softening and guarantees, technical assistance and capacity building, technology transfer, carbon credits, and microfinance schemes.

Brown and Sovacool (2011) list five policy options for supplying renewable energy that have been shown to be effective in at least a number of countries:

1. renewable energy obligations;
2. net metering and improved electricity pricing systems;
3. producer subsidies;
4. reduction of fossil-fuel subsidies;
5. feed-in tariffs for renewable energy technologies.

5.4 Energy efficiency technologies

The consumption of global primary energy is forecast to rise, such that by 2050 the world will need double today's level of energy supply to meet increased demand (Moriarty and Honnery, 2012). 800–1175 EJ yr^{-1} of primary energy use are projected for 2050 (ibid.), from a current global energy consumption of 524 EJ yr^{-1} in 2012 (BP, 2013). Given the economic, social and environmental barriers that would need to be overcome to realise a renewable-intensive contribution to meet this energy demand (see Section 5.3), improvement of energy efficiency has been identified as the most cost-effective, near-term option to support a sustainable future (Johansson *et al.*, 2012). The IEA (2012a) states that energy efficiency can improve energy security, increase economic growth and reduce GHG emissions and other pollutants, but current and planned efforts fall well short of tapping its full potential, mostly owing to non-technical barriers. In addition, there are limits to GHG savings and there is also the paradox that greater efficiency can lead to greater consumption (known as the 'rebound effect'; Binswanger, 2001).

5.4.1 Energy efficiency indicators

Some definitions (WEC, 2010a):

- *Energy conservation and energy efficiency*: Both terms refer to the reduction in energy consumption that can be achieved through technological changes (i.e. more efficient lighting, heating, and transportation), and non-technical factors such as better management, and behavioural changes. Often the term 'negajoules' is used to indicate the avoided energy consumption obtained from energy productivity improvements.
- *Energy efficiency (technical definition)*: This refers to a reduction in the energy use associated with technological changes for a given level of services, such as the purchase of efficient equipment, retrofitting investments to reduce energy consumption of buildings and facilities or avoiding unnecessary energy consumption.
- *Energy efficiency (the economists' definition)*: To economists, energy efficiency refers to all kinds of technological, behavioural and economic changes that reduce the amount of energy consumed per unit of GDP.

The World Energy Council (WEC) uses a list of 39 energy efficiency indicators to identify the recent trends in energy efficiency performance for different countries (WEC, 2013c). At the global scale, the primary energy intensity is considered a reliable indicator of energy efficiency performance, which relates to the total amount of energy necessary to generate one unit of GDP. Trends over the period 1990–2011 show that primary energy intensity has been decreasing at a rate of 1.3 per cent per annum (p.a.). China experienced the highest improvement in energy productivity (around 4.7 per cent p.a. from 1990–2011; WEC, 2013c), despite now being the leading primary energy consumer and emitter of CO_2 (2735 million tonnes oil equivalent and 9208 million tonnes CO_2 in 2012, respectively; BP, 2013).

Another useful global indicator is the final energy intensity, which corresponds to the energy consumed per unit of GDP by final consumers, excluding consumption and losses in energy conversion (power plants, refineries, etc.) and non-energy uses. An estimated 80 per cent of energy is lost during supply, transportation and use (Quaschning, 2009). The ratio between final/primary energy intensity is therefore a more appropriate indicator to assess energy efficiency at the end-use level. In recent years, energy losses have generally been increasing because of the increased use of electricity by final consumers coupled with the fact that most electricity is produced from thermal power generation, which is commonly associated with 60–70 per cent energy losses. In contrast, energy losses in Europe have been decreasing, partly because of an increase in use of renewables that have lower energy losses compared with thermal power (WEC, 2010a).

The World Energy Council provides a database on energy efficiency policies, programmes and targets around the world, which can be consulted at www.wec-policies.enerdata.eu.

5.4.2 Cogeneration

Cogeneration (also combined heat and power, or CHP) is often promoted as a promising candidate for increasing energy efficiency, as this technology simultaneously produces both electricity and useful heat. CHP plants capture waste heat either very close to the plant (as heat cannot be transported efficiently over large distances), or as hot water for district heating, which is known as CHPDH. For typical heating applications, CHP plants can achieve an overall thermal efficiency of 90 per cent, and show considerable fossil fuel and CO_2 savings when compared with typical coal-fired power plants (IEA, 2009).

Cogeneration schemes can have different sizes, ranging from a total electrical output of less than 5 kW$_e$ to over 500 MW$_e$. Small CHP units of less than 5 kW$_e$, known as micro-CHP, are now commercially available and they are typically installed in single-family houses or small businesses. A number of different conversion technologies have been developed for the domestic sector, including reciprocating engines, Stirling engines, low- and high-temperature fuel cells, micro gas turbines, organic Rankine cycle, etc. It is anticipated that the mass market for micro-CHP will be for the replacement of gas heating boilers (Pehnt, 2008).

Mini-CHP units with electrical output between 5 kW$_e$ and 50 kW$_e$, are usually installed in buildings such as hospitals, leisure centres or hotels. The electricity produced can be used internally for the buildings or be exported to the national grid where feed-in-tariffs are in place. Currently, most CHP installations are found in district heating or in industrial plants that need both electricity and heat in large quantities. CHP is widely used in countries such as Denmark and Finland (IEA, 2009). The typical technologies used are steam turbines, gas turbines, combined cycle gas turbines (a combination of the first two plant types) and gas engines. Other more niche technologies are available for mini and micro cogeneration (Tzimas *et al.*, 2011).

In 2011, CHP in the EU-27 accounted for about 11.2 per cent of electricity demand (or about 105.3 GW$_e$). A European Commission study foresees the growth of installed CHP capacity in the EU-27 reaching 225 GW$_e$ in 2020, with avoided CO_2 emissions of up to 10 Mt y^{-1} (COGEN Europe, 2013). The global market for CHP is expected to reach US$90 billion in 2015 from US$55 billion in 2009 (BCC Research, 2011). Micro-CHP in particular represents a potential mass market product. For example, in the UK there are at least 20 million dwellings that could be fitted with a 1 kW micro-CHP unit (Tzimas *et al.*, 2011).

Theoretically almost any fuel is suitable for CHP, though for new systems, natural gas currently dominates the European market (about 40 per cent), followed by solid fossil fuels (35 per cent). Other fuel sources include renewables, mainly biomass (see Section 5.2.1), but also combustible waste, which supplies 12 per cent of the market (Tzimas *et al.*, 2011). CHP plants that use renewable energy can deliver both high energy efficiency and low carbon electricity and heat supply (IEA, 2011c).

Most CHP systems are superior, as far as the reduction of GHG emissions is concerned, when compared to the average electricity and heat supply. This is especially the case where CHP plants are fuelled by renewable energy sources (ibid.). For instance, GHG reductions above 50 per cent can be achieved by micro-CHP compared to separate production with more coal-dominated electricity mixes, such as the German electricity mix (Pehnt, 2008). Environmental impacts of CHP relate specifically to the precise choice of technology that is used. While fuel cells and Stirling engines are associated with low emissions of pollutants (particularly NO_x), if small reciprocating engines are used, their emissions can be somewhat higher than those of centralised gas power plants, owing to more efficient emission control in the latter (ibid.). Economically, under current energy political situations, micro cogeneration is generally favourable compared to non-CHP heat and electricity production in those countries with a favourable regulatory framework (e.g. tax exemptions or feed-in tariffs).

> ### Reflection point
>
> What do you think would be the optimal CHP plant operation and fuelstock to accelerate a transition to a green economy?

5.4.3 Smart grids

Smart grids are another promising candidate to increase energy efficiency and reduce CO_2 emissions (Pratt *et al.*, 2010; IEA, 2011d). Various definitions of Smart Grids (Figure 5.7) have been proposed (Vaziri *et al.*, 2011). According to ETP Smart Grids (2010):

> [A] Smart Grid is an electricity network that can intelligently integrate the actions of all users connected to it – generators, consumers and those that do both (the so-called prosumers) – in order to efficiently deliver sustainable, economic and secure electricity supplies.

According to the IEA (2011d), a smart grid can be characterised as a process that will do the following:

* *Enable informed participation by customers.* Customers will be able to modify the way they use and purchase electricity thanks to new technologies, new information about their electricity use and new forms of electricity pricing.
* *Accommodate all generation and storage options.* A smart grid will be able to integrate the growing array of customer-sited distributed energy resources including renewables, small-scale combined heat and power and energy storage (including electric vehicles).
* *Enable new products, services and markets.* New regulated markets will allow customers to choose among competing services.
* *Provide the power quality for the range of needs.* A smart grid will be able to supply varying grades (and prices) of power through advanced control methods, as not all customers need the same quality of power.

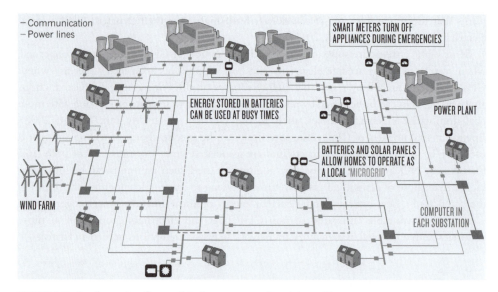

FIGURE 5.7 A schematic of a possible future smart electricity grid

Source: Amin (2013). Reprinted by permission from Macmillan Publishers Ltd: *Nature*, ©2013.

- *Optimise asset utilisation and operating efficiency.* The latest technologies will be able to optimise the use of the grid assets. For example, the use of system control devices will be able to reduce losses and eliminate congestion, increasing energy efficiency.
- *Provide resilience to disturbances, attacks and natural disasters.* A self-healing framework will allow the system to withstand disturbances and major disruptions.

At the core of all smart grids lie information technology (IT) capabilities, since they empower the communication between all connected actors and components. IT includes smart metering, telecommunication and remote control technologies, allowing a more efficient grid operation (Ipakchi and Albuyeh, 2009; Tzimas *et al.*, 2011). Some of the technologies needed to deploy smart grids, such as IT and communications technology and advanced metering infrastructure (including smart meters), are already considered mature in both their development and application (Hledik, 2009). Others, such as the integration of renewables and the electric vehicle-charging infrastructure, require further development (IEA, 2011d).

According to Hledik (2009), a conservative smart-grid approach that incorporates only those technologies that are currently commercially available would lead to a 5 per cent reduction in annual power sector CO_2 emissions by 2030. An expanded smart-grid scenario that accounts for the effects of future technologies (i.e. increased penetration of renewables and deployment of large-scale electricity storage devices) would produce a power sector CO_2 emissions drop in 2030 of 16 per cent relative to a business-as-usual scenario.

Smart meters are devices that allow for a two-way communication between the provider and the meter, so the providers can have access to real-time information on the electricity consumption of each customer (Beyea, 2010). In Europe, smart meters are already being introduced. This has raised concerns, however, about privacy protection, regarding the information that will be collected and stored. Outside Europe, investments have been mainly dedicated to enhancing power transmission and distribution. China, the USA and South Korea are among the forerunners in smart-grid demonstration and deployment efforts.

In 2009, China allocated €5.1 billion for smart-grid development, the United States €4.9 billion and South Korea €580 million; such investments are expected to grow considerably in future (Giordano *et al.*, 2011). It is expected that smart grids will support the development of renewable energy, by assisting its integration and optimal use, while also contributing to energy savings (Hledik, 2009; Amin, 2013). However, there will also be a need for public policies to be adapted both to regulate the new networks and to provide incentives for investors (Clastres, 2011).

Suggested activity

For more information on smart grids, consult the following websites:

- www.smartgrids.eu; link for the European Technology Platform for Electricity Networks of the Future, also called ETP Smart Grids.
- http://smartgrid.ieee.org; link for the Institute of Electrical and Electronics Engineers (IEEE) website that provides information, resources and expertise on smart grids.

5.5 Green buildings

Buildings are key to the development of a green economy because their design, construction, operation and the activities that go on in buildings are significant contributors to energy-related sustainability challenges (UNEP, 2011). The building construction sector and people's activities in buildings are responsible for over one-third of global final energy consumption and are an equally important source of energy-related CO_2 emissions (Ürge-Vorsatz *et al.*, 2012). Energy demand in buildings is set to rise 50 per cent by 2050 (IEA, 2013a), and reducing this demand can play one of the most important roles in solving energy-related sustainability challenges.

Direct energy use in the building sector (residential, commercial and services) typically accounts for 20–40 per cent of an individual country's total final energy use. The energy share of the building sector in 2007 was 34 per cent in the EU-27 and 31 per cent in the USA and Canada. Larger shares of total energy consumption are found in many low-income countries, especially in rural areas (e.g. Sub-Saharan Africa), where energy in buildings is mostly derived from the inefficient burning of firewood and other biomass (UNEP, 2006; Ürge-Vorsatz *et al.*, 2012).

The building sector is the second largest global CO_2 emitter after industry, responsible for 34 per cent of worldwide CO_2 emissions (Price *et al.*, 2006). This partly explains why energy efficiency in buildings has become one of the top priorities for governments to achieve emission reduction targets (Levine *et al.*, 2007). GHG emissions in buildings arise from: (1) the manufacturing of the building materials; (2) the transport of these materials from the production site to the building site; (3) the construction of the building; (4) the operation of the building, which corresponds to the running of the building when it is occupied; and (5) the demolition of the building (UNEP, 2006). Several studies have indicated that over 80 per cent of GHG emissions are produced during the operational phase of a building where the energy is used to meet various people's needs, such as space heating, cooling and ventilation, air conditioning, water heating, appliances, lighting, office equipment, etc. (UNEP, 2006, 2011).

Large GHG savings can be achieved during the operational phase of a building, though the level of potential savings varies according to a wide range of factors, such as the function and use of the building, the climate zone, the level of energy demand, and the supply and source of energy (UNEP, 2006). In some developing countries, a large proportion of the energy used during the running of the building is derived from traditional biomass (i.e. firewood, animal dung) using technologies that are often very inefficient. As countries develop, and traditional fuels are replaced by electricity, the potential for GHG emissions increases significantly. This is because the production of electricity is itself a major source of GHGs (unless derived from renewables), and access to electricity stimulates demand for electrical devices and appliances, increasing energy use (Ürge-Vorsatz et al., 2012).

In developed countries, opportunities for greening the building sector are found mainly in retrofitting existing buildings by reducing energy demand and using renewable energy sources. For the majority of non-OECD countries, which have a significant housing deficit and huge demand for office space, the greatest potential to reduce energy demand will come from new generations of buildings with more efficient design performance standards (UNEP, 2011). Priorities in the building sector highlighting which technologies and policies will have the largest impact at the regional level are presented in Table 5.4.

Although the building sector is the largest GHG emissions contributing sector in the world, it also holds the greatest potential to reduce these emissions. Assuming a cost per tCO_2e of no more than US$100, the global economic mitigation potential ranges between 5.3 and 6.7 $GtCO_2e$ yr^{-1} by 2030, far more than could be achieved in any of the other sectors (see Section 3.7.2, Figure 3.15). The EC, for example, estimated the full energy saving potential of residential and commercial buildings by 2020 to be around 27 per cent and 30 per cent, respectively (EC, 2007). The GEA scenarios exploring possible transformational pathways of the future global energy system (see Section 5.3.2) demonstrate that a reduction of approximately 46 per cent of the global final heating and cooling energy use in the building sector is possible by 2050 (Ürge-Vorsatz et al., 2012).

The largest energy and carbon emission savings occur for new buildings, and can be achieved through a system approach or Integrated Design Process in which the building performance is optimised, involving architects, engineers, contractors and clients (Levine et al., 2007; UNEP, 2011). Passive houses, zero-energy, and energy-plus buildings (all requiring a system approach) are increasingly important in developed countries (particularly in Germany). A *passive house* is a building that manages almost without any heating or cooling system; the house heats and cools itself. This is mainly achieved by architectural decisions regarding the building shape, form and orientation, daylighting, passive solar energy for heating and ventilation and passive heat sinks for cooling (Ürge-Vorsatz et al., 2012). In Europe, a prerequisite to a passive house is an annual heating requirement that is less than 15 Kwh per square metre of living area per annum. For comparison, an old building with poor insulation can require over 300 kWh m^{-2} yr^{-1}, and a new-built standard house needs around 100 kWh m^{-2} yr^{-1} (Quaschning, 2009).

A *zero-energy house* is a house that produces as much energy as it consumes over a full year (Ürge-Vorsatz et al., 2012). This is mainly achieved by careful site selection and orientation, improved insulation, passive heating, cooling and ventilation, appropriately sized and fully commissioned efficient equipment and systems, combined with the installation of a number

Table 5.4 Summary of the regional priorities for green buildings in different regions

Technology	EU and the USA	China	Brazil and Mexico	Russia	India and South Africa
Advanced envelope – cold climate (highly insulating windows, air sealing and insulation)	X	X		X	
Reduced cooling loads – hot climates (reflective technologies, i.e. white or cool roofs, and advanced cooling equipment)			X		
Heat pumps (water heating and/ or space heating and/or space cooling)	X	X		X	
Solar thermal (water heating and/ or space heating)			X		X
More efficient use of biomass (more efficient cooking and water heating, and leading to modern biogas)					X
Policy					
Building codes with supporting infrastructure (education, product ratings, and implementation to pursue an Integrated Design Process)		X	X	X	X
Appliance and equipment standard (promoting advanced appliances, lighting, heat pumps, heat pump water heater, gas condensing boilers, miscellaneous electrical loads, efficient cooling)		X	X		X
Deep retrofitting of existing buildings (systems approach with advanced envelopes and high-performance equipment)	X			X	
Zero-energy new buildings (Integrated Design Process with renewable energy)	X				

Source: IEA (2013a), ©OECD/IEA, 2013, Table ES.1, p. 12, modified by Elena Cantarello.

of microgeneration technologies, such as solar thermal collectors, solar electricity (PV), small-scale wind turbines, biofuels, geothermal heat pumps and micro-cogeneration (see Section 5.2). Zero-energy buildings are usually connected to the national grid, in order to be able to cope with the intermittency of solar and wind energy and fluctuations in demand. A building that is producing a surplus of energy is known as an *energy-plus* building (Voss *et al.*, 2012).

Harvey (2009) shows that significant energy savings in new buildings of all types and in all climate zones are possible using existing technologies, and states that the main obstacles to achieving these savings lie in the lack of knowledge and motivation within the design profession.

With regards to existing buildings, the largest energy and carbon savings occur by retrofitting (Levine *et al.*, 2007; UNEP, 2011). Cost-effective retrofit measures that improve the thermal properties of both domestic and commercial buildings include: sealing points of air leakage around doors, windows, skirting boards, plumbing; upgrades of insulation (in attics, to walls or walls cavities); doors, windows and roofs; external insulation and finishing systems; the replacement and/or reconfiguration of heating, ventilation and air conditioning (HVAS) systems; and the implementation of better control systems.

There are numerous published studies, summarised by Harvey (2009) and Ürge-Vorsatz *et al.* (2012), showing that 50–70 per cent or more energy savings can be achieved through retrofits of commercial buildings throughout the world. Heating energy requirements have been reduced by up to a factor of ten through comprehensive retrofits of residential buildings, especially multi-unit residential buildings.

Further energy and carbon emission savings can be made by replacing energy-demanding lighting and appliances with high efficiency ones. Energy-saving lighting can reduce energy use by a factor of four to five compared to incandescent/halogen lighting. Continuous improvements in lighting efficiency have occurred during the last decade and are expected to continue. A light-emitting diode (LED) light is about 1,000 times more efficient than a kerosene lamp, which is commonly used in low-income countries (Levine *et al.*, 2007). A considerable amount of energy can also be saved with electrical appliances, such as washing machines, refrigerators, freezers and office equipment. Energy efficiency-class labels provide useful information to customers when choosing between different models, and also should be an important criterion in the decision to replace appliances (Quaschning, 2009).

The IEA (2013a) estimates that approximately US$12 trillion of investment in the building sector, including space and water heating, space cooling, lighting, cooking, appliance and other equipment, will realise US$17 trillion in fuel savings. Further significant reductions could be possible through lifestyle, cultural and behavioural changes. Most people spend most of their life in buildings and understanding the rationale of decisions made by individuals and institutions is increasingly considered as fundamental to achieving the development of green buildings (UNEP, 2011). According to Charles (2009), the biggest challenge is not inventing new technology, but persuading people to adopt the technology and practices that have already been proved successful. Humans by their nature are less likely to embrace energy efficiency solutions unless they are aware of the implications, therefore in order to encourage more people to leap the efficiency gap, a mixture of persuasion, regulation and taxation will be necessary (ibid.).

5.6 Green transport

In 2007, the transport sector consumed more than 60 per cent of total oil consumption and accounted for about 26 per cent of all energy-related CO_2 emissions (IEA, 2010). Road transport accounts for the majority of transportation energy consumption, with light duty vehicles (LDVs) representing a 52 per cent share of the total, while medium-sized and heavy trucks account for 21 per cent. Marine and aviation each account for about 10 per cent of the total transport energy use, while railways represent only a 3 per cent share. Transportation is almost entirely powered by petroleum fuels (largely diesel and petrol), while a small share comes from natural gas (LPG/CNG), biofuels and electricity (WEC, 2011). One consequence of this dependence is that globally CO_2 emissions of transport are approximately proportional to transport energy use (Kahn Ribeiro *et al.*, 2007).

Globally, transport energy use and CO_2 trends are strongly related to rising population and income. From 1971 to 2007, global transport energy increased steadily by between 2 per cent and 2.5 per cent a year, closely following patterns of economic growth (IEA, 2010). If income and population continue to rise, then there is little doubt that transport energy use and CO_2 emissions will continue to rise at a rapid pace, unless strong action is taken (IEA, 2012b; Kahn Ribeiro *et al.*, 2012).

According to UNEP (2011), making a decisive shift to green transport requires a holistic strategy known as the 'avoid–shift–improve' strategy (see also IEA, 2012b; Riahi *et al.*, 2012). 'Avoid' focuses on reducing the need to travel, 'shift' on developing more green alternatives to car use, and 'improve' considers technological options that not only take into account GHG emissions, but also local environmental conditions and social concerns (Table 5.5).

Table 5.5 Avoid–shift–improve strategy and examples in green transport businesses

Avoid, shift, improve	*Developed countries*	*Developing countries*	*Examples of sustainable business*
Avoid (or reduce the need to travel)	Reduce vehicle kilometres (VKM) through transport demand management, land use planning, localised production, and shorter supply chains.	Avoid unnecessary generation of VKM through land use and transport planning.	• Teleconferencing and teleworking by major companies in Europe, the USA, etc. • Transit-orientated development in Curitiba (Brazil) enabling people to access housing, jobs, services by walking, biking and bus rapid transport • Car-sharing in Switzerland, the UK, the USA, Australia, Canada, France, Germany, Ireland • Bicycle sharing such as: JC Décaux/Cyclocity, Paris, Clear Channel/SmartBike, Barcelona
Shift	Shift from private vehicles to non-motorised transport (NMT) and public transport (PT) and from aviation to rail/PT. Transfer freight from road to rail and water transport.	Enable conditions for the lowest-emitting modes (both freight and passenger). Prevent shift from NMT and PT to private vehicles by ensuring that attractive alternatives to private vehicles exist.	• Bus Rapid Transit systems in Bogotá, Pereira, Curitiba, Ahmedabad, Guayaquil, Mexico, Léon, Guadalajara, Guatemala • Bus systems in Santiago, São Paulo (and most Brazilian cities) • Metro rail systems in Singapore, etc. • Auto-rickshaws in India, Pakistan • Bicycle rickshaws in India, New York City, San Francisco • Bicycle stations and rentals in Germany, Amsterdam • Intelligent transportation systems in Santiago, Guayaquil

(Continued)

Table 5.5 (Continued)

Avoid, shift, improve	Developed countries	Developing countries	Examples of sustainable business
			• Commercial enterprises in public spaces, advertising and street furniture in Barcelona, Buenos Aires, Guayaquil • Light Rail Transit in Europe
Improve	Improve existing vehicles. Down-scale vehicle engine size. Increase penetration of electric vehicles and carbon-neutral liquid fuels. Electrify rail (for both freight and passengers).	Ensure future vehicles/fuels are cleaner, encouraging small, efficient cars. Design innovations for traditional NMT such as cycle rickshaws.	• Small, lightweight vehicles, ultra-low emission engines, hybrid vehicles, plug-in hybrids linked with sustainable generation of electricity • Biofuels, conforming to stringent and comprehensive sustainability criteria • Annual vehicle checks in, e.g. Indonesia • Used vehicle emissions standards • Rail electrification in Europe, Japan, Russia

Sources: UNEP (2011) and Kahn Ribeiro *et al.* (2012).

According to the IEA (2010), reducing CO_2 emissions from transport will be challenging and will require rapid improvements in transport system efficiency, and further development and adoption of new low-carbon technologies. In addition, government targets will need to be backed by policy action (IEA, 2012b). But if significant decoupling of transport growth from oil is achieved by properly designed investments, the benefits will include not only GHG reductions and energy savings, but also reduced air pollution, congestion, transport accessibility and road safety (Table 5.6).

Many transport technologies and strategies are available to reduce GHG emissions. The most promising strategies are modal shifts and efficiency improvements in the near term, and use of alternative fuels in the medium to long term (IEA, 2010).

Selecting the right means of transport is the best option for a rapid reduction in GHG emissions. For example, rail is less GHG-intensive than air for both freight and passenger movement. Shipping is generally the most GHG-efficient way to move freight, with rail the next most efficient mode. Although studies reveal a wide range of values for each mode of transport, road and air transport tend to be much more energy-intensive (IEA, 2010).

Improving energy efficiency offers another effective alternative to reduce GHG emissions. Several countries have already adopted policies to improve the fuel efficiency of their vehicle fleets through regulatory standards, voluntary targets, financial incentives and consumer information (Onoda, 2009). Common energy efficiency measures include (Kahn Ribeiro *et al.*, 2007):

- materials substitution to reduce vehicle loads;
- aerodynamics improvement;

Table 5.6 Costs and benefits of investing in green transport

	Investments		Benefits				
	Direct investment	Long term costs/investment	Air quality	GHG emissions	Congestion	Transport accessibility	Road safety
Bus Rapid Transit	++	+	++	++	++++	++++	++
Light Rail	+++	++	++	++	++++	+++	++
Rail	++++	++	+	++	+++	++	+
Cleaner & more efficient vehicles	++	+	++++	+++	+/-	+/-	+/-
Non-motorised transport infrastructure	++	+	++	+	+++	+++	+++
City planning/design	++	++	+++	++	++++	++++	+++

Source: UNEP (2011).
Note: The more pluses, the bigger the investment or the benefit associated with the intervention.

- mobile air conditioning systems improvement by using new refrigerants with a much lower global warming potential;
- engine fuel efficiency and transmission improvement;
- expansion of public transport;
- improved driving practices (e.g. eco-driving);
- switching to non-motorised transport (i.e. walking and cycling);
- traffic management through transport demand management programmes.

In the medium to long term, alternative fuels such as biofuels (see Section 5.2), low-carbon electricity and hydrogen will play an important role in decarbonising the transport sector. Bioethanol is already used in large quantities in Brazil and the USA and is receiving increasing attention in various parts of Asia and Africa. Biodiesel is also receiving increasing attention, though compared with bioethanol, the cost and production potential are less favourable (IPCC, 2011). However, the scale-up of biofuels is limited by the amount of available land for energy crops and other competing uses, and by the availability of cost-effective production pathways (e.g. Richard, 2010; IPCC, 2011; Kahn Ribeiro et al. 2012; see also Section 5.2). Advanced biofuels (produced from non-food feedstock) are considered to have a much greater potential in decarbonising the transport sector if managed in the strict context of sustainable development and if food security remains uncompromised (IEA, 2010; Kahn Ribeiro et al., 2012). Recent developments of advanced biofuels derived from agricultural and forestry residues or wastes, energy grasses, algae and other microorganisms (e.g. see Anbarasan et al., 2012; Choi and Lee, 2013; and www.biofuelsdigest.com) suggest that building a bio-economy is not an unrealistic proposition. However, advanced biofuels all need further research, development and demonstration investment and international standardisation before they can become fully commercialised (IPCC, 2011).

Beyond biofuels, electric vehicles, plug-in hybrid electric vehicles and hydrogen fuel cell vehicles (see Box 5.3) will be extremely important in order to meet long-term GHG emission targets, such as those agreed by the Kyoto Protocol (Kahn Ribeiro et al., 2007). Electric vehicles and hydrogen fuel cell vehicles may also be used when they are stationary to help stabilise the electricity grid (Pratt et al., 2010; Simões et al., 2011).

BOX 5.3 ADVANTAGES AND DISADVANTAGES OF ALTERNATIVE FUELS AND VEHICLES

Battery electric vehicles (BEVs) are powered by chemical energy stored in batteries. The battery is recharged by connecting it to an electricity supply. When driving, the energy is drawn from the electric-cells and converted into motive power by the use of an electric motor. Plug-in hybrid electric vehicles (PHEVs) are part battery-electric and part conventional internal combustion engine (ICE) vehicles. PHEVs can take many forms, but the underlying principle is the use of an energy storage device (usually a battery) that optimises the fuel economy. In both BEVs and PHEVs, battery storage also enables the use of recovered energy from braking, which tops up the battery.

Hydrogen fuel cell vehicles (FCVs) use fuel cells to convert the chemical energy contained in hydrogen into electricity, which is then used to power the vehicle. The most suitable fuel cell type for vehicle applications is the proton exchange membrane fuel cell which uses very pure hydrogen. Although the long-term vision is to produce hydrogen by the electrolysis of water using electricity from renewable sources, currently most hydrogen is produced by steam 're-forming' of methane, a process that also produces CO_2. Reformation can take place on board using a portable reformer or hydrogen could be stored on board as part of an extensive hydrogen production and distribution infrastructure. Table 5.7 lists the advantages and disadvantages of alternative fuels and vehicles.

Table 5.7 Advantages and disadvantages of green transport

Technology	Advantages	Disadvantages
Battery-powered electric vehicles (BEV), e.g. Nissan Leaf and other models (see, for example, www.nextgreencar.com/electric-cars/available-models.php)	• Prospect of zero (or near-zero) emissions when the batteries are charged by carbon-free electricity (i.e. nuclear or renewables) • Reduced air and noise pollution • Up to four times the efficiency of traditional ICE	• Limited driving range and maximum speeds owing to the size and weight of the batteries • Battery lifetime and cost • Lack of recharging infrastructure • Battery disposal problem • Will need recycling of lithium batteries for large share of BEV to avoid exhausting the current lithium reserve base • Incremental cost compared to petrol ICE
Plug-in hybrid electric vehicles (PHEVs), e.g. Toyota Prius Hybrid and other models (see, for example, www.nextgreencar.com/hybrid-cars/available-models.php)	• Can switch to ICE when the batteries are depleted, solving the driving range and charging problems of BEV • Have powerful batteries (nickel-metal hydride) that can be charged from the grid and deliver distances of 100 km or more • Improved fuel economy and reduced emissions compared to ICE	• Technology still reliant on the internal combustion engine, therefore entailing higher life-cycle GHG emissions compared to BEV • Higher purchase price than ICE equivalent, but cheaper than BEV • Air pollution due to nickel production which emits nitrogen and sulphur oxides
Hydrogen fuel cell vehicles (FCVs), several hundred prototype vehicles (e.g., Honda, Toyota, General Motors) and buses (e.g. HyFLEET:CUTE project; www.global-hydrogen-bus-platform.com)	• Prospect of zero (or near-zero) emissions when hydrogen is produced from carbon-free sources (i.e. nuclear or renewables) • High quality energy carrier which can be readily converted into electricity • The only by-products of hydrogen combustion are water and a very small amount of nitrogen oxides, addressing GHG emissions, air and noise pollution problems	• Hydrogen does not occur naturally and energy is required for its production • Complex and expensive on-board reforming • Will require a specialist infrastructure • Disadvantage of being a gas with lower energy density of natural gas at atmospheric pressure, making it expensive to transport, store and distribute • Needs further research and development

Sources: Lane (2006), Chapman (2007), Muradov and Veziroglu (2008), Boureima *et al.* (2009), Jacobson and Delucchi (2011) and Kahn Ribeiro *et al.* (2012).

Reflection point

The Italian Fiamm Group is leading in the production of electric cars with nickel sodium chloride technologies (salt battery). The salt battery technology offers great advantages, including 100 per cent recyclability, energy savings, no maintenance, maximum safety, long life and significant reduction in running costs. Do you think salt batteries could be the solution to the renewable energy storage problem?

5.7 Sustainable waste management

In the past century, global waste production has risen tenfold, and it is projected to double again by 2025 (Hoornweg *et al.*, 2013). Waste management is the collection, transport, recovery and disposal of waste, including the managing and monitoring of such operations and the aftercare of disposal sites (Chalmin and Gaillochet, 2009). The term is usually used to refer to waste materials produced by human activity, and management is generally undertaken to reduce their effects on human health and the environment (Wilson, 2007).

A key goal of waste management is to safeguard public health and quality of life, by removing the waste from living and working areas. Historically, the initial focus of waste management was on 'basic waste management', including waste storage, collection, transport and environmentally acceptable disposal (ibid.). Sustainable approaches to waste management extend beyond these activities, to embrace the design of finished products, which ideally enable them to be easily de-manufactured and dismantled for material recovery and recycling. This requires shifts in consumer behaviour (e.g. increasing demand for waste-wise products) as well changes in manufacturing processes (e.g. increasing cleaner production technologies, eco-design and eco-innovation). A genuinely sustainable approach would involve zero waste, which might ultimately be achieved through improvements in production efficiency, a 'cradle-to-cradle' approach and consumer waste awareness. Steps have been made towards this focus on reducing the growth of the waste stream and reducing as much waste as possible at source (by preventing it from being generated) (UNEP, 2013).

Greening the waste management sector – one that shifts from less-preferred waste management approaches, such as incineration and landfilling towards an integrated sustainable waste management – is a central aspect of the development of a green economy. The opportunities for greening the waste sector come from three inter-related sources: (1) the growth of the waste market; (2) the scarcity of resources; and (3) the emergence of new waste management technologies (UNEP, 2011).

Every year, an estimated 1.3 billion tonnes of municipal solid waste is collected worldwide (UNEP, 2013). Solid waste generation rates range from <0.1 tonnes per capita per year (t $cap^{-1}yr^{-1}$) in low-income countries to > 0.8 t $cap^{-1}yr^{-1}$ in high income countries. These rates have been found to be correlated with growing population and affluence, including GDP per capita and energy consumption per capita, especially in developing countries (Bogner *et al.*, 2007). For example, during 1997–2007, India experienced an average GDP growth of 7 per cent and an estimated municipal waste increase of almost 46 per cent during the same period. Developed countries are aiming to decouple waste generation from economic growth and some EU countries such as Germany have to some extent managed to do this (in particular with regards to the household waste sector) (UNEP, 2010). However, waste reduction remains a challenge (Box 5.4), and, at the global level, waste generation is expected to increase to 2.2 billion tonnes by 2025, with almost all of the increase from developing countries (UNEP, 2013). Globally, about one-third of food produced for human consumption is lost or wasted (FAO, 2013).

The global waste market, from collection to recycling, is estimated at €300 billion, shared evenly between municipal waste and industrial waste, but not including the informal sector present in most emerging and developing countries. The four major municipal waste markets are the USA, Europe, Japan and China. The leading industrial waste market would appear to be Japan, though industrial waste is difficult to estimate with precision, because of the lack of reliable data. Electrical and electronic waste products (e-waste) are increasingly profitable as they contain scarce primary resources such as gold, copper and aluminium (Chalmin and Gaillochet, 2009).

Reflection point

What new opportunities might there be for developing new businesses as part of the global waste market? Would such businesses be considered green?

5.7.1 Waste management approaches

The 'waste hierarchy', as described by the International Solid Waste Association (ISWA), is commonly presented as a tool to create sustainable waste management scenarios (Figure 5.8). The measures at the top of the hierarchy should be considered first in order to green the waste sector and achieve sustainable waste management (UNEP, 2011).

BOX 5.4 WASTE AND GHG EMISSIONS ACCOUNTING

According to the IPCC, the waste sector contributes about 5 per cent to global GHG emissions, which compared to percentages of other sectors, might appear to be low (Bogner *et al.*, 2007). However, the IPCC accounting rules do not take into consideration the impacts of reducing, re-using or recycling of waste as well as waste-to-energy strategies on climate mitigation (Eggleston *et al.*, 2006). These effects are either attributed to another GHG industry sector or they are not accounted for at all (Gentil *et al.*, 2009). In addition to the IPCC GHG accounting, other types of accounting mechanisms have been developed for the waste sector, including:

1. corporate accounting, adopted by organisations (either mandatory or voluntary) as part of their annual reporting on environmental issues and social responsibility;
2. Life-Cycle Assessment (see Section 5.9), usually undertaken to compare alternative waste management systems and technologies;
3. carbon trading accounting, introduced by different carbon trading schemes, such as the Clean Development Mechanism and Joint Implementation (see Chapter 3).

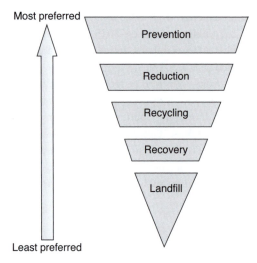

Most preferred

Least preferred

Prevention

Reduction

Recycling

Recovery

Landfill

FIGURE 5.8 The waste management hierarchy
Source: UNEP (2010, 2011).

Waste prevention and reduction are considered the most important measures in the waste hierarchy. All goods and products contain raw materials and energy. Every time we dispose of them, we effectively throw away valuable resources. Waste prevention requires that goods and products be changed in order to reduce valuable resources from being used, through reduced resources demand and more effective use of raw materials. Waste reduction measures include system management, increasing product lifetime, and reducing packaging (UNEP, 2013).

Avoiding and reducing waste generation provides benefits in avoided GHG emissions from less raw resources extraction and manufacturing, transportation and treatment and disposal of the waste. Avoiding and reducing waste generation also has important co-benefits for natural ecosystems as well as public health (Bogner *et al.*, 2007). Benefits from waste prevention generally outweigh benefits derived from any other waste management measure (UNEP, 2010). However, there is general consensus that not enough attention is given to this waste measure (ISWA, 2009). Waste management measures are as follows:

- *Re-use and recycling* both reduce the demand for raw materials and keep valuable resources from waste treatment and disposal, reducing associated GHG emissions. Although recycling requires energy input, generally the energy required to re-manufacture products is lower than that needed to make new products from raw materials (Smith *et al.*, 2001; ISWA, 2009). Many developed countries now have comprehensive recycling programmes. However, the percentage of waste recycled differs greatly between countries owing to a series of factors, including local economics, national policies, regulatory restrictions, public perceptions and infrastructure availability (Bogner *et al.*, 2007).
- *Biological treatment*, including composting and anaerobic digestion, is practised in many developed and developing countries. Both processes are commonly applied to

source-separated waste fractions. Composting decomposes biodegradable waste, such as food waste, bio-waste and garden waste aerobically into CO_2, water and a humic fraction (compost) that is normally used as a soil amendment (ISWA, 2009). Anaerobic digestion of organic waste produces a biogas that can be used to generate power, and a nutrient-rich digestate that can be used as a fertiliser (see Section 5.2.1). In Europe, Germany leads the way with 7,874 large-scale anaerobic digesters, followed by Austria with 586 (IEA Bioenergy, 2013).

- *Mechanical biological treatment (MBT)* of waste refers to a wide range of operations that mechanically separate waste into recyclable materials for recovery and an organic fraction for other treatments, including composting, anaerobic digestion and incineration with energy recovery or co-combustion in industrial furnaces. MBT is largely found in Europe where MBT plants employ sophisticated front-end sorting equipment. MBT is relatively rare in the rest of the world (ISWA, 2009).

- *Incineration and other thermal processes* (i.e. production of refuse-derived fuel and industrial co-combustion) reduce the mass of waste, and when energy is recovered can replace fossil fuel requirements, thus reducing GHG emissions. Metals can also be recovered from incineration, contributing to further GHG savings. Small contributions of CO_2 are emitted as a result of incineration of waste containing fossil carbon (Bogner *et al.*, 2007). Waste incinerators have been widely deployed in Europe and Japan owing to limited space for landfilling and legislation that limits landfilling. In Europe, for example, the Landfill Directive requires Member States to reduce the amount of biodegradable waste that they landfill to 35 per cent of 1995 levels by 2016, and to follow stringent technical requirements for waste and landfills (EC, 1999). In the rest of the world landfilling remains the cheapest and thus preferred option, despite its negative environmental impacts. Typical efficiencies in European waste incinerators are 15–30 per cent for electricity and 60–85 per cent for heat, with more efficient treatments (i.e. pyrolysis and gasification) becoming available (Astrup *et al.*, 2009).

- *Landfilling* (i.e. burial of waste in the ground) is the most common waste management approach around the world. CH_4 emissions from landfills represent the largest source of GHG emissions for the waste sector, whereas N_2O and CO_2 from landfills are believed to be negligible (Bogner *et al.*, 2007). CH_4 emissions are estimated to be 500–800 Mt CO_2-e yr^{-1} at the global scale. For a specific site, values can vary greatly depending on landfill management, waste composition, landfill gas management and climate. For example, where landfill practices are not managed and the waste is not compacted or covered (the situation in many poor countries), the conditions for CH_4 production do not develop easily, and therefore less methane is produced compared to more controlled landfill sites (UNEP, 2010). Common measures to reduce landfill CH_4 include the use of vertical wells and horizontal collectors to capture the landfill gas, which is then used to generate electricity, to fuel industrial boilers or to produce a substitute natural gas. However, compared to anaerobic digestion or conversion of waste to energy in incinerators, the 'lifetime' energy recovery efficiency from landfill processes is generally lower (as low as 20 per cent) (Bogner *et al.*, 2007). CH_4 emissions can also be reduced by CH_4 oxidation by methanotrophic microorganisms in cover soils. The use of cover soils can in some cases function as a sink of CH_4, but does not offer energy recovery. Landfills may also function as a long-term sink of carbon where the original waste contains a high proportion of wood products.

Bahor *et al.* (2009) demonstrate that if the tonnage of municipal solid waste was allocated to recycling, recovery and landfilling in descending order of preference (i.e. following the waste hierarchy), we would be able to reduce GHG emissions by more than 1 Gt C yr^{-1} with current technologies. This could represent one of the seven stabilisation 'wedges' (Pacala and Socolow, 2004; see Chapter 3) that would be needed to stabilise atmospheric concentration of GHG over the next 50 years.

A complementary tool to be used with the waste hierarchy is the *integrated sustainable waste management (ISWM)* framework developed for UN-Habitat (2010). While the waste management hierarchy focuses on the treatment and disposal of waste, the ISWM emphasises the linkages and interdependency of the various activities (waste system elements), stakeholders and sustainability aspects. The framework recognises that waste management problems cannot be solved simply by dealing with the technical, financial and environmental aspects or providing the infrastructure, but users and providers of the waste management services, sound institutions and pro-active policies also need to be considered.

5.7.2 Policies and measures

Much can be done to reduce waste. Examples of recent progress include San Francisco in California, which has a goal of 'zero waste' to be achieved by reduction and recycling, by 2020. Already more than half of its waste is recycled or reused (Hoornweg *et al.*, 2013). Globally, progress towards more sustainable methods of waste management have been made through numerous policies and regulations that: (1) regulate targets for waste reduction, reuse and recycling; (2) require targets limiting the use of certain virgin materials in types of product; (3) regulate the waste management market, (i.e. by setting requirements for waste handling, storage, treatment and final disposal, standards for recycled materials and waste facilities); and (4) relate to land use policies, (i.e. by setting the legal liability for land contamination and planning) (UNEP, 2010).

In industrialised countries, major policies are aimed at waste recycling and minimisation, whereas in developing countries the main goal of legislative instruments is to restrict the uncontrolled dumping of waste for public health reasons as well as environmental benefits. In the non-OECD countries, CH_4 emissions from landfills are expected to increase exponentially (owing to growth in population and affluence); hence policies and regulations, including the Clean Development Mechanism (see Chapter 3), have focused on improving landfilling practices and landfill CH_4 recovery (Bogner *et al.*, 2007). Developing country examples include: India's Municipal Waste Management and Handling Rules in 2000, the Law of the People's Republic of China on the Prevention and Control of Solid Waste Pollution, adopted in 1995, and Indonesia's Act regarding Waste Management in 2008 (UNEP, 2011).

Reflection point

In developing countries, there is often a high level of informal recycling. Those who make their living from this sector often play a large (yet unrecognised) role in reducing the mass of waste. For example, in Jakarta, it has been estimated that waste pickers recover 25 per cent of the city's waste, saving the municipality fuel, equipment and labour costs, and producing an economic impact of more than

US$50 million per year. In Mumbai, the economic impact of waste pickers has been estimated to reach US$1 billion a year (Medina, 2008). Do you think policies and measures should strengthen the position of waste pickers? If so, how might this be reconciled with threats to human health?

In the EU, a number of waste-related policy measures have been put in place since the early 1990s, setting targets limiting the amount of waste going to landfills and targets for the collection and recycling of targeted waste streams. These include the EU Directives Landfill in 1999, End of Life Vehicles (EoLV) in 2000, Waste Electrical and Electronic Equipment (WEEE) in 2002, Packaging and Packaging Waste in 2005 and the revised Waste Framework Directive in 2008 (UNEP, 2011). The WEEE Directive (EC, 2012a), for example, currently requires electronics firms to fund e-waste recycling in line with an annual target of 4 Kg per person, and a 20 kg capita annual target (or 85 per cent of WEEE generated) to be brought in from 2019. It is estimated that by 2020 over 40 per cent of the total waste generated will be regulated by binding EU requirement targets for recycling and recovery (ISWA, 2009). In addition to policies and legislations, mandatory Extended Producer Responsibility programmes have been introduced, requiring that producers of particular goods take back the goods at the end of their lifetime and take responsibility for any waste implications (UNEP, 2011).

Initiatives such as those taken to meet the WEEE targets have been beneficial in greening the waste sector. However, Reck and Graedel (2012) state that we are far away from a closed-loop material system. Metals are infinitely recyclable in principle. However, collection of electronic waste needs the active cooperation of society, which is related to social and governmental factors. Recycling technology, for reasons of scale and economics, focuses on steel and base metals used in large quantities, whereas special and precious metals found in small quantities are often not recovered. Thermodynamics also make elements' separation of many metal phases either very energy-intensive or expensive. Reck and Graedel conclude that to improve metal recycling, increased collection rates, improved products design and enhanced deployments of modern recycling methodology will all be needed.

5.7.3 The circular economy

The long-term vision for greening the waste sector is to shift from a linear economy, in which resources are extracted from the earth for production and consumption on a one-way track to disposal, to a circular economy. According to this concept, also referred to as a 'sound material-cycle society' or a 'cradle-to-cradle' approach, the generation of waste is minimised and any unavoidable waste enters a new cycle at the same or higher level of quality, which is repeated indefinitely (UNEP, 2011, 2013). The concept is described by McDonough and Braungart (2002) and Ellen MacArthur Foundation (2013a).

The circular economy requires careful management of all materials, which must have a known, well-defined chemical composition, and be easy and safe to disassemble. Ideally they should be either 'biological nutrients', designed to re-enter the biosphere safely for decomposition and become 'food' for a new cycle, or 'technical nutrients', designed by intention to retain embedded quality and energy, and to circulate without entering the

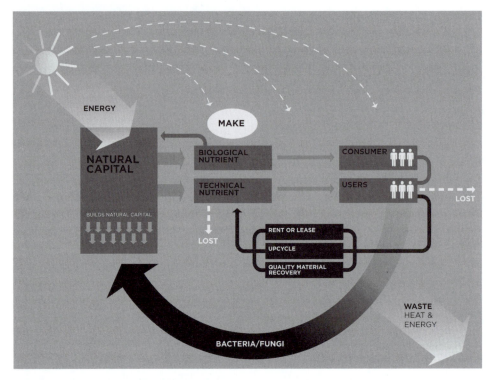

FIGURE 5.9 Schematic of a circular economy

Source: Ellen MacArthur Foundation (2013b).

biosphere (UNEP, 2013) (Figure 5.9). The circular economy concept resonates in many ways with the concept of industrial ecology, which emphasises the benefits of utilising the outputs of an industry as inputs for another industrial product or process (see Chapter 7).

In order to implement the circular economy, radical changes to the supply-chain management are needed. Specifically, the 3R principles (reduction, reuse and recycle, see Section 5.7.1) need to be embedded at all stages of the supply-chain (UNEP, 2011), from the design, manufacturing, retailing and consumption stages to the waste collection, recycling and reprocessing of end-of-life products (ESA, 2013). According to Ellen MacArthur Foundation (2013a), four building blocks are needed:

1. Advanced skills in circular product design and production, including advanced information sets and working methods.
2. New business models accompanied by advertising and awareness campaigns to drive acceptance and adoption by end-consumers; the incorporation of new players within and across the value chains, and intermediary players to help provide information and visibility.
3. Skills in building cascades/reverse cycles, including reverse logistics chains to cascade materials to other applications, in ways that optimise nutrients and value recovery; and innovative technology for reuse of materials.
4. Enablers to improve cross-cycle and cross-sector performance, including governments to facilitate business collaboration and to provide a stable policy framework of environmental

rules, economic incentives, and access to financing; governments, educational institutions and popular opinion leaders to lead by example.

The concept and principles of the circular economy have already been achieved in practice by a range of companies, especially in the clothing industry. Examples include Patagonia and Asos (Ellen MacArthur Foundation, 2013a). Patagonia (www.patagonia.com), a US-based maker of outdoor clothing with sales of US$500 million, produces all clothes that are recyclable. The company is also committed to (1) making clothes that last and serve as many uses as possible; (2) using raw materials that are organic, recycled or produced with minimal environmental and social impact; (3) carrying out repairs on some components for free; and (4) taking back any product made by Patagonia for either donation or recycling. Asos (www.asos.com), a UK-founded US$800 million fashion online retailer, provides a marketplace where anyone from anywhere in the world can sell fashion to anyone else, prolonging the lifetime of clothes and reducing waste.

At the country level, China provides an example of implementing the circular economy. The term is understood there to mean the realisation of a closed loop of material flows in Chinese economic systems, and this was formally accepted in 2002 as a new development model to help China move towards a more sustainable economic structure (Geng and Doberstein, 2008; Su *et al.*, 2013). Ongoing circular economy practices involve three different levels: micro-level (corporate-level), meso-level (inter-firm level) and macro-level (city or regional level). At the micro-level, industries are encouraged or required to adopt cleaner production and eco-design. Cleaner production aims to increase the efficiency of processes, products and services and to reduce the risks to humans and the environment at all stages of the production process (UNEP, 2013). Eco-design refers to a systematic incorporation of environmental aspects into the design of production process and the final product (Su *et al.*, 2013). Demonstration projects have been implemented in 24 provinces and one national, four industrial sector and 11 local cleaner production centres have been established (Geng and Doberstein, 2008).

At the meso-level, eco-industrial parks and eco-agricultural systems have been established where firms share common infrastructure and services and trade industrial by-products such as heat, energy, wastewater and other wastes. It should be noted that China's industrial parks typically have a dual function as both production and residential areas. Therefore planners are encouraged to incorporate 'green design' also in the residential areas (ibid.). At the macro-level, plans have been established to build eco-cities and eco-provinces where infrastructure and industries are redesigned and rearranged according to regional characteristics, and heavy polluting enterprises are phased out in favour of cleaner industries such as bio-farming. In addition, in an eco-city, consumers are encouraged to move away from wasteful forms of consumption in favour of energy preservation and environmental protection (Su *et al.*, 2013).

Reflection point

To what extent do you think that the Chinese concept of the circular economy should be implemented more widely? Can you identify any problems with these ideas?

5.8 Emerging green technologies

This section considers a number of additional green technologies that are still at the research or early development stage. Some of these technologies, such as carbon capture and storage and geoengineering, are considered to offer potential for tackling climate change, but have been the subject of much controversy. Others, such as green chemistry, green nanotechnologies and biomimicry, could potentially solve some of the problems associated with the current scale of fossil fuel use. However, they may require major capital investment, and perhaps some societal adjustments, to become fully operational.

5.8.1 Carbon capture and storage

Carbon capture and storage (CCS) techniques hold considerable potential as part of a series of technologies that could allow countries to continue to use fossil fuels, while mitigating climate change (Brown and Sovacool, 2011; Benson *et al.*, 2012). The IPCC Special Report on CCS (Metz *et al.*, 2005) indicates that a power plant with CCS can reduce CO_2 emissions to the atmosphere by 80–90 per cent compared to a plant without CCS. Therefore, retrofitting existing power plants with CCS is expected to lead to very large CO_2 savings worldwide (IEA, 2012b). In brief, the purpose of CCS is to separate CO_2 from industrial and energy-related sources so that it can be transported in a concentrated form to a 'safe' and 'permanent' storage site (Benson *et al.*, 2012) (Figure 5.10)

CCS is applicable to many stationary CO_2 sources, including power generation and industrial sectors. Technologies combining CCS with biomass hold great potential to achieve negative emissions. However, the greatest focus of CCS so far has been on coal-based electric generation, since this is responsible for nearly 40 per cent of total human-made fossil fuel CO_2 emissions (Benson *et al.*, 2012).

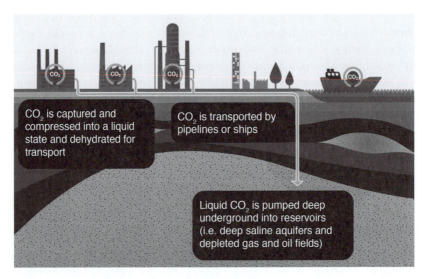

FIGURE 5.10 Representation of carbon capture and storage

Source: www.zeroemissionsplatform.eu.

There are three main processes for capturing CO_2, all requiring a significant amount of energy: (1) pre-combustion; (2) post-combustion; and (3) oxy-fuel combustion (Haszeldine, 2009). At the present time, none of these technologies is superior to another; each has particular characteristics that make it suitable in different cases of power generation (IEA, 2012b). Recent estimates of CO_2 capture costs range from US\$58–US\$112 per tonne of CO_2 avoided for gas-fired plants, and US\$23–US\$36 for coal-fired plants, depending on the technology applied. These costs do not include the additional costs of carbon transport and storage, which are very site-specific (Gibbins and Chalmers, 2008). CCS appears to be a high cost abatement option, especially for gas-fired plants. However, costs are expected to decline once further practical experience from CCS becomes available.

Reflection point

Compare the cost of CO_2 avoided for a power plant with CCS with the current market price of carbon (you can check that at www.theice.com/emissions.jhtml; see also Chapter 3). Do you think the price of carbon will ever increase enough to justify CCS? If not, do you think the incremental cost of CCS will ever decline to a value comparable to the price of carbon?

Following its capture, CO_2 needs to be compressed and transported to the storage site. Transport can be achieved using pipelines or ships, though pipelines are currently considered the preferred option for large-scale systems. According to Neele *et al.* (2013), many thousands of kilometres of new high-pressure pipelines would be needed in the EU if CCS is to play a significant role in achieving CO_2 emission reduction goals. A pipeline network of this scale would be expensive, technically and politically challenging and pose health, safety and environmental risks (ibid.). Although the chances of CO_2 leakage or rupture of a pipeline would be low, exposure to high CO_2 concentration can lead to adverse consequences on human health, plants and animals.

In the final phase of the CCS, CO_2 needs to be trapped and stored. This is typically done by injecting the liquid CO_2 into porous rocks, such as depleted oil and gas fields and saline aquifers deeper than water aquifers (Benson *et al.*, 2012). Injection of CO_2 into depleted or underperforming oil wells has been used since the 1970s by the oil industry as a way to boost production or enhance oil recovery. In fact, many injection and storage technologies employed for storing CO_2 are derived from the oil industry. The US Department of Energy's Carbon Sequestration Program has developed a method to provide quantitative estimates of CO_2 storage resources available in geological formations of the United States and Canada (see www.natcarbviewer.com). At current CO_2 emission rates, it is estimated that the available CO_2 storage capacity would meet the storage needs of the USA for hundreds of years (US DOE and NETL, 2012). Although there is evidence that suggests that for well-selected and managed storage formations, CO_2 retention rates will be very high, concerns remain about CO_2 leakage out of the storage reservoirs.

Currently five large-scale CCS projects are operational, and interest in CCS is growing internationally. However, to make coal and gas combustion 'greener', a significant scale-up in size compared to existing CCS activities would be needed. Haszeldine (2009), for example, estimates that the scale-up would be required from tens of power plants within five years, to hundreds of large plants by 2025, and then to thousands of small power plants by 2035. Several concerns surrounding such a plan have been raised, including (Haszeldine, 2009; Poumadere *et al.*, 2011; Benson *et al.*, 2012):

- lack of funding to start the building of real projects;
- lack of a market to justify the large investments;
- increased cost of generating electricity by 50–100 per cent;
- safety risks of CO_2 leaks;
- contamination of ground water if CO_2 or brine leaks out and migrates into drinking water aquifers;
- effect of local environment near site, including traffic, noise and habitat fragmentation, ecosystem productivity and function;
- long-term viability and who is liable for CO_2;
- ownership of underground space;
- micro-seismicity if injection pressures are very high;
- public opposition.

Furthermore CCS, if successfully implemented, could prove a setback to the progress of developing renewables and facilitate the recovery of further oil reserves through enhanced oil recovery, generating even more CO_2 emissions. Haszeldine (2009) concludes that with no price support or communication, CCS will remain limited to isolated demonstration plants and will not be able to make coal and gas combustion 'green' enough to play a large role in limiting climate change.

5.8.2 Geoengineering

Increasingly attention has been given to the deliberate large-scale manipulation of the climate in order to minimise the effects of the anthropogenic atmospheric changes. This reflects mounting pessimism that countries can effectively cooperate to combat climate change and a desire for a quick artificial fix to the problem (Mulvaney, 2011; Vaughan and Lenton, 2011). The umbrella term for this field of investigation is *geoengineering* or *climate engineering* (Poumadere *et al.*, 2011). Although most scientists agree that geoengineering should only be used as an emergency response to a climate crisis, there is no consensus to what constitutes this crisis (Brown and Sovacool, 2011). Advocates of geoengineering argue that immediate research should be undertaken to support widespread deployment within 20 years (Marshall, 2013). Two main approaches to geoengineering are summarised below. A comprehensive review of climate geoengineering proposals is presented in Vaughan and Lenton (2011).

Solar radiation management (SRM)

Reducing the net incoming short-wave solar radiation reaching the Earth could potentially be achieved by many different technology systems. Three options involving solar radiation management have received particular attention so far (Brown and Sovacool, 2011):

- *Injecting sulphates* into the stratosphere, mimicking the cooling effects of a volcanic eruption, is generally seen as one of the 'cheapest' geoengineering schemes (US$25–50 billion a year) with a relatively high probability of success. It has been estimated that using balloons to deliver sulphur dioxide to the stratosphere could counteract half of the global warming that the world is expected to experience in the next century.

- *Cloud reflectivity enhancement*, also known as cloud brightening or whitening, aims at increasing the reflectivity of solar radiation by spraying seawater in the atmosphere. It has been estimated that using a fleet of 1,900 ships spraying 8 gallons of seawater a second would offset the magnitude of global warming anticipated to occur by the end of the century. The approach would be relatively cheap (US$9 billion) and is expected to be reversible in a matter of days.
- *White roofs and roads* are already being used to increase surface albedo and to cool metropolitan areas (notably in California). This technique has been demonstrated to be effective in these areas, but is expected to be insignificant to counteract global warming owing to the difficulty of scaling up.

Carbon-cycle engineering

Also called carbon dioxide removal (CDR), carbon-cycle engineering comprises a variety of approaches to removing CO_2 from the atmosphere. It tends to be slower than solar radiation management, but of lower risk. Four geoengineering options involving carbon–cycle engineering have demonstrated potential to date: (1) carbon capture via biochar burial; (2) direct capture of CO_2 from air; (3) ocean iron fertilisation; and (4) increase in ocean alkalinity (Brown and Sovacool, 2011). Some scientists, and the IPCC, also include afforestation and reforestation (Vaughan and Lenton, 2011; Marshall, 2013). However, this approach is too slow to qualify as an emergency response to a climate crisis.

1. *Carbon capture via biochar burial* involves creating charcoal by pyrolysis of biomass in a closed container with little or no oxygen. The biochar is then added to topsoil, allowing organic carbon to be stored in larger percentages than is naturally possible. In addition, biochar soil amendments improve soil fertility and increase crop yields, which results in an additional carbon sequestration benefit (Brown and Sovacool, 2011). Woolf et al. (2010) estimate that the sustainable global implementation of biochar could potentially offset 1–1.8 Pg CO_2-C equivalent per year and that over the next 100 years the total net offset from biochar could be 66–130 Pg CO_2-C equivalent (for comparison CO_2 emissions from fossil fuel in 2011 were 34.7 Pg CO_2, according to Le Quéré et al., 2013).
2. A notable example of direct capture of CO_2 is in the form of '*artificial trees*', in which sorbents capture CO_2 molecules from free-flowing air and then release these molecules as a pure stream of CO_2 ready for transport and storage. It has been suggested that 100 million of these would reduce atmospheric CO_2 concentrations by 0.5 ppm per year (Biello, 2013). However, the technology would face similar issues to those examined for carbon storage (see Section 5.8.1).
3. *Ocean iron fertilisation* is the intentional introduction of iron to upper layers of the ocean to accelerate the growth of phytoplankton, which in turn creates carbon compounds by removing CO_2 from the atmosphere. While a number of ocean studies have proved iron fertilisation to be effective, controversy remains over its global potential as well as its ecological effects. For example, Buesseler et al. (2008) indicate that research is needed to evaluate the risks and benefits of ocean iron fertilisation, which could

potentially lead to major changes in marine ecosystems. On the other hand, adding iron into iron-deficient ocean waters could potentially help fisheries recover (Brown and Sovacool, 2011).

4. *Increase in ocean alkalinity* to accelerate natural weathering seeks to remove hydrochloric acid electrochemically from seawater, enhancing the ability of the ocean to absorb CO_2 from the atmosphere. According to House *et al.* (2007), the construction of 100 water-treatment plants where this process would take place could reduce global CO_2 emissions by 15 per cent.

Complications

While visionary plans have been presented that could offset current CO_2 emissions (Marshall, 2013), geoengineering remains highly controversial (Robock, 2008; Poumadere *et al.*, 2011; IPCC, 2013). As a rough estimate, it would cost several trillion dollars per year (a few per cent of global GDP) (Marshall, 2013) to implement, which is orders of magnitude greater than current global renewable-energy subsidies (US$88 billion in 2011, according to the IEA, 2012a). The effectiveness of geoengineering schemes such as SRM is limited by saturation, tropospheric pollution and surface area, whereas CDR is limited by land area availability, ocean physics and chemistry and carbon storage capacity. Geoengineering effectiveness is also constrained by our ability to verify an effect has occurred, which in turn needs detailed understanding and monitoring (Vaughan and Lenton, 2011). Current climate models cannot predict all of the impacts of geoengineering; some consequences could be unexpected (Robock, 2008). Some SRM solutions such as injecting sulphates into the stratosphere would modify the global water cycle (IPCC, 2013), increase acid deposition, contribute to ozone depletion and cause enormous environmental damage (Robock, 2008). A reduction in incoming solar radiation would affect the radiation available for solar power and have impacts on crops and natural vegetation. If SRM were terminated, global surface temperature would rise rapidly, the effects of which would be worse than gradual climate warming. On the other end, in case of unforeseen side effects, there are uncertainties regarding how quickly the intervention could be reversed. Geoengineering schemes could be conducted by one nation and would incur global impacts, which could provoke international tension. A global consensus would have to be attained regulating the control of geoengineering, which, if not reached, could prevent geoengineering altogether (Robock, 2008; Vaughan and Lenton, 2011).

Above all, geoengineering represents an artificial fix rather than a cure for climate change, and given its uncertain cost-effectiveness, side effects and long-term consequences, should not be considered as a replacement for reduction of GHG emissions (Robock, 2008; Vaughan and Lenton, 2011; Marshall, 2013).

5.8.3 Green chemistry

The term 'green chemistry' refers to the idea of making industrial chemistry safer, cleaner and more energy-efficient throughout a product's life-cycle, from synthesis to clean-up and disposal (see Section 5.9). A key goal is to design products and processes that minimise or eliminate toxic waste and the use of hazardous substances (Sanderson, 2011) (Box 5.5). Lancaster (2010) and Poliakoff *et al.* (2002) provide introductions to the topic, and Curzons *et al.* (2001) provide guidance on how to determine whether or not a particular chemical process can be considered green.

BOX 5.5 THE TWELVE PRINCIPLES OF GREEN CHEMISTRY
(POLIAKOFF ET AL., 2002; SANDERSON, 2011)

These principles were formulated by Paul Anastas, one of the principal founders of green chemistry, and John Warner in 1998.

1. *Prevention.* It is better to prevent waste than to treat or clean up waste after it is formed.
2. *Atom economy.* Synthetic methods should be designed to maximise the incorporation of all materials used in the process into the final product.
3. *Safer syntheses.* Wherever practicable, synthetic methodologies should be designed to use and generate substances that possess little or no toxicity to human health and the environment.
4. *Safer products.* Chemical products should be designed to preserve the efficacy of function while reducing toxicity.
5. *Safer auxiliaries.* The use of auxiliary substances (e.g., solvents, separation agents, and so forth) should be made unnecessary wherever possible and be innocuous when used.
6. *Energy efficiency.* Energy requirements should be recognised for their environmental and economic impacts and should be minimised. Synthetic methods should be conducted at ambient temperature and pressure.
7. *Renewable feedstocks.* A raw material or feedstock should be renewable rather than depleting wherever technically and economically practicable.
8. *Derivative reduction.* Unnecessary derivatisation (blocking group, protection/deprotection, temporary modification of physical/chemical processes) should be avoided whenever possible.
9. *Catalysis.* Catalytic reagents (as selective as possible) are superior to stoichiometric reagents.
10. *Degradability.* Chemical products should be designed so that at the end of their function, they do not persist in the environment, and should break down into innocuous degradation products.
11. *Pollution prevention.* Analytical methodologies need to be developed further to allow for real-time in-process monitoring and control before the formation of hazardous substances.
12. *Accident prevention.* Substances and the form of a substance used in a chemical process should be chosen so as to minimise the potential for chemical accidents, including releases, explosions, and fires.

As green chemistry is a relatively new concept, there has been insufficient time for its principles (Box 5.5) to be translated into industrial processes. However, many recently developed processes and products fulfil most of these principles. For example, the waste greenhouse gas N_2O, obtained from the manufacture of adipic acid (a component of nylon), is being reused as the oxidant in a greener process for producing phenol. More benign replacements have been found for the environmentally problematic tri-butyl tin oxide in marine antifouling applications (Poliakoff *et al.*, 2002). Reactions of organic compounds and some alkylation reactions carried out in green solvents (i.e. supercritical CO_2 and ionic liquids) are now widely used in the manufacture of chemical products. Some companies, such as BASF (the world's leading chemical company) have increased the atom efficiency from 40 per cent to 77 per cent in the synthetic production of ibuprofen, using many of the principles of green chemistry (Poliakoff and Licence, 2007).

5.8.4 Green nanotechnology

Nanotechnology refers to the study and manufacturing of things at very small scales, usually between 1–100 nanometres. Green nanotechnology can be defined as nanotechnology for green innovation, thus aiming for products and processes that are safe; energy efficient; reduce waste, GHG emissions and pollution; and use renewable materials (OECD, 2013). Green nanotechnology also focuses on products and processes that are economically and environmentally sustainable. Conceptually, the subject is framed by the principles of green chemistry (Box 5.5) and green engineering (Box 5.6) (Schmidt, 2007).

Green nanotechnology can produce nanomaterial directly, or can be of an enabling nature, by being used as a tool to further boost performance of a process or product. Green developments have been made particularly in the areas of nanoelectronics, synthesis of nanomaterials, nanomanufacturing, and nano-enhanced green technology (Schmidt, 2007). For example:

- Novel devices are being developed based on electromechanical nanosystems and using optical rather than metallic interconnections that reduce energy consumption in the traditional technologies used in electronics (OECD, 2013).

BOX 5.6 THE NINE PRINCIPLES OF GREEN ENGINEERING
(ABRAHAM AND NGUYEN, 2003: WITH PERMISSION FROM JOHN WILEY & SONS)

1. Engineer processes and products holistically, use systems analysis, and integrate environmental impact assessment tools.
2. Conserve and improve natural ecosystems while protecting human health and well-being.
3. Use life-cycle thinking in all engineering activities.
4. Ensure that all material and energy inputs and outputs are as inherently safe and benign as possible.
5. Minimise depletion of natural resources.
6. Strive to prevent waste.
7. Develop and apply engineering solutions, while being cognisant of local geography, aspirations, and cultures.
8. Create engineering solutions beyond current or dominant technologies; improve, innovate, and invent technologies to achieve sustainability.
9. Actively engage communities and stakeholders in development of engineering solutions.

- Scientists in China have demonstrated that it is possible to use low frequency mechanical energy (i.e. sound) as a power source to drive a nanogenerator, which can be used not only to light five commercial LEDs but also to drive biomedical microsystems (Zhang et al., 2013).
- Nanofibres with antimicrobial properties are being developed in the packaging industry to create suitable wrappings that are also biodegradable (OECD, 2013).
- Nanotechnology allows for environment-friendly catalytic nanoparticles to be tailored to perform a series of reactions, such as the synthesis of biodiesel from free fatty acids in vegetable oils (Schmidt, 2007).
- The use of nanogold and nanopalladium catalysts can remove carbon monoxide from the air (Schmidt, 2007).
- Filters with nanometer-scale pores can purify water, and nanoporous sorbents can remove mercury and other toxic metals from wastewater (Schmidt, 2007).
- In the solar technology sector, nanotechnologists are working towards systems that allow a 'printing' of solar cells, similar to that of an inkjet printer, making solar panels thin, flexible and potentially very cheap (Guo, 2012).
- In the auto industry, the use of lightweight nanocomposites in the body, internal and external structure of a car can reduce the amount of fuel required to power it; combining nanomaterials with rubber can improve tyre performance and reduce tyre abrasion; nanotechnologies for lithium batteries with greater storage capacity, lifetime and safety can enable the manufacturing of 'greener' electric vehicles (OECD, 2013).
- Core-shell nanoparticle structures are under investigation that would quickly take up and release hydrogen as needed (Guo, 2012).
- A new kind of proton exchange membrane with nanoscale patterning has been found that outperforms traditional ones and could be used in fuel cells that run directly on methanol, instead of hydrogen (Schmidt, 2007).

While green nanotechnology is increasingly revealing its potential to enhance current technologies or to create entirely new solutions, most of these technologies are still in the research and development stage and very few products have reached the market to date (Jones, 2007). The costs associated with the application of green nanotechnologies need to be offset against their beneficial impacts, taking into account a number of factors such as the timing and distribution of various benefits and costs, interest rates, opportunity costs, and the relative advantages of green nanotechnologies compared with conventional technologies (OECD, 2013). Some scientists point out that while the application of nanotechnology may save energy and reduce GHG emissions, significant amounts of energy may be involved in producing the component materials. Some nanotechnology applications also raise environmental, health and safety risks related to the use and disposal of nanostructures that they employ. Critics argue that green nanotechnology is too dangerous (Mulvaney, 2011), and that above all, it only represents another artificial fix to problems that are ultimately socio-political (Jones, 2007). As the technology is being developed, greater efforts are being made to find ways of monitoring and assessing the impact of nanotechnology. However, this is a very challenging task (OECD, 2013).

5.8.5 Biomimicry

Biomimicry or biomimetics is a scientific discipline that imitates the designs and processes found in nature, to solve human problems in a sustainable way (Benyus, 1997). It is an old concept; Leonardo da Vinci studied how birds fly to better understand how to design flying machines for men (Bhushan, 2009). However, it was Benyus (1997) who popularised the approach. The discipline is framed by life's principles, which is a list of best practices that all organisms have in common (Figure 5.11). Benyus and her team believe that by applying these principles, we can revolutionise how we feed the world, harness energy, invent and design things, heal ourselves, restore the environment, compute and conduct business in a way that is sustainable (Benyus, 1997; Baumeister *et al.*, 2013). Biomimicry can therefore be seen as a tool enabling a transition towards a green economy.

Over the past two years, increasing efforts have been made to integrate designs derived from nature into products, buildings, communities and even investments (Makower, 2013). Two projects provide examples. The first is the Genius of Biome, a report designed to encourage designers, architects and planners to be inspired by nature (Biomimicry 3.8 and HOK, 2013). This translates biological principles and natural patterns into design

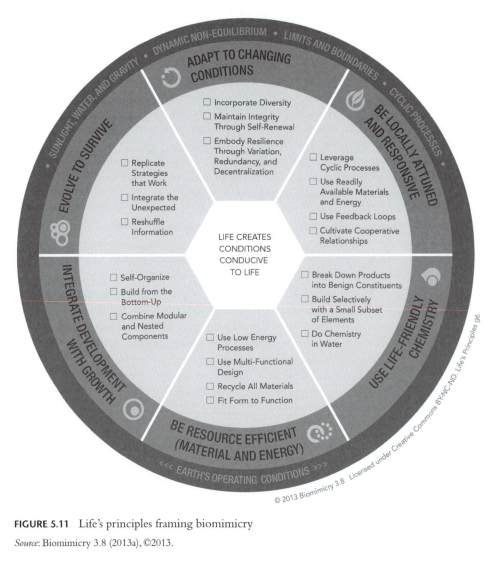

FIGURE 5.11 Life's principles framing biomimicry

Source: Biomimicry 3.8 (2013a), ©2013.

principles that could be used to inspire innovation into the design of buildings, communities and cities. For example, by mimicking trees, structures subject to wind damage, such as streetlights and power poles, could be made to have deep, flexible footing with lateral underground supports to prevent falling. The second is Ethical Biomimicry Finance™, a new investment methodology, designed to identify technologies and businesses accelerating the green transition. This methodology is based on biological principles (see Figure 5.11), and aims to transform the ideology and models of traditional finance (Ethical Markets, 2013).

There are a large number of organisms in nature that have properties of commercial interests (Bhushan, 2009). The website AskNature.org provides a database of more than 2,100 technological innovations and ideas, each inspired by such organisms. Some examples relevant to the green economy are:

- Humpback whales have large, irregular bumps called tubercles across the leading edges of their flippers, which enable them to make very tight turns in manoeuvring to catch krill. Wind tunnel tests demonstrated that blades with tubercles used less energy to turn compared with those without tubercles. Inspired by this, a company called WhalePower can now develop precise designs for retrofit leading edges or fully integrated tubercle technology blades for any turbines. Tubercle blades have been shown to increase annual electrical production by 20 per cent, while greatly reducing noise. The technology also promises greater efficiency in other applications including hydroelectric turbines, irrigation pumps and ventilation fans (WhalePower, 2013).
- A company called PAX Scientific has been developing air and fluid movement techno-logies in fans, mixers, propellers, turbines and pumps based on geometric designs found in nature. Depending on application, the resulting designs reduce energy usage between 10–85 per cent over conventional rotors, and noise by up to 75 per cent (PAX Scientific, 2013).
- The aerodynamic beak of a kingfisher allows the bird to dive down fast to catch the fish, with very little splash. This inspired the chief engineer of the fastest train the world, the Japanese Shinkansen Bullet Train, who modelled the front-end of the train based on the bird's beak. This resulted in a quieter and more energy efficient train (using 15 per cent less energy even when the train travels 10 per cent faster) (Bhushan, 2009).
- The termites *Macrotermes michaelseni* build tall self-cooling mounds by opening and closing vents throughout the mounds to manage convection currents of air. This model was used to design the high-rise Eastgate Building in Harare, Zimbabwe, which uses 90 per cent less energy for ventilation than similar-sized conventional building, while also saving US\$3.5 million dollars in air conditioning costs (Biomimicry 3.8, 2013b).
- The efficient lungs of birds and the swim bladders of fish have inspired the Esser-Kahn group from the University of California to produce a new filtering system, much like blood vessels in a natural lung, to remove CO_2 from electric power station smokestacks (ACS, 2013).

The field of biomimicry has been gaining more traction among business leaders in recent years. However, the discipline remains largely untapped, mainly owing to the difficulty in identifying structures and patterns in nature and then adapting these to solve human problems.

5.9 Assessing the environmental impact of green technology

How can the environmental impact of green technology be assessed in practice? Some approaches are outlined below.

5.9.1 Life-Cycle Analysis (LCA)

A key approach to evaluating the environmental impact of any item of technology is 'Life-Cycle Analysis' (LCA), which is sometimes referred to as 'Life Cycle Assessment'. This aims to evaluate impacts throughout the entire life cycle of a particular product, 'from cradle to grave', in terms of the raw materials, energy and land resources required for construction right through to the disposal of the product at the end of its useful lifespan (Wolf *et al.*, 2012). Legally, LCA is governed by the environmental management standard ISO 14040:2006 outlining LCA principles and framework, and ISO 14044:2006 for requirements and guidelines (ibid.). Further information on the approach is given by Ciambrone (1997), Horne *et al.* (2009), and Curran (2012).

The process of LCA can be divided into four phases according to ISO 14040 standards (Figure 5.12). In the first phase, the *goal and the scope* of the study need to be defined. It is important to clearly define the functional unit, system boundaries, methodological assumptions, and environmental impacts to be covered in order to ensure transparency and allow interpretation and comparison between LCA studies (Kloepffer, 2008). The following phase, *inventory analysis*, consists of data collection on the resources, materials and waste associated with the product throughout its life cycle, within the boundaries specified in the scope definition. In the *impact assessment* stage, these data are translated into indicators of environmental impacts. In the last phase, *interpretation*, the results of the second and third phase are interpreted in relation to the goal of the study. Through a sensitivity and uncertainty analysis, data quality issues or gaps can be identified, which can result in a revised scope of the LCA, and results and conclusions can be put in perspective (Aurich *et al.*, 2013). While a carbon footprint analysis (see Chapter 3) focuses only on GHG emissions and climate change (BSI, 2011), a full LCA must include all of the impacts that are relevant to the product analysed,

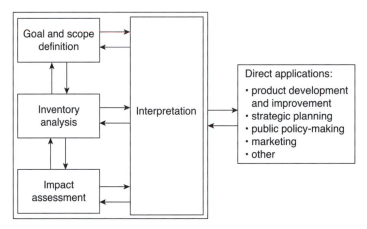

FIGURE 5.12 LCA framework and applications according to ISO 14040:2006

Source: Aurich *et al.* (2013), ©2013, with permission from Elsevier.

including ozone depletion, human toxicity, ecotoxicity, eutrophication, acidification, land use, and resource depletion.

Many green technologies have been subjected to LCA. For example, von Blottnitz and Curran (2007) present an assessment of 47 LCA analyses that compare bioethanol with conventional fuels. Results typically showed that bioethanol results in reductions in resource use and GHG emissions; however, impacts on acidification, human toxicity and ecological toxicity, which mainly occur during the growing and processing of biomass, were more often unfavourable than favourable. Cleary (2009) compared 20 LCAs of solid waste management systems, and found that overall, thermal treatment scenarios had a better environmental performance than landfilling. Boureima *et al.* (2009) performed a comparative LCA of electric, hybrid, LPG and petrol cars in Belgium. The analysis showed that the electric car had the best score and the petrol the worst, in terms of GHG emissions. The hybrid car was slightly better than the LPG car. The assessment of the impact on human health confirmed the best environmental score to the electric vehicle, followed by the LPG, petrol and hybrid.

Pehnt (2006) investigated the LCA of renewable energy (including hydro, PV and solar thermal, wind, geothermal and biomass) and demonstrated that the consumption of renewable energy resources (e.g. for construction) and GHG emissions are significantly lower than those of conventional systems. For other environmental impacts (i.e. material resources, eutrophication, and acidification), no consistent result for or against renewables was obtained; the comparison depends on a large number of context-dependent factors.

LCA methodologies have been evolving over the last decade and are now supported by international initiatives, such as the UNEP/SETAC Life Cycle Initiative (www.lifecycleinitiative. org/), and the European Platform on Life Cycle Assessment (EPLCA) (Sanfélix *et al.*, 2013). However, there are still barriers that inhibit the broader implementation of life cycle thinking. Limitations in LCA include (Finnveden *et al.*, 2009):

- LCA is very data-intensive and lack of data can restrict the conclusions that can be drawn for a specific technology.
- LCA aims to provide coverage of all environmental impacts that are relevant. However, only the most studied impacts (i.e. global warming potential, acidification, and eutrophication) are formally addressed; loss of biodiversity, for example, is often excluded owing to the lack of a quantitative indicator.
- Some LCA methodological challenges exist (especially for renewables) and LCA results can vary depending on the methodologies used.
- Uncertainties need to be addressed through the development of specific tools, which can lead to loss of simplicity.
- Weighting methods need to be evaluated for consistency by scientific methods, which can represent a challenge.

Kloepffer (2008) states that for a product to be truly sustainable, LCA needs to be combined with: (1) life cycle costing (LCC), to take into account all costs associated with the life-cycle of a product including the use- and end-of-life phases and hidden costs; and (2) social life cycle assessment (SLCA), to address the social aspects of the product. The author formalised his perspective into the Life Cycle Sustainability Assessment (LCSA) framework, where LCSA = LCA + LCC + SLCA. However, more research is necessary to make this framework operational (Zamagni, 2012).

5.9.2 Environmental Impact Assessment (EIA)

A second key approach to evaluating the environmental impact of any item of technology is an environmental impact assessment (EIA) (Figure 5.12). The goal of EIA is to anticipate and mitigate the environmental impacts of proposed new projects at the planning and design stages. Ideally, an EIA would be integrated with Environmental Management Systems (EMS, see Chapter 6), though such integration is rather limited in practice (Jay *et al.*, 2007). The two approaches have different origins and regulatory status; for example, within the EU, the ISO 14001 standard for EMS is designed to be adopted *voluntarily* by organisations operating in any sector, whereas EIA is *legally required* for projects listed in the annexes of the EIA Directive (EC, 2012b). EMS activity is also more widespread; for example, almost 10,000 ISO 14001 certificates are held in the UK (ISO, 2009) whereas around 450 EIAs are undertaken in England each year (Barker, 2006).

Jay *et al.* (2007) describe an EIA as an evaluation of the effects on the environment that are likely to arise from a major project (or other action). It can be considered as a systematic process for considering possible impacts prior to a decision being taken on whether or not a proposal should be given approval to proceed. Abaza *et al.* (2004) suggest that EIA should:

- be integrated into existing development planning and approval processes;
- be applied as a tool to implement environmental management;
- be integrated into the project life-cycle to ensure that environmental information is provided at the appropriate decision points and the correct time;
- be applied to all proposed actions that are likely to have a significant adverse effect on the environment and human health;
- include an analysis of feasible alternatives to the proposed action;
- include meaningful opportunities for public involvement;
- be carried out in a multi- or inter-disciplinary manner;
- integrate information on social, economic and biophysical impacts.

A number of research studies have been conducted to examine the effectiveness of EIA, and to identify reasons for failure. Jay *et al.* (2007) conclude that while it is generally accepted that EIA has an important role, it is often less successful than anticipated, partly because of poor integration with decision-making contexts within which it operates (Cashmore *et al.*, 2004). Abaza *et al.* (2004) suggest that the following components must be addressed for the EIA process to be effective:

- self-directed assessment by development proponents and agencies;
- oversight of EIA implementation by a designated body;
- guidance on conducting EIA in accordance with legal and procedural requirements;
- public involvement including measures related to availability of information and opportunity to comment on the content of EIA reports and documentation.

One of the limitations of EIA is the extent to which their recommendations are implemented in practice. For example, one investigation of EIA applications found that 50 per cent of mitigation measures were not translated into planning conditions or obligations (Tinker *et al.*, 2005).

Further information on EIA is provided by the International Association for Impact Assessment (IAIA, www.iaia.org), and in the UK, by the Institute of Environmental Management and Assessment (IEMA, www.iema.net).

Reflection point

Consider the steps in EIA illustrated in Figure 5.13. Which do you think are the weakest parts of this process, or the most difficult to implement? Consider, also, the need to consult a range of potential stakeholders in any EIA. One reason for doing this is to avoid the so-called 'NIMBY' effect. NIMBY stands for 'Not In My Back Yard', and is a common term used to describe people who oppose developments on qualitative, often subjective grounds. Very often a NIMBY argument will be based purely on personal or vested interest, and may be considered by others to be ill-informed or hypocritical. An example is provided by the opposition to wind farms in rural areas.

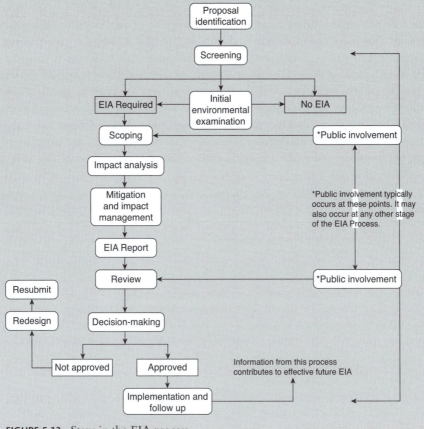

FIGURE 5.13 Steps in the EIA process

Source: UNEP (2002).

5.10 Achieving a green technological revolution

This chapter has profiled a number of different technologies and approaches that can potentially contribute to the green economy. However, their widespread deployment will require a form of technological revolution. Specifically, there will be a need to do the following (UNDESA, 2011):

- Enable countries to access, utilise and afford green technologies. There may be high costs of moving from non-green and non-sustainable technologies, which are 'locked into' existing economic systems.
- Enable further innovation and scaling up to drive down unit costs.
- Transfer technologies and make them accessible, since much innovation takes place in developed countries and in private corporations, who are the main owners of intellectual property rights covering green technologies (Eaton, 2013).
- Improve much existing infrastructure and actively promote green technologies and industries.

Unlike previous technological revolutions, development of the green economy will be different in that it will need to take place quickly, ideally within the next few decades (UNDESA, 2011). This is challenging, given that diffusion of technologies is usually a slow process. It can be argued that governments will have to assume a central role, as an acceleration of technological innovation and diffusion is unlikely to occur sufficiently rapidly if left only to market forces. Government policy, such as procurement policies and provision of incentives (see Table 5.8), can have a major influence on development of markets for green technologies. A radical shift to green technologies will mean improving, adjusting and replacing much existing infrastructure and other invested capital, which will require large-scale long-term

Table 5.8 Examples of green technology policy options for countries at different levels of development and administrative capacity

	Administrative and innovative capacity		
	Weak	*Medium*	*Strong*
Formal education	Primary and secondary education, emphasis on vocational training; begin to strengthen tertiary education, including educating some people abroad	Primary, secondary, and tertiary education; emphasis on vocational training; strengthening of tertiary education	Higher demand for capabilities; greater emphasis on tertiary education, including at the postgraduate and doctorate level
Technology transfer	FDI and global value chains in conjunction with domestic research and policies; encourage joint ventures with foreign firms and mobility between firms	Reverse engineering of imports, FDI and global value chains in conjunction with domestic research and policies; encourage joint ventures with foreign firms, mobility between firms and return of diaspora members	Outward FDI; joint research with international firms; sharing of scientific research

	Administrative and innovative capacity		
	Weak	Medium	Strong
Other industrial policies	Emphasise regulations and quantity-based incentives; possible investment regulations; investments in infrastructure	Wide range of quantity and price-based incentives; possible investment regulations; investments in infrastructure	Wide range of quantity and price-based incentives; focus on domestic and export markets
Additional market formation policies	Public procurement	Public procurement, feed-in tariffs	Public procurement, feed-in tariffs
Other risk-sharing mechanisms	Public–private partnerships; development banks; country funds; equity-linked financing; rural infrastructure funds	Public–private partnerships; development banks; country funds; equity linked financing; rural infrastructure funds	Public–private partnerships; development banks; equity-linked financing; country funds; rural infrastructure funds
Focus on building linkages between …	Universities and firms; regional knowledge networks; science parks; movement of people	Universities and firms; regional knowledge networks; science parks; movement of people	Build international knowledge networks; joint research and development with international firms; outward FDI
Intellectual property rights	Weak intellectual property rights regimes	Advantages to both weak and strong systems	Likely a stronger system; though still encourage knowledge-sharing in key sectors

Source: UNDESA (2011).
Note: FDI, foreign direct investment.

financing. This would require government support and incentives. The process will also need to be facilitated by international cooperation.

Reflection point

Do you believe that a green technological revolution is needed to bring about the green economy? Might that revolution already be underway?

Bibliography

Abaza, H., Bisset, R. and Sadler, B. 2004. *Environmental Impact Assessment and Strategic Environmental Assessment: Towards an Integrated Approach*, [Online], United Nations Environment Programme (UNEP), Nairobi, Kenya. Available at: www.unep.ch/etu/publications/textONUbr.pdf (accessed 2 Dec. 2013).

Abraham, M. A. and Nguyen, N. 2003. 'Green engineering: Defining the principles': results from the Sandestin Conference. *Environmental Progress*, 22: 233–236.

ACS 2013. Artificial lung to remove carbon dioxide—from smokestacks [Online]. Available at: American Chemical Society, Washington, DC. Available at: http://www.acs.org/content/acs/en/pressroom/newsreleases/2013/september/artificial-lung-to-remove-carbon-dioxide-from-smokestacks.html (accessed 15 Nov. 2013).

Adamantiades, A. and Kessides, I. 2009. Nuclear power for sustainable development: current status and future prospects. *Energy Policy*, 37: 5149–5166.

Amin, M. 2013. Energy: the Smart-Grid solution. *Nature*, 499: 145–147.

Anbarasan, P., Baer, Z. C., Sreekumar, S., *et al.* 2012. Integration of chemical catalysis with extractive fermentation to produce fuels. *Nature*, 491: 235–239.

Archer, C. L. and Jacobson, M. Z. 2005. Evaluation of global wind power. *Journal of Geophysical Research*, 110: D12110.

Astrup, T., Møller, J. and Fruergaard, T. 2009. Incineration and co-combustion of waste: accounting of greenhouse gases and global warming contributions. *Waste Management & Research*, 27: 789–799.

Aurich, J. C., Linke, B., Hauschild, M., *et al.* 2013. Sustainability of abrasive processes. *CIRP Annals: Manufacturing Technology*, 62: 653–672.

Baba, A. and Ármannsson, H. 2006. Environmental impact of the utilization of geothermal areas. *Energy Sources, Part B: Economics, Planning and Policy*, 1: 267–278.

Bahaj, A. S. 2013. New research in tidal current energy. *Philosophical Transactions of the Royal Society A: Mathematical, Physical and Engineering Sciences*, 371. Available at: http://rsta.royalsocietypublishing.org/site/2013/1985.xhtml.

Bahor, B., Van Brunt, M., Stovall, J. and Blue, K. 2009. Integrated waste management as a climate change stabilization wedge. *Waste Management & Research*, 27: 839–849.

Baker, A. C. 1991. *Tidal Power*, Peter Peregrinus, London.

Barker, K. 2006. *Barker Review of Land Use Planning: Final Report – Recommendations*. London, HMSO.

Baumeister, D., Tocke, R., Dwyer, J., *et al.* 2013. *Biomimicry Resource Handbook: A Seed Bank of Best Practices*, Biomimicry 3.8, Missoula, Montana, USA.

BCC Research 2011. *Green Technologies and Global Markets* [Online], BCC Research, Wellesley, MA. Available at: www.bccresearch.com/report/green-technologies-markets-env012a.html (accessed 1 Nov. 2013).

BCC Research 2012. *Global Markets and Technologies for Photovoltaic Systems*, BCC Research LLC, Wellesley, MA.

Benson, S. M., Bennaceur, K., Cook, P., *et al.* 2012. Carbon capture and storage, in *Global Energy Assessment: Toward a Sustainable Future*, Cambridge University Press, Cambridge, and the International Institute for Applied Systems Analysis, Laxenburg, Austria.

Benyus, J. M. 1997. *Biomimicry: Innovation Inspired by Nature*, HarperCollins, New York.

Bertani, R. 2010. *Geothermal Power Generation in the World: 2005–2010 Update Report* [Online], Proceedings World Geothermal Congress 2010, Bali, Indonesia, 25–29 April 2010. Available at: www.geothermal-energy.org/pdf/IGAstandard/WGC/2010/0008.pdf (accessed 25 Oct. 2013).

Beyea, J. 2010. The Smart Electricity Grid and scientific research. *Science*, 328: 979–980.

Bhushan, B. 2009. Biomimetics: lessons from Nature – an overview. *Philosophical Transactions of the Royal Society A: Mathematical, Physical and Engineering Sciences*, 367: 1445–1486.

Biello, D. 2013. 400 PPM: can artificial trees help pull CO_2 from the air? *Scientific American*, 16 May 2013. [Online]. Available at: www.scientificamerican.com/article.cfm?id=prospects-for-direct-air-capture-of-carbon-dioxide (accessed 12 Nov. 2013).

Biksey, T. M. and Wu, F. 2009. Biofuels: by-products. *Science*, 326: 1344–1345.

Binswanger, M. 2001. Technological progress and sustainable development: what about the rebound effect? *Ecological Economics*, 36: 119–132.

Biomimicry 3.8 2013a. *Life's Principles* [Online]. Biomimicry 3.8: Missoula, MT. Available at: http://biomimicry.net/about/biomimicry/biomimicry-designlens/lifes-principles/ (accessed 2 Dec. 2013).

Biomimicry 3.8 2013b. *Architecture: Learning from Termites How to Create Sustainable Buildings* [Online]. Available at: Biomimicry 3.8: Missoula, MT. Available at: http://biomimicry.net/about/biomimicry/case-examples/architecture/ (accessed 15 Nov. 2013).

Biomimicry 3.8 and HOK 2013. *Genius of Biome: Temperate Broadleaf Forest*, Biomimicry 3.8 and HOK Group, Inc., Missoula, MT.

Bogner, J., Abdelrafie Ahmed, M., Diaz, C., *et al.* A. (eds) *Climate Change 2007: Mitigation. Contribution of Working Group III to the Fourth Assessment Report of the Intergovernmental Panel on Climate Change.* Cambridge University Press: Cambridge.

Boureima, F. S., Messagie, M., Matheys, J., *et al.* 2009. Comparative LCA of electric, hybrid, LPG and gasoline cars in Belgian context. *World Electric Vehicle Journal*, 3.

Boyle, E. 2012. Solar photovoltaics, in G. Boyle (ed.) *Renewable Energy: Power for a Sustainable Future*, 3rd edn. Oxford University Press: Oxford.

Boyle, E., Everett, B. and Alexander, G. 2012. Introducing renewable energy, in G. Boyle (ed.) *Renewable Energy: Power for a Sustainable Future*, 3rd edn. Oxford University Press: Oxford.

BP 2013. *BP Statistical Review of World Energy June 2013*, BP p.l.c., London.

Brown, M. A. and Sovacool, B. K. 2011. *Climate Change and Global Energy Security: Technology and Policy Options*, The MIT Press, Cambridge, MA.

BSI 2011. *The Guide to PAS 2050:2011: How to Carbon Footprint Your Products, Identify Hotspots and Reduce Emissions in Your Supply Chain*, British Standards Institution, London.

Buesseler, K. O., Doney, S. C., Karl, D. M., *et al.* 2008. Ocean iron fertilization: moving forward in a sea of uncertainty. *Science*, 319: 162.

Cashmore, M., Gwilliam, R., Morgan, R., *et al.* 2004. The interminable issue of effectiveness: substantive purposes, outcomes and research challenges in the advancement of environmental impact assessment theory. *Impact Assessment and Project Appraisal*, 22: 295–310.

Chalmin, P. and Gaillochet, C. 2009. *From Waste to Resources: World Waste Survey*, Economica Ltd., Paris.

Chapman, L. 2007. Transport and climate change: a review. *Journal of Transport Geography*, 15: 354–367.

Charles, D. 2009. Leaping the efficiency gap. *Science*, 325: 804–811.

Choi, Y. J. and Lee, S. Y. 2013. Microbial production of short-chain alkanes. *Nature*, 502: 571–574.

Ciambrone, D. F. 1997. *Environmental Life Cycle Analysis*, Lewis Publishers, Boca Raton, FL.

Clastres, C. 2011. Smart grids: another step towards competition, energy security and climate change objectives. *Energy Policy*, 39: 5399–5408.

Cleary, J. 2009. Life cycle assessments of municipal solid waste management systems: a comparative analysis of selected peer-reviewed literature. *Environment International*, 35: 1256–1266.

Clery, D. 2010. Sending African sunlight to Europe, special delivery. *Science*, 329: 782–783.

COGEN Europe 2013. Time is ripe to harness CHP's energy savings potential [Online]. The European Association for the Promotion of Cogeneration (COGEN Europe): Brussels. Available at: www.cogeneurope.eu/medialibrary/2013 Oct./22/2ff8f20d/Media%20Advisory%20on%20Eurostat%20CHP%20statistics%2022_10_2013.pdf (accessed 1 Nov. 2013).

Curran, M. A. 2012. *Life Cycle Assessment Handbook: A Guide for Environmentally Sustainable Products*, Wiley, Somerset, NJ.

Curzons, A. D., Constable, D. J. C., Mortimer, D. N. and Cunningham, V. L. 2001. So you think your process is green, how do you know?-Using principles of sustainability to determine what is green-a corporate perspective. *Green Chemistry*, 3: 1–6.

da Costa, A. C. A., Pereira, N. and Aranda, D. A. G. 2010. The situation of biofuels in Brazil: new generation technologies. *Renewable & Sustainable Energy Reviews*, 14: 3041–3049.

DEFRA 2011. *Anaerobic Digestion Strategy and Action Plan*, Department for Environment, Food and Rural Affairs, London.

Delucchi, M. A. and Jacobson, M. Z. 2011. Providing all global energy with wind, water, and solar power, Part II: Reliability, system and transmission costs, and policies. *Energy Policy*, 39: 1170–1190.

Duckers, L. 2012. Wave energy, in G. Boyle (ed.) *Renewable Energy: Power for a Sustainable Future*, 3rd edn. Oxford University Press: Oxford.

Duffy, J. E., Canuel, E. A., Adey, W. and Swaddle, J. P. 2009. Biofuels: algae. *Science*, 326: 1345.

Eaton, D. 2013. Technology and innovation for a green economy. *Review of European, Comparative & International Environmental Law*, 22: 62–67.

EBTP 2013. *Energy Crops for Biofuels* [Online]. European Biofuels Technology Platform (EBTP), Newbury, UK. Available at: www.biofuelstp.eu/crops.html.

EC 1999. Council Directive 1999/31/EC of 26 April 1999 on the Landfill of Waste [Online], *Official Journal of the European Union*, Luxembourg. Available at: http://eur-lex.europa.eu/LexUriServ/LexUriServ.do?uri=CELEX:31999L0031:EN:NOT (accessed 7 Nov. 2013).

EC 2007. *2020 Vision: Saving Our Energy*, European Commission, Directorate-General for Energy and Transport, Brussels.

EC 2012a. Directive 2012/19/EU on Waste Electrical and Electronic Equipment (WEEE) (Recast) [Online]. *Official Journal of the European Union*, Luxembourg. Available at: http://eur-lex.europa.eu/LexUriServ/LexUriServ.do?uri=OJ:L:2012:197:0038:0071:EN:PDF (accessed 7 Nov. 2013).

EC 2012b. Directive 2011/92/EU on the Assessment of the Effects of Certain Public and Private Projects on the Environment (Codification) [Online]. Official Journal of the *European Union*, Luxembourg. Available at: http://new.eur-lex.europa.eu/legal-content/EN/TXT/PDF/?uri=CELEX:32011L0092&rid=1 (accessed 16 Nov. 2013).

Eggleston, H. S., Buendia, L., Miwa, K., *et al.* (eds) 2006. *2006 IPCC Guidelines for National Greenhouse Gas Inventories*, IGES: Japan.

Ellen MacArthur Foundation 2013a. *Towards the Circular Economy: Opportunities for the Consumer Goods Sector*, Ellen MacArthur Foundation, Cowes, Isle of Wight.

Ellen MacArthur Foundation 2013b. *The Circular Economy* [Online]. Ellen MacArthur Foundation, Cowes, Isle of Wight. Available at: www.ellenmacarthurfoundation.org/higher_education/global_campus/global-campus-resources (accessed 2 Dec. 2013).

Elliott, D. 1996. Tidal power, in G. Boyle (ed.) *Renewable Energy: Power for a Sustainable Future*, 3rd edn. Oxford University Press: Oxford.

ESA 2013. *Going for Growth: A Practical Route to a Circular Economy* [Online]. Environmental Services Association (ESA) London. Available at: www.esauk.org/esa_reports/Circular_Economy_Report_FINAL_High_Res_For_Release.pdf (accessed 8 Nov. 2013).

Escobar, J. C., Lora, E. S., Venturini, O. J., *et al.* 2009. Biofuels: environment, technology and food security. *Renewable and Sustainable Energy Reviews*, 13: 1275–1287.

ESRI 2013. *World Continents* [Online]. Available at: ESRI: Redlands, CA. Available at: www.arcgis.com/home/item.html?id=a3cb207855b348a297ab85261743351d (accessed 28 Nov. 2013).

Ethical Markets 2013. Ethical Markets rolls out Ethical Biomimicry Finance™ [Online]. Ethical Markets Media, LLC: St. Augustine, FL. Available at: www.ethicalmarkets.com/2013/05/16/ethical-markets-rolls-out-ethical-biomimicry-finance/ (accessed 15 Nov. 2013).

ETP Smart Grids 2010. *Strategic Deployment Document for Europe's Electricity Networks of the Future*, [Online]. European Technology Platform Smart Grids (ETP Smart Grids), Brussels. Available at: www.smartgrids.eu/documents/SmartGrids_SDD_FINAL_APRIL2010.pdf (accessed 1 Nov. 2013).

Everett, B. 2003. Costing energy, in G. Boyle, B. Everett and J. Ramage (eds) *Energy Systems and Sustainability: Power for a Sustainable Future*. Oxford University Press in association with The Open University: Oxford.

Everett, B. and Boyle, G. 2012. Integrating renewable energy, in G. Boyle (ed.) *Renewable Energy: Power for a Sustainable Future*, 3rd edn. Oxford University Press: Oxford.

EWEA 2009. *Economic Benefits of Wind Energy*, European Wind Energy Association (EWEA), Brussels.

EWEA 2011. *Pure Power: Wind Energy Targets from 2020 and 2030*, European Wind Energy Association (EWEA), Brussels.

EWEA 2013. *Wind in Power: 2012 European Statistics*, European Wind Energy Association (EWEA), Brussels.

FAO 2013. *Food Wastage Footprint: Impacts on Natural Resources. Summary Report*, FAO SAVE FOOD Working Group, Rome, Italy.

Finnveden, G., Hauschild, M. Z., Ekvall, T., *et al.* 2009. Recent developments in Life Cycle Assessment. *Journal of Environmental Management*, 91: 1–21.

Frid, C., Andonegi, E., Depestele, J., *et al.* 2012. The environmental interactions of tidal and wave energy generation devices. *Environmental Impact Assessment Review,* 32: 133–139.

Garnish, J. and Brown, G. 2012. Geothermal energy, in G. Boyle (ed.) *Renewable Energy: Power for a Sustainable Future*, 3rd edn. Oxford University Press: Oxford.

GEA 2012. *Global Energy Assessment: Toward a Sustainable Future*, Cambridge University Press, Cambridge, and the International Institute for Applied Systems Analysis, Laxenburg, Austria.

Geng, Y. and Doberstein, B. 2008. Developing the circular economy in China: challenges and opportunities for achieving 'leapfrog development'. *International Journal of Sustainable Development and World Ecology*, 15: 231–239.

Gentil, E., Christensen, T. H. and Aoustin, E. 2009. Greenhouse gas accounting and waste management. *Waste Management & Research*, 27: 696–706.

Gibbins, J. and Chalmers, H. 2008. Carbon capture and storage. *Energy Policy*, 36: 4317–4322.

Giordano, V., Gangale, F., Fulli, G. and Sánchez Jiménez, M. 2011. *Smart Grids Projects in Europe: Lessons Learned and Current Developments. JRC Reference Report 65215*, EC, DG JRC, Institute for Energy, Petten, The Netherlands.

Grecian, W. J., Inger, R., Attrill, M. J., *et al.* 2010. Potential impacts of wave-powered marine renewable energy installations on marine birds. *Ibis*, 152: 683–697.

Greenpeace 2012. *Energy [R]Evolution: A Sustainable World Energy Outlook*, Greenpeace, Global Wind Energy Council (GWEC) and European Renewable Energy Council (EREC), Amsterdam [Online]. Available at: http://www.greenpeace.org/international/Global/international/publications/climate/2012/Energy%20Revolution%202012/ER2012.pdf (accessed 31 Oct.2013).

Green Technology 2013. *Green Technology – What Is It?* [Online]. Pasadena, CA. Available at: www.green-technology.org (accessed 15 Oct. 2013).

Guo, K. W. 2012. Green nanotechnology of trends in future energy: a review. *International Journal of Energy Research*, 36: 1–17.

GWEC 2013. *Global Statistics* [Online]. Global Wind Energy Council (GWEC). Available at: www.gwec.net (accessed 18 Oct. 2013).

Harvey, L. 2009. Reducing energy use in the buildings sector: measures, costs, and examples. *Energy Efficiency*, 2: 139–163.

Hasper, M. 2009. Green technology in developing countries: creating accessibility through a global exchange forum. *Duke Law and Technology Review*, 7: 1–14.

Haszeldine, R. S. 2009. Carbon capture and storage: how green can black be? *Science*, 325: 1647–1652.

Hecht, M. M. 2009. The myth of nuclear 'waste'. *Executive Intelligence Review*, February 13: 14–17.

Hledik, R. 2009. How green is the Smart Grid? *The Electricity Journal*, 22: 29–41.

Hoornweg, D., Bhada-Tata, P. and Kennedy, C. 2013. Waste production must peak this century. *Nature*, 502: 615–617.

Horne, R., Verghese, K. and Grant, T. 2009. *Life Cycle Assessment: Principles, Practice, and Prospects*, CSIRO Pub, Collingwood, Vic.

House, K. Z., House, C. H., Schrag, D. P. and Aziz, M. J. 2007. Electrochemical acceleration of chemical weathering as an energetically feasible approach to mitigating anthropogenic climate change. *Environmental Science & Technology*, 41: 8464–8470.

IEA 2009. *Cogeneration and District Energy: Sustainable Energy Technologies for Today and Tomorrow*, OECD/IEA, Paris.

IEA 2010. *Energy Technology Perspectives 2010*, OECD/IEA, Paris.

IEA 2011a. *Technology Roadmap Geothermal Heat and Power*, OECD/IEA, Paris.

IEA 2011b. *Renewable Energy: Policy Considerations for Deploying Renewables*, OECD/IEA, Paris.

IEA 2011c. *Co-generation and Renewables: Solutions for a Low-Carbon Energy Future*, OECD/IEA, Paris.

IEA 2011d. *Technology Roadmap: Smart Grids*, OECD/IEA, Paris.

IEA 2012a. *World Energy Outlook 2012 Factsheet: How Will Global Energy Markets Evolve to 2035?* [Online]. International Energy Agency, Paris. Available at: www.worldenergyoutlook.org/media/weowebsite/2012/factsheets.pdf (accessed 25 Oct. 2013).

IEA 2012b. *Energy Technology Perspectives 2012: Pathways to a Clean Energy System*, International Energy Agency, Paris.

IEA 2013a. *Transition to Sustainable Buildings: Strategies and Opportunities to 2050. Executive Summary*, OECD/IEA, Paris.

IEA 2013b. *Key World Energy Statistics 2013*, International Energy Agency, Paris.

IEA Bioenergy 2013. *IEA Bioenergy Task 37: Member Country Reports, Bern, Switzerland, April 17–19, 2013* [Online]. IEA Bioenergy, Petten, The Netherlands. Available at: www.iea-biogas.net/country-reports.html (accessed 7 Nov. 2013).

Ipakchi, A. and Albuyeh, F. 2009. Grid of the future. *IEEE Power and Energy Magazine*, 7: 52–62.

IPCC 2011. *Renewable Energy Sources and Climate Change Mitigation*, Cambridge University Press, Cambridge.

IPCC 2013. *Working Group I Contribution to the IPCC Fifth Assessment Report Climate Change 2013: The Physical Science Basis. Summary for Policymakers* [Online]. Available at: www.climatechange2013.org/images/uploads/WGIAR5-SPM_Approved27Sep2013.pdf (accessed 10 Oct. 2013).

ISO 2009. *ISO 14001:2004/Cor 1:2009. Environmental Management Systems. Requirements with Guidance for Use. Technical Corrigendum 1*, International Organization for Standardization, Geneva, Switzerland.

ISWA 2009. *Waste and Climate Change: ISWA White Paper*, International Solid Waste Association (ISWA), Vienna.

Jacobson, M. Z. 2009. Review of solutions to global warming, air pollution, and energy security. *Energy & Environmental Science*, 2: 148–173.

Jacobson, M. Z. and Archer, C. L. 2012. Saturation wind power potential and its implications for wind energy. *Proceedings of the National Academy of Sciences of the United States of America*, 10 September 2012. Available at: http://www.pnas.org/content/early/2012/08/31/1208993109.abstract.

Jacobson, M. Z. and Delucchi, M. A. 2011. Providing all global energy with wind, water, and solar power, Part I: Technologies, energy resources, quantities and areas of infrastructure, and materials. *Energy Policy*, 39: 1154–1169.

Jacobson, M. Z. and Masters, G. M. 2001. Exploiting wind versus coal. *Science*, 293: 1438.

Jay, S., Jones, C., Slinn, P. and Wood, C. 2007. Environmental impact assessment: retrospect and prospect. *Environmental Impact Assessment Review*, 27: 287–300.

Johansson, T. B., Nakicenovic, N., Patwardhan, A. and Gomez-Echeverri, L. 2012. Summary for policymakers, in *Global Energy Assessment: Toward a Sustainable Future*. Cambridge University Press, Cambridge, and the International Institute for Applied Systems Analysis, Laxenburg, Austria.

Jones, R. 2007. Can nanotechnology ever prove that it is green? *Nature Nanotechnology*, 2: 71–72.

Kahn Ribeiro, S., Figueroa, M. J., Creutzig, F., *et al.* 2012. Energy end-use: transport, in *Global Energy Assessment: Toward a Sustainable Future*, Cambridge University Press, Cambridge, and the International Institute for Applied Systems Analysis, Laxenburg, Austria.

Kahn Ribeiro, S., Kobayashi, S., Beuthe, M., *et al.* 2007. Transport and its infrastructure, in B. Metz, O. R. Davidson, P. R. Bosch, *et al.* (eds) *Climate Change 2007: Mitigation. Contribution of Working Group III to the Fourth Assessment Report of the Intergovernmental Panel on Climate Change*, Cambridge University Press: Cambridge.

Kauppi, P. E. and Laura, S. 2009. Biofuels: forests and carbon. *Science*, 326: 1345.

Kaygusuz, K. 2009. The role of hydropower for sustainable energy development. *Energy Sources Part B-Economics Planning and Policy*, 4: 365–376.

Kerr, R. A. 2010. Do we have the energy for the next transition? *Science*, 329: 780–781.

Kloepffer, W. 2008. Life cycle sustainability assessment of products. *The International Journal of Life Cycle Assessment*, 13: 89–95.

Kunz, T. H., Arnett, E. B., Erickson, W. P., *et al.* 2007. Ecological impacts of wind energy development on bats: questions, research needs, and hypotheses. *Frontiers in Ecology and the Environment*, 5: 315–324.

Lancaster, M. 2010. *Green Chemistry: An Introductory Text*, Royal Society of Chemistry, Cambridge.

Lane, B. 2006. *Life Cycle Assessment of Vehicle Fuels and Technologies: Final Report, London Borough of Camden, March 2006* [Online]. Ecolane Transport Consultancy, Bristol. Available at: www.travelfootprint.org/docs/Camden_LCA_Report_FINAL_10_03_2006.pdf (accessed 6 Nov. 2013).

Langton, R., Davies, I. M. and Scott, B. E. 2011. Seabird conservation and tidal stream and wave power generation: information needs for predicting and managing potential impacts. *Marine Policy*, 35: 623–630.

Le Quéré, C., Andres, R. J., Boden, T., *et al.* 2013. The global carbon budget 1959–2011. *Earth System Scientific Data*, 5: 165–185.

Levine, M., Ürge-Vorsatz, D., Blok, K., *et al.* 2007. Residential and commercial buildings, in B. Metz, O. R. Davidson, P. R. Bosch, *et al.* (eds) *Climate Change 2007: Mitigation. Contribution of Working Group III to the Fourth Assessment Report of the Intergovernmental Panel on Climate Change*, Cambridge University Press: Cambridge.

McCartney, M. 2009. Living with dams: managing the environmental impacts. *Water Policy*, 11: 121–139.

McDonough, W. and Braungart, M. 2002. *Cradle to Cradle: Remaking the Way We Make Things*, North Point Press, New York.

MacKay, D. J. C. 2008. *Sustainable Energy – Without the Hot Air*, UIT Cambridge Ltd, Cambridge.

Makower, J. 2013. Biomimicry's growing web of opportunity [Online]. GreenBiz Group Inc.: Oakland, CA. Available at: www.greenbiz.com/blog/2013/09/16/biomimicry-spins-web-opportunity-0 (accessed 15 Nov. 2013).

Marshall, M. 2013. Terraforming Earth: geoengineering megaplan starts now. *New Scientist*, 9 October, 10–11.

Medina, M. 2008. The informal recycling sector in developing countries: organising waste pickers to enhance their impact. *Gridlines*, 44 [Online]. Available at: www.ppiaf.org/sites/ppiaf.org/files/publication/Gridlines-44-Informal%20Recycling%20-%20MMedina.pdf (accessed 8 Nov. 2013).

Metz, B., Davidson, O., de Coninck, H., *et al.* 2005. *Carbon Dioxide Capture and Storage*, IPCC, Cambridge University Press, Cambridge.

Møller, A. P. and Mousseau, T. A. 2011. Conservation consequences of Chernobyl and other nuclear accidents. *Biological Conservation*, 144: 2787–2798.

Møller, J., Boldrin, A. and Christensen, T. H. 2009. Anaerobic digestion and digestate use: accounting of greenhouse gases and global warming contribution. *Waste Management & Research*, 27: 813–824.

Moriarty, P. and Honnery, D. 2012. What is the global potential for renewable energy? *Renewable and Sustainable Energy Reviews*, 16: 244–252.

Mulvaney, D. 2011. *Green Technology: An A-to-Z Guide*, Sage, Thousand Oaks, CA.

Muradov, N. Z. and Veziroglu, T. N. 2008. 'Green' path from fossil-based to hydrogen economy: an overview of carbon-neutral technologies. *International Journal of Hydrogen Energy*, 33: 6804–6839.

Neele, F., Mikunda, T., Seebregts, A., *et al.* 2013. A roadmap towards a European CO_2 transport infrastructure. *Energy Procedia*, 37: 7774–7782.

New, T. and Xie, Z. 2008. Impacts of large dams on riparian vegetation: applying global experience to the case of China's Three Gorges Dam. *Biodiversity and Conservation*, 17: 3149–3163.

NNFCC 2013. *What Is AD? The Official Information Portal on Anaerobic Digestion* [Online]. The National Non-Food Crops Centre (NNFCC), Heslington, York, UK. Available at: www.biogas-info.co.uk/index.php/what-is-anaerobic-digestion.html (accessed 17 Oct. 2013).

NREL 2013. *Levelized Cost of Energy Calculator* [Online]. National Renewable Energy Laboratory (NREL), Golden, CO, USA. Available at: www.nrel.gov/analysis/tech_lcoe.html (accessed 25 Oct. 2013).

OECD 2013. Nanotechnology for green innovation. *OECD Science, Technology and Industry Policy Papers*, No. 5. Available at: http://dx.doi.org Oct..1787/5k450q9j8p8q-en.

Onoda, T. 2009. IEA policies: G8 recommendations and an afterwards. *Energy Policy*, 37: 3823–3831.

Pacala, S. and Socolow, R. 2004. Stabilization wedges: solving the climate problem for the next 50 years with current technologies. *Science*, 305: 968–972.

Pampel, F. C. 2011. Support for nuclear energy in the context of climate change. *Organization & Environment*, 24: 249–268.

Parida, B., Iniyan, S. and Goic, R. 2011. A review of solar photovoltaic technologies. *Renewable and Sustainable Energy Reviews*, 15: 1625–1636.

PAX Scientific 2013. *PAX Scientific: Capturing the Force of Nature* [Online]. PAX Scientific: San Rafael, CA. Available at: http://paxscientific.com/ (accessed 15 Nov. 2013).

Pehnt, M. 2006. Dynamic life cycle assessment (LCA) of renewable energy technologies. *Renewable Energy*, 31: 55–71.

Pehnt, M. 2008. Environmental impacts of distributed energy systems: the case of micro cogeneration. *Environmental Science & Policy*, 11: 25–37.

Phillips, J. 2010. Evaluating the level and nature of sustainable development for a geothermal power plant. *Renewable and Sustainable Energy Reviews*, 14: 2414–2425.

Poliakoff, M. and Licence, P. 2007. Sustainable technology: green chemistry. *Nature*, 450: 810–812.

Poliakoff, M., Fitzpatrick, J. M., Farren, T. R. and Anastas, P.T. 2002. Green chemistry: science and politics of change. *Science*, 297: 807–810.

Poumadere, M., Bertoldo, R. and Samadi, J. 2011. Public perceptions and governance of controversial technologies to tackle climate change: nuclear power, carbon capture and storage, wind, and geoengineering. *Wiley Interdisciplinary Reviews-Climate Change*, 2: 712–727.

Pratt, R., Balducci, P., Gerkensmeyer, C.,*et al.* 2010. *The Smart Grid: An Estimation of the Energy and CO_2 Benefits*. PNNL-19112, Pacific Northwest National Laboratory, Richland, WA.

Price, L., De la Rue du Can, S., Sinton, J. and Worrell, E. 2006. *Sectoral Trends in Global Energy Use and GHG Emissions*, Lawrence Berkeley National Laboratory, Berkeley, CA.

Quaschning, V. 2009. *Renewable Energy and Climate Change*, John Wiley & Sons Ltd, Chichester.

Ramage, J. 2012. Hydroelectricity, in G. Boyle (ed.) *Renewable Energy: Power for a Sustainable Future*, 3rd edn. Oxford University Press: Oxford.

Reck, B. K. and Graedel, T. E. 2012. Challenges in metal recycling. *Science*, 337: 690–695.

RFA 2013a. *The New Fuel: E15* [Online]. Renewable Fuels Association: Washington, DC. Available at: www.ethanolrfa.org/pages/E15 (accessed 17 Oct. 2013).

RFA 2013b. *World Fuel Ethanol Production* [Online]. Renewable Fuels Association: Washington, DC. Available at: http://ethanolrfa.org/pages/World-Fuel-Ethanol-Production (accessed 17 Oct. 2013).

Riahi, K., Dentener, F., Gielen, D., *et al.* 2012. Energy pathways for sustainable development, in *Global Energy Assessment: Toward a Sustainable Future*, Cambridge University Press, Cambridge, and the International Institute for Applied Systems Analysis, Laxenburg, Austria.

Richard, T. L. 2010. Challenges in scaling up biofuels infrastructure. *Science*, 329: 793–796.

Rist, L., Lee, J. S. H. and Koh, L. P. 2009. Biofuels: social benefits. *Science*, 326: 1344.

Robock, A. 2008. 20 reasons why geoengineering may be a bad idea. *Bulletin of the Atomic Scientists*, 64: 14–18.

Rogner, H-H. 2010. Nuclear power and sustainable development. *Journal of International Affairs*, 64: 137–163.

Rogner, H-H., Aguilera, R. F., Bertani, R., *et al.* 2012. Energy resources and potentials, in *Global Energy Assessment: Toward a Sustainable Future*, Cambridge University Press, Cambridge, and the International Institute for Applied Systems Analysis, Laxenburg, Austria.

Saidur, R., Rahim, N. A., Islam, M. R. and Solangi, K. H. 2011. Environmental impact of wind energy. *Renewable & Sustainable Energy Reviews*, 15: 2423–2430.

Sakulniyomporn, S., Kubaha, K. and Chullabodhi, C. 2011. External costs of fossil electricity generation: health-based assessment in Thailand. *Renewable and Sustainable Energy Reviews*, 15: 3470–3479.

Sanderson, K. 2011. Chemistry: it's not easy being green. *Nature*, 469: 18–20.

Sanfélix, J., Mathieux, F., Rúa, C., *et al.* 2013. The enhanced LCA Resources Directory: a tool aimed at improving Life Cycle Thinking practices. *The International Journal of Life Cycle Assessment*, 18: 273–277.

Schiermeier, Q. 2013. Germany's energy gamble. *Nature*, 496: 156–158.

Schmidt, K. F. 2007. *Green Nanotechnology: It's Easier Than You Think*, Project on Emerging Nanotechnologies, Woodrow Wilson International Center for Scholars, Washington, DC.

SEAI 2013. *Gas Yields Table* [Online]. Sustainable Energy Authority of Ireland (SEAI), Dublin. Available at: www.seai.ie/Renewables/Bioenergy/Bioenergy_Technologies/Anaerobic_Digestion/

The_Process_and_Techniques_of_Anaerobic_Digestion/Gas_Yields_Table.pdf (accessed 17 Oct. 2013).

Searchinger, T., Heimlich, R., Houghton, R. A., *et al*. 2008. Use of U.S. croplands for biofuels increases greenhouse gases through emissions from land-use change. *Science*, 319: 1238–1240.

Simões, M. G., Roche, R., Kyriakides, E., *et al*. 2011. Smart-grid technologies and progress in Europe and the USA. Energy Conversion Congress and Exposition (ECCE), 2011 IEEE, 17–22 Sept. 2011, 383–390.

Smith, A., Brown, K., Ogilvie, S., *et al*. 2001. *Waste Management Options and Climate Change: Final Report to the European Commission, DG Environment*, Office for Official Publications of the European Communities, Luxembourg.

Solangi, K. H., Islam, M. R., Saidur, R., *et al*. 2011. A review on global solar energy policy. *Renewable and Sustainable Energy Reviews*, 15: 2149–2163.

Sorensen, B. 2010. *Renewable Energy: Physics, Engineering, Environmental Impacts, Economics & Planning*, 4th edn, Academic Press, New York.

Sovacool, B. K. 2008. Renewable energy: economically sound, politically difficult. *The Electricity Journal*, 21: 18–29.

Sovacool, B. K. 2010. A critical evaluation of nuclear power and renewable electricity in Asia. *Journal of Contemporary Asia*, 40: 369–400.

Stone, R. 2011. The legacy of the Three Gorges Dam. *Science*, 333: 817.

Streimikiene, D., Roos, I. and Rekis, J. 2009. External cost of electricity generation in Baltic States. *Renewable and Sustainable Energy Reviews*, 13: 863–870.

Su, B., Heshmati, A., Geng, Y. and Yu, X. 2013. A review of the circular economy in China: moving from rhetoric to implementation. *Journal of Cleaner Production*, 42: 215–227.

Sundqvist, T. 2004. What causes the disparity of electricity externality estimates? *Energy Policy*, 32: 1753–1766.

Swanson, R. M. 2009. Photovoltaics power up. *Science*, 324: 891–892.

Taylor, D. 2012. Wind energy, in G. Boyle (ed.) *Renewable Energy: Power for a Sustainable Future*, 3rd edn. Oxford University Press: Oxford.

Thorpe, T. W. 1999. *A Brief Review of Wave Energy*. Report ETSU-R-120 for the UK Department of Trade and Industry [Online]. AEA Technology plc, Didcot, UK. Available at: http://www.mech.ed.ac.uk/research/wavepower/Tom%20Thorpe/Tom%20Thorpe%20report.pdf (accessed 16 Nov. 2013).

Tilman, D., Socolow, R., Foley, J. A., *et al*. 2009. Beneficial biofuels—the food, energy, and environment trilemma. *Science*, 325: 270–271.

Tinker, L., Cobb, D., Bond, A. and Cashmore, M. 2005. Impact mitigation in environmental impact assessment: paper promises or the basis of consent conditions? *Impact Assessment and Project Appraisal*, 23: 265–280.

Tsoutsos, T., Frantzeskaki, N. and Gekas, V. 2005. Environmental impacts from the solar energy technologies. *Energy Policy*, 33: 289–296.

Turkenburg, W. C., Arent, D. J., Bertani, R., *et al*. 2012. Renewable energy, in *Global Energy Assessment: Toward a Sustainable Future*, Cambridge University Press, Cambridge, and the International Institute for Applied Systems Analysis, Laxenburg, Austria.

Tzimas, E., Moss, R. L. and Ntagia, P. 2011. *2011 Technology Map of the European Strategic Energy Technology Plan (SET-Plan)*, Publications Office of the European Union, Luxembourg.

UNDESA 2011. *The Great Green Technological Transformation: World Economic and Social Survey 2011*, United Nations Department of Economic and Social Affairs (UNDESA), United Nations, New York.

UNEP 2002. *The Environmental Impact Assessment Training Resource Manual: United Nations Environment Programme*. Nairobi: United Nations.

UNEP 2006. *Buildings and Climate Change: Status, Challenges and Opportunities*, UNEP DTIE, Sustainable Consumption and Production Branch, Paris.

UNEP 2010. *Waste and Climate Change: Global Trends and Strategy Framework*, UNEP DTIE International Environmental Technology Centre, Osaka, Japan.

UNEP 2011. *Towards a Green Economy: Pathways to Sustainable Development and Poverty Eradication*, UNEP, Geneva, Switzerland.

UNEP 2013. *Guidelines for National Waste Management Strategies: Moving from Challenges to Opportunities*, UNEP DTIE International Environmental Technology Centre, Osaka, Japan.

UNESCAP 2012. *Green Technology: Fact Sheet. Low Carbon Green Growth Roadmap for Asia and the Pacific* [Online]. United Nations Economic and Social Commission for Asia and the Pacific, Bangkok. Available at: www.unescap.org/esd/environment/lcgg/ (accessed 16 Oct. 2013).

UN-Habitat 2010. *Solid Waste Management in the World's Cities: Water and Sanitation in the World's Cities 2010*, Earthscan, London.

Ürge-Vorsatz, D., Eyre, N., Graham, P., *et al.*. 2012. Energy end-use: building, in *Global Energy Assessment: Toward a Sustainable Future*, Cambridge University Press, Cambridge, and the International Institute for Applied Systems Analysis, Laxenburg, Austria.

US DOE and NETL 2012. *Carbon Storage: The 2012 United States Carbon Utilization and Storage Atlas*, 4th edn (Atlas IV) [Online]. US Department of Energy (DOE) and National Energy Technology Laboratory (NETL), Pittsburgh, PA. Available at: www.netl.doe.gov/technologies/carbon_seq/refshelf/atlasIV/ (accessed 11 Nov. 2013).

USGS and ESRI 2011a. *Tectonic Plates Lines* [Online]. ESRI: Redlands, CA. Available at: www.arcgis.com/home/item.html?id=357b0e32423f43cebf9f844ae70f7d1c (accessed 28 Nov. 2013).

USGS and ESRI 2011b. *Volcanoes of the World 93 from Shapefiles* [Online]. ESRI: Redlands, CA. Available at: www.arcgis.com/home/item.html?id=430a92d3ff7f4959b5c3a1293629e499 (accessed 28 Nov. 2013).

Vaughan, N. E. and Lenton, T. M. 2011. A review of climate geoengineering proposals. *Climatic Change*, 109: 745–790.

Vaziri, M., Vadhva, S., Oneal, T. and Johnson, M. 2011. Distributed generation issues, and standards. Paper presented at IEEE International Conference on Information Reuse and Integration (IRI), 2011 3–5 Aug., pp. 439–443.

von Blottnitz, H. and Curran, M. A. 2007. A review of assessments conducted on bio-ethanol as a transportation fuel from a net energy, greenhouse gas, and environmental life cycle perspective. *Journal of Cleaner Production*, 15: 607–619.

von Hippel, F., Bunn, M., Diakov, A., *et al.* 2012. Nuclear energy, in *Global Energy Assessment: Toward a Sustainable Future*, Cambridge University Press, Cambridge, and the International Institute for Applied Systems Analysis, Laxenburg, Austria.

Voss, K., Sartori, I. and Lollini, R. 2012. Nearly-zero, net zero and plus energy buildings: how definitions and regulations affect the solutions. *REHVA Journal* [Online]. Available at: http://www.rehva.eu/index.php?id=339 (accessed 4 Nov. 2013).

Walker, S. 1996. Cost and resource estimating, in G. Boyle (ed.) *Renewable Energy: Power for a Sustainable Future*, Oxford University Press in association with The Open University: Oxford.

WEC 2010a. *Energy Efficiency: A Recipe for Success*, World Energy Council, London.

WEC 2010b. *2010 Survey of Energy Resources*, World Energy Council, London.

WEC 2011. *Global Transport Scenarios 2050*, World Energy Council, London.

WEC 2013a. *World Energy Resources, 2013 Survey*, World Energy Council, London.

WEC 2013b. *World Energy Perspective: Cost of Energy Technologies* World Energy Council, London.

WEC 2013c. *Energy Efficiency Indicators Database* [Online]. World Energy Council and Enerdata, London. Available at: http://www.wec-indicators.enerdata.eu/ (accessed 1 Nov. 2013).

WhalePower 2013. *Whale Power: Building the Energy Future on a Million Years of Field Tests*, [Online]. WhalePower, Toronto, ON. Available at: www.whalepower.com (accessed 15 Nov. 2013).

Wilson, D. C. 2007. Development drivers for waste management. *Waste Management and Research*, 25: 198–207.

Wolf, M.-A., Pant, R., Chomkhamsri, K., Sala, S. and Pennington, D. 2012. *The International Reference Life Cycle Data System (ILCD) Handbook: Towards More Sustainable Production and Consumption for a*

Resource-Efficient Europe. JRC Reference Reports, Publications Office of the European Union, Luxembourg.

Woolf, D., Amonette, J. E., Street-Perrott, F. A., *et al.* 2010. Sustainable biochar to mitigate global climate change. *Nature Communications*, 1: 56.

World Commission on Dams 2000. *Dams and Development: A New Framework For Decision-Making*, Earthscan, London.

Wu, J., Huang, J., Han, X., Xie, Z. and Gao, X. 2003. Three-Gorges Dam: Experiment in Habitat Fragmentation? *Science*, 300: 1239–1240.

WWF 2011. *The Energy Report: 100% Renewable Energy by 2050* [Online]. WWF International, Ecofys and OMA, Gland, Switzerland. Available at: http://assets.worldwildlife.org/publications/384/files/original/The_Energy_Report.pdf?1345748859 (accessed 31 Oct. 2013).

Zamagni, A. 2012. Life cycle sustainability assessment. *The International Journal of Life Cycle Assessment*, 17: 373–376.

Zhang, X.-S., Han, M.-D., Wang, R.-X., *et al.* 2013. Frequency-multiplication high-output triboelectric nanogenerator for sustainably powering biomedical microsystems. *Nano Letters*, 13: 1168–1172.

6

ENVIRONMENTAL LAW AND SOCIAL JUSTICE

With Kate Forrester, Chris Shiel and Tilak Ginige

6.1 Introduction

Environmental policy and law are often regarded as being a relatively new area of law, having originated primarily with the growth in environmentalism since the early 1960s. Increasing concern about environmental issues such as climate change, pollution and species extinction has led to increasing emphasis on environmental law, which now impacts on many areas of life. Key issues in environmental law cross boundaries between politics, law, economics and political science. This chapter provides an introduction to the definition, development and application of environmental law, and its implications, specifically in relation to the development of the green economy.

Environmental policy decisions have implications for the environment and the people that reside within, or rely upon, that environment. Such implications may not be equitably distributed among members of society and may therefore be perceived as socially unjust. This is particularly the case where sections of society experience economic loss, greater risk from natural hazards, and a reduced quality of life as a result of a policy choice. These aspects can be considered from the perspective of social and environmental justice, which forms the second part of this chapter.

6.2 What is environmental law?

Although it is widely recognised that law is central to environmental management, and there are now a vast array of laws that relate to environmental protection, the concept of environmental law is not easily defined. This partly stems from the difficulty of defining the environment in precise terms, though generally it is interpreted as encompassing air, water and land, and the organisms associated with them. Simply put, environmental law can be described as the area of law that seeks to manage human impacts on the environment. Generally, environmental law focuses on laws and practices that explicitly support environmental protection (Bell *et al.*, 2013). Many other laws may have an effect on the environment, without explicitly focusing on its protection, such as those influencing tax levels and provision of incentives. Such laws are not explicitly considered here, though clearly they could have a significant influence on development of the green economy.

It is also pertinent to consider what is meant by the term 'law'. Generally this refers to a system of rules that a country or community recognises as regulating the actions of its members, which may be enforced by the imposition of penalties. However, it is important to note that such rules are not limited to legislation or judicial decisions; the issue of how (or whether) the law is enforced can be just as important as what the law actually states (Bell *et al.*, 2013). Consequently there are many different sources of law, such as policy documents, codes of practice and guidance notes, which can have a major influence on how the law operates in practice.

It is also helpful to differentiate different types of law:

1. *Private law*, which involves relationships between individuals, and is relevant to issues such as nuisance and property law.
2. *Public law*, which addresses the relationships between individuals and the government, as well the relationships between individuals that are of concern to society. This includes different forms of state regulation, including setting standards for water and air quality; requirement for authorisation of activities, such as environmental permits and planning; requiring specific procedures to be undertaken, such as an Environmental Impact Assessment; banning activities, such as pollution or waste disposal; and identifying species or habitats to be protected.
3. *Criminal law*, which relates to environmental crime; examples include offences relating to the pollution of water courses.

The sections below provide an introduction to some of the core principles, sources and themes of environmental law. However, environmental law also relates to a range of specific issues not examined here in detail, including air pollution, water pollution and quality, contaminated land, waste management, deforestation and illegal timber harvesting, international trade, transport, genetically modified organisms and energy production. Further details of such aspects are presented by Bell *et al.* (2013), Hughes *et al.* (2002) and McEldowney and McEldowney (2010).

6.3 Environmental values

Most people agree that protection of the environment is an important priority. However, individuals vary greatly in terms of the choices they make when weighting the environment against other factors, such as economic growth. Such choices are a reflection of the environmental values held by individuals.

Reflection point

Consider your own environmental values. Do you believe, for example, that human interests come before those of nature? What has been the main influence on your own values?

Environmental values underpin environmental laws and policies, and many of the controversies surrounding them reflect contrasting values held by different groups of people. These can be considered along a spectrum of opinion, ranging from a belief that environmental protection is of paramount importance to a view that it is inconsequential (Bell *et al.*, 2013). In a sense, therefore, environmental law has to balance these different values.

This highlights a link between environmental law and *environmental ethics*, which may be defined as the moral relationship of human beings to, and also the value and moral status of, the environment and its nonhuman contents. Many environmentalists hold strong ethical views regarding the rights and values of nature, as illustrated by philosophical worldviews such as Deep Ecology (Naess, 1973). An *environmentalist* perspective can therefore be characterised as placing greatest weight on the need to protect the environment, and thereby contribute to human health and well-being. A more anthropocentric perspective suggests that the environment only has a value within the context of its value to people (Bell *et al.*, 2013).

An *economic* perspective is concerned with making rational decisions based on the relative costs and benefits of different options. An economic approach would therefore examine the extent to which people value some aspect of the environment, such as a species or habitat of conservation concern. According to neoclassical economics (see Chapter 1), an economically efficient decision would be one where the benefits outweighed the costs. As explored in Chapter 4, monetary values can potentially be placed on ecosystems and the services that they provide to people, to support economic decision-making. However, some people contest the idea that nature can be valued in this way.

6.4 Forms and sources of environmental law

First, some basic points:

1. Most areas of law seek to control unpredictable human relationships, whereas environmental law seeks to control the relationship between humans and the natural environment.
2. In order to control the relationship between humans and the natural environment, lawyers require the assistance of many disciplines, particularly science.
3. In creating an effective law it is often necessary to seek to predict the effect of the law in the future as well to control the present situation. Some solutions to environmental problems can cause further problems in the future.
4. An integrated approach is required to the development of environmental law, since a particular environmental law cannot be viewed in isolation.
5. Environmental law is constantly changing.
6. Environmental actions can be irreversible.
7. Environmental actions may be cumulative, and only cause harm after a series of events.

One model for environmental law is to enshrine fundamental standards of environmental protection in constitutional documents that guarantee basic human rights. This can happen in various ways. Environmental protection can be enshrined as a specific, separate right in a constitutional document. For example, Article 20a of the German Basic Law states (in translation):

> The state protects – also considering its responsibility for future generations – the natural foundations of life within the framework of the constitutional order through legislation and according to law and order through the executive and the judiciary.

Another method of providing environmental protection with constitutional status is to link the guarantee of fundamental human rights to the protection of the environment. For example, Principle 1 of the 1972 Stockholm Declaration states:

> Man has the fundamental right to freedom, equality and adequate conditions of life, in an environment of a quality that permits a life of dignity and well-being, and he bears a solemn responsibility to protect and improve the environment for present and future generations.

While the idea that individuals should be able to enjoy particular rights and freedoms has a long history, it is only recently that these have been incorporated in binding legal texts (Bell *et al.*, 2013). In Europe, the most important is the 1950 European Convention on Human Rights (ECHR), which provides a variety of different forms of protection. Although it does not provide explicitly for the protection of the environment, a number of articles in the Convention have been successfully used for this purpose.

Environmental human rights have brought a new expectation for citizens. Pressure groups are empowered through test cases and judicial reviews to bring actions against public authorities. For example, in the UK, liberalised laws of standing to sue help empower pressure groups to challenge the legality of decisions that could adversely affect the environment (Gibbons, 2008). This creates a link with the media as a strategy for airing environmental issues and for bringing public notice to environmental problems. Environmental human rights engage with ordinary citizens and provide opportunities for public participation in environmental issues. They also allow individual cases to be taken that claim rights and the law to be enforced.

At the same time, there can be potential conflicts between environmental human rights and the goal of sustainable development. The 1992 Rio Declaration linked the concept of sustainable development with an entitlement to a 'healthy and productive life in harmony with nature'. Potentially, the empowerment of citizens may constrain opportunities for economic development; as a result, there may be a tension between the rights of individuals or communities, and broader societal goals for economic development (McEldowney and McEldowney, 2010). Examples of such tensions are explored later in this chapter.

Additional sources of environmental law include the following:

1. *International environmental law*: This includes treaties, custom, soft law and case law as provided under Statute of the International Court of Justice. (Soft law refers to international norms that are deliberately non-binding in character but still have legal relevance, whereas case law is the body of law set out in judicial decisions.) International environmental law typically addresses environmental concerns that apply across different states, or at the global scale. As a result, international environmental law is characterised by negotiation and the attempt to gain consensus from as many countries as possible (Bell *et al.*, 2013). While having no direct effect on domestic law or individuals, such laws may define generally accepted standards or raise awareness and political will in relation to specific issues. Relevant international treaties are listed in Box 6.1.
2. *European Union (EU) law*: EU law has formed an important body of environmental law in its Member States. EU law tends to adopt a purposive approach, and often defines specific standards in relation to environmental quality and emission levels (ibid.). EU Directives differ from legislation in only specifying objectives but leaving the Member

States some discretion regarding how they are achieved in practice. Examples include Directives for water and air quality standards.

3. *Domestic law*: this includes primary legislation, namely the laws made by governments; secondary legislation, which provides procedures or sets standards; and tertiary legislation, which are usually aids to the interpretation of statutory provisions, as a flexible form of informal guidance or rule. Such legislation also supports the promotion of consistency and transparency in decision-making, as well as providing rules and guidance on procedural or other technical matters.

BOX 6.1 INTERNATIONAL TREATIES AND DECLARATIONS

The main forms of international law are treaties, conventions or agreements. Some of the most important such agreements in relation to the green economy are listed below (after Bell *et al.*, 2013).

Biodiversity conservation

1971 Ramsar Wetlands Convention
1973 Convention on International Trade in Endangered Species (CITES)
1979 Bonn Convention on Migratory Species of Wild Animals
1992 Convention on Biological Diversity
2000 Cartagena Biosafety Protocol

Natural and cultural heritage

1972 UNESCO World Heritage Convention

Climate change

1992 Framework Convention on Climate Change
1997 Kyoto Protocol

Pollution

1979 Convention on Long-Range Transboundary Air Pollution (LRTAP) and associated protocols on sulphur dioxide (1994), nitrous oxides (1988), volatile organic compounds (1991), persistent organic pollutants (1998) and heavy metals (1998)
1989 Basel Transboundary Waste Shipment Convention
1998 Rotterdam Prior Informed Consent to Trade Convention
2001 Stockholm Convention on Persistent Organic Pollutants

Global marine environment

1982 UN Convention on the Law of the Sea

Environmental Assessment

1991   Espoo Transboundary EIA Convention
2004   Kiev Strategic Environmental Assessment Protocol

There are also three key international *declarations*, namely:

*   the 1972 Stockholm Declaration of the UN Conference on the Human Environment
*   the 1992 Rio Declaration on the Environment and Development
*   the 2002 Johannesburg Declaration on Sustainable Development.

At the international scale, the Rio+20 United Nations Conference on Sustainable Development, held in 2012, is of particular importance in the context of the green economy. The Conference adopted new guidelines on green economy policies (Box 6.2).

BOX 6.2 GUIDELINES ON GREEN ECONOMY POLICIES ADOPTED AT RIO+20 (UN, 2012)

Green economy policies in the context of sustainable development and poverty eradication should:

(a) Be consistent with international law.
(b) Respect each country's national sovereignty over their natural resources taking into account its national circumstances, objectives, responsibilities, priorities and policy space with regard to the three dimensions of sustainable development.
(c) Be supported by an enabling environment and well-functioning institutions at all levels with a leading role for governments and with the participation of all relevant stakeholders, including civil society.
(d) Promote sustained and inclusive economic growth, foster innovation and provide opportunities, benefits and empowerment for all and respect of all human rights.
(e) Take into account the needs of developing countries, particularly those in special situations.
(f) Strengthen international cooperation, including the provision of financial resources, capacity-building and technology transfer to developing countries.
(g) Effectively avoid unwarranted conditionalities on official development assistance (ODA) and finance.
(h) Not constitute a means of arbitrary or unjustifiable discrimination or a disguised restriction on international trade, avoid unilateral actions to deal with environmental challenges outside the jurisdiction of the importing country, and ensure that environmental measures addressing transboundary or global environmental problems, as far as possible, are based on an international consensus.
(i) Contribute to closing technology gaps between developed and developing countries and reduce the technological dependence of developing countries using all appropriate measures.

  (j) Enhance the welfare of indigenous peoples and their communities, other local and traditional communities and ethnic minorities, recognizing and supporting their identity, culture and interests, and avoid endangering their cultural heritage, practices and traditional knowledge, preserving and respecting non-market approaches that contribute to the eradication of poverty.
  (k) Enhance the welfare of women, children, youth, persons with disabilities, smallholder and subsistence farmers, fisherfolk and those working in small and medium-sized enterprises, and improve the livelihoods and empowerment of the poor and vulnerable groups in particular in developing countries.
  (l) Mobilize the full potential and ensure the equal contribution of both women and men.
  (m) Promote productive activities in developing countries that contribute to the eradication of poverty.
  (n) Address the concern about inequalities and promote social inclusion, including social protection floors.
  (o) Promote sustainable consumption and production patterns.
  (p) Continue efforts to strive for inclusive, equitable development approaches to overcome poverty and inequality.

6.5 Principles of environmental law

Environmental principles underpin environmental law at all levels, including at both international and national scales. These principles are applied to a very wide range of environmental laws and policies, and for this reason they are flexible in nature. However, this can create a challenge to their application in a specific context, as they sometimes lack clarity and precision. It should also be noted that they are not always mutually supportive. These principles include (Bell *et al.*, 2013):

1. *Sustainable development*, often defined as 'development that meets the needs of the present without compromising the ability of the future generations to meet their own needs' (Brundtland Report, 1987).
2. *The precautionary principle*: 'Where there are threats of serious or irreversible damage, lack of full scientific certainty shall not be used as a reason for postponing cost–effective measures to prevent environmental degradation' (EC (2000) Com (2001)1 on the Precautionary Principle).
3. *The polluter pays principle*: 'The polluter shall bear the expenses of carrying out pollution prevention and control measures to ensure that the environment is in an acceptable state' (Part 2A of the Environmental Protection Act 1990, UK).
4. *Preventative principle*: 'States have the responsibility to ensure that activities within their jurisdiction or control do not cause damage to the environment of other States or of areas beyond the limits of national jurisdiction' (Rio Declaration on the Environment and Development, Principle 2).
5. *The integration principle*: 'Environmental protection requirements must be integrated into the definition and implementation of the Union policies and activities, in particular with a view to promoting sustainable development' (Article 11 of the Treaty on the Functioning of the European Union (TFEU)).

6. *The public participation principle*: 'Environmental issues are best handled with the participation of all concerned citizens, at the relevant level. At the national level, each individual
shall have appropriate access to information concerning the environment that is held by
public authorities, including information on hazardous materials and activities in their
communities, and the opportunity to participate in decision-making processes. States
shall facilitate and encourage public awareness and participation by making information
widely available. Effective access to judicial and administrative proceedings, including
redress and remedy, shall be provided' (1992 Rio Declaration on the Environment and
Development, Principle 10).

7. *The substitution principle*: 'Chemicals that are unsafe should be substituted with safer
alternatives including technologies' (Commission White Paper on Strategy for a New
Chemicals Policy, COM (2001) 88).

The following sections provide greater detail on selected principles that are of particular
importance to the green economy.

6.5.1 Sustainable development

The concept of sustainable development is central to environmental law and policy. Yet its
application continues to be the focus of much debate (see Lélé, 1991; Beckerman, 1994; Doyle,
1998; Jamieson, 1998; Luke, 2005, Redclift, 2005; Bratt, 2009, for different commentaries on
the concept). Part of this uncertainty relates to the precise definition of the principle, and what
it actually entails in practice (Chapter 1). A key issue is the concept of *intergenerational equity*,
which refers to fairness across generations. According to the widely used definition of
sustainable development provided by the Brundtland Report (WCED, 1987), future generations
should be able to meet their own needs. This implies an ethical dimension: essentially, we need
to bequeath forthcoming generations a fair share of resources. But who knows what the needs
of future generations will actually be? Further, the definition is based on the assumption that
we can identify the impact of current activities on future availability of resources, yet this is
highly uncertain (Bell *et al.*, 2013).

> **Reflection point**
>
> Do you think that it is appropriate to define sustainability in terms of the needs of
> future generations? How would you define it?

This definition of sustainable development was created as an attempt to reconcile the tension
between environmental and developmental concerns that were at the heart of
global policy-making. It is as much concerned with economic and social development as it is
with environmental protection. The concept has been widely incorporated into policy, for
example, many countries have developed strategies for sustainable development. However,
problems with definitions have hindered the use of sustainable development as a working legal
principle. The concept has been discussed and developed by international agreements, applied in
courts of law, referred to in statutory provisions and therefore can be said to impose provisions
and objectives on public and private bodies. However, there is a general consensus that sustainable
development has not achieved the status of an enforceable legal principle. Rather, sustainable

development is mostly found in 'soft law' documents, namely, those that are not legally binding. An example is Agenda 21, which was signed at the 1992 Earth Summit in Rio de Janeiro, and provides guidance on how sustainable development might be achieved in practice.

> ### Reflection point
>
> If sustainable development is not a fully working legal principle, do you think that this might hinder its implementation? Or does its strength lie in the fact that it is not merely confined to legal issues, but encompasses political, social and economic issues?

There is ongoing debate regarding how the principle of sustainable development should be implemented, which reflects contrasting environmental values, as described earlier. Relatively 'strong' approaches to sustainability emphasise the extent to which natural resources are irreplaceable, whereas 'weak' sustainability accepts that natural assets can be used so long as the stocks available to future generations are not diminished (Bell *et al.*, 2013). There is an ethical dimension to the choice between these approaches; while some people consider nature to be irreplaceable, and therefore of very high value, it could be argued that strong sustainability is morally abhorrent because it places the interests of nature above those of people.

A further issue relates to the use of technology, and specifically whether current environmental problems can be addressed through technological progress. The Brundtland Report advocated solutions within the current economic system, leading to a widespread belief that technological progress can both solve environmental problems, and enable natural resources to be managed more efficiently. This concept of a 'win–win' solution from which both the economy and the environment benefit through technological progress has been termed 'ecological modernisation' (Hajer, 1995), and is central to many perceptions of the green economy. A contrary view would suggest that an overhaul of the current economic system is required to deliver a genuinely green economy (Cato, 2009).

> ### Reflection point
>
> Based on the guidelines in Box 6.2, which values do you think have informed the concept of the green economy as agreed by the UN? Does this constitute 'weak' or 'strong' sustainability, in your opinion? Is there a commitment here to ecological modernisation?

6.5.2 Public participation principle

People have the right to take part in decisions that have an effect on their environment. But in order to do this, they need to be able to access the information on which the decisions are based, they need to have the chance to express their opinions about the decision, and they need to be able to influence the direction of the final result (Foti *et al.*, 2008). Access to information brings with it power. When people are denied the right to information, voters may make uninformed choices and politicians cannot be held to account. When government control prevents the media from reporting the facts, then this withholding of information from the public can negatively affect trust and accountability and in turn can cause dissatisfaction (Transparency International, 2011). Meaningful participation is assured through access rights – the rights of public access to information, to public participation in government decision-making and of access to justice (Foti *et al.*, 2008).

Access to information needs to be two-way: namely a government's duty to supply access needs to be matched by civil society's capacity and interest to demand access. Governments can supply access through freedom of information laws, and people can send petitions to courts, file requests for information and can attend government meetings. But people must have the right information about the decision if their participation is to be meaningful, and for this reason awareness-raising is needed for civil society, as well as for administrators and legislators, so that engagement may be productive (ibid.).

In the Rio Declaration on Environment and Development of 1992, 178 governments pledged to open environmental decision-making to public input and scrutiny. This gave the undertaking that every person should have access to information about the environment, opportunities to participate in the decision-making processes affecting the environment, and access to redress and remedy. Access to information, public participation, and access to justice are keys to more transparent, inclusive, and accountable decision-making in matters affecting the environment, and can be referred to as 'environmental democracy' (ibid.).

In 1998, the states present at the UNECE Environment for Europe Conference adopted the Aarhus Convention, which is known formally as the Convention on Access to Information, Public Participation in Decision Making, and Access to Justice in Environmental Matters. This has been seen as a milestone in the development of procedural environmental rights and of an expanded notion of democracy in an open, transparent society (Rehbinder, 2002).

Suggested activity

Explore further information about the Aarhus Convention provided on the internet (e.g. www.unece.org/env/pp/treatytext.html). Implementation of the Convention is further considered by Morgera (2005), Mason (2010) and Nadal (2008).

As a result of the Rio Declaration and the Aarhus Convention, many countries have created rights-based framework laws on freedom of information. In addition, there has been a trend of increasing public participation in decision-making, which can improve the quality as well as the acceptance of resulting decisions (Petkova *et al.*, 2002). An example is public participation in an Environmental Impact Assessment (EIA), which is a key aspect of many large-scale planning applications (see Section 5.9.2). An EIA is designed to identify, predict, evaluate and mitigate the biophysical and social effects of development proposals before major decisions are taken and commitments made. It can therefore be considered as an important mechanism to ensure that planning proposals are environmentally 'green'. Public participation in EIA is further considered by Hartley and Wood (2005) and Bond *et al.* (2004).

Reflection point

How important do you think that public participation is for development of the green economy? Do you think that it might be a problem that even in democratic societies, a large part of society does not engage with democratic processes, even at the level of national government elections?

6.5.3 The precautionary principle

The precautionary principle (or approach) has emerged in recent decades as a widely accepted general principle of environmental policy and law. It provides for action to avoid serious or irreversible environmental harm when scientific certainty of such harm is lacking. It is therefore an approach to support decision-making under conditions of uncertainty (Cooney, 2004). While it is an important and intuitively sensible concept, its acceptance into both law and policy has been highly controversial. On one hand, it has been described as the fundamental principle underlying all environmental policy, and a crucial tool to support sustainable development. Conversely, it has also been heavily criticised for being anti-scientific, subject to abuse, anti-innovation, and anti-sustainable use (ibid.).

Examples of the precautionary principle in international law include:

- The 1992 Framework Convention on Climate Change states:

    The Parties should take precautionary measures to anticipate, prevent or minimise the causes of climate change and mitigate its adverse effects. Where there are threats of serious or irreversible damage, lack of full scientific certainty should not be used as a reason for postponing such measures.

    (Art. 3(3))

- The 1992 Convention on Biological Diversity states, 'where there is a threat of significant reduction or loss of biological diversity, lack of full scientific certainty should not be used as a reason for postponing measures to avoid or minimise such a threat' (Preamble).

The concept can be viewed as a mechanism to counter the widespread regulatory presumption in favour of allowing development or economic activity to proceed, even when there is a lack of clear evidence about its impacts. The potential for controversy lies in the fact that applying precaution will typically involve restrictions on human actions that may impose substantial costs. Yet, by definition, when the principle is invoked, scientific evidence in support of such restrictions is lacking.

Application of the principle has varied markedly among different contexts. Relatively 'weak' versions of the principle attempt to balance the benefits and costs of taking action; this is how the EU implements the principle at present. A 'strong' application of the principle might prohibit any action, which could result in significant environmental damage, regardless of the cost of doing so (Bell *et al.*, 2013). This could lead to beneficial activities being prohibited simply because of a lack of understanding of associated risks.

Cooney (2004) highlights that the precautionary principle can result in significant equity issues. The livelihood and socio-economic impacts of the principle can be negative, particularly for those dependent on utilisation of biological resources to support their livelihoods. Highly restrictive or protectionist approaches, which may be supported by application of the principle, raise particular problems in this respect.

Reflection point

Research has highlighted the difficulties of applying the precautionary principle in practice. How do you think such difficulties might be overcome?

6.6 International trade

6.6.1 Regulation of trade

The total value of international trade has increased markedly in recent years (Figure 6.1), raising concerns about its potential environmental impact. A key development in relation to regulation of international trade was the Marrakesh Declaration of 1994, which affirmed the establishment of the World Trade Organization (WTO). This essentially shifted the international community from the General Agreement on Tariffs and Trade (GATT) framework to the WTO system. The WTO deals with regulation of trade between participating countries, by providing a framework for negotiating and formalising trade agreements, and a dispute resolution process to enforce participants' adherence to WTO agreements. One of the goals of the WTO was to integrate developing countries into the international trade community while also preserving the environment. While sustainable development was identified as a primary objective, it was stated that this should reflect the 'needs and concerns' of countries 'at different levels of economic development' (Skinner, 2010).

In practice, the WTO has illustrated the problem of striking a balance between the situations of developing countries and preserving environmental values. Significant cases included a dispute centred around restrictions on the import of tuna fish by the USA, because of concerns about the impacts of fishing methods on dolphin populations. The US action was judged unlawful, because the fishing activities related to international waters, rather than those under jurisdiction of the USA. A further case challenged another attempt by the USA to limit imports of shrimps to suppliers who could demonstrate that harvesting methods did not endanger sea turtles. This was also adjudged to be discriminatory (ibid.).

These cases highlight the concerns of some developing countries that green protectionist measures are merely disguised barriers to international trade. These concerns relate to a

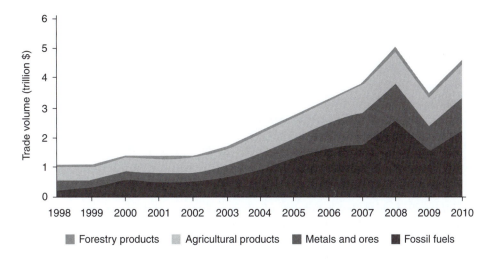

FIGURE 6.1   Trends in global trade by value

Source: UNEP (2013), based on information provided by Chatham House Resource Trade Database, BACI, and COMTRADE (Lee *et al.*, 2012), with permission from UNEP (www.unep.org).

potential abuse of power, and eco-imperialism, relating to imposition of environmental values by developed countries upon developing countries. As the measures frequently impose stricter standards for environmental protection, developing countries maintain that the gaps in environmental standards have resulted in 'green barriers' to trade. The potential environmental impacts of WTO decisions have led to widespread concerns among environmentalists. However, according to Skinner (ibid.), the WTO, because of its amenability and application of interpretive sources of law, is a valuable forum for encouraging sustainable development.

The role of international trade in the green economy is examined in detail by UNEP (2013), which makes the following points:

- Trade, when accompanied by appropriate regulation, can facilitate the transition to a green economy by fostering the exchange of environmentally friendly goods and services (including environmentally sound technologies). In order to contribute to poverty eradication, the additional wealth generated by international trade should provide income opportunities to reduce inequalities, rather than exacerbate them.
- The transition to a green economy has the potential to create enhanced trade opportunities by opening new export markets for environmental goods and services, by increasing trade in products certified for sustainability and promoting certification-related services, and by greening international supply chains.
- Rio+20 initiated a shift of focus, from the potential risk of trade protectionism associated with green economy policies, towards improving the trade performance of developing countries through the implementation of green economy policies. As a result, the green economy is increasingly being seen as a gateway to new opportunities for trade, growth and sustainable development.
- While a shift to more sustainable trade practices may advance economic and social development, achieving such a shift will also require effective policies to mitigate the adverse impacts that often arise from trade, including pollution and emissions from transport, increased pressure on natural resources for production and processing, and social marginalisation. Addressing these effects, while reducing income inequalities, are key elements for improving the sustainability of international trade.

Reflection point

Do you agree that the green economy should provide new opportunities for trade? Or should international trade be limited or reduced, for a green economy to be achieved?

UNEP (2013) identifies a number of opportunities to support sustainable development through trade. Sustainable trade opportunities may arise, for example, from trading environmental goods and services (EGS) (Figure 6.2), by complying with sustainability standards and by greening global supply chains. However, UNEP (2013) notes that realisation of these opportunities is often challenging, particularly for developing countries.

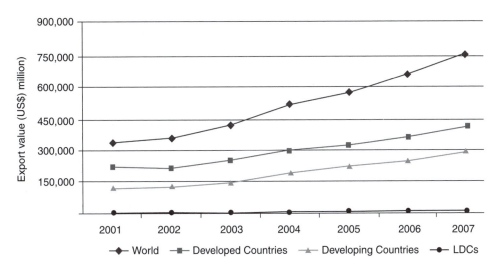

FIGURE 6.2   Growth in the export of environmental goods, defined as 'activities which produce goods and services to measure, prevent, limit, minimise or correct environmental damage to water, air and soil as well as problems related to waste, noise and ecosystems' (OECD, 2005)

Source: UNEP (2013) based on information provided by UNDP. With permission from UNEP (www.unep.org).
Note: LDC: Least Developed Countries.

6.6.2 Fair trade

Another aspect of trade with particular relevance to the green economy is *fair trade*. This is a social movement that aims to help producers, particularly those in developing countries, by improving trading conditions and promoting sustainability. In particular, fair trade advocates the payment of a higher price to exporters, which is linked to higher social and environmental standards. According to Fairtrade International (2012), by the end of 2011, the total number of small-scale farmers in the Fairtrade system had reached 1.24 million. Fair trade is growing rapidly in terms of both participation and revenue generated, for example, the total sales revenue increased by 22 per cent between 2010 and 2011. Consumer demand for fair trade products is driven by concern over improving the socio-economic conditions of farm workers in developing countries. Fair trade agricultural products such as bananas, cocoa, coffee, honey and tea therefore present a potentially green economic opportunity for developing countries (UNEP, 2013).

6.6.3 Environmental standards

International trade has encouraged the development and implementation of international standards. These can be defined as non-tariff measures aimed at setting requirements related to issues such as product quality, safety and environmental protection (UNEP, 2013). Standards are often developed by international technical committees. The International Organization for Standardization (ISO) is a non-governmental federation of national standardisation bodies from more than 160 countries. The ISO has developed a number of standards that are relevant to the green economy, including (ibid.):

- ISO 19011 on auditing of environmental management systems;
- ISO 14031 on the evaluation of environmental performance;

- ISO 14020 on environmental labels and declarations;
- ISO 14064 on greenhouse gas accounting and verification.

As an indicator of the uptake of these standards, the implementation of ISO 14001 on environmental management systems (see Chapter 7) increased exponentially in the period 1999–2009 (ibid.).

Environmental quality standards have also been developed, which focus on the impact of pollutants on the environment. Examples include air quality standards relating to the maximum or minimum concentration of substances in air, and water quality standards, referring to the concentration of pollutants in water. Emission standards regulate the amount of pollutants emitted, rather than the effects on the environment; examples include the amounts emitted from pipes or sewers, or from a chimney or exhaust pipe (Bell *et al.*, 2013).

Despite their value for improving environmental quality, environmental quality standards require constant environmental monitoring, which can be impractical or expensive. Enforcement can also present challenges, as the failure to reach a standard does not necessarily identify how the problem can be remedied. They also provide no incentive to polluters to improve performance in areas where the standard is being met. In general, they tend to be set as objectives rather than as legal requirements. In contrast, emission standards are relatively easy to control, monitor and enforce. Their main limitation relates to the difficulty of controlling diffuse, or non-point emissions (ibid.).

The setting of environmental standards depends strongly on scientific analysis, which includes consideration and definition of risks. Such risks are usually presented in the form of probabilities and likelihoods, emphasising the fact that there is often considerable scientific uncertainty about human impacts on the environment (McEldowney and McEldowney, 2010).

6.7 Social and environmental justice

6.7.1 Introduction

The concept of environmental justice has developed rapidly in recent years, and is now widely recognised as a key element of the green economy. In other words, an economy cannot be considered to be genuinely 'green' unless issues relating to social justice, and environmental justice in particular, are adequately addressed (Jones, 2009).

6.7.2 Social justice

Social justice is about creating a society, or world, based on principles of equality, solidarity and human rights (Box 6.3). The concept of social justice is at the heart of the Millennium Development Goals (MDG) (see Chapter 1). The MDGs have been developed with the aim of securing a world that is more equitable in terms of equality of opportunity and life chances. If the MDGs were achieved, the world would essentially be fairer for many of the world's poor, particularly women and children. However, it is worth noting that 'fair' is a relative concept, as is social justice. What is socially just to one group may well be an injustice from another's perspective.

BOX 6.3 LINKING PLANETARY BOUNDARIES WITH SOCIAL BOUNDARIES

The concept of planetary boundaries has received widespread attention as a way of envisioning human impacts on the Earth system (see Chapter 2). Recently, attempts have been made to combine this idea with the complementary concept of social boundaries (Raworth, 2012). This is based on recognition that the achievement of sustainable development requires ensuring that all people have the resources that they need, including food, water, health care, and energy.

Integration of this concept with planetary boundaries is illustrated in Figure 6.3. In Figure 6.3, the social foundation forms an inner boundary, inside which are different dimensions of human deprivation. The environmental ceiling forms an outer boundary,

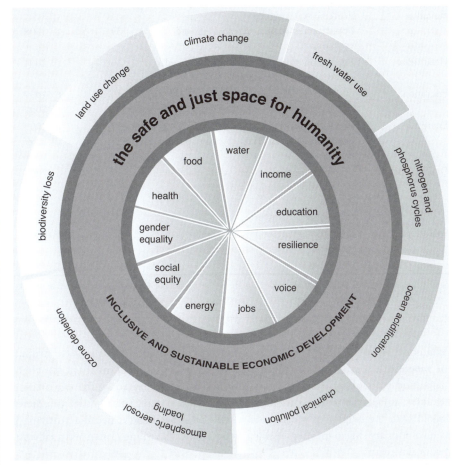

FIGURE 6.3   Conceptual diagram integrating planetary environmental boundaries with social boundaries

Source: Raworth (2012), Figure 1, with the permission of Oxfam GB (www.oxfam.org.uk). Oxfam GB does not necessarily endorse any text or activities that accompany this material.

beyond which are various dimensions of environmental degradation. Between the two boundaries lies a doughnut-shaped area that represents an environmentally safe and socially just space for humanity (Raworth, 2012). It is in this space where inclusive and sustainable economic development, and the green economy, can take place.

How far is humanity from this space, from a social perspective? This is illustrated in Table 6.1.

Table 6.1 An illustrative assessment indicating the current distance from social boundaries

Social foundation	Extent of global deprivation	(%)	Year
Food security	Population undernourished	13	2006–8
Income	Population living below US$1.25 (PPP) per day	21	2005
Water and sanitation	Population without access to an improved drinking water source	13	2008
	Population without access to improved sanitation	39	2008
Health care	Population estimated to be without regular access to essential medicines	30	2004
Education	Children not enrolled in primary school	10	2009
	Illiteracy among 15–24-year-olds	11	2009
Energy	Population lacking access to electricity	19	2009
	Population lacking access to clean cooking facilities	39	2009
Gender equality	Employment gap between women and men in waged work (excluding agriculture)	34	2009
	Representation gap between women and men in national parliaments	77	2011
Social equity	Population living on less than the median income in countries with a Gini coefficient exceeding 0.35	33	1995–2009

Source: Adapted from Raworth (2012), Table 1, with the permission of Oxfam GB (www.oxfam.org.uk). Oxfam GB does not necessarily endorse any text or activities that accompany this material.

As a concept, social justice is relatively new. It can be considered to have originated in the nineteenth century when industrialisation gave rise to concerns about the plight of the poor, and particularly about the conditions of hardship created by the exploitation of the workers, as factories were set up under the capitalist system. Social justice can therefore be linked with the origins of socialism as a political movement; it became a driving goal and a revolutionary slogan for those seeking to overthrow the ruling classes, and a rallying cry for political activists.

The issue today is much broader than simply a response to capitalism, as the MDGs illustrate. The Copenhagen Declaration and Programme of Action adopted by the World Summit for Social Development in 1995 makes explicit reference to social justice. In many other international legal or quasi-legal texts (such as the Universal Declaration of Human Rights, www.un.org/en/documents/udhr/), social justice is implied rather than stated explicitly, though references may be couched in broader terms or simply phrased as 'justice'. Today, social justice is therefore something that is widely held as an ideal, but is often not achieved in practice.

Social justice is based on the notion of fairness or egalitarianism, where all participants in a society work towards equality of outcomes. Part of the reason why this is difficult to achieve is that people have different perceptions of what is fair; human beings will all make different calculations in terms of the effort/reward bargain. Social justice is difficult to achieve within a country; achieving social justice across the globe represents an even greater challenge.

Social justice is typically taken to mean *distributive justice*. The critical question is: how can an equitable distribution (e.g. of wealth, of goods and of resources) be achieved? It is worth reflecting on this question, as there are no easy solutions. It is also worth remembering that the literature relating to social justice is presented from a variety of different disciplinary perspectives, where it is sometimes difficult to suspend personal beliefs, values, emotive language and moral views.

Reflection point

Do you think that social justice is something that is achievable in a society where individualism often prevails? How do you think we might move towards a society where everyone shares the same opportunities?

6.7.3 Environmental justice

The concept of environmental justice is more recent than social justice, and has gathered momentum in recent years (e.g. see Pellow, 2000; Agyeman and Evans, 2004; Schlosberg, 2004; Walker, 2007; Elvers *et al.*, 2008; Schroeder, 2008; Sze and London, 2008; Walker, 2009, 2010; Pedersen, 2011). Environmental justice has taken a civil rights and social justice approach to environmental problems (ESRC, 2001). It began as an 'offshoot' of social justice, specifically in the USA in the 1970s. From the basic observation that not all people experience equal treatment in the environments where they live and work, a broader pattern quickly became clear: that working–class, Native American, African American, and Latino communities were routinely denied equal protection from polluting factories and waste sites (Schroeder, 2008).

Since then, the concept of environmental justice has continued to evolve beyond its origins and initial scope, and is now applied to a wide range of environmental and social concerns and political contexts (Walker, 2009; Walker and Burningham, 2011). Agyeman and Evans (2004) explain that the concept was initially based on the problems of siting waste facilities, such as transfer, storage and disposal facilities, and other issues such as lead contamination, pesticides, water and air pollution, workplace safety and transportation. More recently, issues such as urban sprawl, 'smart growth' and 'climate justice' have become issues of concern. In addition, the geography of environmental justice has also broadened, triggered by the explosions in Bhopal and Mexico City in 1984 and by various scandals surrounding the issue of international toxic waste dumping. These incidents have shown that environmental justice is an issue with global dimensions.

Suggested activity

The explosions in Bhopal, India and San Juanico, Mexico City, in 1984 offer powerful case studies illustrating the issues surrounding environmental justice; they are among the deadliest industrial disasters in history. You are encouraged to increase your awareness of these events by exploring the resources available on the internet. In reviewing these materials, consider the issue of justice in terms of the people who were affected by these disasters, and the extent to which they received adequate compensation from the companies involved.

Some authors have drawn links between environmental justice and sustainability. For example, Agyeman and Evans (2004) argue that environmental justice and equity should be at the heart of policies for sustainability at every level. These authors point out that environmental justice movements have begun to address sustainability as an issue. In contrast, environmentalist movements have tended to ignore social justice issues in the past. The importance of integrating social justice and environmental concerns is emphasised by Jones (2009), who identifies this integration as one of the key features of the green economy.

ESRC (2001) identify some key aspects of environmental justice, from a UK perspective:

- Environmental impacts are unevenly distributed.
- Access to environmental resources is often similarly uneven.
- Generally, poorer people live in worse environments. For example, of 11,400 tonnes of carcinogenic chemicals emitted to the air from large factories in England in 1999, 82 per cent were from factories located in the most deprived 20 per cent of local areas.
- There are also ethnic inequalities. For example, there is a statistically significant bias towards sites with hazardous substances being located in areas with a higher proportion of an ethnic minority population. Some 70 per cent of all people from ethnic minorities live in the 88 most deprived local districts. As deprivation is associated with worse environmental conditions, it is likely that this indicates disproportionately large impacts on ethnic communities.
- Environmental health impacts are also unequally distributed. Respiratory problems in London have been found to be concentrated in the poorest areas and correlate with high traffic levels. The responsibility for the cause of problems is also unequal: car ownership is lower in areas with worse traffic levels.
- In the UK there are 4.5 million households living in fuel poverty, which means they lack affordable warmth. Millions of homes are energy inefficient and have poor heating systems, and their occupants cannot afford to make improvements or keep their homes warm. Damp and cold homes increase the likelihood of lung and heart illnesses. Fuel poverty is linked to higher rates of winter mortality, with an estimated 30,000 unnecessary extra winter deaths occurring each year.
- There is also a problem of 'food poverty' in the UK, where 20 per cent of the population cannot afford healthy food, especially where fuel and rent take priority. This situation is exacerbated by lack of access to shops selling healthy food. Again, poorer areas tend to be further from shops selling fresh fruit and vegetables, partly because the growth of out-of-town superstores has caused many inner-city food stores to close. People in poorer communities are less likely to have transport options to enable them to access more distant shops.

> ### Reflection point
>
> While this report refers explicitly to the UK, to what extent do you believe that these findings might relate to other countries? Note also how these different factors link together, leading to feedbacks. For example, poverty limits access to resources, which can damage health and well-being, which can negatively affect earning potential. Consider how a 'green' approach to urban planning might address these problems.

ESRC (2001) also highlight the international dimension of environmental justice. Because of patterns of consumption and the ecological footprint (see Chapters 2 and 7), the social and environmental impact of the UK's economy extends to many parts of the globe. This can cause environmental problems in other countries, such as contamination of land and water, and environmental degradation. Economists have introduced terms such as 'race to the bottom', the 'pollution haven hypothesis' and 'regulatory chill' to describe situations where poor countries might deliberately weaken their environmental policies in order to attract industry. A further argument is that not only do industrialised countries currently take far more than a 'fair share' of resources, but they are historically responsible for a wide range of over-use of environmental resources, which has been referred to as the 'ecological debt' (ESRC, 2001).

How can such problems be addressed? Part of the solution lies in considering the social dimension in the formulation of an implementation of policies, an issue that has been neglected in the past (Bulkeley and Walker, 2005). There is also a need to recognise that environmental justice can play a role in the wider agenda for sustainable development and social inclusion, as illustrated by the concept of 'just sustainability' (Agyeman and Evans, 2004). Policy processes need to consider not only what the environmental impacts of a new policy or regulation might be, but how these impacts are likely to be distributed across different social groups. Appraisal tools have the potential to ensure that policy is made on a more informed basis, and that social issues are taken into consideration before decisions are made (Walker et al., 2005; Walker, 2007).

An example is provided by the case of flooding, as a distinct form of environmental risk. Many countries are experiencing an increase in the occurrence of large-scale flooding events, which may be attributable to climate change (Milly et al., 2002). It was only in the wake of the devastating impact of Hurricane Katrina on the City of New Orleans, USA, that the impacts of flooding began to be considered from an environmental justice perspective. In this case, ethnic minorities and the poorer sections of society experienced disproportionate suffering as a result of the floods. In addition, socially and economically vulnerable storm victims recovered less quickly than other sections of society (Colten, 2007; Stivers, 2007; Morse, 2008). This outcome was partly attributable to patterns of settlement, with racial segregation and poverty leading many African Americans to live in less-desirable flood-prone areas (Morse, 2008). This highlights a need to consider inequalities in flood exposure, flood impacts and vulnerability when making decisions about investing in flood protection and the development of emergency plans (Walker and Burningham, 2011).

6.8 Globalisation

6.8.1 Introduction

Globalisation can be seen as one of the defining features of the modern world. It has been identified as one of the causes of current environmental problems, but is also considered by some to be a potential solution to such problems. Any efforts to develop a green economy will need to take place within the context of globalisation, as explored in this section.

6.8.2 Defining globalisation

Many definitions of globalisation have been proposed, such as:

- a process that encompasses the causes, course, and consequences of transnational and transcultural integration of human and non-human activities (Al-Rodhan and Stoudmann, 2006);
- all those processes by which the peoples of the world are incorporated into a single world society (Albrow and King, 1990);
- a process that embodies a transformation in the spatial organisation of social relations and transactions, generating transcontinental or interregional flows and networks of activity, interaction and power (Giddens, 1999).

Globalisation is characterised by four types of change (Common and Stagl, 2005):

- a stretching of social, political and economic activities across political frontiers, regions and continents;
- intensification of interconnectedness and flows of trade, investment, finance, culture, etc.;
- speeding up of global interactions and processes, supported by developments of global transportation and communication infrastructure;
- increased impact of events; for example, events at the local scale can have major consequences at the global scale.

Globalisation provides obvious benefits for global trade. For example, small companies can now potentially reach a global market by selling their products via the internet. However, the phenomenon of globalisation has been highly contested, as illustrated by the development of many social protests and campaigns. Social justice lies at the heart of these concerns, arising from the perceived role of globalisation in increasing inequality. Other issues that have been raised include the increasing power of transnational corporations; the erosion of wages and social welfare standards for the sake of international trade; and a decline in the security of supply of food and energy, as they are increasingly obtained from other countries (Cato, 2009).

Reflection point

Although the focus here is primarily on social and economic aspects of globalisation, consider also its environmental dimension. Many human impacts on the environment that we have considered in other chapters, such as emission and distribution of pollutants and anthropogenic climate change, have a global dimension. For example, improved transport links across the globe have directly contributed to the spread of invasive species, and the spread of pest and disease organisms. Critics of globalisation also highlight a potential 'race to the bottom', as production shifts to countries that have the lowest environmental standards.

Suggested activity

Explore the internet resources relating to anti-globalisation campaigns to understand who is participating in such action, and what activists are actually protesting about (e.g. search for 'anti-globalisation'). As you explore these links, consider the aims of these different organisations. To what extent do they coincide? In what ways do the issues that they raise relate to the green economy? Some suggested links are provided below:

* Alliance for Global Justice (http://afgj.org/)
* Campaign Against the Arms Trade (www.caat.org.uk/)
* Grassroots Global Justice Alliance (http://ggjalliance.org/)
* International of Anarchist Federations (http://i-f-a.org/)
* No Sweat (http://www.nosweat.org.uk/)
* People's Global Action (www.nadir.org/nadir/initiativ/agp/en/)
* Urban75 (www.urban75.org/photos/protest/)
* World Social Forum (http://www.fsm2013.org/en)

6.8.3 Neoliberalism and globalisation

It is important to recognise that many economists firmly believe that globalisation, and the policies that support it, are crucial to future economic development and the alleviation of poverty. To understand this context, it is first important to understand the concept of *neoliberalism* (see Chapter 1). This is an economic philosophy or ideological belief, which focuses on providing economic freedom to all people, including free choice in economic matters and an emphasis on private property as the means of production. Neoliberalism therefore promotes private enterprise, liberalised trade and open markets to promote globalisation, and maximises the role of the private sector in setting both political and economic priorities.

Williamson (1990) describes the fundamentals of neoliberalist policies, referred to as the 'Washington consensus'. These have been supported by Washington-based international economic organisations such as the International Monetary Fund (IMF) and the World Bank. Williamson's list included ten points:

* *Fiscal policy*: governments should not run large deficits that have to be paid back by citizens in the future; large and sustained fiscal deficits are the primary source of macro-economic dislocation in the forms of inflation, payments deficits, and capital flight.

- *Redirection of public spending* from subsidies towards provision of pro-growth services such as primary education, primary health care and infrastructure investment. Subsidies, especially indiscriminate subsidies (including subsidies to cover the losses of state enterprises) should be reduced or preferably eliminated.
- *Tax reform*: overall, tax revenues are seen as less preferable than reduced public expenditure to reduce fiscal deficits. Where taxes are applied, the tax base should be broad and marginal tax rates should be moderate.
- *Interest rates* should be determined by the market, and should be positive and moderate, so as to discourage capital flight and to increase savings, promote productive investment and avoid the threat of an explosion in government debt.
- *Exchange rates* should be competitive, for example, by being determined by market forces.
- *Trade liberalisation*: including liberalisation of imports, with particular emphasis on elimination of quantitative restrictions such as licensing; any trade protection to be provided by low and relatively uniform tariffs, to encourage competition and long-term growth. A policy of protecting domestic industries against foreign competition is viewed as creating costly distortions that end up penalising exports and impoverishing the domestic economy.
- *Encourage foreign direct investment*, by removing barriers to capital flows.
- *Privatisation of state enterprises*, based on the belief that private industry is managed more efficiently than state enterprises, because of the more direct incentives faced by a manager who either has a direct personal stake in the profits of an enterprise or else is accountable to those who do.
- *Deregulation*: abolition of regulations that impede market entry or restrict competition, except for those justified on safety, environmental and consumer protection grounds, and prudent oversight of financial institutions.
- *Legal security for property rights*.

Reflection point

Consider the extent to which the points identified by Williamson (1990) still underpin political decision-making today.

So how does the 'Washington consensus' relate to neoliberalism and globalisation? The term 'Washington consensus' is now often used in a way that is synonymous with neoliberalism; it has also become a focus of anti-globalisation protestors, who believe that Washington-based international financial institutions have imposed neoliberal policies on other countries.

Neoliberal movements have changed the global economy in many ways, as illustrated by Cohen and Centeno (2006) and Rapley (2004):

- increased growth in international trade and cross-border capital flows;
- elimination of trade barriers;
- cutbacks in public sector employment;
- widespread privatisation of previously public-owned enterprises;
- an increasing share of a country's economic wealth concentrated in the top economic percentiles of the population.

6.8.4 Impacts of globalisation

Globalisation has fostered international trade links and facilitated the international movement of financial capital. Globalisation can therefore be seen as leading to the increased integration of societies and economies around the world. Links between the economies of different countries have a history as long as that of international trade, but the pace of this global integration has become much more rapid in recent decades because of unprecedented advances in technology, communications, science, transport and industry.

Has globalisation contributed to improvements in human well-being and the alleviation of poverty? There is no doubt that the rapid economic development of countries such as China and India has been facilitated by the process of globalisation, and such countries have made significant progress in reducing poverty. However, others have not, for example, many African countries have failed to benefit significantly. The reasons for such disparity between countries are not always clear, but poor policies and infrastructure, weak institutions and corrupt governance have been contributory factors. Geographical factors can also be influential, for example, land-locked countries can find it more difficult to compete in global manufacturing and service markets.

Globalisation can therefore be seen as a catalyst for and a consequence of human progress, but it also creates significant challenges and problems. The fact that the pace of change has been so rapid has itself become one of these challenges; many societies, institutions and political structures are finding it difficult to adapt to the pace of change, and can feel powerless to prevent further change. Recent examples include the current global economic crisis, and the role of social media in supporting political activism, as observed in the 'Arab Spring' of 2011.

Stiglitz (2002) published a major critique of globalisation and the economic theory that underpins it. This publication is particularly significant, given that Stiglitz won the Nobel Prize in economic sciences, and was also for a time the chief economist at the World Bank. As a result of this experience, he became disillusioned with the IMF and other international institutions, which he believes act against the interests of relatively poor developing countries. Stiglitz suggests that the neoliberal assumptions that underpin the policies pursued by institutions such as the IMF are unsound. Specifically, he criticises policies such as high interest rates, trade liberalisation, the privatisation of state assets and the liberalisation of capital markets. He attributes financial crises in East Asia and Argentina, as well as low levels of development in Sub-Saharan Africa, to the policies of the IMF. Stiglitz also highlights the lack of evidence in support of 'trickle down economics', namely the belief that wealth will trickle down from the top to all segments of society, as many adherents of neoliberalist policies believe.

Another notable critic of neoliberalism is Noam Chomsky, a well-known American linguist and philosopher, who stated (Chomsky, 2006): 'Globalization that does not prioritize the rights of people will very likely degenerate into a form of tyranny, perhaps oligarchic and oligopolistic, based on concentrations of tightly-linked state-private power, largely unaccountable to the public.' With more than one billion people living in extreme poverty, one of the main concerns of globalisation's critics is its impact on the poor. Although a number of studies have been undertaken of such impacts, most of the evidence is indirect; very few studies have examined direct links between poverty and globalisation. A recent synthesis of research reached the following conclusions (Harrison, 2007):

• Globalisation produces both winners and losers among the poor. Such contrasting outcomes can occur even within a single country. In Mexico, for example, while most

medium-sized corn farmers saw their incomes fall by half in the 1990s, the incomes of large corn farmers increased.
- Export growth and incoming foreign investment have reduced poverty in countries such as Mexico, India and Zambia.
- The poor are more likely to share in the gains from globalisation when there are complementary policies in place, such as trade reforms implemented in conjunction with reducing impediments to labour mobility.
- The poor in countries with an abundance of unskilled labour do not always gain from trade reform, in contrast to the belief of many economists.
- Financial crises are costly to the poor. For example, in Indonesia, poverty rates increased by at least 50 per cent after the currency crisis in 1997.

A further issue is the equality of income distribution. Neoliberal economists maintain that the distribution of income between the world's people has become more equal over the past two decades, owing to increased economic integration between countries (Wade, 2004). Evidence for this contention depends critically on the measures that are used to assess income distribution, and a variety of different conclusions can be drawn from the information available. However, based on a review of such evidence, Wade concluded that income inequality has actually been rising during the past three decades, particularly when incomes are measured at market-exchange rate incomes. Absolute income gaps are also widening. Income inequality between countries affects the ability of poorer countries to repay their debts, to import capital goods and to participate in the international negotiations that affect them directly. Within countries, increasing inequality of income distribution is a major contributor to social and political unrest. As an illustration of the magnitude of the problem, 0.7 per cent of the world's population (32 million) currently hold 41 per cent of the global wealth (US$98.7 trillion) (Credit Suisse, 2013).

6.8.5 A green perspective

Porritt (2007) suggests that the anti-globalisation protests are essentially anti-corporate, and questions the idea that what is good for business – less regulation, more mobility, more access – will trickle down into benefits for everybody. Most protestors are not calling for a return to narrow nationalism, but for the borders of globalisation to be expanded, and for trade to be linked to labour rights, environmental protection and democracy. These could be viewed as elements of the green economy.

Further, Porritt suggests that most people acknowledge that the world is generally a better place for improved global communications, the development of the internet and improved understanding between nations. Also, global problems demand global solutions mediated through accountable global initiatives and institutions. With respect to globalisation, he suggests that there is a need for 'increased decentralisation of power, global and national regulation of large corporations, community-based and local enterprise as a complement to international trade, and a passionate belief in development as freedom rather than development as growth'.

Cato (2009) suggests that local, self-reliant communities are the most positive way forward, rather than supporting inequitable global trade. In this context she cites Gandhi, whose political action was directed at liberation from the neo-colonialism that he identified in the global trade system. Gandhi promoted a concept of 'Swadeshi', or self-reliance, which, according to Cato (2009), offers a prototype for the localisation of the economy.

> **Reflection point**
>
> Note here the concept of 'localisation' as the converse of 'globalisation' (see also Chapter 8). The development of locally based economies, in which products and services are sourced locally, is a central concept in green thinking, as explored further by Cato (2009, 2011) and Schumacher (1973), among others.

6.8.6 Governing globalisation

Three international economic organisations (IEOs) have played a leading role in supporting the process of globalisation, namely, the International Monetary Fund (IMF), the World Bank, and the World Trade Organization (WTO, previously GATT). The role, coverage and mandate of these organisations have expanded significantly over the past six decades, which has generated significant controversy. In particular, they have been criticised for the negative impacts of globalisation, as the World Bank and the IMF have urged countries to open up their markets as a precondition for financial assistance (Bhagwati, 2004; Hessami, 2011). In addition, the IMF and the World Bank have been accused of not having fulfilled their missions, given that poverty and financial instability are still widespread. This failure has been widely attributed to the promotion of a 'market fundamentalist' ideology, which has adversely affected poor countries while rich countries have prospered (Stiglitz, 2002; Bhagwati, 2004; Hessami, 2011). Furthermore, these IEOs have been criticised for their lack of democratic accountability, which has led to a lack of trust and has undermined their legitimacy (Hessami, 2011). As a consequence, though these organisations have a major impact on the protection of human rights worldwide, there is no mechanism to hold them accountable for their respective human rights obligations (Lafont, 2010).

Allegations of a lack of democratic accountability are based on the fact that influence at the World Bank and the IMF depends on economic size and power. Specifically, the USA, the UK, Japan, Germany and France hold 40 per cent of the votes, while the remaining votes are divided among about 180 countries (Hessami, 2011). This situation has been criticised by many countries from the Global South, who have also complained about how the WTO negotiations are conducted (Bøås and McNeill, 2003).

Businesses also play a major role in global governance. For example, 51 of the largest 100 economies in the world are those of transnational corporations, rather than states. Some 500 of these corporations control around 70 per cent of global trade (Cato, 2009), highlighting a major concentration of power. It is pertinent to consider who controls such corporations, and who they are accountable to. Further, many non-governmental organisations (NGOs) also play a significant role in global governance, particularly in areas such as advocacy for environmental justice, and consultation in policy development (Gemmill and Bamidele-Izu, 2002). It is now increasingly being recognised that the effectiveness of global governance is strongly dependent on enabling the constructive participation of such civil society organisations (Gemmill *et al.*, 2002).

> **Reflection point**
>
> Given that many problems facing the world are global in nature, do you think that some kind of global governance is required to bring about the green economy? If so, what features should it have?

6.9 Environmental justice in practice

6.9.1 Introduction

How can problems or issues relating to environmental justice be identified? And how can such problems be solved?

6.9.2 Advocacy and activism

The concept of social or environmental justice essentially relates to fairness: achieving an equitable distribution or outcome. There are very many situations where such a fair outcome is not being achieved in practice; these provide examples of injustice. How should such injustice be addressed or resolved? One option would be to try to persuade governments to change laws, if these are the source of the injustice in question. Alternatively, the problem may lie in the lack of enforcement of the laws that already exist.

How might an individual or organisation persuade a government to change its laws, or improve its law enforcement? One way might be to engage in some form of direct action, or *activism*. This can take many different forms, such as conducting a media campaign, for example, by writing letters to newspapers or TV stations, or by using the internet; by undertaking economic activism such as boycotts of particular businesses; or by organising or engaging in public demonstrations such as rallies, street marches, strikes or sit-ins. Such activities can potentially involve people from any walk of life; many who engage in campaigns do not necessarily think of themselves as activists. The anti-globalisation protests considered above provide an example of such campaigns.

> **Reflection point**
>
> Consider how the internet is revolutionising how people engage in activism, by providing powerful tools for rapid communication between large numbers of people. A good example is provided by 38 degrees (www.38degrees.org.uk/), a website designed to facilitate action, which has already been successful in changing government policies in the UK by mobilising mass support.

Another approach is *advocacy*. This is a political process pursued by an individual or group of people, which typically aims to influence public policy or laws, and affect decisions regarding the activities of political, economic or social institutions. Advocacy can be undertaken through a wide range of activities, including media campaigns, commissioning and publishing research or conducting opinion polls (Box 6.4). *Lobbying* (which is often undertaken by lobby groups

BOX 6.4 ENVIRONMENTAL JUSTICE ORGANISATIONS

Some organisations campaigning for environmental justice are listed below. You are encouraged to explore these websites to discover learning resources and information on how campaigns are being conducted.

1. Capacity Global: www.capacity.org.uk. Capacity Global provides an example of an organisation that focuses explicitly on promoting environmental justice, with the aim of influencing policy and marginalised community action. Examples of current initiatives include development of a greener jobs programme, and 'Big Local', a ten-year programme to support local communities in making their areas better places to live.
2. Greenpeace: www.greenpeace.org/international/en. Greenpeace is a well-known environmental campaigning organisation, with a particular focus on undertaking direct action. Environmental justice is increasingly featuring in their portfolio of activities. This organisation has campaigned particularly on the global trade in waste, and its impact on poor people; they are also campaigning for greener electronics.
3. Friends of the Earth (FoE): www.foei.org. FoE are also well known for their environmental campaigns, which have a strong focus on sustainable development. In the UK, FoE played a major role in establishing environmental justice as an issue through research that they conducted. FoE is currently campaigning for equitable responses to climate change, environmental health issues and green energy.
4. Environmental Justice Resource Center, Clark Atlanta University, USA: www.ejrc.cau.edu. This is a university-based centre that provides support to community-based organisations and environmentally impacted communities. Their focus is primarily Black Americans in the USA. Current major concerns include environmental health, pollution and energy.
5. Environmental Justice Foundation (EJF): www.ejfoundation.org.EJF provides training to individuals and grassroots organisations in the Global South, enabling them to document, expose and create long-term solutions to environmental abuses. Based in London, the organisation works internationally with a number of partners in other countries. Current initiatives focus on illegal fishing, shrimp farming, ethical and sustainable cotton production, and climate refugees.
6. Ejolt (Environmental Justice Organisations, Liabilities and Trade): www.ejolt.org. This is a collaborative research project funded by the European Union, involving a partnership between a large number of environmental justice organisations (EJOs), which are civil society groups involved in conflicts over resource extraction or waste disposal. Current themes include energy, mining, environmental health and consumption.
7. Oxfam International: www.oxfam.org.Oxfam is an international confederation of organisations spread over more than 90 countries, which focuses on freeing people from the injustice of poverty. While not exclusively an environmental justice organisation, current campaigns focus on climate change, agriculture and environmental disasters, as well as health and education.

or special interest groups) is a form of advocacy, where a direct approach is made to legislators on a particular issue; this plays a very significant role in modern politics.

Social justice advocates might typically address power relations and people's participation, and promote a vision of a more just society. They might question how existing laws or policies are implemented, target political systems that do not respond to people's needs, suggest policy options, and provide a forum for public dialogue and debate. Different forms of advocacy can usefully be identified. For example, media advocacy is 'the strategic use of the mass media as a resource to advance a social or public policy initiative' (Jerningan and Wright, 1996), whereas legislative advocacy is the 'reliance on the state or federal legislative process' in the strategy to create change (Loue *et al.*, 2003).

How does advocacy differ from activism? The two concepts are related, but many authors on advocacy (Tusinski, 2007; Masner, 2008) consider it to be the act of publicly representing an individual, organisation or idea, with the aim of persuading people to look favourably on it. Cohen *et al.* (2001) defines advocacy as the pursuit of influencing outcomes in society. While advocacy can be considered as showing active support, pleading or arguing for something, activism is a policy of taking direct action to achieve a political or social goal (Zeitz, 2008). Activism can therefore be best described as part of the advocacy process where some kind of direct and deliberate action is taken to bring about political or social change.

Reflection point

In the context of environmental justice, why do you think advocacy or activism might be necessary? Might they be a response to some form of political or social failure? Also, to what extent do you consider such campaigns to be democratic, and truly representative of majority opinion?

6.9.3 Access to justice

Activist organisations typically encourage mass participation in protest activity and in political action, and encourage community groups to organise protests, demonstrations, and even to engage in civil disobedience. But why is this course of action preferred over pursuing litigation in the courts? This issue is explored by Marshall (2010), who notes that the goals of lawyers – 'appropriate juridical arguments and winning'– may contrast to those of activists –'recruitment and political mobilization'. Moreover, lawsuits are rarely successful, except when environmental laws have been clearly violated. On the other hand, some environmental justice organisations in the USA have pursued litigation through a participatory strategy that helps mobilise grassroots' interest in the movement (ibid.).

This raises the issue of *access to justice*. Pursuing litigation in the courts can be very expensive, and this can result in the poorer sections of society being excluded from the legal process. This is explored by Millner (2011), who notes that having good laws that facilitate consultation will not ensure that members of the public will have access to environmental justice. There is also a need for appropriate institutions and the education of members of the public, so that the public is aware of its rights and opportunities to participate in government decisions and knows how to utilise these opportunities.

Even if people are educated and aware of how they may access tribunals and other decision-making fora, doing this in practice can be difficult. This is because courts and tribunals can be intimidating, and gaining an understanding of their procedures can be difficult (ibid.). There are also geographical barriers to access to environmental justice. For example, people in rural and remote communities are often a significant distance from where decisions are made. Most courts and tribunals that make decisions on environmental law matters are based in capital cities.

> ### Reflection point
>
> Consider how access to justice is itself an aspect of social justice. The rural poor, for example, are likely to be in a disadvantaged position in terms of accessing the legal system, compared to the urban rich.

6.9.4 Governance and corruption

A further reason for engaging with activism as a means of seeking justice may be that the legal system itself is weak. It is widely recognised that good governance is essential to sustainable development. In turn, good governance is dependent on well-functioning legal institutions and governments that are bound by the rule of law. However, many countries are characterised by weak legal and judicial systems, where laws are not adequately enforced, and where non-compliance and corruption are common. Such situations undermine respect for the rule of law, and can undermine progress towards the green economy, for example, by causing environmental degradation.

Morita and Zaelke (2006) note that good governance promotes accountability, transparency, efficiency, and rule of law in public institutions at all levels. In addition, it allows for sound and efficient management of human, natural, economic and financial resources for equitable and sustainable development. Under good governance, clear decision-making procedures exist at the level of public authorities, civil society participates in decision-making processes, and there is an ability to enforce rights and obligations through legal mechanisms. An absence of such aspects of good governance can significantly impede progress towards sustainable development. For example, a lack of properly functioning institutions of governance based on the rule of law can act as a disincentive for investment, and encourage high rates of corruption. This can include paying and receiving bribes, fraud, embezzlement, self-dealing, conflicts of interest, and providing a quid pro quo in return for gifts. Introduction of good governance and rule of law, however, can take time to implement, requiring changes in long-standing practices, entrenched interests, cultural habits, social and even religious norms.

Corrupt activities are illegal in most countries, but are nevertheless widespread. Researchers at the World Bank estimate that worldwide bribery totals at least US$1 trillion per year, and represented around 3 per cent of world income in 2002. This issue was reviewed by Rose-Ackerman (2004), who noted that poor governance is itself one of the reasons that some countries are poor and have low or negative growth rates. Demands for greater democracy, transparency, and integrity in government often become more insistent as per capita income rises. However, those who benefit from a corrupt status quo often try to impede reform. High levels of corruption lead to increases in inequality, and can persuade people that it is acceptable not to pay taxes because the government is being run by corrupt officials and their supporters. Another key factor is the security of property rights, which can have a major influence on inward investment. The security of property rights is indicated by the ability of the state to enforce its own rules impartially. Property rights are less secure if bribery and protection payments are common and if the courts do not enforce contracts.

To address the problems of corruption and poor governance, Rose-Ackerman (2004) suggests:

- Implementation of programmes that improve accountability at the grassroots. Relatively simple, inexpensive reforms can have large benefits if the political will to do so exists.
- Attempts to develop benchmark cost estimates can help constrain procurement fraud and corruption.
- Reform of revenue collection through tax simplification and incentive-based reforms.
- Streamlining of business regulations to reduce the economic costs of 'red tape.' However, policy must balance the benefits and costs of regulations, as there may be costs to society of eliminating regulations that provide social and environmental benefits.
- International initiatives to track down the assets of corrupt officials. It is estimated that this could provide multi-billion dollar benefits with minimal costs.

Reflection point

How dependent do you think the green economy might be on good governance?

6.10 Environmental justice and indigenous peoples

6.10.1 Introduction

Many indigenous groups have engaged in long political struggles to defend their rights; many of these groups have been the subject of illegal action, oppression and persecution. Access to environmental resources, including oil, water (Box 6.5), mineral and genetic resources, has been the focus of particular conflict. Indigenous peoples therefore provide a powerful example of issues relating to environmental justice.

It is estimated that there are around 370 million indigenous people living in 90 countries (Doyle, 2009). As pressure on global resources increases, indigenous peoples can bear disproportionate costs from resource-intensive and resource-extractive industries and activities, such as mining (Box 6.6), oil and gas development, large dams and other infrastructure projects, logging and plantations, bio-prospecting, industrial fishing and farming, and also eco-tourism and imposed conservation projects (UNDESA, 2009). In many cases, the issues centred on distributive environmental justice, since indigenous peoples often have strong spiritual attachments to particular places and their environmental attributes. At the same time, indigenous peoples often lack a voice and are often not represented in decision-making bodies (Forest Peoples Programme, 2009).

BOX 6.5 CASE STUDY: WATER PRIVATISATION

In many countries, water resources have been privatised in recent years. This has been highly controversial, especially from a social justice standpoint. For example:

- In India, from the mid-1980s onward, companies such as the Coca-Cola Company, PepsiCo, Suez, Vivendi and Bechtel became involved in a highly profitable water market. This ranged from the outright privatisation of urban water supplies and wastewater management, to joint contracts with cities and public sector entities to manage water infrastructure and delivery to industries and consumers. Control of water resources by such companies reduced the water available to resource-poor farmers, increased contamination and impacted negatively on crop yields. This led to a development of a major protest movement and the imposition of government bans on company products (Aiyer, 2007).
- In Colombia, water privatisation was found to lead to an improvement in the quality of water, and a positive effect on health outcomes in both urban and rural areas. However, it also resulted in a strong negative effect on access to water in rural areas (Barrera-Osorio et al., 2009).
- Like many other indebted developing countries, the Philippines was pressurised by the World Bank to privatise its government-controlled water services through loan conditions and technical assistance programmes. The results were very mixed, and led to the bankruptcy of one of the companies involved (Li, 2011).
- In Belize, consumers complained bitterly about an increase in water tariffs and excessive disconnection rates following water privatisation. Policy-makers accused the company involved of front-loading profits and not making strategic investments in infrastructure (Mustafa and Reeder, 2009).

In a review of the impacts of water privatisation, Link (2010) identified the need: (1) to create norms and guidelines relating to the human right to water at national and international scales; (2) to collaborate between governments and companies to ensure that citizens' needs are met; and (3) to increase citizen participation.

Suggested activity

You are encouraged to explore some of the case studies documented in the UNDESA (2009) report, which provides an overview of the current state of the world's indigenous peoples. A good example is the San of the Kalahari, who for many years have been struggling with forced relocation from their homelands, without any substantive address of their fundamental human rights. Another resource is provided by Survival International, which campaigns on behalf of tribal people such as the San (www.survivalinternational. org/tribes). (Note, however, that not all indigenous peoples are 'tribal'.)

BOX 6.6 CASE STUDY: MINING

Mining provides another powerful example of widespread social injustice, which has sometimes led to conflict. Over the past two decades, the mining industry has come under intense pressure to improve its social, developmental and environmental performance (Wellmer and Becker-Platen, 2002; Bridge, 2004). This reflects the environmental pollution caused by mining waste, the contribution of mining to biogeochemical processes, and the role of mining in driving regional land-cover conversion, habitat fragmentation, and associated effects on biodiversity. In addition, the conditions of the mine working environment have long been a source of socio-political struggle (Bridge, 2004). From a social perspective, many mining areas are centres of intense poverty, despite the fact that the companies involved often make substantial profits.

A particular area of concern in recent years has been the impact of multinational mining operations on indigenous peoples. Common features of such examples (1) stress the asymmetries of power between mining firms and indigenous peoples; (2) focus on the political struggles that take place between firms, indigenous peoples and the state over resource access, land rights, revenue distribution and environmental impacts; and (3) involve infringements of justice, human rights and indigenous rights.

Specific examples include:

- The development of a new mining code in the Philippines in 1995; impacts of a surge in gold mining exploration on the Guianan Shield during the 1990s; and controversies over large-scale mining operations in Melanesia (Ok Tedi and Porgera in Papua New Guinea, Grasberg in Irian Jaya, and the Gold Ridge mine in the Solomon Islands) (Bridge, 2004; Kirsch, 2007).
- Muradian *et al.* (2003) describe the social clash over a gold mining project in Peru, which 85 per cent of the local population were against. Sources of the conflict included disagreement between experts, the local population and the mining company; distrust in institutions; and the lack of a participatory procedure for deciding local development strategies.
- Keeling and Sandlos (2009) examine the negative social, economic and environmental consequences of mining in Canada's territorial north, which has impacted on aboriginal communities in the region since the early twentieth century. Many of these historical impacts persist, and include toxic sites associated with abandoned mines located within traditional territories, which have become a source of great concern.

6.10.2 International treaties, conventions and declarations

In recent years, the rights to land and natural resources of indigenous peoples have begun to appear in international law-making. However, international environmental law, with its treaty-based framework built on the premise of state sovereignty, is ill equipped to deal with indigenous peoples who demand rights equivalent to states. The challenge for indigenous peoples is to assert their sovereign rights to their lands and the natural resources they provide. Some key milestones in international law relating to indigenous peoples include (UNDESA, 2009):

- The first international treaty to specifically deal with indigenous rights was ILO (International Labour Organisation) Convention No. 107 (superseded by Convention No. 169 in 1989) concerning the Protection and Integration of Indigenous and other Tribal and Semi-Tribal Populations in Independent Countries, adopted in 1959. This Convention recognised the indigenous peoples' rights of ownership, collective or individual, of the lands they traditionally occupy (Article 11).
- Agenda 21 gives extensive and formal recognition to indigenous peoples and recommends the incorporation of indigenous peoples' rights and responsibilities into national legislation.
- In 2007, the General Assembly passed the UN Declaration of the Rights of Indigenous Peoples (UNDRIP), drafted in part by the rights holders themselves. While not legally binding, UNDRIP consolidates existing international rights, laws and jurisprudence as applicable to indigenous peoples and is the most comprehensive expression of the collective and individual rights of indigenous peoples. The policy condemns forcibly removing indigenous peoples from their lands, and promotes fair local benefit from the use of mineral, water, or other resources (Finley-Brook and Thomas, 2010).
- Since 1988, indigenous peoples have participated in UNFCCC Conferences of the Parties (COP) and have released statements expressing concerns on the implications of climate change policies on their livelihoods and cultures. However, they are admitted only as observers, not as peoples.
- The Convention on Biological Diversity (CBD) was the first international environmental convention to develop measures for the use and protection of traditional knowledge, related to the conservation and sustainable use of biodiversity.

6.10.3 Issues affecting indigenous peoples

Some key issues where indigenous peoples are vulnerable to environmental injustices are listed below.

- *Conservation and national parks.* Dispossession of traditional lands and territories is one of the major problems faced by indigenous peoples globally. Some advocates of wilderness preservation fiercely oppose the presence of people in protected areas, while others argue that local residents are some of the best custodians that valuable habitats could have (Colchester, 2004; Schmidt-Soltau and Brockington, 2007; Schroeder, 2008).
- *Dams.* Large dams have disproportionately impacted indigenous peoples. They have suffered from loss of lands and livelihoods, culture and identity, and have been the victims of human rights abuses. Dam planning and projects are often characterised by procedural injustices that relate directly to indigenous communities (UNDESA, 2009). The benefits of a large dam (e.g. electricity, irrigation) are rarely enjoyed by the peoples most affected by it (Sneddon and Fox, 2008; Finley-Brook and Thomas, 2010).
- *Mining and oil extraction.* Extractive industries such as mining and oil drilling often lead to depletion of resources necessary for physical and cultural survival, destruction and pollution of the traditional environment, social and community disruption, and long-term

negative health, all of which can cause indigenous peoples to migrate (UNDESA, 2009; Orta-Martinez and Finer, 2010; see also Box 6.6).

- *Forests.* For many indigenous peoples, forests have a vital role in maintaining their physical, cultural, spiritual and economic well-being. However, this can be threatened by logging, agri-business, large-scale infrastructure projects, oil exploration and mining operations (UNDESA, 2009). There are concerns that new initiatives such as REDD+ (see Chapter 7) could also impact negatively on indigenous peoples (Lyster, 2011).
- *Bioprospecting and biopiracy.* This refers to the commercial development of natural resources, such as plant extracts or genetic cell lines, without fair compensation to the people who live where the materials were discovered. This has become a major issue for many indigenous groups (Takeshita, 2000; DeGeer, 2003; Argumedo and Pimbert, 2006; Cloatre, 2006; Grenier, 2010).

Potentially such issues can be addressed by ensuring that indigenous peoples receive a greater degree of justice concerning their lands and livelihoods (Box 6.7). One key approach is 'Free, prior and informed consent (FPIC)', which can be used in defining and regulating contractual

---

BOX 6.7 CASE STUDY: ENVIRONMENTAL JUSTICE FOR FIRST NATION PEOPLES IN CANADA

Environmental justice is not only an issue for indigenous peoples in developing countries, but also in developed countries, where indigenous peoples consistently lag behind in terms of most indicators of human well-being (UNDESA, 2009). An example is provided by the First Nation peoples in Canada:

- Mascarenhas (2007) provides an analysis of water management at Walpole Island First Nation in Canada's Chemical Valley in south-western Ontario. He illustrates how the recognition of environmental injustices and participation in environmental governance has become much more difficult for First Nation communities. New forms of neoliberal governance have exacerbated historically derived disparities in health, environmental pollution, and well-being.
- Page (2007) focuses on salmon farming on the British Columbia coast in western Canada. Salmon have an important traditional place in West Coast First Nation cultures, not only as food and an economic mainstay, but also as the foundation of their entire culture and way of life. Fishing therefore has importance for the social cohesion of many West Coast communities. This is threatened by the intensive salmon farming that is developing along the Pacific coast. Page demonstrates why the disputes over salmon aquaculture should be considered a case of environmental justice for reasons greater than the environmental impacts of the farming.
- Robinson *et al.* (2007) analyse environmentalism in British Columbia and its potential support for First Nations' land claims. Specifically, these authors highlight how environmental justice provides an appropriate frame for different organisations and stakeholders to come together in a unified environmentalist and environmental justice movement.

relationships, to ensure an open and equitable relationship between the different stakeholders. Negotiating consent means that forest peoples have the right to refuse any proposed interventions on their territories (Lewis *et al.*, 2008). Cariño and Colchester (2010) consider FPIC in the context of large dams, and how it has been affirmed as a right of indigenous peoples under international human rights law and as best practice for the extractive industries. These authors note that for FPIC to be effective, it must respect indigenous peoples' rights to control their customary lands, enable them to represent themselves through their own institutions, and to make decisions according to procedures of their choosing. Lewis *et al.* (2008) document the findings of a preliminary study that was conducted in the Congo Basin to test how FPIC can be implemented in practice.

6.11 Environmental justice and gender

Environmental justice has tended to focus on race and class or wealth. However, gender is also an important issue in relation to environmental justice (Buckingham, 2004), despite the fact that it has often been marginalised in the past (Buckingham and Kulcur, 2009).

An example of how environmental impacts can disproportionately affect women is provided by Hurricane Katrina, where 80 per cent of people left in New Orleans following the storm were women (Women's Environmental Network, 2010). Women and children living in poverty are the most vulnerable to the negative impacts of climate change (Nelson *et al.*, 2002; Aguilar *et al.*, 2008). Furthermore, 70 per cent of farmers worldwide are women, but they often have little access to decision-making structures. Globally, women only hold title to less than 2 per cent of private land (Women's Environmental Network, 2010). Female-headed households, both in developed and developing countries, are also more likely to be poor. For example in Bangladesh, 95 per cent of female-headed households are living below the poverty line (ibid.).

Buckingham (2010) observes that representative democracy, with its rights-based approach grounded in models of patriarchy, has not served women well in the development of environmental programmes. This situation has led to the development of *ecofeminism*, which is a social and political movement that highlights links between the health of humans and the health of the environment. Ecofeminism maintains that there are strong parallels between the oppression of and control over both women and the environment, particularly by a patriarchal society (Buckingham, 2004). Examples of women's participation in the environmental justice movement are provided by Kurtz (2007) and Bell and Braun (2010).

A commentary on a gender perspective in the green economy is provided by the Women Rio+20 Steering Committee (2011), which calls for policy and legislative changes that will do the following:

- secure women's property rights, land tenure, and control over natural resources;
- promote women's access to services and technologies needed for water, energy, agricultural production, family care, household management and business enterprises;
- provide safe health care facilities, including for sexual and reproductive health;
- enable women – and men – to combine their jobs with childcare;
- support investments in women's economic empowerment; and
- promote women's participation in government and business leadership.

Bibliography

Aguilar, L., Araujo, A. and Quesada-Aguilar, A. 2008. *Gender and Climate Change*, IUCN, Gland, Switzerland.

Agyeman, J. and Evans, B. 2004. 'Just sustainability': the emerging discourse of environmental justice in Britain? *The Geographical Journal*, 170: 155–164.

Aiyer, A. 2007. The allure of the transnational: notes on some aspects of the political economy of water in India. *Cultural Anthropology*, 22: 640–658.

Albrow, M. and King, E. (eds) 1990. *Globalization, Knowledge and Society*, Sage, London.

Al-Rodhan, R. F. N. and Stoudmann, G. 2006. *Definitions of Globalization: A Comprehensive Overview and a Proposed Definition* [Online]. Program on the Geopolitical Implications of Globalization and Transnational Security, Geneva. Available at: www.sustainablehistory.com/articles/definitions-of-globalization.pdf (accessed 28 Nov. 2013).

Argumedo, A. and Pimbert, M. 2006. *Protecting Indigenous Knowledge against Biopiracy in the Andes*, IIED, London.

Barrera-Osorio, F., Olivera, M. and Ospino, C. 2009. Does society win or lose as a result of privatization? The case of water sector privatization in Colombia. *Economica*, 76: 649–674.

Beckerman, W. 1994. Sustainable development: is it a useful concept? *Environmental Values*, 3: 191–209.

Bell, S., McGillivray, D. and Pedersen, O. 2013. *Environmental Law*, 8th edn, Oxford University Press, Oxford.

Bell, S. E. and Braun, Y. A. 2010. Coal, identity, and the gendering of environmental justice activism in Central Appalachia. *Gender and Society* 24: 794–813.

Bhagwati, J. 2004. *In Defense of Globalization*, Oxford University Press, Oxford.

Bøås, M. and McNeill, D. 2003. *Multilateral Institutions: A Critical Introduction*, Pluto Press, London.

Bond, A., Palerm, J. and Haigh, P. 2004. Public participation in EIA of nuclear power plant decommissioning projects: a case study analysis. *Environmental Impact Assessment Review*, 24: 617–641.

Bratt, L. 2009. The Brundtland link between poverty and environmental degradation, and other questionable opinions. *International Journal of Innovation and Sustainable Development*, 4: 74–92.

Bridge, G. 2004. Contested terrain: mining and the environment. *Annual Review of Environment and Resources*, 29: 205–259.

Buckingham, S. 2004. Ecofeminism in the twenty-first century. *Geographical Journal*, 170: 146–154.

Buckingham, S. 2010. Call in the women. *Nature*, 468: 502.

Buckingham, S. and Kulcur, R. 2009. Gendered geographies of environmental injustice. *Antipode*, 41: 659–683.

Bulkeley, H. and Walker, G. 2005. Environmental justice: a new agenda for the UK. *Local Environment*, 10: 329–332.

Cariño, J. and Colchester, M. 2010. From dams to development justice: progress with 'free, prior and informed consent' since the World Commission on Dams. *Water Alternatives*, 3: 423–437.

Cato, M. S. 2009. *Green Economics. An Introduction to Theory, Policy and Practice,* Earthscan, London.

Cato, M. S. 2011. *Environment and Economy*, Routledge, London.

Chomsky, N. 2006. Globalisation: Noam Chomsky interviewed by Maria Ahmed [Online]. Available at: www.chomsky.info/interviews/2006----.htm (accessed 3 Oct. 2013).

Cloatre, E. 2006. From international ethics to European Union policy: a case study on biopiracy in the EU's biotechnology directive. *Law & Policy*, 28: 345–367.

Cohen, D., De la Vega, R. and Watson, G. 2001. *Advocacy for Social Justice: A Global Action and Reflection Guide*, Kumarian Press, Bloomfield, CT.

Cohen, J. N. and Centeno, M. A. 2006. Neoliberalism and patterns of economic performance, 1980–2000. *Annals of the American Academy of Political and Social Science*, 606: 32–67.

Colchester, M. 2004. Conservation policy and indigenous peoples. *Environmental Science & Policy*, 7: 145–153.

Colten, C. E. 2007. Environmental justice in a landscape of tragedy. *Technology in Society*, 29: 173–179.

Common, M. and Stagl, S. 2005. *Ecological Economics: An Introduction*, Cambridge University Press, Cambridge.

Cooney, R. 2004. *The Precautionary Principle in Biodiversity Conservation and Natural Resource Management: An Issues Paper for Policy-Makers, Researchers and Practitioners*, IUCN, Gland, Switzerland.

Credit Suisse 2013. *Global Wealth Report 2013*, Credit Suisse AG, Zurich, Switzerland.

DeGeer, M. E. 2003. Biopiracy: the appropriation of indigenous peoples' cultural knowledge. *New England Journal of International and Comparative Law*, 9: 179–207.

Doyle, C. 2009. Indigenous peoples and the Millennium Development Goals: 'sacrificial lambs' or equal beneficiaries? *The International Journal of Human Rights*, 13: 44–71.

Doyle, T. 1998. Sustainable development and Agenda 21: the secular bible of global free markets and pluralist democracy. *Third World Quarterly*, 19: 771–786.

Elvers, H. D., Gross, M. and Heinrichs, H. 2008. The diversity of environmental justice towards a European approach. *European Societies*, 10: 835–856.

ESRC 2001. *Environmental Justice: Rights and Means to a Healthy Environment for All. Special Briefing No 7*, ESRC Global Environmental Change Programme, London.

Fairtrade International 2012. *Monitoring the Scope and Benefits of Fairtrade*, Fairtrade International (FLO), Bonn, Germany.

Finley-Brook, M. and Thomas, C. 2010. From malignant neglect to extreme intervention: treatment of displaced indigenous populations in two large hydro projects in Panama. *Water Alternatives*, 3: 269–290.

Forest Peoples Programme 2009. *Applying Free, Prior and Informed Consent in the Democratic Republic of Congo*, Forest Peoples Programme, London.

Foti, J., de Silva, L., McGray, H., Shaffer, L., Talbot, J. and Werksman, J. 2008. *Voice and Choice: Opening the Door to Environmental Democracy*, World Resources Institute, Washington, DC.

Gemmill, B. and Bamidele-Izu, A. 2002. The role of NGOs and civil society in global environmental governance, in D. C. Esty and M. H. Ivanova (eds) *Global Environmental Governance: Options and Opportunities*. Yale School of Forestry and Environmental Studies, Connecticut.

Gemmill, B., Ivanova, M. and Chee, Y. L. 2002. *Designing a New Architecture for Global Environmental Governance: World Summit for Sustainable Development Briefing Papers*, International Institute for Environment and Development (IIED), London.

Gibbons, S. 2008. Group litigation, class actions and Lord Woolf's three objectives: a critical analysis. *Civil Justice Quarterly*, 27: 208–243.

Giddens, A. 1999. *Runaway World: How Globalisation Is Reshaping Our Lives*, Profile Books Ltd, London.

Grenier, E. 2010. A new protocol to stop biopiracy: worth a standing ovation? [Online]. Available at: www.legalfrontiers.ca/2010/11/special-contribution-a-new-protocol-to-stop-biopiracy-worth-a-standing-ovation/ (accessed 3 Oct. 2013).

Hajer, M. A. 1995. *The Politics of Environmental Discourse: Ecological Modernization and the Policy Process*, Clarendon Press, Oxford.

Harrison, A. 2007. Globalization and poverty: an introduction, in A. Harrison (ed.) *Globalization and Poverty*. University of Chicago Press: Chicago.

Hartley, N. and Wood, C. 2005. Public participation in environmental impact assessment: implementing the Aarhus Convention. *Environmental Impact Assessment Review*, 25: 319–340.

Hessami, Z. 2011. What determines trust in international organizations? An empirical analysis for the IMF, the World Bank, and the WTO. *Munich Personal RePEc Archive*, MPRA Paper No. 34550 [Online]. Available at: http://mpra.ub.uni-muenchen.de/34550/ (accessed 28 Nov. 2013).

Hughes, D., Jewell, T., Lowther, J., Parpworth, N. and de Prez, P. 2002. *Environmental Law*, 4th edn, Butterworths, London.

Jamieson, D. 1998. Sustainability and beyond. *Ecological Economics*, 24: 183–192.

Jerningan, D. H. and Wright, P. 1996. Media advocacy: lessons from community experiences. *Journal of Public Health Policy*, 17: 306–330.

Jones, V. 2009. *The Green Collar Economy. How One Solution Can Fix Our Two Biggest Problems*, HarperCollins, New York.

Keeling, A. and Sandlos, J. 2009. Environmental justice goes underground? Historical notes from Canada's northern mining frontier. *Environmental Justice*, 2: 117–125.

Kirsch, S. 2007. Indigenous movements and the risks of counterglobalization: tracking the campaign against Papua New Guinea's Ok Tedi mine. *American Ethnologist*, 34: 303–321.

Kurtz, H. 2007. Gender and environmental justice in Louisiana: blurring the boundaries of public and private spheres. *Gender, Place and Culture*, 14: 409–426.

Lafont, C. 2010. Accountability and global governance: challenging the state-centric conception of human rights. *Ethics & Global Politics*, 3: 193–215.

Lee, B., Preston, F., Kooroshy, J., Bailey, R. and Lahn, G. 2012. *Resources Futures. A Chatham House Report*, The Royal Institute of International Affairs, London.

Lélé, S. M. 1991. Sustainable development: a critical-review. *World Development*, 19: 607–621.

Lewis, J., Freeman, L. and Borreill, S. 2008. *Free, Prior and Informed Consent and Sustainable Forest Management in the Congo Basin*, Intercooperation/Swiss Foundation for Development and International Cooperation, Berne.

Li, M. 2011. 'Walking on the tightrope': can water TNC tackle the drinking water crisis in developing countries? *Asian Social Science*, 7: 122–131.

Link, A. D. 2010. The perils of privatization: international developments and reform in water distribution. *Global Business and Development Law Journal*, 22: 379–399.

Loue, S., Lloyd, L. S. and O'Shea, D. J. 2003. *Community Health Advocacy*, Kluwer Academic Publishers, New York.

Luke, T. W. 2005. Neither sustainable nor development: reconsidering sustainability in development. *Sustainable Development*, 13: 228–238.

Lyster, R. 2011. REDD+, transparency, participation and resource rights: the role of law. *Environmental Science & Policy*, 14: 118–126.

McEldowney, J. F. and McEldowney, S. 2010. *Environmental Law*, Longman, Harlow.

Marshall, A.-M. 2010. Environmental justice and grassroots legal action. *Environmental Justice*, 3: 147–151.

Mascarenhas, M. 2007. Where the waters divide: First Nations, tainted water and environmental justice in Canada. *Local Environment*, 12: 565–577.

Masner, C. M. 2008. *The Ethic of Advocacy*, Universal Publishers, Boca Raton, FL.

Mason, M. 2010. Information disclosure and environmental rights: the Aarhus Convention. *Global Environmental Politics*, 10: 10–13.

Millner, F. 2011. Access to environmental justice. *Deakin Law Review*, 16: 189–207.

Milly, P. C. D., Wetherald, R. T., Dunne, K. A. and Delworth, T. L. 2002. Increasing risk of great floods in a changing climate. *Nature*, 415: 514–517.

Morgera, E. 2005. An update on the Aarhus Convention and its continued global relevance. *Review of European Community & International Environmental Law*, 14: 138–147.

Morita, S. and Zaelke, D. 2006. Rule of law, good governance and sustainable development. Paper presented at the Seventh International Conference on Environmental Compliance and Enforcement [Online]. Available at: www.inece.org/conference/7/vol1/05_Sachiko_Zaelke.pdf (accessed 3 Oct. 2013).

Morse, R. 2008. *Environmental Justice through the Eye of Hurricane Katrina*, Joint Center for Political and Economic Studies, Health Policy Institute, Washington, DC.

Muradian, R., Martinez-Alier, J. and Correa, H. 2003. International capital versus local population: the environmental conflict of the Tambogrande Mining Project, Peru. *Society & Natural Resources*, 16: 775–792.

Mustafa, D. and Reeder, P. 2009. 'People is all that is left to privatize': water supply privatization, globalization and social justice in Belize City, Belize. *International Journal of Urban and Regional Research*, 33: 789–808.

Nadal, C. 2008. Pursuing substantive environmental justice: the Aarhus Convention as a 'pillar' of empowerment. *Environmental Law Review*, 10: 28–45.

Naess, A. 1973. The shallow and the deep, long range ecology movement: a summary. *Inquiry*, 16: 95–100.

Nelson, V., Meadows, K., Cannon, T., Morton, J. and Martin, A. 2002. Uncertain predictions, invisible impacts, and the need to mainstream gender in climate change adaptations. *Gender and Development*, 10: 51–59.

OECD. 2005. *Trade that Benefits the Environment and Development: Opening Markets for Environmental Goods and Services.* OECD Trade Policy Studies, OECD, Paris.

Orta-Martinez, M. and Finer, M. 2010. Oil frontiers and indigenous resistance in the Peruvian Amazon. *Ecological Economics*, 70: 207–218.

Page, J. 2007. Salmon farming in First Nations' territories: a case of environmental injustice on Canada's West Coast. *Local Environment*, 12: 613–626.

Pedersen, O. W. 2011. Environmental justice in the UK: uncertainty, ambiguity and the law. *Legal Studies*, 31: 279–304.

Pellow, D. N. 2000. Environmental inequality formation: toward a theory of environmental injustice. *American Behavioral Scientist*, 43: 581–601.

Petkova, E., Maurer, C., Henninger, N., Irwin, F., Coyle, J. and Hoff, G. 2002. *Closing the Gap: Information, Participation and Justice in Decision Making for the Environment*, World Resources Institute, Washington, DC.

Porritt, J. 2007. *Capitalism as if the World Matters*, Earthscan, London.

Rapley, J. 2004. *Globalization and Inequality: Neoliberalism's Downward Spiral*, Lynne Rienner, Boulder, CO.

Raworth, K. 2012. A safe and just space for humanity. Can we live within the doughnut? Oxfam Discussion Papers [Online]. Oxfam, Oxford. Available at: http://policy-practice.oxfam.org.uk/publications/a-safe-and-just-space-for-humanity-can-we-live-within-the-doughnut-210490 (accessed 28 Nov. 2013).

Redclift, M. 2005. Sustainable development (1987–2005): an oxymoron comes of age. *Sustainable Development*, 13: 212–227.

Rehbinder, E. 2002. *Democracy, Access to Justice and Environment at the International Level*, CIDCE, Limoges, France.

Robinson, J. L., Tindall, D. B., Seldat, E. and Pechlaner, G. 2007. Support for First Nations' Land claims amongst members of the Wilderness Preservation Movement: the potential for an environmental justice movement in British Columbia. *Local Environment*, 12: 579–598.

Rose-Ackerman, S. 2004. Governance and corruption, in B. Lomborg (ed.) *Global Crises, Global Solutions*. Cambridge University Press: Cambridge.

Schlosberg, D. 2004. Reconceiving environmental justice: global movements and political theories. *Environmental Politics*, 13: 517–540.

Schmidt-Soltau, K. and Brockington, D. 2007. Protected areas and resettlement: what scope for voluntary relocation? *World Development*, 35: 2182–2202.

Schroeder, R. A. 2008. Environmental justice and the market: the politics of sharing wildlife revenues in Tanzania. *Society & Natural Resources*, 21: 583–596.

Schumacher, E. F. 1973. *Small Is Beautiful*, Abacus, London.

Skinner, J. 2010. A green road to development: environmental regulations and developing countries in the WTO. *Duke Environmental Law and Policy Forum*, 20: 245–270.

Sneddon, C. and Fox, C. 2008. Struggles over dams as struggles for justice: the World Commission on Dams (WCD) and anti-dam campaigns in Thailand and Mozambique. *Society & Natural Resources*, 21: 625–640.

Stiglitz, J. E. 2002. *Globalization and Its Discontents*, Penguin, London.

Stivers, C. 2007. 'So Poor and So Black': Hurricane Katrina, public administration, and the issue of race. *Public Administration Review*, 67: 48–56.

Sze, J. and London, J. K. 2008. Environmental justice at the crossroads. *Sociology Compass*, 2/4: 1331–1354.

Takeshita, C. 2000. Bioprospecting and indigenous peoples' resistances. *Peace Review*, 12: 555–562.

Transparency International 2011. *Annual Report 2011*, Transparency International, Berlin.

Tusinski, K. 2007. A description of lobbying as advocacy public relations. Originally published in the *Proceedings of 2007 International Public Relations Research Conference*: 563–570.

UN 2012. *United Nations Conference on Sustainable Development, Rio+20. A/RES/66/288. Green Economy in the Context of Sustainable Development and Poverty Eradication* [Online]. United Nations Department of Economic and Social Affairs, Division for Sustainable Development: New York. Available at: http://sustainabledevelopment.un.org/index.php?menu=1225 (accessed 28 Nov. 2013).

UNDESA 2009. *State of the World's Indigenous Peoples*, UNDESA, New York.

UNEP 2013. *Green Economy and Trade: Trends, Challenges and Opportunities* [Online]. Available at: www.unep.org/greeneconomy/GreenEconomyandTrade (accessed 2 Oct. 2013).

Wade, R. H. 2004. Is globalization reducing poverty and inequality? *World Development*, 32: 567–589.

Walker, G. P. 2007. Environmental justice and the distributional deficit in policy appraisal in the UK. *Environmental Research Letters,* 2: 045004.

Walker, G. 2009. Beyond distribution and proximity: exploring the multiple spatialities of environmental justice. *Antipode*, 41: 614–636.

Walker, G. 2010. Environmental justice, impact assessment and the politics of knowledge: the implications of assessing the social distribution of environmental outcomes. *Environmental Impact Assessment Review*, 30: 312–318.

Walker, G. and Burningham, K. 2011. Flood risk, vulnerability and environmental justice: evidence and evaluation of inequality in a UK context. *Critical Social Policy*, 31: 216–240.

Walker, G., Fay, H. and Mitchell, G. 2005. *Environmental Justice Impact Assessment: An Evaluation of Requirements and Tools for Distributional Analysis*, Institute for Environment and Sustainability Research, Staffordshire University, UK.

Walker, G. P. 2007. Environmental justice and the distributional deficit in policy appraisal in the UK. *Environmental Research Letters*, 2: 045004.

WCED 1987. *Our Common Future*, Oxford University Press, Oxford.

Wellmer, F. W. and Becker-Platen, J. D. 2002. Sustainable development and the exploitation of mineral and energy resources: a review. *International Journal of Earth Sciences*, 91: 723–745.

Williamson, J. 1990. What Washington means by policy reform, in J. Williamson (ed.) *Latin American Adjustment: How Much Has Happened?* Institute for International Economics: Washington, DC.

Women Rio+20 Steering Committee 2011. *A Gender Perspective on the 'Green Economy'. Equitable, Healthy and Decent Jobs and Livelihoods*, WECF, Utrecht.

Women's Environmental Network 2010. *Gender and the Climate Change Agenda. The Impacts of Climate Change on Women and Public Policy*, Women's Environmental Network, London.

Zeitz, P. 2008. What is advocacy? What is activism? [Online]. George Washington University, USA. Available at: www.ccaba.org/wp-content/uploads/Paul-Zeitz-What-is-Advocacy-and-What-is-Activism-Compatibility-Mode1.pdf (accessed 3 Oct. 2013).

7

THE GREEN ECONOMY IN PRACTICE

With Kate Forrester and Kathy Hodder

7.1 Introduction

While the green economy is a relatively recent concept, it is closely linked with sustainable development, which has been the focus of international policy initiatives for more than 40 years. In this chapter, we will therefore examine how the green economy can be achieved in practice, based on the lessons learned from attempts to support sustainable development. The chapter is structured around some different elements of the green economy.

7.2 Sustainable agriculture

7.2.1 Introduction

Global food production is increasing (Sachs *et al.*, 2010), and is keeping up with population growth (IAASTD, 2009). Despite this, almost 1 billion people are undernourished, more than half of whom are in rural households. The expansion and intensification of farming systems have led to widespread environmental degradation, causing loss of biodiversity and ecosystem services, and producing significant quantities of greenhouse gases and other pollutants (UNEP, 2011a). Sachs *et al.* (2010) claim that over a billion hectares of wild land will need to be converted to farmland by 2050, if the needs of the growing human population are to be adequately met. It is clear that a transformation from conventional farming needs to be made in order to develop a green economy.

It is useful to differentiate between two main types of agriculture: the industrial approaches that predominate in higher-income countries, and the more traditional, subsistence approaches that are more prevalent in lower-income countries. Over the past few decades, there have been substantial gains in productivity in industrial agriculture, through what has been termed the 'Green Revolution'. These gains were primarily obtained through the development of higher-yield varieties of major cereal crops (i.e. wheat, rice and corn/maize), together with an increase in the use of irrigation, inorganic fertilisers, pesticide/herbicide use and fossil fuel-based farm machinery (UNEP, 2011a). Industrial agriculture is therefore highly demanding in terms of energy and other inputs, including extensive use of petrochemical fertilisers, herbicides, pesticides, fuel and water.

Reflection point

How green was the Green Revolution?

The intensification and expansion of agriculture have led to significant negative impacts on the environment. Conversion of land to agriculture is one of the main causes of biodiversity loss (Millennium Ecosystem Assessment, 2005), with some 0.5 billion ha land area converted since the 1960s (Pretty, 2008). During the same period, livestock production has also increased substantially, with a fourfold increase in numbers of chickens, twofold increase in pigs and 40–50 per cent increase in numbers of cattle, sheep and goats (Pretty, 2008). Increased use of fertilisers, pesticides, fungicides and herbicides has also had major negative impacts on biodiversity (Millennium Ecosystem Assessment, 2005: Chapter 4). The contamination of water courses as a result of the nitrogen applied to farmland has become a major environmental and public health issue. Irrigation for agriculture has caused widespread waterlogging and salinisation, as well as diverting water from other uses (Pretty, 2008).

Evidence suggests that current approaches to agricultural production have reached critical environmental limits (ibid.). Many agricultural systems are now becoming vulnerable because of the effects of declining soil and water availability. While there is clearly a need to increase food production to avoid the problems of hunger, there is also a need to adjust how food is produced in order to increase the flow of other ecosystem services. Foley *et al.* (2011) note the need to halt agricultural expansion, close 'yield gaps' on underperforming lands, increase cropping efficiency, shift diets and reduce waste. According to these authors, such approaches could double food production while greatly reducing the environmental impacts of agriculture. However, meeting the increasing demand for food in ways that are environmentally sustainable, while ensuring that people do not go hungry, represents a significant challenge (Godfray *et al.*, 2010; Mueller *et al.*, 2012). How might this challenge be addressed?

7.2.2 Approaches to sustainable agriculture

A wide range of different approaches to sustainable agriculture have been identified, including biodynamic, community-based, environmentally sensitive, free range, low input, organic and permaculture approaches. However, the extent to which such approaches are genuinely sustainable remains the subject of debate. Pretty (2008) identifies key principles that genuinely sustainable approaches should meet:

1. Harness biological and ecological processes such as nutrient cycling, nitrogen fixation, soil regeneration, competition, predation and parasitism, and integrate them into food production processes.
2. Minimise the use of non-renewable inputs, technologies and practices that cause harm to the environment or to the health of farmers and consumers.
3. Make productive use of the knowledge and skills of farmers, thus improving their self-reliance and substituting human capital for costly external inputs.

4. Make productive use of people's collective capacities to work together to solve common agricultural and natural resource problems, such as pests, watershed, irrigation and credit management.
5. Minimise the impacts of management on externalities such as greenhouse gas emissions, clean water availability, carbon sequestration, conservation of biodiversity, and dispersal of pests, pathogens and weeds.

A number of different technologies and practices are used by sustainable agricultural approaches, including (Pretty, 2008; Godfray *et al.*, 2010):

1. *Integrated pest management (IPM)*, which encourages the use of natural pest control mechanisms and aims to use pesticides only when other options are ineffective (Kogan, 1998; Hassanali *et al.*, 2008).
2. *Integrated plant nutrient management*, which aims to use nutrients in a more targeted way that is site- and soil-specific; to use combinations of mineral and organic fertilisers; to encourage use of waste through recycling; and to reduce nutrient losses through erosion control (Gruhn *et al.*, 2000; Goulding *et al.*, 2008).
3. *Conservation, reduced or zero tillage*, which reduces the amount of tillage to help conserve soil structure, nutrient status and available moisture (Holland, 2004; Knowler and Bradshaw, 2007; Hobbs *et al.*, 2008).
4. *Agroforestry*, which is an integrated approach for combining tree species with crops and/ or livestock, with the aim of producing more diverse and sustainable land-use systems (Leakey *et al.*, 2005; Batish *et al.*, 2008; Wojtkowski, 2010).
5. *Aquaculture*, which incorporates fish, shrimps and other aquatic resources into farm systems, such as into irrigated rice fields and fish ponds, thereby increasing production of protein (Bunting, 2007).
6. *Water harvesting* in dryland areas, which involves improving rainwater retention through construction of contour ridges, terraces, bunds or pits, thereby improving crop productivity (Morison *et al.*, 2008). Contour farming, mulches, and cover crops can similarly improve water and soil conservation.
7. *Precision agriculture*, which incorporates a series of technologies that allow the application of water, nutrients, and pesticides only to the places and at the times they are required, thereby optimising the use of inputs (Day *et al.*, 2008).

Together, such approaches can help enhance soil fertility, reduce soil erosion and increase the efficiency of water use, while reducing use of chemical pesticides and herbicides (UNEP, 2011a). The implementation of sustainable agriculture can also increase crop yields. For example, Pretty *et al.* (2006) examined the impact of 286 agricultural sustainability projects in developing countries, and found an average yield increase of 79 per cent.

As noted by Godfray *et al.* (2010), there is no single solution to sustainable agriculture; a range of options will need to be pursued simultaneously. Barriers to the implementation of such approaches include lack of information and management skills, and the fact that the biological processes that make sustainable agroecosystems productive also take time to become established (Pretty, 2008; Godfray *et al.*, 2010). Ultimately, sustainable agriculture can be seen as any combination of approaches that achieves an appropriate balance between provision of food and other goods for farmers and markets, together with other services.

> **Reflection point**
>
> Given that an increase in food production will be needed in the future, should this be achieved through expanding the area of agricultural land, or by increasing yields on existing land? Which is the greenest solution? This is the 'land sharing versus land sparing' debate (Phalan *et al.*, 2011).

Does sustainable agriculture require a reduction in inputs? Not necessarily. In some situations, it may actually be preferable to focus on making better use of existing resources, such as land, water and biodiversity. Localisation of agriculture through some form of intensification could potentially reduce the pressure for conversion of natural ecosystems. Tscharntke *et al.* (2005) note that the environmental impacts of agricultural intensification are not always negative; for example, higher productivity of land use may provide more food resources for birds, mammals and butterflies. A key question is the type of intensification involved; approaches that could be considered sustainable would need to minimise or eliminate harm to the environment (Pretty, 2008).

Dietary preferences are the key factor influencing agricultural businesses. As the efficiency of converting plant to animal matter is about 10 per cent, more people could be supported from the same amount of land if they were vegetarians (Godfray *et al.*, 2010). However, the demand for meat and dairy products is increasing rapidly in many areas, particularly in countries such as China and India, as a result of increasing affluence and the perception of meat as a high status food. Sustainable approaches to agriculture should arguably focus on increasing the efficiency of livestock production, as well as reducing meat consumption.

The transition to sustainable agriculture requires a number of enabling conditions, including (UNEP, 2011a):

* investments to strengthen supply-side capacities, such as farmer training, extension services, and demonstration projects focusing on green farming practices;
* investments to scale up production and increase access to green agricultural inputs (e.g. organic fertilisers, biopesticides), no-tillage cultivation equipment, etc.;
* secure land rights, good governance and appropriate infrastructure development;
* public policies that provide subsidies to encourage adoption of more environmentally friendly agriculture practices;
* increased public awareness and education to strengthen consumer demand for sustainably produced food, including the nutritional, health, environmental and social implications of dietary behaviour.

7.2.3 Organic agriculture

Organic farming differs from conventional farming because of the absence of synthetically compounded fertilisers, pesticides, growth regulators, and livestock feed additives. It is based on the recycling of plant nutrients, biological nitrogen fixation, hand weeding and husbandry methods to control pests (Jansen, 2000). Organic agriculture is growing rapidly in popularity, for example, in the USA, organic food sales now total more than US$7 billion per year (Pimentel *et al.*, 2005).

Organic agriculture does not merely refer to a form of farming that avoids the use of chemicals. Rather, it implies understanding the farm as an integrated system, in which all the components, the soil minerals, organic matter, microorganisms, insects, plants, animals and humans interact to create a coherent, self-regulating and stable whole (IFOAM, 2010).

Lobley *et al.* (2005) point out that sometimes organic farming is presented as a panacea for the problems facing the food and farming sector. As well as the potential environmental and health benefits, there are frequent claims that organic farming can contribute to rural development and economic growth. But how effective is organic farming? A number of research studies have examined this question, for example:

- Pimentel *et al.* (2005) described 22-year experiments that compared organic animal-based, organic legume-based, and conventional agricultural systems. Environmental benefits were consistently greater in the organic systems than in the conventional systems.
- Norton *et al.* (2009) found that organic farms produced greater field and farm complexity than non-organic farms, with consequent benefits for biodiversity.
- Crowder *et al.* (2010) demonstrated that the communities of predator and pathogen biological control agents, that are typical of organic farms, exerted the strongest pest control and yielded the largest plants.
- Bengtsson *et al.* (2005) showed that organic farming often has positive effects on species richness and abundance, but that its effects differ between organism groups and landscapes.
- Pretty (2008) showed that organic farming can lead to lower energy use and improved nutrient retention, though greater nutrient losses have occurred in some situations.

Given these potential benefits, why is organic agriculture not more widely practised? Smit *et al.* (2009) examine the situation in the Netherlands, and identify a number of barriers that are limiting conversion to organic dairy production. In the short term, conversion can have negative financial consequences, and can result in the termination of long-term relationships with suppliers and buyers. Prices of organic food products tend to be relatively high, as costs of organic production are often higher. Organic agriculture may also lack the benefits of scale available to conventional agricultural production. Pretty (2008) indicates that food productivity can be lower for organic farming systems, though UNEP (2011a) present evidence that this is not always the case. Seufert *et al.* (2012) present a comprehensive meta-analysis to compare the relative yield performance of organic and conventional farming systems globally, and show that overall, organic yields are typically lower than conventional yields, but these differences depend strongly on system and site characteristics. Under some conditions, with particular crop types and with appropriate management, organic systems can nearly match conventional yields.

7.2.4 Locally or community-based food production

Another approach to developing green agriculture focuses on locally produced food. Feenstra (2002) summarises experience with community-based food production approaches in California, and highlights three outcomes in particular: (1) increased public participation in food production; (2) development of new partnerships; and (3) a commitment to social, economic and environmental justice (see Chapter 6).

Local food systems are an alternative to conventional corporate models where producers and consumers are separated through a chain of processors/manufacturers, distributors and retailers. Local food markets such as 'farmers' markets', in which the producers sell directly to consumers, are growing rapidly in countries such as the USA and Canada, and in many parts of Europe (Guthrie *et al.*, 2006; Martinez *et al.*, 2010). Increasingly, consumers can now purchase such products online. Such trends can be considered as a form of grassroots or 'bottom-up' movement, which can be supported by distinctive branding and marketing of food produced within a particular geographic area. Related initiatives are the 'slow food' movement, which promotes traditional and regional cuisine as an alternative to fast food, and the use of 'food miles' to assess the distance food is transported before it reaches the consumer.

> ## Reflection point
>
> Is locally produced food always likely to be greener, do you think?

Locally produced food could potentially deliver a number of benefits, including reduction of greenhouse gas emissions from transporting the food, reduction of waste along the supply chain, and increased financial returns to producers of sustainable or organic food. Relatively little research has examined whether locally produced food actually delivers such benefits. Weber and Matthews (2008) compared the life-cycle GHG emissions associated with food production against long-distance distribution, or 'food miles'. Results indicated that though food is often transported long distances, the GHG emissions associated with food are dominated by the production phase, with transport representing only 11 per cent of emissions. These authors suggest that dietary shift can be a more effective means of lowering an average household's food-related climate footprint than 'buying local'. Similarly, Åström *et al.* (2013) found that a vegetarian diet was associated with lower GHG emissions; for non-vegetarian diets, the amount of beef consumed had a major influence on emission levels. From a climate change perspective, these results show that dietary choice is more important than whether it is locally grown or how it was produced. Such results highlight the value of a complete life-cycle analysis for informing consumer decisions (see Chapter 5).

7.2.5 Genetically modified organisms (GMOs)

The use of genetically modified crop plants, or GMOs, has proved highly controversial. Potentially, they could play a major role in helping to increase agricultural productivity, but there are widespread concerns about their possible impacts on human health and the environment.

GMOs are produced by introducing novel genes into a crop plant. The genes may be derived either from the same or another species, the latter being referred to as transgenics (Royal Society, 2009). There are now around 170 million ha of GM crops being grown worldwide, but their cultivation is largely restricted to five countries: the United States, Argentina, Brazil, India and Canada. They are absent from most of Europe and Africa (*Nature*, 2013). The potential benefits and negative impacts of GMOs vary depending on the nature of the gene being transferred and the crop species involved (Royal Society, 2009).

In the 20 years since GMOs were introduced, it is argued that they have increased agricultural production by more than US$90 billion and reduced pesticide application by an estimated 473 million kg (*Nature*, 2013). However, the environmental, social and economic aspects of GMOs have been widely questioned (WWF, 2005). The debate has been highly polarised, partly because the scientific evidence is often lacking or contradictory.

Reflection point

Do you believe that GMOs should be considered a green technology, or not?

Evidence suggests that as some critics predicted, use of GMOs has led to the evolution of 'superweeds' that can be very difficult to eradicate. For example, 24 weed species have now developed resistance to glyphosate herbicide (*Nature*, 2013). In response, new technologies are being developed involving resistance to multiple herbicides, which are predicted to lead to a significant increase in herbicide use (Mortensen *et al.*, 2012). A further concern is spread of genes from GMOs to wild crops, which has been reported in maize in different parts of Mexico (Dyer *et al.*, 2009).

A further concern is an ethical one, relating to the protection of intellectual property rights to biotechnology by companies. This has led to a widespread belief that the technology purely benefits commercial interests and is of limited value to consumers (Godfray *et al.*, 2010). There are also widespread concerns about food safety, particularly in Europe, though evidence in support of such concerns is lacking (Royal Society, 2009). New developments in GMOs could potentially make a significant contribution to improving human livelihoods; for example, the development of Golden Rice that includes a precursor to vitamin A that is lacking in many East Asian diets (*Nature*, 2013). Godfray *et al.* (2010) suggest that GMOs offer a potentially valuable technology whose advantages and disadvantages need to be considered rigorously on a case-by-case basis.

7.2.6 Waste reduction

Almost half of the human edible calories that are produced by global agriculture are currently lost because of crop losses to pests and hazards, and losses in storage, distribution and marketing. For these reasons, a reduction in losses and wastage in the production and consumption chain is an important element of greening agriculture (UNEP, 2011a).

In the developing world, losses are mainly attributable to the absence of food-chain infrastructure and the lack of knowledge or investment in food storage technologies (Godfray *et al.*, 2010). For example, it is estimated that 35–40 per cent of fresh produce is lost in India because of a lack of cold storage in wholesale or retail outlets (Nellemann *et al.*, 2009). In such countries, investment in transport infrastructure and cold storage is required to reduce spoilage. In the developed world, while pre-retail losses are relatively low, there has been a rapid increase in losses occurring at the retail and home stages of the food chain. Wastage of food is encouraged by relatively low food prices, and by consumer preference for cosmetically attractive food (Godfray *et al.*, 2010). Addressing this problem may require education of consumers, advocacy and perhaps legislation such as that relating to sell-by dates.

7.2.7 Agriculture and biofuel production

In recent years, there has been rapid growth of the production of biofuels from food crops such as maize, sugarcane, soybeans and palms (see Chapter 5). Extensive areas of cropland are now devoted to biofuel production, particularly in the Americas and parts of South-east Asia. Growth of the biofuel industry is also increasing conversion of ecosystems to agricultural land use, resulting in biodiversity loss (Fargione *et al.*, 2008). Examples include the cultivation of palm oil in Indonesia, soybeans in the Brazilian Amazon and maize in the United States. Such conversion can release CO_2 as a result of burning or microbial decomposition of the organic carbon stored in soils and plant biomass. Fargione *et al.* (2008) demonstrated that as a result of such emissions, biofuels can potentially be much greater net emitters of greenhouse gases than fossil fuels (see also Chapter 5). According to these authors, biofuels should be grown from perennials in degraded cropland or obtained from waste biomass, which would minimise habitat destruction and reduce competition with food production.

Significant efforts are now being made to develop second-generation biofuels, which can be produced from non-food biomass feedstock such as wood and crop-residue wastes, switch grass and algae (see Chapter 5; UNEP, 2011a). Such technologies can potentially enable biofuels to be produced with fewer negative impacts on food supplies.

7.3 Forest management

7.3.1 Introduction

Forests are of high ecological, socio-economic and cultural importance. As the principal biomass component of forest ecosystems, they provide habitat for at least half of Earth's terrestrial species (Millennium Ecosystem Assessment, 2005). Forest ecosystems play a major role in the Earth's biogeochemical processes, and contain about 50 per cent of the world's terrestrial carbon stocks (Millennium Ecosystem Assessment, 2005; FAO, 2010). Trees provide a wide range of other benefits to people including production of timber, fuelwood, food and fibre, maintenance of water yields and quality, flood protection and prevention of soil erosion, as well as being of high cultural and spiritual value (Millennium Ecosystem Assessment, 2005; UNEP *et al.*, 2009). Some 1.6 billion people depend directly on forests for their livelihoods (World Bank, 2004), and forest industries contribute around US$468 billion annually to the global economy (FAO, 2011).

The widespread loss and degradation of native forests are now recognised as a major environmental issue (Spilsbury, 2010). Results from the latest global forest assessment indicate that during the first decade of the twenty-first century, global forest area declined by around 13 million ha^{-1} yr^{-1} (FAO, 2010). Hansen *et al.* (2010) reported a substantially higher annual forest loss of approximately 20 million ha^{-1} yr^{-1} for 2000–2005, based on analysis of satellite imagery. FAO (2010) also report that during the decade 2000–2010, the area of undisturbed primary forest declined by an estimated 4.2 million hectares per year (or 0.4 per cent annually), largely because of the introduction of selective logging and other forms of human disturbance.

7.3.2 Sustainable forest management

In recent decades, global policy initiatives have focused on the implementation of sustainable forest management (SFM). Traditionally in forestry, sustainability concepts focused on sustained yield of timber; in recent years the concept has broadened to include environmental and socio-economic aspects (Wiersum, 1995). SFM has been defined in a variety of different ways but most authors agree that it comprises three main components: environmental, social and economic (Nussbaum and Simula, 2005). Environmental sustainability requires that a forest ecosystem be able to support healthy organisms, while maintaining its productivity, adaptability and capability for renewal; social sustainability requires that an activity not stretch a community beyond its tolerance for change; and economic sustainability requires that some form of equivalent capital (such as a forest resource) be handed down from one generation to the next (Newton, 2007).

International policy dialogue has led to the development of a wide variety of different criteria and indicators (C&I), designed to assess progress towards SFM. Criteria may be defined as the essential elements or major components that define SFM. Indicators are qualitative or quantitative parameters of a criterion, which provide a basis for assessing the status of, and trends in, forests and forest management. C&I have been developed under a series of international processes, including ITTO, the Pan-European (or 'Helsinki') Process, the Montreal Process, and the Tarapoto, Lepaterique, Near East, Dry Zone Asia and Dry Zone Africa processes, each of which have generated sets of C&I (ibid.). Although the processes share similar objectives and overall approach, the C&I that they have developed are different. This highlights the difficulty of defining and assessing SFM in a way that applies to all forests, in different parts of the world.

These processes provide a valuable source of information on the indicators that are considered important for forests in different regions. However, it is important to note that most processes have focused on developing C&I for application at the regional or national scale. Only four of the nine processes – ATO, ITTO, Lepaterique and Tarapoto – have produced sets of C&I for application at the forest management unit (FMU) scale, which is the scale most likely to be of value in supporting practical forest management.

The development of indicators at the FMU level has primarily been driven by the growth of interest in *forest certification*. Certification is a tool for promoting responsible forestry practices, and involves certification of forest management operations by an independent third party against a set of standards. Typically, forest products (including timber but also non-timber forest products) from certified forests are labelled so that consumers can identify them as having been derived from well-managed sources. There are now many different organisations certifying forests against a variety of different standards, including the Sustainable Forestry Initiative Program, the American Tree Farm System, the Canadian Standards Association Sustainable Forest Management Program and the Forest Stewardship Council (FSC). The latter is probably the best known, and was originally created by the conservation organisation WWF.

How can SFM be assessed in practice? Essentially, the process involves checking whether the standards are being met, through some form of field survey or evaluation. The process of verification differs between organisations and from place to place (Rametsteiner and Simula, 2003). Further details are given by Nussbaum and Simula (2005).

Has the process of certification actually improved forest management? Based on a review of the available evidence, Rametsteiner and Simula (2003) concluded that the main impact of certification appears to have been some improvement in internal auditing and monitoring of forest organisations, and increased sensitivity of forest managers to issues such as natural regeneration, reduced impact harvesting, road construction and the use of fertilisers and pesticides. However, impacts on biodiversity conservation appear to have been slight.

Nevertheless, this remains potentially an important mechanism for increasing the sustainability of forest management, and at the very least, it has raised awareness among timber businesses and consumers regarding the importance of sourcing sustainable supplies of timber.

For forest management to be genuinely sustainable, appropriate indicators should be used as a basis for monitoring, to support a process of adaptive management. Methods of applying such indicators are described by Newton (2007). Higman *et al.* (2005) provide a useful guide to how SFM can be achieved in practice, and Nussbaum and Simula (2005) provide an authoritative account of forest certification, including a description of relevant standards.

> ### Reflection point
>
> Consider the process of forest certification. In order to succeed, consumers would need to prefer to purchase products that have been certified as sustainably produced. What do you think could be done to encourage consumers to make such choices?

7.3.3 Participatory forest management (PFM)

Participatory forest management (PFM) is a generic term for a variety of similar approaches to forest management, which include shared forest management, joint forest management, collaborative forest management, social forestry and community forestry. PFM can be defined simply as 'any situation that intimately involves local people in forestry activities' (Arnold, 2001). The aim of PFM is to safeguard the livelihoods of local communities who depend on the forests they live in or around, by involving stakeholders in the process of forest management (Mustalahti and Lund, 2010). A community may manage the forest without outside assistance or control (community-based forest management), or the management may be in a partnership, for example, with government (joint forest management).

Various approaches to PFM have become increasingly popular in recent years. This is because engaging local communities and 'users' in the management and control of forests can lead to improved forest condition and better conservation outcomes. In Nepal, for example, evidence suggests that illegal logging, forest fires and overgrazing have declined in areas under community management, and forest condition has improved (Arnold, 2001). In addition, transferring power and access rights back to communities can help to improve livelihoods. PFM has become particularly widespread in Africa and is recognised as a significant route towards sustaining and securing forests (Wily, 2002). However, realisation has grown that working with local communities to manage their forests is not sufficient by itself; there may also be a need to seek alternative sources of income to improve local livelihoods, in order to reduce pressure on forests (Mustalahti and Lund, 2010).

Examples of PFM in practice include Nepal, where Community Forest User Groups have been established with management control formally handed over after approval of an operational plan. Through these groups, communities can plan and implement the management of forests for an indefinite period (McDermott and Schreckenberg, 2009). There are now over 14,000 such groups in Nepal, who are part of a formal network (Schreckenberg and Luttrell, 2009). Several decades of learning through practice have enabled Nepal to develop a relatively fair and transparent system, supported by clear legislation that has overcome some of the challenges encountered in other countries (ibid.). A further example is Tanzania, which passed key forest laws and policy changes in 2002, providing an enabling environment for PFM. Mainland Tanzania now has one of the most progressive community forestry jurisdictions in Africa, as reflected in policy, law and practice (Wily, 2000).

Reviews of PFM indicate that it can succeed in making improvements to rural livelihoods, governance and forest condition; however, many initiatives have failed to deliver these benefits (Lawrence, 2007). For success to be achieved, there needs to be a supportive policy environment, providing security of tenure, together with appropriate institutional and administrative support. Lawrence also highlights the need for a more interconnected and interactive approach, linking social, cultural and political factors together with their ecological context, as part of an integrated social-ecological system.

7.3.4 REDD+ (Reducing Emissions from Deforestation and Forest Degradation)

One recently developed policy initiative has particular potential to support the sustainable development of forest resources: 'REDD+' (see Chapter 3). This aims to offer incentives for developing countries to invest in low-carbon approaches to sustainable development. Developed within the UN Framework Convention on Climate Change (UNFCCC), this provides a potential funding mechanism for supporting forest conservation and restoration activities, as a contribution towards the goal of enhancing forest carbon stocks. Revenues could be generated from the global market in carbon, which had reached US$125 billion by 2008; funding for REDD+ itself has already reached US$6 billion (Stickler *et al.*, 2009). REDD+ essentially offers an opportunity for stakeholders around the world to contribute financially to the restoration of tropical forests. The mechanism has been criticised, however, for its focus on a single ecosystem service (carbon); there is a possibility that other services and social issues could be neglected or adversely affected (ibid.). Potential negative social impacts include loss of livelihoods or access to lands undergoing forest restoration, a risk that is particularly high in areas where land tenure is insecure. Nevertheless, this is an important initiative, because it represents a major potential source of funding to support SFM in developing countries.

7.3.5 Case studies

UNEP (2011b) provide an overview of forests in the green economy, and highlight the following examples:

- Many large cities, including Tokyo and New York, manage surrounding forests for water services.
- India has recently approved a national mission for a Green India, which aims to increase forest cover on 5 million ha of land, and improve forest quality on an additional 5 million ha, while increasing incomes for 3 million forest-dependent families.
- Ecological restoration in the Loess Plateau of China has resulted in a doubling of income for people living within the area, with 2.5 million people lifted out of poverty. In addition, sediment loads to the Yellow River decreased by 10 million tonnes yr^{-1}, reducing risk of flooding. Similarly the restoration of natural mangrove forests in Vietnam at a cost of US$1.1 million resulted in annual savings of US$7.3 million in sea dyke maintenance.

7.4 Sustainable fisheries

7.4.1 Introduction

Fish are an important renewable resource, contributing to the livelihoods and survival of a large percentage of the world's population. UNEP (2011a) estimates that fish provide food security to over 1 billion people globally, and that 170 million jobs are directly or indirectly supported by fishery industries, equal to about US$35 billion per year. It is important to remember that fish are an important source of protein for many people, and if fisheries collapse (as they demonstrably can do, see Chapter 4), this raises the question of how such people will meet their nutritional needs in future.

The fisheries sector and the oceans in general are being exploited unsustainably, creating what is often considered as a global crisis. It is increasingly acknowledged that fisheries should operate so that fishing can continue without over-exploiting the resource, the productivity of the ecosystem should be preserved, and local, national and international laws should be recognised (Jacquet *et al.*, 2010). However, in many areas, this understanding is not translating into effective action to prevent further over-exploitation.

Reviews of the sustainability of global fisheries are provided by Pauly *et al.* (2002), Costello *et al.* (2012) and Tacon *et al.* (2010). The use of ecolabelling schemes for fish is evaluated by Gulbrandsen (2009) and Parkes *et al.* (2010).

7.4.2 Current status and trends of global fisheries

The current state of the world's fisheries is monitored by the UN Food and Agriculture Organisation (FAO). The following points are derived from the latest report (FAO, 2012):

- Capture fisheries and aquaculture supplied the world with about 148 million tonnes of fish in 2010 (Figure 7.1), with a total value of US$217.5 billion, an all-time high. Of this, approximately 128 million tonnes was used as human food, representing a mean per capita supply of about 18.6 kg.
- Of the total food fish supply, aquaculture accounted for about 41 per cent, having increased from 34 per cent in 2006.
- In 2009, fish accounted for 16.6 per cent of the global population's intake of animal protein and 6.5 per cent of all protein consumed, highlighting their dietary importance. Globally, fish provides 3.0 billion people with almost 20 per cent of the animal protein that they consume.

> **Reflection point**
>
> Note the important distinction between the harvest of wild fish populations and aquaculture, which involves the rearing of fish by people. Which approach is likely to be the greenest, do you think?

FAO (2010) also highlight that more than half of the wild fish stocks have been fully exploited, with no room for further expansion. The remaining stocks are considered either to be over-exploited (28 per cent), depleted (3 per cent) or recovering from depletion

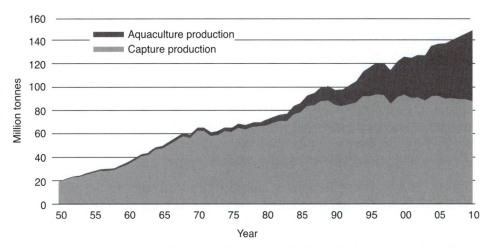

FIGURE 7.1 Trends in amount of fish being harvested, both from wild (capture) and farmed (aquaculture) sources

Source: FAO (2012), with permission from Food and Agriculture Organisation of the United Nations.

(1 per cent). The maximum wild capture fisheries potential from the world's oceans has probably therefore been reached (FAO, 2008).

This gives an indication of the extent of the global fisheries crisis. But what can be done to address the problem? Some of the different approaches currently being explored are presented below.

7.4.3 Marine protected areas (MPAs)

One recommendation for dealing with the problem of declining fish stocks is to set up marine protected areas (MPAs). The FAO defines a marine protected area as

> any area of intertidal or subtidal terrain together with its overlying water and associated flora, fauna, historical and cultural features, which has been reserved by law or other effective means to protect part or all of the enclosed environment.
>
> *(Cochrane, 2005)*

MPAs are established with several aims in mind, but principally to conserve resources and to assist in rebuilding exploited fish stocks. This can benefit surrounding areas through species migration and recruitment, and can protect critical habitats and their biodiversity, although there often appears to be a trade-off between achieving conservation and fishery goals (Gaines *et al.*, 2010).

MPAs can offer varying degrees of protection to the selected area, from total exclusion of all fishing ('no take areas') to more flexible regimes that permit fishing at certain times of the year, or by permitting certain fishing gear types, while maintaining regulations against other practices ('multiple use protected areas'). The extent of protection usually depends on the conservation objectives and the socio-economic context of that particular MPA (Cochrane, 2005). Currently, MPAs account for around 1 per cent of the world's oceans, but under the current targets of the CBD, the aim is to increase this to 10 per cent of coastal and marine habitats by 2020.

> **Suggested activity**
> You can explore information on MPAs on this website: www.wdpa-marine.org.

Wood *et al.* (2008) reviewed the current status of the world's MPAs and considered the requirements of the global targets, including the distribution and coverage of MPAs, network characteristics, representativeness and growth of the network. These authors concluded that only 0.08 per cent of the world's oceans, and 0.2 per cent of the total marine area under national jurisdiction, is 'no-take' (i.e. fishing is prohibited). The global distribution of protected areas is currently uneven and unrepresentative at multiple scales, and only half of the world's marine protected areas are part of a coherent network. However, since 1984, the spatial extent of marine area protected globally has grown at an annual rate of 4.6 per cent.

Sumaila *et al.* (2000) discuss the role of MPAs as an approach to address the negative impacts of fishing, and argue that they have an important part to play as part of a management strategy for fisheries. However, they also include an assessment of the socio–economic impacts of MPAs, which can sometimes be negative. Others who consider the human aspect of MPAs include Charles and Wilson (2009), Pollnac and Seara (2011) and Ferse *et al.* (2010). The latter authors highlight the poor performance of many MPAs, which is attributed to a failure to include local communities in their design and implementation. A key challenge therefore is to develop frameworks that enable the effective participation of local communities in MPA management.

> **Reflection point**
>
> Consider the factors that would need to be addressed to ensure the success of an MPA. How do you think MPAs might contribute to increasing the sustainability of fisheries?

7.4.4 Small-scale fisheries (SSF)

Both large-scale industrial fisheries and small-scale fisheries (SSF) can have a major impact on fish stocks. SSFs are characterised by being more labour-intensive and less capital-intensive than industrial fishing, and are bound to their own coastal communities. Small-scale fisheries are found along most coasts, and they provide vital food supplies and support the social values of these areas. However, they are threatened by a variety of factors (UNEP, 2011a):

- Depletion of coastal fish stocks by industrial fleets.
- Degradation of coastal environments and fish habitat, often as a result of land-based activities such as development of urban areas, destruction of mangroves, etc.
- Limitations on the ability to transport fish and fish products.
- Long-standing policy support for industrialisation of fisheries and neglect of the small-scale sector (Allison and Ellis, 2001).
- Climate change.

Salas *et al.* (2007) provide a summary of the key characteristics of small-scale coastal marine fisheries in Latin America and the Caribbean, and identify as a key constraint the lack of institutional frameworks to manage fisheries effectively. These authors conclude that greater attention needs to be directed to the 'people side' of fishery systems. There is a need for integrated approaches that aim to improve fishery governance at a local scale, and encourage the involvement of coastal fishers in developing their own management measures.

Despite the risks of a 'tragedy of the commons' scenario (see Chapter 2), many successes have been recorded in community-based fisheries management in different parts of the world (Jentoft, 2000; Cudney-Bueno and Basurto, 2009). Viable fishing communities can potentially contribute to the preservation of healthy fish stocks, but may also need to rebuild fish stocks where these have been depleted (Jentoft, 2000). Effective community-based management practices include the establishment of local marine reserves, but such approaches can be undermined if communities fail to form linkages with higher levels of governance that legitimise their efforts (Cudney-Bueno and Basurto, 2009).

Effective local governance is also vital. The development of strong leadership, robust social capital and consensus within communities are key elements to successful community-based fisheries management (Guenette and Alder, 2007; Gutierrez *et al.*, 2011). However, political and administrative obstacles and resistance to change can be challenging (Guenette and Alder, 2007). Allison and Ellis (2001) argue that a livelihoods approach to understanding natural resource management systems can assist in the search for solutions to small-scale fisheries management problems, by focusing on the adaptive strategies of fishers themselves.

> ### Reflection point
>
> Consider the factors that contribute to successful community-based fisheries. How might such approaches succeed in terms of delivering sustainable fish harvesting? Or are they doomed to failure, given the widespread advance of larger-scale industrial fishing?

7.4.5 Integrated Coastal Management (ICM)

Rather than simply focusing on the traditional approach of managing a single species, more holistic approaches have been developed, such as ecosystem-based fisheries management. This focuses on maintaining the ecosystem rather than the target species (Pikitch *et al.*, 2004). This approach is linked to integrated coastal management (ICM), or integrated coastal zone management (ICZM). The goals of such approaches are to achieve the sustainable development of coastal and marine areas, to reduce their vulnerability to natural hazards and to preserve ecological processes and biodiversity. Cicin-Sain and Belfiore (2005) argue that MPAs are often designed and implemented without recognition of the larger system within which they are located. These authors make a number of recommendations, including guiding principles for managing MPAs within an ICM context, and the need for collaboration of diverse actors in national-level ocean and local planning. AIDEnvironment *et al.* (2004) provide guidance on incorporating the conservation and sustainable use of marine and coastal biodiversity into integrated management programmes. A critique of the principles of ICZM is presented by McKenna *et al.* (2008).

7.5 Sustainable water management

7.5.1 Introduction

Water is one of the basic requirements of human life. Yet the amount of fresh water on Earth is finite. There have always been floods and droughts, but now human activities are influencing water systems in unprecedented ways. There is a strong linkage between water resources development, human development and economic growth (Vörösmarty *et al.*, 2010). Water is unique among natural resources since problems with availability can lead to crises connected with energy, human health, food supplies and prices, and can ultimately cause political insecurity and conflict (World Water Assessment Programme, 2009). Although water is inextricably linked with other sectors of the economy, it is rarely managed in a coordinated way with these other sectors (Lenton and Muller, 2009).

7.5.2 Status and distribution of the world's water resources

Consideration of the global distribution of water (Figure 7.2) emphasises how little of the Earth's water resources are actually available for human consumption.

The Millennium Ecosystem Assessment (2005) noted that prior to the twentieth century, global demand for fresh water was small compared with natural flows in the hydrologic cycle. Demand for water-related goods and services has since increased dramatically, putting pressure on the ecosystems that sustain these services. Although demand is increasing, supplies of clean water are diminishing owing to increasing pollution and contamination. As a result, there is increasing competition for water in many areas. Meeting even the most basic of needs for safe drinking water and sanitation continues to be an international development priority, as some 1.1 billion people lack access to clean water supplies

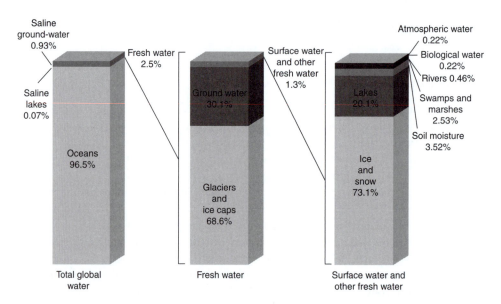

FIGURE 7.2 Distribution of the Earth's water

Source: Shiklomanov (1993), with permission of Oxford University Press.

and more than 2.6 billion lack access to basic sanitation (Millennium Ecosystem Assessment, 2005).

Groundwater is located beneath the ground surface, in the pores or fractures of soil and rock. It can be replenished by surface water from precipitation, streams and rivers. Fossil water is groundwater that has remained sealed for a long period of time. As fossil water is no longer being replenished from precipitation, its extraction represents non-sustainable water use. Such non-sustainable use of water can also occur when total withdrawals of water for human use exceed the rate at which groundwaters are replenished. The renewable water supply is therefore the amount of water consumption that could occur in a region on a sustained basis.

The amount of water available for human extraction is limited by the need to maintain minimum flows in rivers for navigation, hydropower, fish, and other uses. At a global scale, non-sustainable water use is widespread. For example, around 15–35 per cent of irrigation withdrawals are estimated to be non-sustainable (ibid.).

7.5.3 Sustainable development of water resources

Given the problems of excessive water use and pollution, and increasing water scarcity, how can sustainable development of water resources be achieved in practice?

Figure 7.3 illustrates the links between different human activities and impacts on water resources, and how these relate to achievement of different sustainability goals. Lenton *et al.* (2008) argue that water is not confined to the Millennium Development Goal relating explicitly to water supply, but is crucial to ensure that many of the other targets are met. However, activities undertaken to achieve specific goals, such as development of crop production to alleviate hunger, can potentially have negative impacts on others, such as those relating to drinking water supplies and environmental sustainability (Figure 7.3).

UNEP (2011a) present some suggestions regarding how the sustainable use of water resources can be achieved in practice:

• Increases in water supply can be achieved through the construction of dams and desalination plants, coupled with actions such as increased recycling. Other key actions

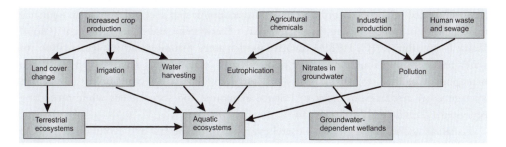

FIGURE 7.3 Links between human activities and impacts on water. Increased crop production and use of agricultural chemicals contribute to the Millennium Development Goal of hunger alleviation, whereas industrial production contributes to poverty alleviation, and human waste relates to the sanitation goal. Impacts on ecosystems link to the goal of environmental sustainability.

Source: Redrawn from information presented in the World Water Assessment Programme, 2009.

that can be taken include increased investment in infrastructure and water-policy reforms that improve the efficiency of water use.

- Large dams are often highly controversial and can lead to substantial negative environmental impacts (see Chapter 5). However, there are alternatives, such as the construction of smaller storages that are built by and serve local communities. At this scale, community engagement and management of infrastructure are easier and adverse environmental impacts tend to be fewer (Winpenny, 2003).

- Investment can usefully be targeted on river restoration (see Chapter 4). For example, in July 2009, the Republic of Korea announced a Five-Year Plan for Green Growth that includes a US$17.3 billion investment in a Four Major Rivers Restoration Project. Overall, it is expected that the project will create 340,000 jobs and generate an estimated US$31.1 billion of positive economic effects as rivers are restored to health.

- Returns to investment in the provision of water and sanitation services to the poor can be high. In China's Gansu Province, for example, investment in the collection of local rainwater at a cost of US$12 per capita was sufficient to enable a significant upgrade of domestic water supplies and to supplement irrigation.

- Sewage recycling is cheaper than desalination as it requires about half as much energy per unit of water treated. Public opposition to household use of recycled sewage water is strong, however.

- Other approaches include the harvesting of rainwater and reuse of domestic water ('greywater'), which are increasingly being incorporated into green building designs (see Chapter 5).

Recent analyses of how water resources can be used sustainably are provided by Bernhardt *et al.* (2005), Elimelech and Phillip (2011), Gleick (2003), Grant *et al.* (2012), Oki and Kanae (2006) and Vörösmarty *et al.* (2010). Selected approaches are considered further below.

Integrated water resources management (IWRM)

IWRM is 'a process which promotes the coordinated development and management of water, land and related resources, in order to maximise economic and social welfare in an equitable manner without compromising the sustainability of ecosystems and the environment' (Global Water Partnership, 2010). IWRM involves participatory planning and implementation for water resources, and functions in the opposite way to traditional sector-based top-down management. Its aim is to bring stakeholders together with a cross-sectoral policy approach to manage water resources, in order to balance economic and social needs while protecting ecosystems (Lenton and Muller, 2009).

Rahaman and Varis (2005) give a useful overview of the origins and evolution of IWRM and identify central challenges in current practice. Anderson *et al.* (2008) consider experiences and lessons learnt from the practice of IWRM in developing countries, and discuss six themes that have emerged from these experiences. Lenton and Muller (2009) present a problem-solving approach to address the development challenges associated with water resources, and illustrate them through a series of case studies, examining the different contexts in which IWRM principles have been applied.

Water governance

Governance is a key issue in water management, being crucial for the allocation of water resources, the settlement of disputes, the financial mechanisms of infrastructure and quality regulation. Water resource management can occur at a variety of scales, from a single stream at village level to huge catchments spanning regions, but all require some level of cooperation and coordination between stakeholders. Twelve criteria have been identified for effective water governance (Lautze *et al.*, 2011). Franks and Cleaver (2007) examine the links between water governance and poverty, with references to marginalised communities and gender issues.

Vörösmarty *et al.* (2010) use a spatial framework to analyse the levels of threat to water security and conclude that policy and management responses are necessary to tackle threats at their source, rather than taking expensive remedial action at a later date. Johnson *et al.* (2001) argue that water is undervalued as a resource and that market-oriented mechanisms should be introduced to counter this.

7.6 Green urban development

7.6.1 Introduction

Over half of the world's population now lives in urban areas. As recently as 1950, this figure stood at 30 per cent, but by 2050, it is expected that almost 80 per cent of the global population will live in cities, with around two billion people moving to urban centres (Bettencourt and West, 2010). Urban areas occupy less than 2 per cent of the Earth's surface, but they concentrate 80 per cent of economic output, 60–80 per cent of energy consumption and around 75 per cent of carbon emissions (UNEP, 2011a). There is huge potential for cities to contribute to sustainable development goals through effective green planning and strategy, in order to reduce resource consumption and carbon emissions.

In many cases, cities can be seen to present both the challenges and the solutions to the problems of sustainability (Grimm *et al.*, 2008). Factors contributing to increased sustainability in cities include greater energy efficiency through more compact urban layouts, reduced travel distances and green transport systems, lower heating/cooling loads through reduced surface-to-volume ratios of denser buildings, energy-efficient utilities, rainwater harvesting, efficient recycling of waste products and effective governance and planning (UNEP, 2011a). The future of urban development is considered by Bettencourt and West (2010) and Rosenzweig *et al.* (2010).

7.6.2 Green cities

Satterthwaite (1997) presents a list of goals of sustainable development as applied to cities. Potential benefits of greening cities include:

* *economic benefits* including agglomeration (where many things are brought together in one small area), lower infrastructure costs, reduced congestion costs;
* *social benefits* including creation of employment, poverty reduction, improved equity and quality of life;
* *environmental benefits* including reduced pollution and carbon emissions, improvements in public health, improvements in urban ecosystems.

An overview of sustainable cities is provided in UNEP (2011a), which notes that the greening of cities requires:

- controlling diseases and their health burden;
- reducing chemical and physical hazards;
- developing high quality urban environments;
- minimising transfers of environmental costs to areas outside the city; and
- ensuring progress towards sustainable consumption.

UNEP (2011a) also note that cities of different wealth impact the environment differently. Local environmental threats are most severe in poorer cities and relate to issues such as fresh water availability, sewage, health and the degradation of the living environment. As cities become more prosperous, with wider and deeper patterns of consumption and production, their environmental impacts are increasingly felt at the global scale.

Another key issue is the pattern of urban development. Many rapidly urbanising areas are characterised by uncontrolled horizontal expansion, often associated with a division between affluent populations occurring at lower densities and the peripheralisation of the urban poor, who may suffer from declining access to infrastructure. Other common developments include the emergence of socially divisive neighbourhoods such as gated communities, shopping centres and business districts, and the spread of informal development with extensive slum housing and limited access to basic services, infrastructure and sanitation (UNEP, 2011a). There is therefore a social equity issue within the concept of a 'green city' – ideally, everyone should have equal access to high environmental quality (see Chapter 6).

UNEP (2011a) highlights a number of opportunities for greening cities:

- Many of the challenges can be addressed by appropriate planning, involving the design and management of urban areas to limit resource consumption and carbon emissions. Compact urban environments may be preferable, with higher-density buildings supported by a transport system based on public transport, walking and cycling.
- More compact urban designs can lead to reduced travel distances, which together with investment in green transport can lead to greater energy efficiency (see Chapter 5). Greater utilisation of energy-efficient buildings can contribute to lower energy demand for urban infrastructure.
- Cities can be structured to make use of green grid-based energy systems such as combined heat and power and micro-generation of energy (see Chapter 5), as well as rainwater harvesting, access to clean water and efficient waste management.
- Green cities can benefit greatly from *synergies* between their constituent parts. This relates to the concept of industrial ecology (Lowe and Evans, 1995). By optimising and synergising different industrial sectors and resource flows, outputs of one sector become the input of another, to create a circular economy (McDonough and Braungart, 2002; see Section 7.8.6). São Paulo's Bandeirantes landfill, for example, is sufficiently large to provide biogas that generates electricity for an entire city district. Such opportunities have led to intensified efforts in designing cross-sectoral green-city strategies when developing new districts or 'eco-cities'.

Examples of cities around the world that have attempted to undergo some form of 'green' development include (UNEP, 2011a):

- Copenhagen, Oslo, Amsterdam, Madrid and Stockholm in Europe, together with Curitiba, Vancouver and Portland in the Americas, have all prioritised compact urban development, creating 'walkable' urban neighbourhoods supported by accessible public transport systems.
- Car-free neighbourhoods have been developed in Freiburg and in London (Beatley, 2004). In the latter case, new homes achieved an 84 per cent reduction in energy and ecological footprints related to mobility decreased by 36 per cent. Recycling reduced waste by between 17–42 per cent.
- Green-city districts have been established in Amsterdam (Ijburg), Copenhagen (Orestad) and Stockholm (Hammerby Sjostad; see Box 7.1).
- Eco-cities have become fashionable in several rapidly urbanising Asian countries. In recent years, high profile investments have been made in sustainable 'new towns', including Tianjin Eco-City in North China, the Songdo Eco-City in Incheon, South Korea, and Masdar Eco-City in Abu Dhabi. However, it is premature to make a comprehensive assessment of their long-term sustainability, especially given the very high capital and development costs of these showcase projects.

7.6.3 Transition Towns

One movement that began in the UK, and which is increasingly spreading to other countries, is the Transition Town movement (Smith, 2011). This offers a holistic approach for community-based action in response to the challenges of climate change and peak oil. This is based on the

---

BOX 7.1 EXAMPLES OF GREEN CITIES

- Freiburg, a city in Germany with a population of 200,000, has aimed for sustainability for many years. It reduced its CO_2 emissions per capita by 12 per cent between 1992 and 2003 (UNEP, 2011a), and has instituted car-free neighbourhoods, earning itself the name of European capital of environmentalism. Evidence relating to the effectiveness of Freiburg in achieving its goals is presented by Ryan and Throgmorton (2003) and Mehaffy (2008).
- Masdar is a planned carbon-neutral city in Abu Dhabi, UAE. Initiated in 2008, it aims to be free of greenhouse gas emissions, to ban petroleum-powered vehicles and to use energy-efficient design, waste reduction strategies and renewable energy. It is an ambitious project and provides an insight into the challenges of designing genuinely carbon-neutral cities for the future. Accounts are given by Crampsie (2008), Reiche (2010) and Nader (2009).
- Hammarby Sjöstad, Stockholm, Sweden (www.hammarbysjostad.se), provides an example of a kind of 'circular economy' (see Chapter 5). For example, combustible waste is incinerated to produce both electricity and district heating, whereas waste heat from the treated wastewater is used for heating water in the district heating system, and food waste is composted and turned into soil (see Figure 7.4).

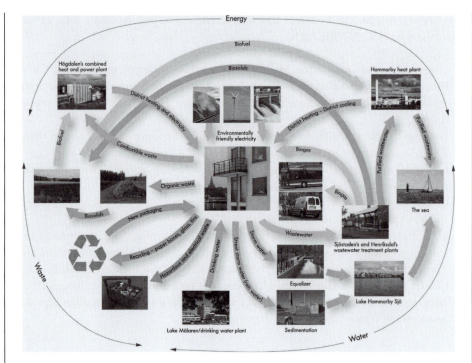

FIGURE 7.4 The 'circular economy' model being adopted in Hammarby Sjöstad, Stockholm. Note the linkage between different sectors, for example, how waste becomes a resource for energy production.

Source: GlashusEtt (2007).

idea that in the event of food and oil shortages, a self-sufficient community would be more resilient to external shocks (Wallace, 2010).

Further information about the Transition Town concept is provided on www.transitionnetwork.org, and in the *Transition Town Handbook* (Hopkins, 2008) (see also http://transitionculture.org). One of the most important features of the approach is that it is 'bottom-up', and community-led. Smith (2011) explores the movement's aims and evolution since its inception, and Scott-Cato and Hillier (2010), in their study of social innovation in response to climate change, examine Transition Towns as a test case of their ideas.

Reflection point

What do you think might be the strengths and weaknesses of a grassroots initiative such as Transition Towns?

7.6.4 The peri-urban interface

Any urban area is intimately linked with the areas that surround it; it is therefore misleading to consider it in isolation. As pointed out by Allen (2003), urban areas such as cities are highly dependent on resources extracted from their immediate hinterland. In many areas undergoing rapid urbanisation, such as areas of India and China, rural areas can progressively become urbanised at a very high rate, with consequent social, economic and environmental problems. Understanding the linkage between urban areas and their hinterlands is therefore an important element of their sustainable development, but remains relatively little researched. Solutions to development of the 'peri-urban interface' may require approaches to planning that are distinct from those currently employed in either urban or in rural areas (ibid.).

> **Reflection point**
>
> Consider how the development of a green economy might be achieved by integrated planning of rural and urban areas. For example, if urban dwellers preferentially consumed food produced locally, this might reduce the environmental impacts of food production ('food miles') while supporting economic development of local rural areas. This kind of approach is central to the 'small is beautiful' concept (Schumacher, 1973).

7.7 Green tourism

7.7.1 Introduction

Tourism is one of the world's largest industries, representing 5 per cent of world GDP. It is also an industry that is growing steadily in size and importance. However, while tourism is a vital source of income for many countries, it can also result in pollution, environmental degradation, deforestation, inefficient energy use and cultural exploitation (UNEP, 2011a). In response, new policies are being developed to encourage sustainable practices in tourism (GSTC Partnership, 2008).

Key points relating to the global tourism industry are presented by UNEP (2011a):

- Tourism has significant potential as a driver for growth for the world economy. International tourism ranks fourth (after fuels, chemicals and automotive products) in global exports, with an industry value of US$1 trillion a year. It is the main source of foreign exchange for one-third of developing countries.
- The development of tourism is accompanied by significant challenges. The sector contributes 5 per cent of global GHG emissions. Other challenges include excessive water consumption, the generation of waste, damage to biodiversity, and the threats to the survival of local cultures, built heritage and traditions.
- Green tourism has the potential to create new jobs and reduce poverty. Travel and tourism are human-resource-intensive, employing 8 per cent of the global workforce. The greening of tourism, which involves efficiency improvements in energy, water, and waste systems, is expected to reinforce the employment potential of the sector.

Such issues highlight both the contribution that tourism could potentially make to the global green economy (Box 7.2), but also the challenges that need to be overcome.

BOX 7.2 TOURISM CASE STUDIES: BHUTAN AND NEPAL

Nepal is a well-known tourist destination, which has in the past suffered environmental degradation as a result. Efforts have been made to involve local communities in the management of protected areas, such as the Annapurna Conservation Area. This provides an exceptional example of how local communities can benefit from tourist revenues to a protected area, and research has documented benefits both to wildlife and to local communities (Bajracharya *et al.*, 2005, 2006).

In Bhutan, the number of visitors has been kept low for many years. However, a new strategy has been adopted to allow for the doubling in number of tourists. There are fears that such growth, if not managed properly, may damage the uniqueness of Bhutan and could jeopardise the very qualities that are the selling points of Bhutanese tourism. Rinzin *et al.* (2007) examine the current state of tourism and the possibilities for future development in this country.

UNEP (2011a) points out that green tourism is not a special form of tourism. Rather, all types of tourism could become greener through various means, e.g. by becoming more energy efficient, using less water, generating less waste, conserving biodiversity, supporting culture and traditions, and improving local livelihoods by providing income. This implies significant improvements in the performance of conventional tourism, as well as growth and improvements in smaller, niche areas centred on natural, cultural and community resources (ibid.).

Reflection point

Note the need to consider not only the needs of tourists, but those people whose livelihoods are affected by tourism projects, which raises an ethical dimension. Consider also the suggestion that tourism can generate local income, and reduce poverty. How might this be achieved in practice?

7.7.2 International criteria of sustainable tourism

Fennell and Weaver (2005) argue that sustainable tourism, and ecotourism in particular, have had issues of low credibility because of two factors. These are the marketing of products as ecotourism that do not fulfil recognised criteria, and the fact that many ecotourism products conform to a model that hampers the potential of this sector to promote environmental, socio-cultural and economic sustainability. As a result of such factors, there have been a number of international meetings that have sought to define the minimum criteria that practitioners can use for guidance.

Three examples of such international meetings are:

- The World Ecotourism Summit, organised by the UN World Tourism Organisation and UNEP, held in 2002. The Quebec declaration that emerged as a result of this meeting provides a template for policy-makers to formulate an official policy on ecotourism.

- The Cape Town Conference in 2002 was organised by the 'Responsible Tourism Partnership' as an event preceding the WSSD in Johannesburg, and produced a declaration that later fed in to the WSSD (ICRT, 2002).
- More recently, the Global Sustainable Tourism Criteria (GSTC) were launched at the World Conservation Congress in 2008. The criteria mainly address the issues of poverty alleviation and environmental sustainability, providing guidance in these areas for the tourism industry (GSTC Partnership, 2008).

Although none of the recommendations of these initiatives are binding, they nonetheless provide an indication of the direction in which the tourism industry needs to move in order to become greener.

> ### Reflection point
>
> Consider any tourism that you have engaged in yourself. How sustainable do you think that it was? How could it have been greener?

7.7.3 Accreditation and certification

How would you be sure whether any tourism that you engaged in, as a consumer, was actually sustainable? One approach is offered by accreditation and certification schemes.

It is helpful to clarify the difference between accreditation and certification. According to Jarvis *et al.* (2010), accreditation is the process by which an organisation endorses a certification agency to ensure that it conforms to a certain set of criteria. Such accreditation is important because it sets quality standards for both industry and markets, and adds credibility and validity to the different certification schemes. There are now many tourism certification schemes around the world, including (following Jarvis *et al.*, 2010):

- Green Globe 21, a global benchmarking and certification programme for travel and tourism;
- Green Key, an international eco-label for leisure that operates in more than 16 countries;
- the Certificate for Sustainable Tourism, a programme to encourage environmental practice in hotels in Costa Rica; and
- STEP, the Sustainable Tourism Eco-certification Standard.

At present, there is no formal global regulation of the certification process for global tourism, though the GSTC criteria provide a potential approach by which global standards might be identified.

7.7.4 Ecotourism

UNEP (2011a) note that ecotourism is not synonymous with sustainable tourism. Ecotourism has, however, attracted a great deal of attention from both researchers and decision-makers, given its apparently high potential to deliver sustainable tourism. Fennell (2008) suggests that three elements of ecotourism can be distinguished: (1) the experience of close contact with nature and people from different cultures; (2) the choice of forms of tourism that maximise revenues for poorer people rather than large tourism companies; and (3) reducing the overall environmental impact of travel.

There is a variety of conflicting views about the effectiveness and practicability of ecotourism. Balmford *et al.* (2009) report that across southern Africa, nature-based tourism generates almost the same revenue as farming, forestry and fisheries combined. Furthermore, Balmford *et al.* (2002) provide evidence that natural habitats can generate economic benefits, including returns from tourism, that are higher than alternative uses of such areas. However, the practicalities can be challenging. Briedenhann and Wickens (2004) note that though governments assume that tourism will generate new jobs and revitalise the economies of rural areas, in reality, the revenues may turn out to be negligible and benefits unequally distributed, leading to high social costs to local communities. Sometimes it is simply cheaper to pay for conservation than to attempt to pay for something indirectly related to it, such as ecotourism, in the expectation that it will conserve the environment (Ferraro and Kiss, 2002).

Conservation through involving the community, or 'community-based ecotourism' (CBET), is a theme examined by some authors. The attraction of CBET is the linking of conservation and local livelihoods, enabling conservation of biodiversity at the same time as reducing rural poverty (Kiss, 2004). However, in practice, there are many issues which prevent CBET from functioning smoothly. For example, Stronza and Gordillo (2008) reported interviews with local leaders associated with ecotourism projects in the Amazon, and found that although ecotourism brings costs, there are also benefits which are not always purely economic. However, Garrod (2003) explains that the full and effective participation of local communities in the planning and management of ecotourism rarely occurs. Contrasting evidence regarding the benefits of ecotourism is presented by Kiss (2004), Briedenhann and Wickens (2004), Sandbrook (2010) and Butcher (2011).

Reflection point

Who actually receives the financial income from ecotourists? Do you think such income typically reaches the poorest sectors of society? If not, how might this be changed?

Reflection point

Some evidence suggests that nature-based tourism is declining because of an increase in the popularity of electronic entertainment media, such as video games and movies (Pergams and Zaradic, 2006, 2008). Might this be a problem for the green economy? If so, what do you think might be done to address it?

7.8 Sustainable consumption and production

7.8.1 Introduction

Victor (2010) states that 'throughput' – the weight of materials, including fuel, that feed the world's economies – increased 800 per cent during the twentieth century. There has been a correspondingly large increase in waste. In this context, progress towards sustainable consumption and production (SCP) is clearly a priority. SCP is a cross-cutting issue, which arises at many points in this book. Here, we focus primarily on practical steps that can be undertaken towards SCP, in the context of recent policy initiatives. Further perspectives on how SCP can be achieved in practice are provided by Dauvergne (2010), Fedrigo and Hontelez (2010), and Mont and Plepys (2008).

7.8.2 Definitions

SCP is commonly considered to be 'the use of goods and services while minimising the use of natural resources, toxic materials and emissions of waste and pollutants over the life-cycle, so as not to jeopardise the needs of future generations' (Prinet, 2011). The emphasis of sustainable production is on the supply side, and focuses on improving environmental performance in key economic sectors. Sustainable consumption addresses the demand side, and considers how the goods and services needed by people can be delivered in ways that reduce the burden on the Earth's carrying capacity (Robins and Roberts, 1997).

7.8.3 The Marrakech Process and the 10-Year Framework of Programmes (10YFP)

Achieving SCP has become a global challenge. This requires building cooperation between a wide range of stakeholders and sectors, at the international scale (Clark, 2007). In recognition of this, governments at the WSSD Johannesburg Summit in 2002 called for the development of a 10-year framework of programmes to support SCP. Actions that were identified included the following (Clark, 2007):

- identify activities, tools, policies, and monitoring and assessment mechanisms, including life-cycle analysis (see Chapter 5);
- develop awareness-raising programmes, particularly for youth through education, consumer information, and advertising;
- develop and adopt consumer information tools;
- increase eco-efficiency for capacity-building and technology transfer.

The Marrakech Process is a global multi-stakeholder process to support these objectives (http://esa.un.org/marrakechprocess/). Its goals are (UNEP, 2009):

- to assist countries in their efforts to green their economies;
- to help corporations develop greener business models;
- to encourage consumers to adopt more sustainable lifestyles.

Reflection point

Note the three elements to this policy initiative, namely nation states, corporations and consumers. Which of these three do you think are more important for the development of a green economy? Or are each of these equally important?

Further information on these initiatives is provided by Clark (2007), UNEP (2009), and UNEP and UNDESA (2011).

> ### Reflection point
>
> The UN's greatest success in terms of dealing with environmental problems is generally agreed to be the Montreal Protocol, which has successfully reduced the emission of pollutants that adversely affect the ozone layer. Do you think the UN will have similar success in terms of securing sustainable production and consumption? Why?

7.8.4 National programmes for sustainable consumption and production

Over 30 countries have drawn up national SCP programmes, using a variety of approaches. Berg (2011) provides a case study of three European countries that have been at the forefront of developing SCP strategies: Finland, Sweden and the UK. Pape *et al.* (2011) consider the range of policy instruments that have been adopted in Ireland, with suggestions of how the country can move forward. These suggestions indicate two important factors: the significance of behavioural change, and the role of government in providing essential infrastructure for people to move to more sustainable lifestyles.

Seyfang (2004) argues that government policy in the UK is dominated by an individualistic culture and a market-led approach to sustainable consumption, and therefore can only respond to a small part of the problem. Hargreaves *et al.* (2008) consider the potential of the Global Action Plan's facilitated team-based approach to changing consumption practices for working with low-income communities. They conclude that while pro-environmental behaviour change can be facilitated through social interaction as well as direct intervention, innovative social experiments of this nature need more support to expand and consolidate their activities.

> ### Reflection point
>
> What do you see as the problems of developing and implementing a national strategy for SCP? What elements would you consider should be included in such a strategy?

A number of authors have noted that there is limited understanding of why people consume as they do, even when it does not seem to bring increased satisfaction (Myers, 2002). For example:

- Dauvergne (2010) suggests that the core of the problem is the inability of environmental governance to alter the global drivers of consumption.
- Mont and Plepys (2008) emphasise that the concept of sustainable consumption calls for changes in the levels and patterns of consumption. So far there has been a lack of strategies that envisage ways of moving from a material-intensive consumer culture to a society with less materialistic aspirations.

- Fedrigo and Hontelez (2010) suggest that the transition to sustainable consumption and production patterns must mean more than just enabling consumers to buy products that are a little more sustainable.

7.8.5 Means of encouraging sustainable consumption

A range of measures have been suggested to encourage sustainable consumption in various contexts. For example:

- Muster (2011) argues that sustainable consumption needs to become part of daily life. One way of achieving this is by promoting sustainable consumption in everyday settings, such as the workplace, which is an important focal point of people's daily lives.
- Seyfang (2006) explains that integrating SCP principles into everyday patterns of behaviour is a major policy challenge for governments seeking long-term sustainability, yet there is an acknowledged need for new tools and instruments to put this into practice.
- Horne (2009) examines the topic of eco-labelling. This is a way to encourage consumers to adopt more sustainable consumption patterns through buying products that are more resource- and energy-efficient. While the author concludes that there is a role for eco-labelling, particularly if supported by governments, eco-labels can only usefully form part of a sustainable consumption strategy. The most environmentally sustainable option is no purchase at all, which carries no label.
- One of the mantras of the sustainable consumption movement is the 3Rs: 'reduce, reuse, recycle' (DEFRA, 2007). Charity shops play an important but often unrecognised role in this, providing an opportunity for genuinely green retailing, promoting reuse and recycling and minimising waste (Klouda, 2007).
- Education and awareness-raising play a major role in bringing about behaviour change towards SCP and need to be used in conjunction with other methods of reducing consumption (Horne, 2009).

7.8.6 Sustainable production: industrial ecology

The methods by which the environmental impact associated with the production of goods can be reduced are explored further in Chapter 5. One specific approach is considered here, namely industrial ecology. This concept first emerged in the late 1980s, partly as a result of a publication by Frosch and Gallopoulos (1989). This considered whether an industrial system could be considered to behave like an ecosystem, where the outputs of an industry might be the inputs of another, thus reducing use of raw materials, pollution, and saving on waste treatment. This led to the idea of industrial ecology, in which businesses might seek to link up with others to minimise their environmental impacts (Figure 7.5). This has since developed into an academic discipline.

A useful introduction to ecology is provided by Garner and Keoleian (1995), who define industrial ecology as the study of the physical, chemical and biological interactions and interrelationships both within and between industrial and ecological systems. Additionally, some researchers suggest that industrial ecology involves identifying and implementing strategies for industrial systems to more closely emulate ecological systems, a form of biomimicry (see Chapter 5).

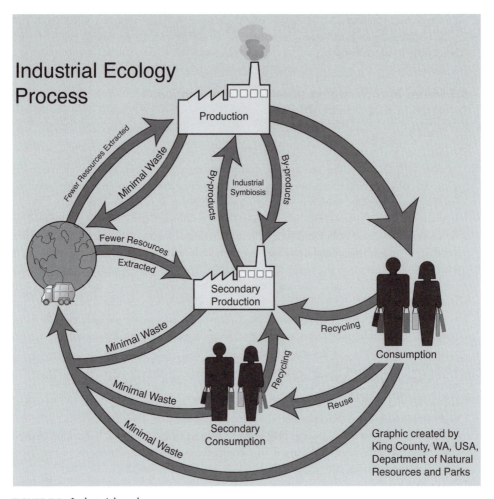

FIGURE 7.5 Industrial ecology

Source: Graphic courtesy of King County, WA, USA, Department of Natural Resources and Parks.

Reflection point

Garner and Keoleian (1995) focus strongly on systems approaches, advocating a 'holistic view' of environmental problems. Does such an approach make environmental problems easier to solve? Why might this be?

One goal of industrial ecology is to change the linear nature of industrial system, where raw materials are used and products, by-products and wastes are produced, to a cyclical system where the wastes are reused as energy or raw materials for another product or process (Garner and Keoleian, 1995). An eco-industrial park in Kalundborg, Denmark, provides an example of attempting to achieve this in practice (Ehrenfeld and Gertler, 1997; Jacobsen, 2006) (Figure 7.6). This example illustrates some of the key features of industrial ecology: to identify and trace flows of energy and materials through industrial systems. This can help to identify their negative

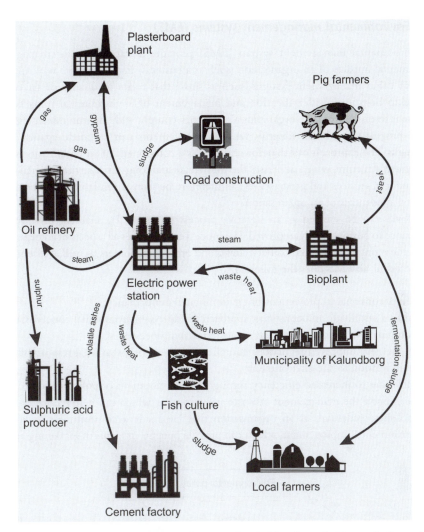

FIGURE 7.6 Industrial ecology in practice: the example of Kalundborg in Denmark. Steam, heat and various raw materials such as sulphur, fly ash and sludge are exchanged between different elements of this industrial ecosystem, providing an example of 'industrial symbiosis'. Participating firms each benefit economically from reduced costs for waste disposal, improved efficiencies of resource use and improved environmental performance.

Source: Figure drawn from information presented in Ehrenfeld and Gertler (1997) and Jacobsen (2006); see also www.symbiosis.dk.

impacts on ecological systems, and provide a basis for both minimising such impacts and optimising the resource efficiency of material and energy use within the industrial system.

7.9 Green business

It is widely recognised that businesses play a central role in the green economy, through the development and marketing of green goods and services. Many companies are also striving to become greener, by reducing the environmental impact of their activities. This section highlights some approaches that can support this process.

7.9.1 Environmental management systems (EMS)

An environmental management system (EMS) provides a framework for managing the environmental impacts of an organisation (such as a business) in a systematic way. An EMS is similar to other management systems, such as those that relate to quality or safety, but is designed to help in the identification and management of environmental impacts. A key objective is to ensure that the organisation's activities comply with environmental legislation, but the process should also identify where improvements can be made against current benchmarks. The approach can therefore be seen as a component of an organisation's overall management structure, which addresses the immediate and long-term environmental impacts of its products, services and processes. It can therefore be seen as fundamental to establishing the 'green' credentials of an organisation.

An EMS can be viewed as an iterative process (Figure 7.7), enabling environmental performance to be continually improved. The process encompasses all aspects of an organisation, and can therefore include its customers, clients and other stakeholders, as well as its employees.

If successful, an EMS does the following:

- delivers continual improvement of environmental performance;
- enables a systematic and consistent approach to address environmental concerns, through a continual evaluation of practices, procedures and processes;
- helps achieve improved regulatory compliance, by ensuring that legal responsibilities are met in relation to the environment;
- contributes to increased efficiency, through the development of policies and procedures that improve the management of waste and resources, which can help reduce cost;
- establishes credentials as an organisation that has made a commitment to continual environmental improvement, which can provide benefits in terms of marketing and sales.

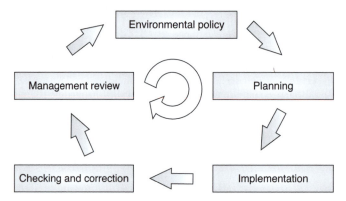

FIGURE 7.7 Illustration of the key elements and process constituting an environmental management system (EMS), as typically employed when following the ISO 14001 EMS standard

What are the steps involved in EMS? These may include:

- *Setting the baseline.* This involves undertaking an assessment of the organisation in terms of its current situation relating to the environment. Areas that might be examined include:

- the environmental impacts of the organisation's products and services, both positive and negative;
- a survey of environmental legislation relevant to the organisation;
- an assessment of current and future environmental risks, based on an assessment of the potential environmental impacts of all of the activities undertaken by the organisation.

In setting the baseline, it can be useful to benchmark (or compare) the organisation's environmental performance with that of others. Analysis of risks should enable those that are most significant to be identified, which should then be addressed by other elements of the plan.

- *Compliance with legal and other requirements.* This involves identifying the environmental legislation that applies to the activities of the organisation, and making sure that it complies with what is required. If areas of non-compliance with regulatory requirements or codes of practice are identified, these will need to be addressed immediately, and an action plan might usefully be addressed to deal with them.
- *Create a policy, and set targets and objectives.* A clear statement of objectives is fundamental to any form of management plan. Such objectives can usefully be underpinned by a statement of policy, which states the guiding principles for the EMS. The policy statement should detail how the environmental impact of the organisation will be managed, and should identify the commitments that it seeks to make. Short-term targets and longer-term objectives will need to be identified, and a process put in place to monitor progress towards them.

An organisation might wish to demonstrate that environmental standards have been reached, both internally and to external clients or customers. This can be achieved through external certification. There are a number of certification schemes that are available, including ISO 14001, BS 8555, the Seren Scheme and the Eco-Management and Audit Scheme.

A key issue is whether implementation of environmental standards actually improves the performance of organisations, in terms of reducing their environmental impacts (see Potoski and Prakash, 2005; Darnall *et al.*, 2008; Zobel, 2008; Yin and Schmeidler, 2009). Ultimately, such approaches depend on the active participation of the workforce, who might range from being highly engaged to being non-supportive; some individuals may perceive it as pointless or simply as extra work for them. The changing of attitudes and expectations is therefore one of the greatest challenges to effective implementation of EMS, especially in maintaining the momentum within the workplace once the management standard has been awarded. It is also worth noting that EMS is not without criticism; because of the self-selection of elements of the system, the result may be an overly positive view of the environmental impacts of an organisation (Yin and Schmeidler, 2009).

7.9.2 Corporate social responsibility (CSR)

The high level of wealth and influence that large corporations have achieved in the last century highlights the need for businesses to adopt a sense of social responsibility. The decisions made by business can have massive impacts upon local communities and national and global policy, as well as the environment.

Business strategies have traditionally focused primarily on meeting the needs of shareholders. The term corporate social responsibility (CSR) implies that the business sector also has a responsibility to society. CSR is the set of practices that are part of a company's corporate strategy that complement and support its main business activities, explicitly seek to avoid damage, and promote compliance with the law, and voluntarily going beyond it (Peinado-Vara, 2006). CSR can therefore be seen as a method by which businesses can contribute to sustainable development goals.

There are a number of national and global initiatives underway to encourage CSR among businesses, which include:

*   *The United Nations Global Compact* (www.unglobalcompact.org), which is a policy initiative for businesses that are committed to aligning their operations and strategies with ten principles in the areas of human rights, labour, environment and anti-corruption.
*   *The Global Leadership Network* (www.gln-online.org), which is a business-led, peer-to-peer global network that aims to support the development of corporate practices on societal, environmental and governance issues.
*   *The European Business Network for Corporate Social Responsibility* (www.csreurope.org), which provides a platform for businesses wishing to engage in CSR, and currently involves more than 5000 companies.
*   ISO 26000, which is a recognised international standard for CSR, providing guidelines on how it can be achieved in practice.

How does CSR affect financial performance? In a detailed review, McWilliams and Siegel (2000) conclude that the impact is generally neutral, suggesting that the conflicting evidence provided by previous studies can be attributed to flawed methods. While large numbers of companies have embraced the concept of CSR, many have found it challenging to implement in practice (Lindgreen *et al.*, 2009).

An important element of CSR is *social accounting*, which involves assessing and communicating the social and environmental effects of a company's economic actions. Typically this is undertaken by companies on a voluntary basis. The concept is reviewed by Gray (2001). The *triple bottom line* has emerged as a popular way of reporting CSR performance. This concept refers to adding social and environmental concerns to the economic 'bottom line' traditionally reported in financial statements, which shows net income or loss. Often paraphrased as 'profit, people, planet', the triple bottom line has been widely adopted as a reporting framework. Much effort has been directed towards the development of appropriate metrics that can be used in such reports (Brown *et al.*, 2006). The concept highlights the responsibility of a company not only to its shareholders, but to its 'stakeholders', which includes anyone who is influenced by actions of the firm.

Suggested activity

You are encouraged to explore the CSR statements produced by different organisations. You will find many examples by searching the internet. As you examine such examples, you should critically evaluate them: how comprehensive are they?

7.9.3 Greenwash

The term 'greenwash' refers to the situation whereby an organisation seeks to mislead people regarding its environmental practices, or the environmental benefits of a product or service that it offers. The potential benefits to this are clear: consumers might be encouraged to purchase a particular product, in the mistaken belief that it is somehow benefiting the environment. Futerra (2008) highlights the fact that consumers often rely on advertising and other corporate messaging to inform their purchasing choices. Greenwash reduces confidence among consumers wishing to engage in green purchasing, and therefore represents a significant factor limiting development of the green economy. Consequently, exposing potential cases of 'greenwash' has become a major focus of some environmental organisations, as well as attracting attention in the media.

Suggested activity

Search the internet for examples of greenwash – there are many! Examples include:

- http://sinsofgreenwashing.org/
- http://stopgreenwash.org/
- www.greenwashingindex.com/
- www.guardian.co.uk/environment/series/greenwash

As you explore these examples, consider the extent to which the claims of greenwash are justifiable. What evidence is provided in support of such claims? How reliable is this evidence?

Some indications of greenwash are summarised in Table 7.1.

Table 7.1 Signs of greenwash

Problem	Explanation
Fluffy language	Words or terms with no clear meaning – e.g. 'eco-friendly'
Green products made by dirty company	For example, efficient light bulbs made in a factory that pollutes rivers
Suggestive pictures	Green images that indicate (unjustified) green impact, e.g. flowers blooming from exhaust pipes
Irrelevant claims	Emphasising one tiny green attribute when everything else is 'un-green'
Best in class	Declaring you are slightly greener than the rest even if the others had very poor performance
Just not credible	'Eco-friendly' cigarette anyone? Greening a dangerous product does not make it safe
Gobbledegook	Jargon and information that only a scientist could check or understand, or is meaningless
Imaginary friends	A label that looks like a third party endorsement – except that it is made up
No proof	It could be right, but where's the evidence?
Outright lying	Total fabrication of claims or data

Source: Adapted from Futerra (2008).

> **Reflection point**
>
> How does the issue of greenwash relate to the issue of environmental standards that we considered earlier in this chapter?

7.10 Sustainability frameworks and approaches

This section considers some frameworks and other approaches that can help provide an understanding of how the green economy can be achieved in practice.

7.10.1 The Sustainable Livelihood Framework (SLF)

The sustainable livelihood approach was originally developed by staff at the Institute of Development Studies, and the Overseas Development Institute, UK. Ashley and Carney (1999) and DFID (1999) describe the approach as a way of thinking about the objectives, scope and priorities for sustainable development, in order to enhance progress in poverty elimination. Although the concept could in principle be applied to the livelihood of any person, it is important to note that its origins lie in the need to alleviate poverty, which has become a major international policy goal in recent years. For example, 'Eradicate extreme poverty and hunger' is the first of the Millennium Development Goals. As a central element of sustainable development, poverty alleviation must also be an objective of the green economy.

Livelihood frameworks are designed to assist with analysing and understanding the livelihoods of the poor and to assess the effectiveness of current efforts aimed at reducing poverty. Such frameworks have been widely used in development planning and policy (Carney, 2002). The Sustainable Livelihood Framework (SLF) assumes that people require a range of assets (including both material and social resources) in order to achieve positive livelihood outcomes. Five different types of capital asset are considered: natural, physical, human, financial and social (DFID, 1999):

1. *Natural capital*, which includes the natural resource stocks from which products and services useful for livelihoods are derived. Note that it is not just natural capital that is required by people, but the ecosystem services that are provided by this capital (Chapter 4). Such services are not only provided by natural ecosystems, but also by human-created ecosystems such as agro-ecosystems.
2. *Physical capital*, which comprises the basic infrastructure and producer goods needed to support livelihoods (e.g. shelter and buildings; tools and equipment used for farming or forest management; transportation, energy and communications; etc.).
3. *Human capital*, which includes the skills, knowledge, ability to work and health that people need to pursue different livelihood strategies and achieve their objectives.
4. *Financial capital*, which includes the financial resources that people use to achieve their livelihood objectives, including savings in various forms, access to credit, earnings and remittances.
5. *Social capital*, which refers to the social resources that people draw upon to help meet their livelihood objectives, including networks and connections between people, and the rules, norms and sanctions associated with different institutions.

The identification of these different types of capital asset required by people for their livelihoods is a very powerful one. However, this forms just one part of the SLF, as illustrated in Figure 7.8. In this context, livelihoods are defined as sustainable (Ashley and Carney, 1999) when:

- they are resilient in the face of external shocks and stresses;
- they are not dependent upon external support;
- they maintain the long-term productivity of natural resources;
- they do not undermine the livelihoods of, or compromise the livelihood options open to, others.

Reflection point

Consider how economic activity might affect the five types of capital asset. For example, exploitation of a forest or a fishery would involve conversion of a natural asset into a financial asset; social, human and physical capital might be required to bring this conversion about.

7.10.2 Application of the 'five capitals' framework

The concept of five types of capital has been applied much more widely than solely to poverty alleviation (e.g. see Porritt, 2007). The Business and the Environment Programme (2006) suggests that it can also be a useful tool for conceptualising sustainable development from a business perspective (Figure 7.9). Specifically, these authors suggest that businesses should seek to identify and implement practices that increase the stocks of these capital assets, by living off the income rather than depleting the capital. While businesses can clearly play a role in the transition to a green economy, this will require changes in social and cultural values, as well as changes in economic and political policies (Business and the Environment Programme, 2006) (Figure 7.10).

Further, Porritt (2010) suggests that what is required is a mix of investment and consumption that maintains and enhances the balance between all the different stocks of capital on which

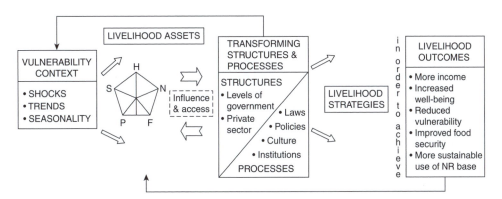

FIGURE 7.8   Sustainable livelihood framework

Source: Ashley and Carney (1999). Courtesy of the Department for International Development (DFID).

Note: H, human capital; S, social capital; N, natural capital; P, physical capital; F, financial capital.

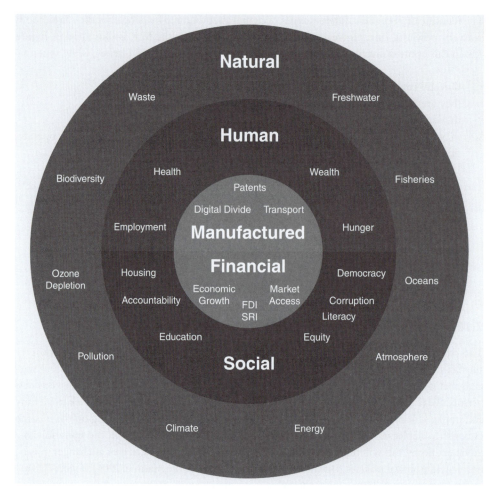

FIGURE 7.9   An alternative conception of the five capitals model. (Note how four of these types of capital are here nested within natural capital, which essentially therefore underpins the green economy.)

Source: Business and the Environment Programme (2006), with permission from Business and Sustainability Programme, Cambridge Programme for Sustainability Leadership.

everyone depends. This represents a shift from a single focus on financial capital, to one that embraces all five capital types. As noted by Porritt (2010), this would require being explicit about the trade-offs between the different types of capital that occur. Specifically, he suggests that a new kind of economy is required, in which human well-being is 'decoupled' from the provision of resource-intensive goods.

Reflection point

How might the five-capitals approach actually assist with identifying how to make the transition to a green economy?

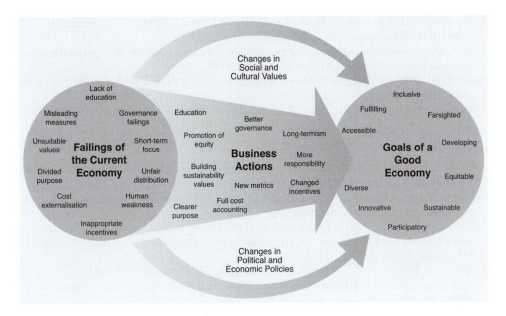

FIGURE 7.10   Illustration of how business actions can contribute to a green or 'good' economy.

Source: Business and the Environment Programme (2006), with permission from Business and Sustainability Programme, Cambridge Programme for Sustainability Leadership.

7.10.3 Measuring and monitoring sustainability

Monitoring progress towards the green economy requires the use of indicators, which can be defined as quantified pieces of information that help to explain how things are changing. The development of such indicators for the green economy is considered in Chapter 8. However, substantial efforts have also been made to develop indicators for sustainable development. Bossel (1999) provides a detailed review of how such indicators can be developed. Bohringer and Jochem (2007) cite key criteria for selecting appropriate indicators, including a rigorous connection to the definitions of sustainability, and reliability and measurability of data for quantification over longer time horizons.

The UN Commission on Sustainable Development (UNCSD) developed a list of indicators for sustainable development designed to be used by decision-makers at national scales. These were designed to facilitate national reporting to UNCSD on sustainable development (UNCSD, 1996, 2007). A wide variety of other sets of indicators and assessment tools have been developed for use at a variety of scales. Ness *et al.* (2007) provide an overview of such approaches, including both indicators and indices (which are aggregated indicators), product-related assessment tools (such as life-cycle analysis, see Chapter 5), and integrated tools for monitoring project implementation. These authors also evaluate the effectiveness of these different approaches.

Bibliography

AIDEnvironment, National Institute for Coastal and Marine Management and RIKZ Coastal Zone Management Centre 2004. *Integrated Marine and Coastal Area Management (IMCAM) Approaches for*

Implementing the Convention on Biological Diversity. CBD Technical Series No. 14, Secretariat of the Convention on Biological Diversity, Montreal.

Allen, A. 2003. Environmental planning and management of the peri-urban interface: perspectives on an emerging field. *Environment and Urbanization*, 15: 135–147.

Allison, E. H. and Ellis, F. 2001. The livelihoods approach and management of small-scale fisheries. *Marine Policy*, 25: 377–388.

Anderson, A., Eiman Karar, K. and Farolfi, S. 2008. Synthesis: IWRM lessons for implementation. *Water SA*, 34: 665–669.

Arnold, J. 2001. *Forests and People: 25 Years of Community Forestry*, Food and Agricultural Organisation, Rome.

Ashley, C. and Carney, D. 1999. *Sustainable Livelihoods: Lessons from Early Experience*, Department for International Development (DFID), London.

Åström, S., Roth, S., Wranne, J., *et al.* 2013. *Food Consumption Choices and Climate Change*, Swedish Environmental Research Institute, Göteborg.

Bajracharya, S. B., Furley, P. A. and Newton, A. C. 2005. Effectiveness of community involvement in delivering conservation benefits to the Annapurna Conservation Area, Nepal. *Environmental Conservation*, 32: 239–247.

Bajracharya, S. B., Furley, P. A. and Newton, A. C. 2006. Impacts of community-based conservation on local communities in the Annapurna Conservation Area, Nepal. *Biodiversity and Conservation*, 15: 2765–2786.

Balmford, A., Beresford, J., Green, J., *et al.* 2009. A global perspective on trends in nature-based tourism. *Plos Biology*, 7.

Balmford, A., Bruner, A., Cooper, P., *et al.* 2002. Economic reasons for conserving wild nature. *Science*, 297: 950–953.

Batish, D. R., Kohli, R. K., Jose, S. and Singh, H. P. (eds) 2008. *Ecological Basis of Agroforestry*, CRC Press: Boca Raton, FL.

Beatley, T. 2004. Planning for sustainability in European cities: a review of practice in leading cities, in S. M. Wheeler and T. Beatley (eds) *The Sustainable Development Reader*. Routledge: London.

Bengtsson, J., Ahnstrom, J. and Weibull, A. C. 2005. The effects of organic agriculture on biodiversity and abundance: a meta-analysis. *Journal of Applied Ecology*, 42: 261–269.

Berg, A. 2011. Not roadmaps but toolboxes: analysing pioneering national programmes for sustainable consumption and production. *Journal of Consumer Policy*, 34: 9–23.

Bernhardt, E. S., Palmer, M. A., Allan, J. D., *et al.* 2005. Ecology: synthesizing US river restoration efforts. *Science*, 308: 636–637.

Bettencourt, L. and West, G. 2010. A unified theory of urban living. *Nature*, 467: 912–913.

Bohringer, C. and Jochem, P. E. P. 2007. Measuring the immeasurable: a survey of sustainability indices. *Ecological Economics*, 63: 1–8.

Bossel, H. 1999. *Indicators for Sustainable Development: Theory, Method, Applications*, International Institute for Sustainable Development, Manitoba, Canada.

Briedenhann, J. and Wickens, E. 2004. Tourism routes as a tool for the economic development of rural areas: vibrant hope or impossible dream? *Tourism Management*, 25: 71–79.

Brown, D., Dillard, J. and Marshall, R. S. 2006. *Triple Bottom Line: A Business Metaphor for a Social Construct*, Departament d'Economia de l'Empresa, Universitat Autònoma de Barcelona, Bellaterra, Spain.

Bunting, S. W. 2007. Confronting the realities of wastewater aquaculture in peri-urban Kolkata with bioeconomic modelling. *Water Research*, 41: 499–505.

Business and the Environment Programme 2006. *The Sustainable Economy Dialogue: Report and Reflections*, University of Cambridge Programme for Industry, Cambridge University.

Butcher, J. 2011. Can ecotourism contribute to tackling poverty? The importance of 'symbiosis'. *Current Issues in Tourism*, 14: 295–307.

Carney, D. 2002. *Sustainable Livelihoods Approaches: Progress and Possibilities for Change* [Online]. Department for International Development (DFID), London. Available at: www.livelihoods.org (accessed 28 Sept. 2013).

Charles, A. and Wilson, L. 2009. Human dimensions of Marine Protected Areas. *ICES Journal of Marine Science*, 66: 6–15.

Cicin-Sain, B. and Belfiore, S. 2005. Linking marine protected areas to integrated coastal and ocean management: a review of theory and practice. *Ocean & Coastal Management*, 48: 847–868.

Clark, G. 2007. Evolution of the global sustainable consumption and production policy and the United Nations Environment Programme's (UNEP) supporting activities. *Journal of Cleaner Production*, 15: 492–498.

Cochrane, K. L. 2005. *Fisheries and Aquaculture Topics: Marine Protected Areas. Topics Fact Sheets* [Online]. FAO Fisheries and Aquaculture Department: Rome. Available at: http://www.fao.org/fishery/topic/13502/en (accessed 27 Sept. 2013).

Costello, C., Ovando, D., Hilborn, R., *et al.* 2012. Status and solutions for the world's unassessed fisheries. *Science*, 338: 517–520.

Crampsie, S. 2008. City of dreams. *Engineering and Technology*, 3: 50–55.

Crowder, D. W., Northfield, T. D., Strand, M. R. and Snyder, W. E. 2010. Organic agriculture promotes evenness and natural pest control. *Nature*, 466: 109–123.

Cudney-Bueno, R. and Basurto, X. 2009. Lack of cross-scale linkages reduces robustness of community-based fisheries management. *Plos One*, 4.

Darnall, N., Henriques, I. and Sadorsky, P. 2008. Do environmental management systems improve business performance in an international setting? *Journal of International Management*, 14: 364–376.

Dauvergne, P. 2010. The problem of consumption. *Global Environmental Politics*, 10: 1–13.

Day, W., Audsley, E. and Frost, A. R. 2008. An engineering approach to modelling, decision support and control for sustainable systems. *Philosophical Transactions of the Royal Society B: Biological Sciences*, 363: 527–541.

DEFRA 2007. *Waste Strategy for England*, DEFRA, London.

DFID 1999. *Sustainable Livelihoods Guidance Sheets* [Online]. DFID, London. Available at: www.livelihoods.org (accessed 28 Sept. 2013).

Dyer, G. A., Serratos-Hernandez, J. A., Perales, H. R., *et al.* 2009. Dispersal of transgenes through maize seed systems in Mexico. *Plos One*, 4.

Ehrenfeld, J. and Gertler, N. 1997. Industrial ecology in practice: the evolution of interdependence at Kalundborg. *Journal of Industrial Ecology*, 1: 67–79.

Elimelech, M. and Phillip, W. A. 2011. The future of seawater desalination: energy, technology, and the environment. *Science*, 333: 712–717.

FAO 2008. *The State of World Fisheries and Aquaculture*, FAO, Rome.

FAO 2010. *Global Forest Resources Assessment*, FAO, Rome.

FAO 2011. *State of the World's Forests 2011*, FAO, Rome.

FAO 2012. *The State of World Fisheries and Aquaculture* [Online]. FAO, Rome. Available at: www.fao.org/docrep/016/i2727e/i2727e.pdf (accessed 28 Nov. 2013).

Fargione, J., Hill, J., Tilman, D., *et al.* 2008. Land clearing and the biofuel carbon debt. *Science*, 319: 1235–1238.

Fedrigo, D. and Hontelez, J. 2010. Sustainable consumption and production. *Journal of Industrial Ecology*, 14: 10–12.

Feenstra, G. 2002. Creating space for sustainable food systems: lessons from the field. *Agriculture and Human Values*, 19: 99–106.

Fennell, D. A. 2008. *Ecotourism*, Routledge, London.

Fennell, D. A. and Weaver, D. 2005. The ecotourism concept and tourism-conservation symbiosis. *Journal of Sustainable Tourism*, 13: 373–390.

Ferraro, P. J. and Kiss, A. 2002. Ecology: direct payments to conserve biodiversity. *Science*, 298: 1718–1719.

Ferse, S. C. A., Costa, M. M., Manez, K. S., *et al.* 2010. Allies, not aliens: increasing the role of local communities in marine protected area implementation. *Environmental Conservation*, 37: 23–34.

Foley, J. A., Ramankutty, N., Brauman, K. A., *et al.* 2011. Solutions for a cultivated planet. *Nature*, 478: 337–342.

Franks, T. and Cleaver, F. 2007. Water governance and poverty: a framework for analysis. *Progress in Development Studies*, 7: 291–306.

Frosch, R. A. and Gallopoulos, N. 1989. Strategies for manufacturing. *Scientific American*, 261: 144–152.

Futerra 2008. *The Greenwash Guide*, Futerra, London.

Gaines, S. D., White, C., Carr, M. H. and Palumbi, S. R. 2010. Designing marine reserve networks for both conservation and fisheries management. *Proceedings of the National Academy of Sciences of the United States of America*, 107: 18286–18293.

Garner, A. and Keoleian, G. A. 1995. *Industrial Ecology: An Introduction*, National Pollution Prevention Center for Higher Education, University of Michigan.

Garrod, B. 2003. Local participation in the planning and management of ecotourism: a revised model approach. *Journal of Ecotourism*, 2: 33–53.

GlashusEtt 2007. *Hammarby Sjöstad: A Unique Environmental Project in Stockholm* [Online]. GlashusEtt, Stockholm. Available at: http://bygg.stockholm.se/Alla-projekt/hammarby-sjostad/ (accessed 28 Nov. 2013).

Gleick, P. H. 2003. Global freshwater resources: soft-path solutions for the 21st century. *Science*, 302: 1524–1528.

Global Water Partnership 2010. *Water Security for Development: Insights from African Partnerships in Action*, GWP, Stockholm.

Godfray, H. C. J., Beddington, J. R., Crute, I. R., et al. 2010. Food security: the challenge of feeding 9 billion people. *Science*, 327: 812–818.

Goulding, K., Jarvis, S. and Whitmore, A. 2008. Optimizing nutrient management for farm systems. *Philosophical Transactions of the Royal Society B: Biological Sciences*, 363: 667–680.

Grant, S. B., Saphores, J-D., Feldman, D. L., et al. 2012. Taking the 'waste' out of 'wastewater' for human water security and ecosystem sustainability. *Science*, 337: 681–686.

Gray, R. 2001. Thirty years of social accounting, reporting and auditing: what (if anything) have we learnt? *Business Ethics: A European Review*, 10: 9–15.

Grimm, N. B., Faeth, S. H., Golubiewski, N. E., et al. 2008. Global change and the ecology of cities. *Science*, 319: 756–760.

Gruhn, P., Goletti, F. and Yudelman, M. 2000. *Integrated Nutrient Management, Soil Fertility, and Sustainable Agriculture: Current Issues and Future Challenges*, International Food Policy Research Institute, Washington, DC.

GSTC Partnership 2008. *Global Sustainable Tourism Criteria*, United Nations Foundation, Washington, DC.

Guenette, S. and Alder, J. 2007. Lessons from marine protected areas and integrated ocean management initiatives in Canada. *Coastal Management*, 35: 51–78.

Gulbrandsen, L. H. 2009. The emergence and effectiveness of the Marine Stewardship Council. *Marine Policy*, 33: 654–660.

Guthrie, J., Guthrie, A., Lawson, R. and Cameron, A. 2006. Farmers' markets: the small business counter-revolution in food production and retailing. *British Food Journal*, 108: 560–573.

Gutierrez, N. L., Hilborn, R. and Defeo, O. 2011. Leadership, social capital and incentives promote successful fisheries. *Nature*, 470: 386–389.

Hansen, M. C., Stehman, S. V. and Potapov, P. V. 2010. Quantification of global gross forest cover loss. *Proceedings of the National Academy of Sciences of the United States of America*, 107: 8650–8655.

Hargreaves, T., Nye, M. and Burgess, J. 2008. Social experiments in sustainable consumption: an evidence-based approach with potential for engaging low-income communities. *Local Environment*, 13: 743–758.

Hassanali, A., Herren, H., Khan, Z. R., et al. 2008. Integrated pest management: the push-pull approach for controlling insect pests and weeds of cereals, and its potential for other agricultural systems including animal husbandry. *Philosophical Transactions of the Royal Society B: Biological Sciences*, 363: 611–621.

Higman, S., Mayers, J., Bass, S., et al. 2005. *Sustainable Forestry Handbook*, 2nd edn, Earthscan, London.

Hobbs, P. R., Sayre, K. and Gupta, R. 2008. The role of conservation agriculture in sustainable agriculture. *Philosophical Transactions of the Royal Society B: Biological Sciences*, 363: 543–555.

Holland, J. M. 2004. The environmental consequences of adopting conservation tillage in Europe: reviewing the evidence. *Agriculture Ecosystems & Environment*, 103: 1–25.

Hopkins, R. 2008. *The Transition Handbook: From Oil Dependency to Local Resilience*, Chelsea Green Publishing, Vermont.

Horne, R. E. 2009. Limits to labels: the role of eco-labels in the assessment of product sustainability and routes to sustainable consumption. *International Journal of Consumer Studies*, 33: 175–182.

IAASTD 2009. *Agriculture at a Crossroads*, International Assessment of Agricultural Knowledge, Science and Technology for Development (IAASTD), Washington, DC.

ICRT 2002. *Cape Town Declaration*, International Centre for Responsible Tourism (ICRT), Cape Town, South Africa.

IFOAM 2010. *Organic Food and Farming: A System Approach to Meet the Sustainability Challenge*, IFOAM EU GROUP, Brussels.

Jacobsen, N. B. 2006. Industrial symbiosis in Kalundborg, Denmark: a quantitative assessment of economic and environmental aspects. *Journal of Industrial Ecology*, 10: 239–255.

Jacquet, J., Pauly, D., Ainley, D., *et al.* 2010. Seafood stewardship in crisis. *Nature*, 467: 28–29.

Jansen, K. 2000. Labour, livelihoods and the quality of life in organic agriculture in Europe. *Biological Agriculture & Horticulture*, 17: 247–278.

Jarvis, N., Weeden, C. and Simcock, N. 2010. The benefits and challenges of sustainable tourism certification: a case study of the Green Tourism Business Scheme in the West of England. *Journal of Hospitality and Tourism Management*, 17: 83–93.

Jentoft, S. 2000. The community: a missing link of fisheries management. *Marine Policy*, 24: 53–59.

Johnson, N., Revenga, C. and Echeverria, J. 2001. Ecology: managing water for people and nature. *Science*, 292: 1071–1072.

Kiss, A. 2004. Is community-based ecotourism a good use of biodiversity conservation funds? *Trends in Ecology & Evolution*, 19: 232–237.

Klouda, L. 2007. Charity retailing: the future of sustainable shopping? *European Retail Digest*, 56: 16–20.

Knowler, D. and Bradshaw, B. 2007. Farmers' adoption of conservation agriculture: a review and synthesis of recent research. *Food Policy*, 32: 25–48.

Kogan, M. 1998. Integrated pest management: historical perspectives and contemporary developments. *Annual Review of Entomology*, 43: 243–270.

Lautze, J., de Silva, S., Giordano, M. and Sanford, L. 2011. Putting the cart before the horse: water governance and IWRM. *Natural Resources Forum*, 35: 1–8.

Lawrence, A. 2007. Beyond the second generation: towards adaptiveness in participatory forest management. *CAB Reviews*, 2: 1–15.

Leakey, R. B., Tchoundjeu, Z., Schreckenberg, K. and Shackleton, S. E. 2005. Tree products (AFTPs): targeting poverty reduction and enhanced livelihoods. *International Journal of Agricultural Sustainability*, 3: 1–23.

Lenton, R., Lewis, K. and Wright, A. M. 2008. Water, sanitation and the Millennium Development Goals. *Journal of International Affairs*, 61: 247–258.

Lenton, R. and Muller, M. (eds) 2009. *Integrated Water Resources Management in Practice: Better Water Management for Development*, Earthscan, London.

Lindgreen, A., Swaen, V. and Johnston, W. J. 2009. Corporate social responsibility: an empirical investigation of US organizations. *Journal of Business Ethics*, 85: 303–323.

Lobley, M., Reed, M. and Butler, A. 2005. *The Impact of Organic Farming on the Rural Economy in England: Final Report to DEFRA. CRR Research Report No. 11*, DEFRA, London.

Lowe, E. A. and Evans, L. K. 1995. Industrial ecology and industrial ecosystems. *Journal of Cleaner Production*, 3: 47–53.

McDermott, M. H. and Schreckenberg, K. 2009. Equity in community forestry: insights from North and South. *International Forestry Review*, 11: 157–170.

McDonough, W. and Braungart, M. 2002. *Cradle to Cradle: Remaking the Way We Make Things*, North Point Press, New York.

McKenna, J., Cooper, A. and O'Hagan, A. M. 2008. Managing by principle: a critical analysis of the European principles of Integrated Coastal Zone Management (ICZM). *Marine Policy*, 32: 941–955.

McWilliams, A. and Siegel, D. 2000. Corporate social responsibility and financial performance: correlation or misspecification? *Strategic Management Journal*, 21: 603–609.

Martinez, S., Hand, M., Da Pra, M., *et al.* 2010. *Local Food Systems: Concepts, Impacts, and Issues. ERR 97 May 2010*, U.S. Department of Agriculture, Economic Research Service, Washington, DC.

Mehaffy, M. 2008. Going to town: three European cities – Berlin, Freiburg, and Warsaw – tackle urban vitality and climate change with varying approaches to town center redevelopment. *Urban Land*, 67: 84–89.

Millennium Ecosystem Assessment 2005. *Ecosystems and Human Well-being: Current State and Trends*, Volume 1, Island Press, Washington, DC.

Mont, O. and Plepys, A. 2008. Sustainable consumption progress: should we be proud or alarmed? *Journal of Cleaner Production*, 16: 531–537.

Morison, J. I. L., Baker, N. R., Mullineaux, P. M. and Davies, W. J. 2008. Improving water use in crop production. *Philosophical Transactions of the Royal Society B: Biological Sciences*, 363: 639–658.

Mortensen, D. A., Egan, J. F., Maxwell, B. D., *et al.* 2012. Navigating a critical juncture for sustainable weed management. *BioScience*, 62: 75–84.

Mueller, N., Gerber, J. S., Johnston, M., *et al.* 2012. Closing yield gaps through nutrient and water management. *Nature*, 490: 254–257.

Mustalahti, I. and Lund, J. F. 2010. Where and how can participatory forest management succeed? Learning from Tanzania, Mozambique, and Laos. *Society & Natural Resources*, 23: 31–44.

Muster, V. 2011. Companies promoting sustainable consumption of employees. *Journal of Consumer Policy*, 34: 161–174.

Myers, N. 2002. The price of consumerism. *Nature*, 418: 819–820.

Nader, S. 2009. Paths to a low-carbon economy; the Masdar example. *Greenhouse Gas Control Technologies* 9(1): 3951–3958.

Nature 2013. Tarnished promise. GM crops: promise and reality. Special issue. *Nature*, 497: 21–29.

Nellemann, C., MacDevette, M., Manders, T., *et al.* (eds) 2009. *The Environmental Food Crisis: The Environment's Role in Averting Future Food Crises. A UNEP Rapid Response Assessment*, United Nations Environment Programme, GRID-Arendal, Arendal, Norway.

Ness, B., Urbel-Piirsalu, E., Anderberg, S. and Olsson, L. 2007. Categorising tools for sustainability assessment. *Ecological Economics*, 60: 498–508.

Newton, A. C. 2007. *Forest Ecology and Conservation: A Handbook of Techniques*, Oxford University Press, Oxford.

Norton, L., Johnson, P., Joys, A., *et al.* 2009. Consequences of organic and non-organic farming practices for field, farm and landscape complexity. *Agriculture Ecosystems and Environment*, 129: 221–227.

Nussbaum, R. and Simula, M. 2005. *The Forest Certification Handbook*, Earthscan, London.

Oki, T. and Kanae, S. 2006. Global hydrological cycles and world water resources. *Science*, 313: 1068–1072.

Pape, J., Rau, H., Fahy, F. and Davies, A. 2011. Developing policies and instruments for sustainable household consumption: Irish experiences and futures. *Journal of Consumer Policy*, 34: 25–42.

Parkes, G., Young, J. A., Walmsley, S. F., *et al.* 2010. Behind the signs: a global review of fish sustainability information schemes. *Reviews in Fisheries Science*, 18: 344–356.

Pauly, D., Christensen, V., Guenette, S., *et al.* 2002. Towards sustainability in world fisheries. *Nature*, 418: 689–695.

Peinado-Vara, E. 2006. Corporate social responsibility in Latin America. *The Journal of Corporate Citizenship*, 21: 61–69.

Pergams, O. R. W. and Zaradic, P. A. 2006. Is love of nature in the US becoming love of electronic media? 16-year downtrend in national park visits explained by watching movies, playing video games, internet use, and oil prices. *Journal of Environmental Management*, 80: 387–393.

Pergams, O. R. W. and Zaradic, P. A. 2008. Evidence for a fundamental and pervasive shift away from nature-based recreation. *Proceedings of the National Academy of Sciences of the United States of America*, 105: 2295–2300.

Phalan, B., Onial, M., Balmford, A. and Green, R. E. 2011. Reconciling food production and biodiversity conservation: land sharing and land sparing compared. *Science*, 333: 1289–1291.

Pikitch, E. K., Santora, C., Babcock, E. A., *et al.* 2004. Ecosystem-based fishery management. *Science*, 305: 346–347.

Pimentel, D., Hepperly, P., Hanson, J., *et al.* 2005. Environmental, energetic, and economic comparisons of organic and conventional farming systems. *BioScience*, 55: 573–582.

Pollnac, R. and Seara, T. 2011. Factors influencing success of marine protected areas in the Visayas, Philippines as related to increasing protected area coverage. *Environmental Management*, 47: 584–592.

Porritt, J. 2007. *Capitalism as if the World Matters*, Earthscan, London.

Porritt, J. 2010. *Towards a Sustainable Economy: Business Leadership and UK Government Policy*, University of Cambridge Programme for Sustainability Leadership, Cambridge University.

Potoski, M. and Prakash, A. 2005. Green clubs and voluntary governance: ISO 14001 and firms' regulatory compliance. *American Journal of Political Science*, 49: 235–248.

Pretty, J. 2008. Agricultural sustainability: concepts, principles and evidence. *Philosophical Transactions of the Royal Society B: Biological Sciences*, 363: 447–465.

Pretty, J. N., Noble, A. D., Bossio, D., *et al.* 2006. Resource-conserving agriculture increases yields in developing countries. *Environmental Science & Technology*, 40: 1114–1119.

Prinet, E. 2011. *Sustainable Consumption and Production: Background Paper No. 1*, One Earth, Vancouver.

Rahaman, M. and Varis, O. 2005. Integrated water resources management: evolution, prospects and future challenges. *Sustainability: Science, Practice and Policy*, 1: 15–21.

Rametsteiner, E. and Simula, M. 2003. Forest certification: an instrument to promote sustainable forest management? *Journal of Environmental Management*, 67: 87–98.

Reiche, D. 2010. Renewable energy policies in the Gulf countries: a case study of the carbon-neutral 'Masdar City' in Abu Dhabi. *Energy Policy*, 38: 378–382.

Rinzin, C., Vermeulen, W. J. V. and Glasbergen, P. 2007. Ecotourism as a mechanism for sustainable development: the case of Bhutan. *Environmental Sciences*, 4: 109–125.

Robins, N. and Roberts, S. 1997. *Changing Consumption and Production Patterns: Unlocking Trade Opportunities*, International Institute for Environment and Development, London.

Rosenzweig, C., Solecki, W., Hammer, S. A. and Mehrotra, S. 2010. Cities lead the way in climate-change action. *Nature*, 467: 909–911.

Royal Society 2009. *Reaping the Benefits: Science and the Sustainable Intensification of Global Agriculture*, Royal Society, London.

Ryan, S. and Throgmorton, J. A. 2003. Sustainable transportation and land development on the periphery: a case study of Freiburg, Germany and Chula Vista, California. *Transportation Research*, Part D: 37–52.

Sachs, J., Remans, R., Smukler, S., *et al.* 2010. Monitoring the world's agriculture. *Nature*, 466: 558–560.

Salas, S., Chuenpagdee, R., Seijo, J. C. and Charles, A. 2007. Challenges in the assessment and management of small-scale fisheries in Latin America and the Caribbean. *Fisheries Research*, 87: 5–16.

Sandbrook, C. G. 2010. Local economic impact of different forms of nature-based tourism. *Conservation Letters*, 3: 21–28.

Satterthwaite, D. 1997. Sustainable cities or cities that contribute to sustainable development? *Urban Studies*, 34: 1667–1691.

Schreckenberg, K. and Luttrell, C. 2009. Participatory forest management: a route to poverty reduction? *International Forestry Review*, 11: 221–238.

Schumacher, E. F. 1973. *Small Is Beautiful*, Abacus, London.

Scott-Cato, M. and Hillier, J. 2010. How could we study climate-related social innovation? Applying Deleuzean philosophy to Transition Towns. *Environmental Politics*, 19: 869–887.

Seufert, V., Ramankutty, N. and Foley, J. A. 2012. Comparing the yields of organic and conventional agriculture. *Nature*, 485: 229–232.

Seyfang, G. 2004. Consuming values and contested cultures: a critical analysis of the UK strategy for sustainable consumption and production. *Review of Social Economy*, 62: 323–338.

Seyfang, G. 2006. Ecological citizenship and sustainable consumption: examining local organic food networks. *Journal of Rural Studies*, 22: 383–395.

Shiklomanov, I. 1993. World fresh water resources, in P. H. Gleick (ed.) *Water in Crisis: A Guide to the World's Fresh Water Resources*, Oxford University Press: New York.

Smit, A. A. H., Driessen, P. P. J. and Glasbergen, P. 2009. Conversion to organic dairy production in the Netherlands: opportunities and constraints. *Rural Sociology*, 74: 383–411.

Smith, A. 2011. The Transition Town network: a review of current evolutions and renaissance. *Social Movement Studies*, 10: 99–105.

Spilsbury, R. 2010. *Deforestation Crisis (Can the Earth Survive?)*, The Rosen Publishing Group, New York.

Stickler, C. M., Nepstad, D. C., Coe, M. T., *et al.* 2009. The potential ecological costs and cobenefits of REDD: a critical review and case study from the Amazon region. *Global Change Biology*, 15: 2803–2824.

Stronza, A. and Gordillo, J. 2008. Community views of ecotourism. *Annals of Tourism Research*, 35: 448–468.

Sumaila, U. R., Guenette, S., Alder, J. and Chuenpagdee, R. 2000. Addressing ecosystem effects of fishing using marine protected areas. *ICES Journal of Marine Science*, 57: 752–760.

Tacon, A. G. J., Metian, M., Turchini, G. M. and De Silva, S. S. 2010. Responsible aquaculture and trophic level implications to global fish supply. *Reviews in Fisheries Science*, 18: 94–105.

Tscharntke, T., Klein, A. M., Kruess, A., *et al.* 2005. Landscape perspectives on agricultural intensification and biodiversity: ecosystem service management. *Ecology Letters*, 8: 857–874.

UNCSD 1996. *Indicators of Sustainable Development: Guidelines and Methodologies*, UNCSD, New York.

UNCSD 2007. *Indicators of Sustainable Development: Guidelines and Methodologies*, 3rd edn, UNCSD, New York.

UNEP 2009. *Frequently Asked Questions: The Marrakech Process. Towards a 10-Year Framework of Programmes on Sustainable Consumption and Production*, UNEP, Nairobi.

UNEP 2011a. *Towards a Green Economy: Pathways to Sustainable Development and Poverty Eradication*, UNEP, Geneva.

UNEP 2011b. *Forests in a Green Economy: A Synthesis*, UNEP, Geneva.

UNEP, FAO, GRID-Arendal and UNFF 2009. *Vital Forest Graphics*, UNEP, GRID-Arendal, Arendal, Norway.

UNEP and UNDESA 2011. *10-Year Framework of Programmes on Sustainable Consumption and Production (10YFP): Identifying Potential Programmes. Draft for Consultation with UN Delegations. Background Paper No. 2*, UNEP and UNDESA, Panama City, Panama.

Victor, P. 2010. Questioning economic growth. *Nature*, 468: 370–371.

Vörösmarty, C. J., McIntyre, P. B., Gessner, M. O., *et al.* 2010. Global threats to human water security and river biodiversity. *Nature*, 467: 555–561.

Wallace, L. 2010. Transition Towns. *Alternatives Journal*, 36: 29–30.

Weber, C. L. and Matthews, H. S. 2008. Food-miles and the relative climate impacts of food choices in the United States. *Environmental Science & Technology*, 42: 3508–3513.

Wiersum, K. F. 1995. 200 years of sustainability in forestry: lessons from history. *Environmental Management*, 19: 321–329.

Wily, L. A. 2000. Forest law in Eastern and Southern Africa: moving towards a community-based forest future? *Unasylva*, 203: 19–26.

Wily, L. A. 2002. Participatory forest management in Africa: an overview of progress and issues, in FAO (ed.) *Proceedings of the Second International Workshop on Participatory Forestry in Africa, 18–22 February 2002*, FAO: Rome.

Winpenny, J. 2003. *Financing Water for All: Report of the World Panel on Financing Water Infrastructure*, World Water Council, Marseilles.

Wojtkowski, P. A. 2010. *The Theory and Practice of Agroforestry Design*, Science Publishers Inc., Enfield, NH.

Wood, L. J., Fish, L., Laughren, J. and Pauly, D. 2008. Assessing progress towards global marine protection targets: shortfalls in information and action. *Oryx*, 42: 340–351.

World Bank 2004. *Sustaining Forests: A Development Strategy*, World Bank, Washington, DC.

World Water Assessment Programme 2009. *The United Nations World Water Development Report 3: Water in a Changing World*, UNESCO and Earthscan, Paris and London.

WWF 2005. *Genetically Modified Organisms (GMOs): A Danger to Sustainable Agriculture*, WWF, Gland, Switzerland.

Yin, H. and Schmeidler, P. J. 2009. Why do standardized ISO 14001 environmental management systems lead to heterogeneous environmental outcomes? *Business Strategy and the Environment*, 18: 469–486.

Zobel, T. 2008. Characterisation of environmental policy implementation in an EMS context: a multiple-case study in Sweden. *Journal of Cleaner Production*, 16: 37–50.

8

OUTLOOK FOR THE GREEN ECONOMY

This chapter provides a brief overview of how the green economy might develop in future, to help integrate the information presented in previous chapters of the book. Consideration is given to a range of challenges that might affect the development of the green economy, and some of the key issues that will need to be addressed.

8.1 Some future trends

As mentioned in Chapter 2, the world is changing very rapidly in many different and unpredictable ways, and this change might intensify in future. The green economy will therefore need to develop in the context of such change, and might even help to drive it.

Some anticipated future changes are listed by Gupta and Sanchez (2012):

- By 2050, the global population may be 9 billion, consuming at higher rates, living mostly (75 per cent) in urban areas, often with high migration to other parts of the world, leading to the rise of new multi-ethnic societies with different value systems. These trends may be affected by climate change, natural disasters, wars or pandemics, as well as major social transitions.
- Despite the recent economic crisis, global world output is expected to increase by as much as three times by 2050, by which time 19 of the top 30 economies will be from the current group of emerging economies.
- Poverty and income inequality will continue to increase, in developed as well as developing countries.
- Partners in international trade will change, associated with increasing trade in services via cyberspace, outsourcing of employment to the changing cheapest economies and to automated systems, with increasing demand for skills and education in the workplace.
- Technological changes, including development of eco-, nano-, bio- and information-technologies, are expected to dramatically change the way we live. The rapid expansion in use of the internet and gadgets (such as mobile devices) will continue to transform the way we communicate and may even influence the rise and fall of governments, while

knowledge may no longer be filtered for its accuracy, secrets may leak, intellectual property rights may be disrespected, and cybercrime and espionage may increase.

- The rising population, growing life expectancy, technological developments and increased income may result in a significant increase in energy use and mineral extraction (especially copper, aluminium, rare metals, platinum). Furthermore, there may be substantial increases in water withdrawals and pollution. Global temperatures may rise by 1.5–2 °C above pre-industrial values by 2050.
- To meet the increasing global food demand, an additional 10–20 per cent of land may be converted to agriculture, transforming habitats, increasing nutrient loading, reducing edible fish populations by 90 per cent in comparison to pre-industrial levels, and reducing plant species richness by 10–15 per cent.
- Economic power may shift to the BRIC countries (Brazil, Russia, India and China), and military power to China. These countries may shape the principles of governance at the global level, and may question the current vision of democracy. A change in value systems may occur as these countries take on a more dominant role in global politics.
- The global market for clean energy and energy efficiency investment opportunities will triple to US$2.2 trillion by 2020 (Robins *et al.*, 2010). This increase will be led by hybrid and full electric vehicles, China's growing clean energy market and the need for capital investment in new green technologies.

Reflection point

Predicting the future is notoriously difficult. How likely do you think these changes are? What other unexpected events could have a major impact on the green economy, as a global social-ecological system? Do you think it possible that global problems might become even more acute, because of positive feedbacks between environmental and development trends?

8.2 Principles of the green economy

One way of supporting future development of the green economy would be to identify a set of principles, to help guide future decision-making. A variety of different organisations have developed sets of principles, which were reviewed by UNDESA (2012). The most commonly identified principles were that the green economy:

- is a means for achieving sustainable development;
- should create decent work and green jobs;
- is resource- and energy-efficient;
- respects planetary boundaries or ecological limits or scarcity;
- uses integrated decision-making;
- measures progress beyond GDP using appropriate indicators/metrics;
- is equitable, fair and just – between and within countries and between generations;
- protects biodiversity and ecosystems;
- delivers poverty reduction, well-being, livelihoods, social protection and access to essential services;

- improves governance and the rule of law; and it is inclusive, democratic, participatory, accountable, transparent and stable;
- internalises externalities (referring to a situation where the costs of environmental damage are borne by producers or consumers).

Interestingly, while these green economy principles encompass the social, economic and environmental of sustainable development, the most common emphasis is on the social dimension. This illustrates how various organisations and stakeholders are currently interpreting the green economy (UNDESA, 2012). It is also interesting to compare these principles, which were produced in the run-up to Rio+20, with those that were recognised in the Rio+20 outcome document (UNCSD, 2012). The latter included explicit reference to economic growth, but no mention of planetary boundaries or ecological limits (see Chapter 2). The idea of using economic measures other than GDP was also not recognised by the deliberations at Rio+20.

Another set of principles is presented by Cato (2011), adapted from Milani (2000), which come from a 'deeper green' perspective:

- The primacy of use-value, intrinsic value and quality: the primary objective as the meeting of need rather than the generation of profit.
- Following natural flows and working with the grain of nature, rather than engaging in a battle for domination of nature.
- Waste equals food: the by-product from one production process should become an input to another production process.
- Elegance and multifunctionality: the search for energy-efficient design and synergies in all economic processes.
- Appropriate scale: rejecting the quest for economies of scale in favour of a size that is sustainable and just.
- Diversity: seeking a range of forms of organisation in place of the uniformity of the global marketplace.
- Self-reliance, self-organisation and self-design.
- Participation and direct democracy.
- Valuing and encouraging human creativity and development.
- The strategic role of the built environment, the landscape and spatial design.

Reflection point

What do you think about these sets of principles? Which best captures your vision of the green economy? Do you think that there are any significant omissions, or that some of the principles listed are inappropriate?

8.3 Measuring progress

As the green economy is now widely established as a policy objective, there is a need to be able to measure progress to assess whether policy goals are being met. Such monitoring is typically achieved through development of appropriate *indicators*. While there have been substantial efforts to develop indicators of sustainable development (see Chapter 7), relevant indicators are now being developed explicitly for the green economy (Chen *et al.*, 2011).

Currently, economic activity is often associated with high emissions, heavily polluting, waste-generating, resource-intensive, and ecosystem-damaging activities. A green economy requires a shift towards low carbon, clean, waste-minimising, resource efficient, and ecosystem-enhancing activities (UNEP, 2012a). Indicators are therefore needed to monitor (UNEP, 2012a):

- how investments are targeted;
- the growth of environmentally friendly or enhancing goods and services;
- employment and jobs in the green economy;
- improved resource efficiency, including the use of materials, energy, water, land, changes to ecosystems, generation of waste, and emissions of hazardous substances related to economic activities;
- human well-being, such as the extent to which basic human needs are fulfilled, the level of education achieved, the health status of the population, and access by the poor to social safety nets.

Conventionally, gross domestic product (GDP) (see Chapter 1) has been used to measure economic activity, but this has been widely questioned. There are four main criticisms (Cato, 2009):

- Unpaid domestic work, which is often undertaken primarily by women, is excluded. As a result, subsistence-based economies, and the core economies in more developed economies, are not recognised.
- Environmental and social catastrophes add to GDP. For example, a major pollution event caused by wreckage of an oil tanker would actually increase GDP, through increased economic activity that might result, such as that associated with the clean-up operation and medical work for damage to health. Similarly, economic activity can be increased by a social breakdown such as an increase in the divorce rate.
- No measure is provided of how equally the goods produced are shared out. There is therefore no measure of inequality, and little indication of the quality of life of any given individual.
- It measures movement, not stores of wealth; in other words, it focuses on flows, not stocks.

The problems with GDP are perhaps illustrated most graphically by Herman Daly, a leading ecological economist, who stated that 'the current national accounting system treats the earth as a business in liquidation' (cited in Cobb *et al.*, 1995). He also highlighted that if virgin forests were cut down and turned into gambling chips, this would register in GDP as an economic improvement (cited in Cato, 2009).

Therefore, there is a need for measures that assess the degree to which society's goals (such as to sustainably provide basic human needs for food, shelter, freedom, participation, etc.) are met, rather than measures such as GDP that assess solely the volume of marketed economic activity (Costanza *et al.*, 2009). Hoffmann (2011) similarly highlighted the need for economic indicators that can be used to monitor human well-being, noting that:

- Income, consumption and wealth should be measured, rather than solely production.
- The household perspective should be emphasised.
- The distribution of income, consumption and wealth should be assessed.

- Measures of people's health, education, personal activities and environmental conditions must be improved.
- Quality-of-life indicators should assess inequalities in a comprehensive way.

The need for such measures is increasingly being recognised, and has been the focus of international dialogue. For example, OECD (2011) proposed indicators of green growth in four inter-related groups:

- monitoring the environmental and resource productivity of production and consumption;
- describing the natural asset base;
- monitoring the environmental dimension of quality of life;
- describing policy responses and economic opportunities.

Examples of alternative indicators that have already been developed include the Genuine Progress Indicator (GPI), the Happy Planet Index (HPI) and the Index of Sustainable Economic Welfare (ISEW) (Lawn, 2003; Abdallah *et al.*, 2012; Kubiszewski *et al.*, 2013). A Global Green Economy Index (GGEI) has also been developed (Dual Citizen Inc., 2011), which seeks to measure both perception and performance of national green economies as judged by experts. Chen *et al.* (2011) describe use of a range of existing indicators, such as the ecological footprint (see Chapter 2), to assess development of the green economy in Taiwan.

Suggested activity

You can calculate your own Happy Planet Index, using online tools available at www.happyplanetindex.org/survey/. As you do so, evaluate how well the index represents your own well-being, as you perceive it.

8.4 Policy and governance

Development of the green economy will require an enabling environment, in terms of appropriate policies, institutions and governance (Box 8.1). Considering national governments in particular, UNEP (2011) identified the following key enabling conditions for a green economic transition:

BOX 8.1 THE ROLE OF CIVIL SOCIETY IN THE GREEN ECONOMY (AFTER UNEP, 2012b)

Increasingly, it is being realised that traditional governance structures are poorly positioned to address current social and environmental challenges, which require long-term rather than short-term solutions. Part of the solution may lie in the fact that global governance is increasingly becoming open to a broad range of civil society actors, including non-governmental organisations, businesses, faith groups and academic institutions. Many of the solutions described in this book require collective action by civil society, including the private sector, the media and academic institutions, as well as governments. By participating in global governance, civil society groups have the opportunity to communicate concerns from local stakeholders to the international scale. They can also facilitate informed public debate about international governance, and can potentially offer rapid support for seeking and implementing solutions. With the rapid development of the internet and telecommunications, decision-makers now possess a wide range of ways to involve civil society, for example through social networks and crowdsourcing. Such approaches can potentially support democratic global engagement.

- *Establishing sound regulatory frameworks.* Regulatory frameworks can regulate unsustainable behaviour, either by creating minimum standards or prohibiting certain activities entirely. An adequate regulatory framework can also reduce regulatory and business risks, and increase market confidence.
- *Spending prioritised in areas that stimulate the greening of economic sectors.* This could include provision of subsidies that have public–good characteristics or positive externalities.
- *Spending limited in areas that deplete natural capital.* Many subsidies currently are associated with a significant environmental, as well as economic cost. For example, artificially lowering the price of goods through subsidisation can encourage inefficiency, waste and over-use, leading to the degradation of renewable resources and ecosystems. Reform of subsidies should be undertaken with careful attention to impacts on the poor.
- *Employing taxes and market-based instruments to shift consumer preference and promote green investment and innovation.* Taxes and market-based instruments can be an efficient means of stimulating investments. Green investments can be discouraged by price distortions. Also, in many economic sectors, negative externalities such as pollution, health impacts or loss of productivity are typically not reflected in costs, thereby reducing the incentive to shift to more sustainable goods and services. A solution is to incorporate the cost of the externality in the price of a good or service via a corrective tax, charge or levy or, by using other market-based instruments, such as tradable permit schemes.
- *Investing in capacity building and training.* A shift towards a green economy could require the strengthening of capacity to analyse challenges, identify opportunities, prioritise interventions, mobilise resources, implement policies and evaluate progress.
- *Strengthening international governance.* International environmental agreements can facilitate and stimulate a transition to a green economy, supported by an active role by governments in international processes. This includes governance of the international trading system, which can influence the flow of green goods, technologies and investments.

As noted by UNEP (2011), many of these policy options are already being implemented by different countries. Babonea and Joia (2012) group the policy instruments that are required into the following categories:

- Fair pricing.
- Procurement policies.
- Ecological tax reform.
- Public investment in infrastructure development.

- Public support for research and development in clean technologies.
- Social policies for combining social objectives with economic policies.

Barbier (2011) notes that green growth will not mean sustainable growth as long as the world continues to face worsening problems of ecological scarcity, because of global ecosystem degradation and loss. He therefore explores the major policy challenges that need to be overcome in order to address this problem. These fall into two main areas:

- While economic development provides benefits to people, it often results in negative impacts on ecosystems and the benefits that they provide. Therefore there is a need to convince global policy-makers that economic development must take into account the worsening ecological scarcity that it causes.
- There is a huge gap between the global benefits that humankind receives from ecosystems and the amount that we currently pay to maintain and conserve them. The global benefits of ecosystem goods and services are likely to be orders of magnitude larger than what is spent annually on ecosystem conservation and restoration. Efforts to halt global biodiversity loss and ecosystem degradation have so far been ineffective, and need to be supported by appropriate financing mechanisms.

According to Barbier (2011), policy interventions are required to address the vicious cycle of unsustainable growth, in which the failure of environmental values to be reflected in markets and policy decisions leads to economic development with excessive environmental degradation (Figure 8.1). If environmental values are not reflected in market and policy actions, then any increasing ecological scarcity will also be ignored in decision-making. The result is that the

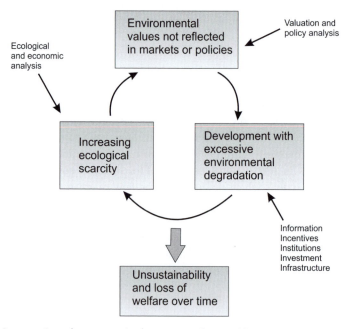

FIGURE 8.1 Interventions that are required to support the transition to a green economy

Source: After Barbier (2011), redrawn with permission from John Wiley & Sons Inc.

current pattern of economic development will continue on its unsustainable path. To address this problem, Barbier suggests that the following steps are required:

- Improvements in environmental valuation and policy analysis are required to ensure that markets and policies incorporate the full costs and benefits of environmental impacts (see Chapter 4). Environmental valuation, specifically of ecosystem goods and services, must be fully integrated into economic development policy and strategy.
- Implementation of effective and appropriate information, incentives, institutions, investments and infrastructure is required to control excessive environmental degradation (Figure 8.1). Market-based instruments, the creation of markets and regulatory measures can help incorporate this information in economic decisions, and thereby address market and policy failures. Encouraging more effective property rights, good governance and support for local communities is also critical, together with reducing government inefficiency, corruption and poor accountability. Governments also have a positive role to play through public investment, protecting critical ecosystems and supporting biodiversity conservation, devising new incentive mechanisms such as payment for ecosystem services, and fostering the technologies and knowledge necessary for improving ecosystem restoration.

Reflection point

Recall that the monetary valuation of nature is controversial, and is rejected by some commentators as unethical (see Chapter 4). Given this, to what extent do you agree with the policy recommendations made by Barbier (2011)?

At what scale are policy interventions needed? Huberman (2010) notes that to date, policy recommendations have primarily been formulated at the macro-economic level, reflecting the need for global action. Although some have argued that environmental crises cannot be effectively addressed at the global scale (Lawn, 2008), it can also be argued that macro-economic analyses are useful for outlining the main trends and sectors that need to be addressed (Huberman, 2010).

Barbier (2012) highlights the need for a mixture of short- and long-term policies, as well as different mixtures of policies and instruments for rich and poor countries. It is also important to note that there may be potential trade-offs between different policies, even if they share a common overall goal of supporting development of the green economy (Table 8.1).

The choice of which policy options are required to develop the green economy depends on how it is conceived and defined (see Chapter 1). For many decision-makers, there is no conflict between the way our economy and society function and a healthy environment, and therefore there is no need for fundamental social or economic change. This position is referred to as 'ecological modernisation', and entails development of a green economy where economic structures such as corporations and markets are maintained, but products are produced in a way that uses less energy and materials (Cato, 2011). A contrasting viewpoint is that the changes required to deliver a genuinely green economy are so deep and fundamental, that an alternative to capitalism might need to be found (Cato, 2009). Other commentators have

Table 8.1 Overview of selected policies designed to support green economic development

Difficulty of implementation	Trade-offs between local, short-term benefits versus global, long-term benefits		
	Fewer trade-offs	*Some trade-offs*	*More trade-offs*
Relatively easy	Energy conservation	Improved drinking water and sanitation	Carbon sequestration projects
	Land use planning	Development of fuel-efficient vehicles	Ocean conservation and fisheries management
Intermediate	Public urban transportation	Low-cost clean energy supply	International payment for ecosystem services
		Removal of fossil fuel subsidies	Large-scale water management projects
		Subsidies for clean energy R&D	
Relatively difficult	Pollution regulation and pricing	Natural resource management and pricing	Global carbon tax
		Sustainable intensification of agriculture	High-cost clean energy supply
		Water pricing	Removal of agricultural subsidies
		Removal of water subsidies	
		Carbon pricing	

Source: Adapted from Barbier (2012).

suggested that if capitalism is to survive, then it must change very significantly (Porritt, 2007). This spectrum of opinion underlies the debates about policy relating to the green economy (Cato, 2011).

Reflection point

Consider your own views on this key point. Having read this book, how fundamental are the changes needed to the current economic system, to achieve a green economy?

8.5 Capital investment

How much might the green economy cost, and how will the money be raised? In response to the financial and economic crisis of 2007–2008, a number of countries launched fiscal stimulus packages. Some US$445 billion, or at least 15 per cent of total investment, was allocated to sectors and activities that can broadly be considered green, including infrastructure such as electric grids, railways, water and waste, energy efficiency, renewable energies and low-carbon vehicles (UNEMG, 2011). A number of countries have expanded investment beyond the stimulus packages, as part of strategies or plans for developing the green economy, for example:

* Germany is aiming to increase the share of renewable energy in total electricity consumption to at least 30 per cent by 2020, supported by investments in energy production and distribution infrastructure.
* The Republic of Korea has allocated US$83.6 million (about 2 per cent of GDP) to be spent in the area of climate change and energy, sustainable transportation and the development of green technologies, including promotion of low-carbon vehicles.
* China is planning to invest US$468 billion on greening the economy over a five-year period, with a focus on waste recycling and reutilisation, clean technologies and renewable energy.

Recent studies on the prospects of green investments forecast a possible tripling to US$2.2 trillion per annum by 2020, with an annual growth rate of 11 per cent (UNEMG, 2011). Is this enough? UNEP (2011) suggested that investing 2 per cent of global GDP per year in ten economic sectors between 2010 and 2050 could potentially be enough to support a transition towards a green economy. Currently, 2 per cent of global GDP amounts to approximately US$1.3 trillion (UNEMG, 2011). Ultimately, however, it is recognised that most investment in the green economy will ultimately need to come from the private sector, rather than from governments.

Brockington (2012) raises two questions about the potential increase in investment that might be required to deliver the green economy. First, does the environmental sector – the NGOs, businesses and government departments who might promote green economy – have the capacity to absorb the kind of increase that is required? Second, on what sort of schemes might such investment usefully be spent?

Reflection point

How do you think money should best be invested, to support a transition to the green economy?

Barbier (2012) suggests that the international community must establish new financial mechanisms for long-term funding of the green economy, highlighting the substantial amounts that could potentially be raised through fuel and tobacco taxes, financial transaction taxes, and investments from dedicated bond and sovereign wealth funds. The idea of a financial transaction tax is currently being explored by the European Commission. UNEP (2011) similarly suggest that the required finance can be mobilised by public policy and innovative financing mechanisms, such as carbon markets, and the use of the sizeable assets controlled by long-term investors, such as public financial institutions, development banks, pension funds and insurance funds.

One financing option that is being widely explored is through the monetary valuation of ecosystem services, and their inclusion in markets, for example through the development of payment schemes for ecosystem services (PES) (see Chapter 4). One problem with this approach is that such commodities are 'fictitious', in that they are not tangible goods that are the product of human labour (Brockington, 2012). The social and ecological values of such ecosystem services are therefore unlikely to be reflected in market prices. For example, the social and ecological value of a forest may often be much higher than the market value of the carbon that it contains. How markets behave with respect to the commodities they feature therefore depends very much on the social structures in which they are embedded. Such issues have led to concerns about the risks of 'commodity fetishism', and more broadly to the effectiveness of market solutions to environmental degradation (Kosoy and Corbera, 2010).

A further potential source of revenue is taxation. As noted by Cato (2009), green taxation has now moved to the mainstream of political debate, as politicians become increasingly aware that they can use national taxation strategically to help support green economic development. This is the subject of much controversy, reflecting the debate about what kinds of lifestyles should be encouraged as part of the green economy. Cato (2009) highlights questions relevant to green taxation, such as:

- Should airline companies be encouraged to purchase more efficient planes or be encouraged to fill those they own to the maximum? Or should passengers be discouraged from flying, because of its impact on GHG emissions?
- Should taxes be used to encourage small, locally based businesses rather than global corporations?
- To address social inequity, should taxes be used to redistribute wealth, reducing the share of assets held by very wealthy people?
- Should the value of land be taxed, because its value derives from nature and from the demands of society as a whole, rather than to the efforts or skill of individual landowners?
- Should there be a tax on pollution? If so, how heavy should it be?

> **Reflection point**
>
> How would you answer these questions?

8.6 Employment

The foundation of any sustainable economic system is employment, and therefore a functional green economy will need to ensure that it provides jobs that are both decent and meaningful (Huberman, 2010). The projected increase in the global human population highlights the ongoing need to create new employment opportunities. Major shifts in employment and the workforce are occurring throughout the world, partly in response to the continual emergence of new technologies. Such shifts occur (1) across sectors (or industries); (2) across enterprises within the same or similar sector (industry); and (3) within enterprises (UNEP, 2012c). The speed and the degree of job creation and loss across these three levels determine the overall effects on the number of jobs, as well as income.

A key question is what the impact of developing the green economy will be on the number, type and quality of jobs. According to UNEP (2012c), employment will be affected in at least four ways:

- In some cases, additional jobs will be created, such as in the manufacturing of newly developed green technology (see Chapter 5).

- Some employment will be substituted, for example, resulting from the shift from fossil fuels to renewables, or from waste disposal to recycling.
- Some jobs may be eliminated without being replaced, for example, when some polluting technology or industrial process is phased out.
- Many existing jobs may be transformed and redefined, as skill sets, work methods and profiles become greener. For example, many construction workers and electricians may need retraining in order to retro-fit or construct green buildings (see Chapter 5).

The net effect of the green economy on employment will depend on the relative importance of these four elements. There is widespread hope that in many countries, green policies and investment will stimulate new economic growth and lead to higher income and employment (Borel-Saladin and Turok, 2013). Large-scale investment in new technologies, equipment, buildings and infrastructure could be a major stimulus for new employment (UNEP, 2012c). However, such positive outcomes will only be achieved if the labour market is supported by appropriate policies, such as those providing retraining in relevant skills, including entrepreneurship and apprenticeships for green jobs. Further, there may be a need to facilitate the reallocation of workers from contracting to expanding sectors of the economy, such as renewable energy (Borel-Saladin and Turok, 2013). Many estimates of green job growth give little recognition to the significant societal problems that can arise from job losses in industries that go out of favour, such as heavy manufacturing and coal mining (Morriss et al., 2009). Also, there is concern that the development of a green economy will not automatically lead to more decent or rewarding work, highlighting the need for policy-makers to take into account people's livelihoods and working conditions.

8.7 Economic growth

As noted previously in this book (e.g. see Chapters 1 and 2), one of the central issues in the debate concerning the green economy is whether or not it is consistent with economic growth. This is related to the idea that the Earth's natural resources, on which the global economy ultimately depends, are finite. The concept of planetary boundaries is currently the focus of particular attention in this context, but as examined in Chapter 2, this idea is derived from the concept of ecological limits to growth, which has a longer ancestry. This debate connects with a deeper question, regarding whether a truly green economy can be successfully developed within the existing capitalist system, or whether a fundamental revolution in the economic system is required.

As noted by Cato (2011), growth is a basic and unavoidable feature of the global economy as it is currently structured. The neoclassical economic view is that innovation and technological development will lead to progressively more efficient use of resources, which is equated with increasing consumption rates and improved quality of life (see Chapter 1). It is assumed by most neoclassical economists that neither pollution nor natural resource limitations should constrain the possibility of perpetual economic growth (Cato, 2011).

A perspective based on the scientific understanding of ecological systems would suggest that in reality, economic activity takes place within a complex social-ecological system. In this system, commodities and the people that demand them, together with the systems that produce them, are interlinked in complex and often unpredictable ways (Chapters 2 and 4). This is one of the reasons why standard economic models have failed to predict the serious environmental consequences of economic growth (Cato, 2011). To provide a simple example, an increase in food production might lead to an increase in human population size, which could lead to a further increase in demand for both agricultural land and food production through a process of positive feedback. Therefore the relationship between food production and population size is not a simple one of supply and demand, which according to neoclassical economic models would eventually reach an equilibrium. Rather, demand can result in more demand (Cato, 2011). A further characteristic of complex systems is that potentially they can undergo irreversible change by crossing a tipping point, which could even lead to their collapse (see Chapter 2). The possibility of such collapse occurring in the global social-ecological system, for example because of climate change (see Chapter 3), is one of the main factors driving the need for a green economy.

Instead of a steadily growing economy, some ecological economists have argued the need for a 'steady state economy', in which human population and stocks of capital remain constant over time (Daly and Farley, 2011). Such stocks would not be static, but instead would vary in a dynamic equilibrium, according to variation in rates of births, deaths, production and consumption. Some proposals for development of the green economy are grounded in this concept. For example Jenkins and Simms (2012) suggest that the following challenges would provide the foundations of a systemic change to a green economy:

* Don't start from a growth perspective.
* Develop a national transition plan that puts countries on paths to operate within planetary boundaries, and on timescales sufficiently quick to preserve key, ecological life support functions.
* Agree to develop and implement new measures of economic success, other than GDP.
* Commit to reduce income and wealth inequalities between and within countries.
* Put fiscal policy and public expenditure centre stage in managing economic transition.
* Recapture the financial sector for the public good, by creating a new financial structure to support the green economy. The banking system should be reformed so that it operates more like a public utility, and is regulated accordingly.

Concerns about economic growth have also led to the development of a social movement called the Degrowth movement, which advocates the downscaling of production and consumption, and economic contraction. This is based on the idea that human happiness and well-being can be increased through approaches other than increased consumption, such as by consuming less, sharing work, and devoting more time to cultural and community pursuits (Fournier, 2008). Degrowth is also increasingly becoming the focus of academic debate. For example:

* Kallis et al. (2012) suggest that economic degrowth is ecologically desirable and possibly inevitable, yet standard economic theories ignore it. Key questions include: under what conditions can it become socially sustainable? How can we have full employment and economic stability without growth? How would production be organised in a degrowing economy?
* Douthwaite (2012) argues that degrowth is going to happen whether governments want it or not because, as fossil fuels run out, incomes will shrink along with the energy supply. This degrowth can either be unplanned and catastrophic or managed and relatively benign. This author suggests that three tools are essential to avoid degrowth becoming a

catastrophic collapse: (1) a system to share the benefits from using increasingly scarce fossil fuels; (2) new ways of financing businesses; and (3) the introduction of debt-free regional and local currencies.

- Tokic (2012) argues that any early indications of degrowth would cause the stock market to crash, which would trigger further contagion and deflation. As a result, the global economy would implode. This might eventually allow for a new rapid growth cycle, as a result of fiscal and monetary policy responses to the implosion. This author concludes that the degrowth idea of 'living better with less' is not economically sustainable in a market economy, because it leads to deflation.

- In contrast, van den Bergh (2011) suggests that degrowth may not be an effective or efficient strategy to reduce pressure on the environment. Rather, being indifferent about growth is a more logical position, given that GDP is an imperfect indicator of social welfare. Focusing on public policy is considered to be more likely to obtain the necessary democratic–political support for change than an explicit degrowth strategy.

Kallis (2011) notes that the concept of degrowth is a radical political project, which would require substantive cultural and political change to be brought about. This would need to include fundamental reform of those institutions that currently make growth an imperative. However, Tokic (2012) highlights the difficulty of fundamentally changing the current financial system, because central banks can create virtually unlimited amounts of money, which is a key safeguard of capitalism.

> **Reflection point**
>
> Do you think that the green economy requires a strategy of degrowth? Or rather, as suggested by van den Bergh (2011), might being indifferent about growth be a more logical aim?

> **Reflection point**
>
> Ultimately, our degree of concern about the impact of economic growth on the environment is a reflection of how we each conceive the environment. The arguments against economic growth depend strongly on the idea of ecological limits or boundaries that should not be transgressed (Chapter 2). Do you think that such limits are real, or might they be better considered as a metaphor? The role of metaphors in environmental sustainability, and how they influence our thinking, is explored in detail by Larson (2011).

8.8 Globalisation versus localisation

As noted in Chapter 6, in recent decades the economies of the world have increasingly become more integrated and interdependent, a process referred to as 'globalisation'. This has resulted in benefits to some individuals, such as increased wealth, a wider range of consumer goods, facilitation of international travel and improved communication links. International corporations have also benefited, through access to larger markets and cheaper labour, and payment of lower taxes by choosing countries accordingly (Cato, 2011).

According to neoclassical economic theory, a freely functioning global market should help growth and development in poorer countries, and therefore contribute to poverty alleviation. In reality, some developing countries have been able to achieve much higher rates of growth than others, and globalisation has widely been implicated as a cause of increasing inequity (see Chapter 6). An increasingly globalised economy is also one that is more energy-intensive, reflecting the lengthy supply chains between producers and consumers, and higher GHG emissions through the combustion of fossil fuels (Cato, 2011).

Might therefore a green economy be more readily achieved through a process of localisation, rather than globalisation? This reflects the ideas in E. F. Schumacher's classic book *Small Is Beautiful* (1973), which continues to exert a powerful influence over much green thinking (Porritt, 2007). Its emphasis on the local scale, on embedding economic activity in neighbourhoods, communities and local culture, and on keeping supply chains short, is central to many concepts of the green economy (Cato, 2009).

This also relates to increasing recognition of the role that 'grassroots innovations' can play in achieving the transition to a green economy. This refers to community-led, value-driven initiatives that respond to local problems and develop innovative socio-economic solutions (Seyfang and Smith, 2007). Such grassroots initiatives are proliferating rapidly in many countries (see Chapter 7). Examples include (Cato, 2009):

• local currency systems
• food cooperatives
• micro-enterprise and micro-finance
• farmers' markets
• permaculture
• car-sharing schemes
• barter systems
• co-housing and eco-villages
• community corporations and banks
• localist business alliances.

Reflection point

Do you think that 'bottom-up' approaches to developing the green economy, led by civil society organisations and rooted in local communities (see Box 8.1), are more likely or less likely to be successful than 'top-down' approaches led by governments?

The concept of 'bioregions' further develops the potential offered by localisation, by seeking to embed economic activity within the specific environmental characteristics of a particular area. Bioregionalism is also a cultural concept, emphasising the contribution, knowledge and solutions of local populations. Cato (2013) suggests that the bioregion approach will support the transition to the green economy by strengthening the links between economic activity and ecosystems, and thereby ensuring that economic development does not exceed environmental limits. This provides a vision of how the green economy might be achieved in practice, through the development of the global economy as a system of largely self-sufficient local economies.

> **Reflection point**
>
> Do you agree that small is beautiful? Might small, local economies be more resilient to environmental change than larger ones? Or might the converse be true?

8.9 Coda

In providing you with an introduction to the green economy, this book might have left you feeling a little dazed and confused. After all, the world in which we live is a large and complex place, which is changing all the time. At its heart, though, the idea of the green economy is a simple one: it is about making the world a better place for everybody. That's what makes it worthwhile. The reason that there is such disagreement and debate is because of uncertainty about the best way of achieving this goal. That's what makes it interesting. At the end of the day, if the green economy is to succeed, it has to benefit everybody. Given the widespread inequalities that exist in the world today, in terms of economic status and power, that won't be easy. That's what makes it challenging.

So, can it be done? Can the green economy offer us genuine hope for the future, or is it just a utopian dream or a passing fad? Hopefully this book has helped you imagine the world as a large and integrated social-ecological system. Changing a system of this magnitude and complexity might seem like an insurmountable challenge. But a remarkable feature of this system, despite its complexity, is that individual behaviour matters. It is the daily decisions that each of us takes that can help make the world a better place. Whether we try to consume less, reduce our carbon emissions, recycle our waste, support the greening of our communities and institutions, campaign for change or develop green goods and services, it can all make a difference. Although our individual actions might seem trivial, they can be multiplied by the positive feedbacks that characterise the interconnected global system of which we are a part. What is wonderful is that increasing numbers of individuals are already taking such action, because they believe that it is the right thing to do. And that's why there is hope.

Bibliography

Abdallah, S., Michaelson, J., Shah, S., Stoll, L. and Marks, N. 2012. *The Happy Planet Index: 2012 Report*, New Economics Foundation, London.

Babonea, A. M. and Joia, R. M. 2012. Transition to a green economy: a challenge and a solution for the world economy in a crisis context. *Theoretical and Applied Economics* 19: 105–114.

Barbier, E. 2011. The policy challenges for green economy and sustainable economic development. *Natural Resources Forum*, 35: 233–245.

Barbier, E. B. 2012. The green economy post Rio+20. *Science*, 338: 887–888.

Borel-Saladin, J. M. and Turok, I. N. 2013. The green economy: incremental change or transformation? *Environmental Policy and Governance*, 23: 209–220.

Brockington, D. 2012. A radically conservative vision? The challenge of UNEP's *Towards a Green Economy. Development and Change*, 43: 409–422.

Cato, M. S. 2009. *Green Economics: An Introduction to Theory, Policy and Practice*, Earthscan, London.

Cato, M. S. 2011. *Environment and Economy*, Routledge, London.

Cato, M. S. 2013. *The Bioregional Economy: Land, Liberty and the Pursuit of Happiness*, Routledge, London.

Chen, Y. K., Chen, C. Y. and Hsieh, T. F. 2011. Exploration of sustainable development by applying green economy indicators. *Environmental Monitoring and Assessment*, 182: 279–289.

Cobb, C., Halstead, T. and Rowe, J. 1995. If the GDP is up, why is America down? *The Atlantic Monthly*, 276: 59–78.

Costanza, R., Hart, M., Posner, S. and Talberth, J. 2009. *Beyond GDP: The Need for New Measures of Progress*. The Pardee Papers, No. 4, Boston University, Boston.

Daly, H. E. and Farley, J. 2011. *Ecological Economics: Principles and Applications*, Island Press, Washington, DC.

Douthwaite, R. 2012. Degrowth and the supply of money in an energy-scarce world. *Ecological Economics*, 84: 187–193.

Dual Citizen Inc. 2011. *The 2011 Global Green Economy Index* [Online]. Dual Citizen Inc., Washington, DC. Available at: http://www.dualcitizeninc.com/ (accessed 23 Sept. 2013).

Fournier, V. 2008. Escaping from the economy: the politics of degrowth. *International Journal of Sociology and Social Policy*, 28: 528–545.

Gupta, J. and Sanchez, N. 2012. Global green governance: embedding the green economy in a global green and equitable rule of law polity. *RECIEL*, 21: 12–22.

Hoffmann, U. 2011. *Some Reflections on Climate Change, Green Growth Illusions and Development Space: Papers No. 205 UNCTAD/OSG/DP/2011/5*, United Nations Conference on Trade and Development Discussion (UNCTAD), Geneva, Switzerland.

Huberman, D. 2010. *A Guidebook for IUCN's Thematic Programme Area on Greening the World Economy (TPA5)*, IUCN, Gland, Switzerland.

Jenkins, T. and Simms, A. 2012. *Paper 1: The Green Economy: Global Transition 2012* [Online]. NEF (New Economics Foundation), London. Available at: www.stakeholderforum.org (accessed 23 Sept. 2013).

Kallis, G. 2011. In defence of degrowth. *Ecological Economics*, 70: 873–880.

Kallis, G., Kerschner, C. and Martinez-Alier, J. 2012. The economics of degrowth. *Ecological Economics*, 84: 172–180.

Kosoy, N. and Corbera, E. 2010. Payments for ecosystem services as commodity fetishism. *Ecological Economics*, 69: 1228–1236.

Kubiszewski, I., Costanza, R., Franco, C., *et al.* 2013. Beyond GDP: measuring and achieving global genuine progress. *Ecological Economics*, 93: 57–68.

Larson, B. 2011. *Metaphors for Environmental Sustainability: Re-defining our Relationship with Nature,* Yale University Press, New Haven, CT.

Lawn, P. A. 2003. A theoretical foundation to support the Index of Sustainable Economic Welfare (ISEW), Genuine Progress Indicator (GPI), and other related indexes. *Ecological Economics*, 44: 105–118.

Lawn, P. A. 2008. Macroeconomic policy, growth, and biodiversity conservation. *Conservation Biology*, 22: 1418–1423.

Milani, B. 2000. *Designing the Green Economy: The Post Industrial Alternative to Corporate Globalisation*, Rowman and Littlefield, Lanham, MD.

Morriss, A., Bogart, W., Dorchak, A. and Meiners, R. 2009. *Green Jobs Myths.* University of Illinois Law and Economics Research Paper Series No. LE09-001 College of Law, University of Illinois.

OECD 2011. *Towards Green Growth: A Summary for Policy Makers*, OECD, Paris, France.

Porritt, J. 2007. *Capitalism as if the World Matters*, Earthscan, London.

Robins, N., Singh, S., Clover, R., *et al.* 2010. *Sizing the Climate Economy, September 2010*, HSBC Global Research, New York.

Schumacher, E. F. 1973. *Small Is Beautiful*, Abacus, London.

Seyfang, G. and Smith, A. 2007. Grassroots innovations for sustainable development: towards a new research and policy agenda. *Environmental Politics*, 16: 584–603.

Tokic, D. 2012. The economic and financial dimensions of degrowth. *Ecological Economics*, 84: 49–56.

UNCSD 2012. *Report of the United Nations Conference on Sustainable Development. A/CONF.216/16*, United Nations, New York.

UNDESA 2012. *A Guidebook to the Green Economy, Issue 2: Exploring Green Economy Principles*, United Nations Division for Sustainable Development (UNDESA), New York.

UNEMG 2011. *Working towards a Balanced and Inclusive Green Economy: A United Nations System-Wide Perspective*, United Nations Environment Management Group (UNEMG), Geneva, Switzerland.

UNEP 2011. *Towards a Green Economy: Pathways to Sustainable Development and Poverty Eradication*, UNEP, Geneva, Switzerland.

UNEP 2012a. *Metrics and Indicators: Green Economy Briefing Paper*, UNEP, Geneva, Switzerland.

UNEP 2012b. *GEO5. Global Environment Outlook 5: Environment for the Future We Want*, UNEP, Nairobi.

UNEP 2012c. *Employment: Green Economy Briefing Paper*, UNEP, Geneva, Switzerland.

van den Bergh, J. C. J. M. 2011. Environment versus growth: a criticism of 'degrowth' and a plea for 'a-growth'. *Ecological Economics*, 70: 881–890.

INDEX

Locators in *italic* refer to figures and tables

uncertainty, and human behaviour 59
United Arab Emirate, green cities 297
United Kingdom: adaptation to climate change
102; carbon management trade-offs 107;
environmental justice 255; sustainable
consumption and production 304–5; tidal
energy 177, 178; waste management 209
United Nations Conference on Sustainable
Development. *see* Rio+20
United Nations Conference on Trade and
Development (UNCTAD) 2
United Nations Convention to Combat
Desertification (UNCCD) 119
United Nations Convention on the Law of the
Sea 240
United Nations Declaration of the Rights of
Indigenous Peoples (UNDRIP) 269
United Nations Department of Economic and
Social Affairs (UNDESA) 267, 325, 326
United Nations Economic and Social
Commission for Asia and the Pacific
(UNESCAP) 4
United Nations Educational, Scientific and
Cultural Organization (UNESCO) 240
United Nations Environment for Europe
Conference (UNECE) 245
United Nations Environmental Programme
(UNEP) 1, 2; employment 334; green cities
296; green economy governance 328–9;
international trade 248; tourism 299, 300, 301
United Nations Framework Convention on
Climate Change (UNFCCC) 4, 67, 74, 82,
87–8, 160, 269, 287; biodiversity 119;
greenhouse gas measurement 88–9, *89*;
mitigation/adaptation measures 99, 103, 105
United Nations Global Compact 310
United Nations Millennium Declaration. *see*
Millennium Development Goals
United Nations Population Division 19, 21
United States: buildings 193, *195*; carbon capture
and storage 211; environmental justice 255,
263; environmental law 247; farmers markets
282; geothermal energy 180; green cities 297;
payments for ecosystem services 159;
population growth 52; Regional Greenhouse
Gas Initiative 97; smart grids 192; transport
197, 200; waste management 206, 209; water
services 287; wind energy 175
Universal Declaration of Human Rights 252
University of the United Nations (UNU-IHDP) 3
urban areas: complex adaptive systems 30; future
trends 324; green 295–9, *298*; planning 245,
255; pollution 39; population growth *20*;
vulnerability 38

VALID (Verifiability, Additionality, Leakage,
Impermanence, Double-counting) 98

valuation, environmental 18–19, 331; ecosystem
services 14, 140–7, *143*, *144*, *145*, *146*;
intrinsic value 142, 146, 147, 326
'The value of the world's ecosystem services and
natural capital' (Costanza et al.) 141–2, *143*
values: environmental law 237–8; moral 10.
see also ethics
Vancouver Olympic and Paralympic Winter
Games 94, *94*
vegetable oil (bio-oil) 169
vegetarian diets 282
vegetation types, succession 34, *35*, 155
verified emissions reductions (VERs) 99
viability, green technology goals 167
Vietnam, sustainable forest management 287
vitamin A, genetically modified rice 283
volcanic eruptions 26, *26*
voluntary carbon market 94–9, *95*, *96*, *98*, *99*
vulnerability: measures *82*, 83; sustainability
science 38–43, *40*, *41*, *42*

Washington consensus, neoliberalism 258
waste electrical and electronic equipment
(WEEE) 207
waste management: agriculture 283; green
technology 202–9, *204*, *208*; hierarchy 203–4,
204; principles 326; progress measures 327;
urban infrastructure 30
waste pickers 206–7
waste sinks *12*, 13
water courses. *see* rivers
water resources management *20*, 39, 292–5, *293*;
agriculture 278; biofuels *170*; climate change
80; global distribution *292*, 292–3; impact on
indigenous peoples 270; payments for
ecosystem services 159; privatisation 267;
sanitation *252*, 292–3, *293*, 294, 296, *332*;
social justice 294; sustainability 279, 287, *292*
water vapour, greenhouse effect 67
wave energy *176*, 176–7; cost-effectiveness *184*;
environmental footprint *186*; impacts *188*
weak precautionary principle 246
weak sustainability 244
weather systems *26*, 27
WEC (World Energy Council) 176, 189–90
WEEE (waste electrical and electronic
equipment) 207
weed species 156, 279, 283
well-being 3; ecosystem disbenefits/disservices
139, 152; ecosystem services 137, 138, *140*,
146; five capitals framework 314; globalisation
259; progress measures 327. *see also* socio-
economic and environmental impacts
whales, biomimetics 219
white roofs and roads, geoengineering 213
wildlife impacts: fishing 247; industrial agriculture
280; tidal energy 178; wind energy 175